MW00559907

COURAGEOUS CONVERSATIONS

The Teaching and Learning of Pastoral Supervision

Edited by

William R. DeLong

University Press of America,® Inc.
Lanham · Boulder · New York · Toronto · Plymouth, UK

Copyright © 2010 by
University Press of America,® Inc.
4501 Forbes Boulevard
Suite 200
Lanham, Maryland 20706
UPA Acquisitions Department (301) 459-3366

Estover Road
Plymouth PL6 7PY
United Kingdom

All rights reserved
Printed in the United States of America
British Library Cataloging in Publication Information Available

Library of Congress Control Number: 2009939541
ISBN: 978-0-7618-5015-1 (paperback : alk. paper)
eISBN: 978-0-7618-5016-8

⊖™ The paper used in this publication meets the minimum
requirements of American National Standard for Information
Sciences—Permanence of Paper for Printed Library Materials,
ANSI Z39.48-1992

With thanksgiving for the wisdom, supervision, and friendship of the Clinical Pastoral Education faculty at Wake Forest North Carolina Baptist Medical Center, who taught me to engage in courageous conversations.

And for Alice Marie, Meredith, Kyle, and Jordan, who keep me engaged in them.

CONTENTS

FOREWORD

Donald Capps

Reading the engaging and thoughtful chapters in this timely text appropriately titled *Courageous Conversations* brought back memories of my CPE summer in 1961 at St. Elizabeth's Hospital in Washington, D.C. I had just completed my junior year at Yale Divinity School and like many of my classmates, I was struggling with the question of whether I was cut out for ministry. A particularly memorable experience was my exit interview with Ernest Bruder, head of the Protestant chaplains. I knew, of course, that he was one of the most highly regarded and influential hospital chaplains throughout the country. This knowledge, plus the fact that he had not been around much during the summer due to illness, made me quite anxious as I entered his office. After a few pleasantries, he asked me to identify the most important thing I had learned about myself through my experience at St. Elizabeth's. I hesitated, then replied that I was giving serious thought to becoming a hospital administrator because it seemed to me that mental institutions like St. Elizabeth's needed to be changed from the top down and chaplains were powerless to effect the changes needed. Not surprisingly, I gained the distinct impression that this was not the answer he was expecting.

At the time, I had not heard of Erving Goffman whose contention that the most important factor in the formation of a mental-hospital patient is not the illness but the institution. This contention, which was derived from his field work at St. Elizabeth's in 1955-1956, had been articulated that very year in his book *Asylums*.[1] If I *had* heard of him, I would have realized that the observation I made in my exit interview had the support of a distinguished sociologist. On the other hand, I was also unaware that Karl Menninger had recently given his presidential address to the American Psychiatric Association on the subject of hope and that this address had so inspired Fr. William F. Lynch that he had decided to spend a year at St. Elizabeth's in preparation for writing his book, *Images of Hope*, which emphasizes that hope "is an act of community, whether the community be a church or a nation or just two people struggling together to produce liberation in each other."[2] Had I known of Lynch at the time, I would have had an answer to my rather cavalier dismissal of the role of the chaplain, an answer that I would have greatly welcomed.

Through much of my own career, I have been trying, as it were, to redeem myself by emphasizing that the pastor, wherever located, is an agent of hope. I may perhaps be forgiven, therefore, for suggesting that the book that editor DeLong has orchestrated here is fundamentally a hopeful book and furthermore, it *is* hopeful precisely because the authors are aware that hope is an act of community. Each in his or her way is mindful of the fact that the profession to which they have chosen to devote themselves is currently confronted with many challenges. At the same time, they have written chapters reflecting their belief that what they do is tremendously important—not only for those they supervise but also for what their work teaches us about what one author refers to as the world's need for healing.

As a reader, I was especially struck by the fact that the work of the pastoral supervisor is no longer grounded in a theological discourse shared by the great majority of supervisors, but that, on the contrary, one of the hallmarks of pastoral supervision today is the theological diversity that informs it. At the same time, I was impressed by the evidence presented in these pages that there are a set of common convictions about the work of pastoral supervision—how one goes about it, what one hopes to accomplish, and what makes it both difficult and rewarding.

One such conviction that seemed especially notable is that the pastoral supervisor has an important role to play in assisting students in their struggles to realize their personal and professional identities. A book that I *did* read at the time I was applying to St. Elizabeth's (I was motivated to do so because a church historian of international renown had informed our junior class that this was a terrible book) was Erik H. Erikson's *Young Man Luther*.[3] One of the things that impressed me about the book was its emphasis on the role that meaningful work can play in assisting young persons in discovering their identities. In this regard, I was moved by Erikson's testimony to the influence on young Martin of his "spiritual mentor," Dr. Johann von Staupitz, who helped him find work to do that, although undertaken "not with pious eagerness, but with a sense of tragic conflict," enabled him to become "affectively and intellectually alive."[4] As a young man who had sat in classes through the preceding nine months, I felt that I experienced a similar sense of coming alive that summer at St. Elizabeth's. This was not, I believe, because I found a single mentor there, but because, as Lynch says of hope, mentoring itself was an act of community.

Perhaps, therefore, the other authors whose reflections grace this volume will forgive me if I draw particular attention to a chapter that emphasizes the student chaplain as work—Mark Hart's chapter, "Focusing Upon Skill Development." He shows how the lessons he learned from his father's efforts to teach him and his brother the art of carpentry have become his guiding principles of pastoral supervision: 1) passion for the work, 2) improvisation in the face of impasse, 3) grace in the face of failure, and 4) confidence in the learner. When I was about the same age as Mark the fledgling carpenter, I asked my father, an accountant with the Union Pacific Railroad, what his work has taught him about life in general. He said that a major issue for accountants is what to do when a station master's books don't quite balance. I asked, "What do you do then?" He shrugged and said, "Accountants have a saying, 'Don't go chasing rabbits.' In other words, sometimes you just have to let it go." If his "don't go chasing rabbits" advice were formulated into a guiding principle for pastoral supervision, it might be something like, "Do the best you can with what you have to work with." Perhaps this fifth guiding principle becomes especially valuable on those occasions when, as Hart notes, his father would experience the limits of the utility of these "key lessons."

Especially noteworthy, however, is the fact that the two brothers were learning these lessons together, which suggests that the search for one's identity ("Who am I?" and "What is becoming of me?") is inseparable from the question "What is becoming of us?" As Francis Rivers Meza might put it, identity is *de conjunto*. Here, then, is where I would simply but unreservedly endorse Bill DeLong's observation in the preface that these chapters represent a conversation through which he hopes "we may all gain greater awareness, new skills, and tools to do our work and perhaps a greater appreciation for the ministry we do and the work still left to us." As Erikson says of the time when, having quit his monastery cell to begin teaching the students at the University of Wittenberg, young Martin became affectively and intellectually alive: "This is not works; it is work, in the best sense."[5]

For another young man who spent the summer of 1961 at St. Elizabeth's Hospital in Washington, D.C., Clinical Pastoral Education under skilled pastoral supervision was the best form of occupational therapy imaginable. Much has changed in the ways in which pastoral supervision is understood, but that it elicits students' desire and capacity to engage in work—*in the best sense*—has remained remarkably constant and consistent throughout the years.

NOTES

1. Erving Goffman, *Asylums: Essays on the Social Situation of Mental Patients and Other Inmates* (New York: Anchor Books, 1961).

2. William F. Lynch, S. J., *Images of Hope: Imagination as Healer of the Hopeless* (New York: Mentor-Omega, 1965), 19.

3. Erik H. Erikson, *Young Man Luther: A Study in Psychoanalysis and History* (New York: W.W. Norton, 1958).

4. *Ibid.*, 220.

5. *Ibid.*, 220.

PREFACE

Professional spiritual care continues to grow as greater attention to spirituality and religious awareness increases throughout the globe. What used to be called the "pastoral care movement" is now clearly an identifiable professional career path with established organizational structures, national and international meetings, and detailed codes of ethics. Ministry in specialized areas is no longer a fringe opportunity or placement for those retired from pulpit ministry. Professional spiritual care has come of age.

I began thinking about this book as I also was making a transition in professional ministry. In 1993, I was working as a staff chaplain at the University of Arizona Medical Center. I had long thought of going into training as a supervisor of Clinical Pastoral Education. I had benefited so much from this type of learning through my internship and then residency at the University of Arizona Medical Center. But now, after serving eight years as a staff chaplain, after a painful divorce, and with a keen awareness of the limits on life, I decided to apply for a supervisory CPE residency.

Typical of me, I began to look for some literature that would tell me about becoming a CPE supervisor. What is it that they actually did? How did one become prepared to supervise the complex intersection of professional development and personal growth? I knew from my own experience that insight was hard work and that, had it not been for supervised encounters, I might never had become the person I am. So I wondered: how do you learn to do that? I searched for literature that centered on pastoral care. As you might guess, there was very little. Thankfully, I stumbled upon *The Supervision of Pastoral Care*, edited by David Steere. As I read, I predictably felt comforted that there were identifiable methods involved in supervising theology students and organizations dedicated to ensuring that competence in that area was achieved. But I also became alarmed that much of what was talked about seemed very foreign or seemed to rely upon psychotherapy. It seemed I would never become proficient at it.

Today there are a myriad of books about pastoral care and counseling and there are numerous books which approach supervision from the perspective of training psychotherapists; most of them are quite helpful. There are an equally large number of books on adult education and group process. Yet, there are few books that speak to the specialized practice and profession of pastoral supervision, which I partly see as the integration of each of these areas. This book is an attempt to fill that gap.

I have intended to create a conversation among the individual authors in this text. We are a diverse group to begin with, and that diversity is apparent in the chapters presented here. But there are also some very clear identifiable themes. One theme that is explicitly and implicitly dealt with is postmodern perspectives in supervision. Several chapters deal exclusively with the implications of post-modern thinking and its effect upon pastoral supervision. Another theme is about pastoral formation itself—that is, how it is understood in a variety of clinical contexts. Finally, and perhaps most importantly, this book does not only look to the past of pastoral supervision, but it presents a clear trajectory of where supervision might be headed in the future. Several authors are attempting to understand theoretical aspects of supervision in order to provide the ground work for future development of theory. Others are looking at national and global themes to understand how these themes might impact pastoral supervision and the organization of the Association for Clinical Pastoral Education.

In all, I see this book as standing in the tradition of Steere's book and others like his. So, I offer this book to men and women who are seeking to understand the process of supervising the formation of pastoral identity. I include in this individuals in congregations who are supervising students in a field education experience. I am hopeful that my colleagues in Clinical Pastoral Education will benefit from the perspectives presented here. Those engaged in the supervision of pastoral counselors and spiritual direction will also find a recognized voice in this conversation.

Spiritual care and competent pastoral formation are needed now more than ever. The world is aware, now more than ever, that our deeply held religious convictions have the power to bring us together to engage in respectful dialogue or they hold the power to send us against each other filled with anger, resentment, and righteous certainty. Now more than ever we need competent supervision of spiritual formation. Now more than ever we need to be looking at how our supervision of individual students may have an effect on an increasingly broken and tragic world. Through the conversation represented here, I hope we may all gain greater awareness, new skills, and tools to do our work and perhaps a greater appreciation for the ministry we do and the work still left to us.

William DeLong
Bloomington, Illinois

Acknowledgments

William DeLong

I am indebted to many colleagues and students who have helped shape my thoughts, theory, and practice of pastoral supervision. My initial unit of Clinical Pastoral Education (CPE) at the University of Arizona Health Sciences Center in Tucson provided me a firm grounding in how to care for those in crisis. My supervisor for that unit and my subsequent residency was with The Rev. Harold Nelson. Harold taught me much about the human condition, about how to learn in a clinical environment, but most importantly, he ignited a spark in me to supervise CPE. I learned from the patients, families, and staff on the Cardio-Vascular Intensive Care Unit. In particular, I learned from the cardiac transplant team at the University of Arizona, who accepted a young chaplain into their midst to teach me about the world of sanctity and scarcity called medicine.

An acknowledgment in any edited book requires, of course, an acknowledgment to the many supervisors and teachers who wrote chapters for this book. Their critical reflections upon the theory and practice of supervision have made this book a reality. To each of these colleagues, I extend my gratitude and respect. I feel privileged to call each of them friend as well as colleague. I wish to especially thank Dr. Donald Capps, William Harte Felmeth Professor of Pastoral Theology at Princeton Theological Seminary, for graciously agreeing to write a foreword to this text. I also acknowledge with immense gratitude the work of Ms. Sara Scheffert, who labored over every paragraph and every endnote to make this book possible. Editing this book would not have been possible without her dedication, skill, and timely sense of humor.

I am indebted to the faculty of Wake Forest University Baptist Medical Center's Department of Pastoral Care where I undertook my supervisory CPE training. Not only did the CPE faculty provide me a supportive and safe environment in which I could integrate personal and professional learning, they also provided a stimulating and challenging intellectual environment where theory development and critical purchase of theory was expected and cultivated.

To be more personal, I wish to acknowledge Jay Foster, Sharon Engebretson, Jane Litzinger (who first coined the term *courageous conversation*), Mark Jensen, Morris Briggs, as well as my training peers, Anna Nobeck, Francis Rivers Meza, and John Titus, all of whom invested countless hours in dialogue around theory development and clinical practice.

Finally, I owe a debt to the administration of BroMenn Healthcare System, who for the past 13 years have provided for and insisted upon a quality Clinical Pastoral Education program in central Illinois. Their dedication to faith-based medical care shows in many ways throughout this organization, but perhaps is nowhere more clearly demonstrated than in providing quality spiritual care to patients, families, and staff. Through this program, and the many students who have participated in CPE at BroMenn Healthcare, I have learned and am learning the art of pastoral supervision.

CHAPTER ONE

Focusing Upon Skill Development

Mark Hart

As many of us have learned in the pastoral integrative process, much of who we are may well be connected to who we were and whose we were. Themes from our families of origin are lived out not only in personal and professional relationships, but also in what our attitude is in learning something new. This chapter revolves around skill development in relation to how any one of us may be involved in the pastoral supervision of others or on the receiving end of someone else's pastoral supervision. However, before that conversation takes place, I need to set the stage for where and how I learned the fundamentals of developing an unknown or new skill set.

My father grew up in the Texas Panhandle oil boomtown of Borger and worked for a refinery from the time he was sixteen until he retired. He was one of those practical, self-made men who learned by action/reflection/action, even though he never even thought about using those terms. He learned by observing the senior operators, being given the task of doing a job himself, and then having his "mentors" review his work with him. In addition to his job at the refinery, my father was a carpenter who contracted himself out around the community for a variety of homebuilding or home improvement projects. My brother and I worked alongside him during our childhood and adolescent years, learning the carpentry skills that seemed to have come so naturally for him. Making the connection between those childhood "skill" lessons and the educational focus in pastoral supervision is an easy one. I learned four key lessons from my father that has influenced how I do pastoral supervision now: 1) "If it's worth doing, it's worth doing right."—passion for the work, 2) "We'll figure out a way to make it work."—improvisation in the face of impasse, 3) "That's okay, just get another board."—grace in the face of failure, and 4) "You can do that."—confidence in the learner. In the interest of full disclosure, I'll be the first to admit my own father's inconsistency when he did not exhibit the aforementioned "key lessons" and when the limits of these lessons pushed past their utility. They are used here for illustration only and I do not begin this writing with an exaggerated sense of his saintliness nor sinfulness.

A PRELIMINARY WORD

As any of us can easily recite, the litany of learning goals of first unit students go something like this: "I need to learn how to listen better," "I've never been around a death before and so I want to learn how to cover everything at a death that I need to cover," "I need to acquire basic knowledge and skill for spiritual ministry to the sick." Assisting students in the writing of their initial learning goals related to pastoral competence to also include pastoral reflection and pastoral formation is nothing new to us. The occasionally overlooked component in goal writing is their dialogue/awareness regarding *how* they came to be the kind of learners they are today. What were the processes surrounding the student's learning in those crucial developmental stages? Were they encouraged or ignored, ridiculed or praised, over-taught or minimalized as they ventured into the initial steps of learning something new?

I am reminded of the enjoyable pastime of watching new parents with their child when the first steps are taken. One parent kneels down with the child on wobbly legs, facing the other parent just a few feet away. The baby, with a big smile on her face, knows her parents are close and begins the awkward journey. She falls. There is laughter, but not ridicule. The parent says, "That's okay, honey. Let's try it again." The baby takes a few more steps and falls into her father's arms with more laughter and applause. What all is present in this picture that can help us understand the dynamics in skill building? There is encouragement, playfulness, no harsh recriminations when "failure" takes place, and, ultimately, celebration when the first walk is successful. Later, parents lose some of the playfulness and get very serious about their child's learning. Parents become police and the earlier enjoyment of those first skills of walking is replaced by harping about homework or, worse yet, neglect/abuse and rendering the child invisible. Before we can get to the question of skill development in pastoral ministry, we must ask the question, "How has that student learned in the past about their own capacity and motivation in learning?"

There's the intriguing story of Milton Erickson, the father of modern hypnotherapy, who, at the age of 17, was severely crippled with polio. His year long recovery provided him lessons that remained with him the rest of his life. Lying paralyzed, Erickson watched his baby sister learning to walk and closely observed how his parents communicated with his sister and how the unconscious mind works. There was focus on the potential for the child to walk versus statements commanding, "Don't fall!" He focused on recalling and visualizing those same movements in himself. He gave himself direct commands: "Move legs! Rock the chair!" Nothing happened. Finally, he gave up, sank back into his daydreams, and once more imagined playing outside. Again, the chair began to rock! It was the indirect suggestion—that vivid imaging—which produced a response. Using this discovery, over the following two years, Milton taught himself to walk. Consequently, one of the hallmarks of hypnotherapy was born: indirect suggestion.[1]

PASSION FOR THE WORK

The hospital system to which I belong has undergone a cultural change within the last six years by integrating the "service excellence" concept by the Studer Group, recognizing what motivates people toward doing the best possible work they can do. The language that Studer uses regarding the essential value of passion provides the self-motivation toward a person's sense of "purpose, worthwhile work, and making a difference."[2] In relation to pastoral supervision, the question of passion involves both the student and the supervisor. What do students report regarding their sense of "passion for ministry" under your supervision? Do they know what you are enthusiastic about? Is there a theoretical rationale for withholding that segment of your supervisory identity in order for the student to write upon the *tabula rasa* of their transference upon you? Students often report that a portion of their decision-making in choosing one CPE center over another has to do with their "feel" about the place. "I just felt a connection with them" or "You seemed to be excited about the program that you have" or "They have a good reputation for having a strong program" are not unfamiliar responses to questions we might raise with students. In relation to pastoral supervision, how contagious is that element of enjoyment that can't help but be noticed by those around you? These are intuitive, less definable variables that suggest the power of one's passion about ministry and supervision and that positively and negatively impact those around you.

My father's passion about doing the best job possible seemed to be motivated by how he viewed his own performance versus how others might view his performance from the outside. Time would have a tendency to slip away and he would often "get lost" in his own project he was working on. The question of the difference between passion and obsession is a good one to ask, but there was an element of enjoyment in what he put his hands to do versus a sense of dogged "oughtness" that seemed to breed an attitude of resentment and blame. What are the implications of the student's own passion, or their sense of "call," that informs our own supervision of their ministry?

I'm reminded of Edwin Friedman's concept of self-definition that eases the burden of expertise with our own cultural momentum toward an anxiety of appearing incompetent.[3] So which came first, the passion (or call) or the competence? One former student, whom I'll call M, captured a sense of this anxiety we often experience in students. M's learning in his clinical assignments came as he confronted his anxiety of being incompetent while in the chaos with families. He reflected that his analytical, distancing persona served as a defense when he became anxious of being found out as inept. He operated from a self-reliant stance, which insisted that he should always know the right thing to say and the right way to be. He thought his passion or call was primarily experienced in this evidence of competence. His assumptions about his pastoral role undervalued the present. He began to reframe what "bearing witness" with persons meant—that is, accepting and celebrating the present moment. He changed his perspective of "witnessing" to patients and families, which consequently kept the onus of responsibility on his own performance to "bearing witness" of their story, struggle, and expression, which helped him become a participant with the other. His scope of learning expanded from being centered on himself to more realistically assessing and providing pastoral care to specific, hurting people.

IMPROVISATION IN THE FACE OF IMPASSE

I also learned from my father, "We'll figure out a way to make it work"—better known as improvisation in the face of impasse. I saw him on more than one occasion take the materials he had on hand and work within the constraints that presented themselves to bring about an acceptable result. What he could do with bailing wire, a few nails, and a few pieces of lumber was amazing! A mark of competence is the ability to think outside of the box when a more obvious solution is not presenting itself, whether the improvisation is applied to carpentry, music, drama, or ministry. Samuel Wells in *Improvisation: The Drama of Christian Ethics* states, "Improvisation in the theater is a practice through which actors seek to develop trust in themselves and one another, in order that they may conduct unscripted dramas without fear."[4]

Often in pastoral supervision, students expect to receive *the* definitive list of how to make an initial visit, manage a conflictual situation, attend their first death, or provide advance directive information. While there are definite skill sets that can be applied to any and all of these scenarios, it is often the student's own flexibility in the moment that will help them retain their own sense of their pastoral authority. Isn't much of what is done in ministry unscripted? That sense of the unknown can be part of the very attraction to ministry because of the limitless presentation of similar themes in people's lives. How many of us have attended countless deaths and crisis situations, but can we say that they presented themselves in the same fashion with the same predictable results? If those moments in ministry do begin to feel like the same old mundane repetition, then those moments may speak more directly to our own attitudes of compassion fatigue, need for renewal, or reassessment.

Even with the challenge of remaining flexible in ministry when rigidity seems to be driving the momentum around the event, students have a right to expect skill sets from their pastoral supervisory context. We have certainly seen the pendulum swing in the volume of information provided to first unit CPE students in the form of student handbook and orientation material. I remember the story from an older supervisor who told of his first day of CPE in the early sixties when his supervisor entered the classroom on the first day of the unit, welcomed them all to the unit, and said, "I'm now going to write on the board the most important word you need to remember this unit." He then proceeded to write the word "LISTEN." Students dutifully pulled out their notebooks, expecting more to follow in their day of orientation. The supervisor laid the chalk down, asked if there were any questions and then began to walk out of the classroom. The students began to ask then, "Well, what's next? What do we do now?" The supervisor's response was, "I think you can figure that out." The students asked, "What are our assignments? What else do we need to cover?" The supervisor again responded, "I think you can figure that out." That was the end of the classroom orientation and the students began their first day of clinical ministry. It is certainly arguable that the supervisor then did not adequately prepare them with a base of knowledge that would then assist them to "figure out" what came next. In our current complex environments of ministry, pastoral supervision constantly deals with the tension of the students' anxiety that can both paralyze and/or energize. If what Malcolm Knowles said about the adult tendency to learn is task-oriented, then the student handbook and orientation must address their need for a certain amount of skill building information.[5]

Students feel anxious because they do not know a particular skill and assume that once they are immersed with more information, they will then be qualified as a professional. This tendency in students can be honored by dialoguing with them about the need to utilize their own selfhood as an avenue, alongside the skills, to help them become a better minister. William McElvaney talks of the task of ministry formation in relation to three partially intersecting circles entitled being, doing, and knowing. Being includes such things as selfhood, life in the spirit, passion, and soul. Knowing includes such things as content, analysis, and cognition. Doing includes such things as function, task, and methodology. If students learn exclusively by their knowing, then, theologically, they try to seek salvation by their own knowledge. If students learn exclusively by their doing, they try to seek salvation through their works and not by faith. If students learn exclusively by their being, they insist that their personal experience is the greatest criteria.[6] The place where they intersect is the critical learning for students as they integrate their whole selves into ministry. This integration helps students balance their orientation to tasks with the rest of their pastoral selves. For example, M, again, wanted to learn the "skills of ministry" so that he would be qualified as a pastor. M operated out of the assumption that his authority came out of his ability to know and do. A supervisory intervention with M helped him address his focus on skill development by utilizing his peer group's feedback and the clinical method of learning to provide examples where he could reflect on what he based his authority—knowing and doing or being/creating relationship with people.

This less defined reality of being is where improvisation resides. Let's assume for the moment that sufficient pastoral skill and knowledge has been demonstrated. As a student moves through the unit, building on their growing awareness that all of ministry cannot be prepared for and that ambiguity is a pastoral reality, the student begins to demonstrate more ease in being in pastoral encounters that are unscripted. From the Christian tradition, Jesus' ministry was constantly interrupted, greatly irritating his disciples. The interruptions became Jesus' platform to teach, heal, and proclaim. He utilized the resources on hand, like an accomplished carpenter. Jesus possessed an element of trust in himself and in God that allowed for the improvisation that disquieted the complacent people around him who needed the challenge. He also provided comfort to those who needed sanctuary, something different than what they had received from the religious authorities.

Pragmatically, let's look at a curriculum component that offers a twist on the use of role-play. Beginning in the second unit of a residency, a student is asked to present a clinical vignette in which they take on the role of the patient, not the chaplain. They solicit a volunteer peer to play their part as chaplain in the pastoral encounter. The student is able to think outside the box now as they participate as the patient/client/parishioner and receive other variations of what might have been possible within that pastoral encounter. Students have positively reported that this twist is a useful tool and has helped them hear what all might be possible that they did not consider and what it might feel like on the part of the patient/client/parishioner or family member.

GRACE IN THE FACE OF FAILURE

In my office I have a fabric board behind my computer in which I have put a variety of quotes that attempt to keep me honest about my own ego needs. Among those quotes is one from Walter Wangerin, a teacher and Lutheran pastor who has a great website in which he says, "Finally, I am convinced that we are not called upon to succeed at anything in the ministry. We are called upon to love. Which is to say, we are called upon to fail—both vigorously and joyfully."[7] The paradox of a statement like this not only challenges the disturbing prosperity theology of some contemporary churches but also, closer to home, challenges my own measuring stick of success. Any one of us would want to experience success in ministry as seen in a CPE program being financially strong, a church growing and meeting the needs of the community or, more to the point, a pastoral encounter having a positive outcome. An unnerving component of ministry is that awful awareness that much of what we do is immeasurable. I currently provide CPE in a clinical context highly committed to initial visits, even to the point of integrated goals developed by the Pastoral Care Department and electronically monitored on a daily basis. While these tools assist in giving a snapshot on the numbers of initial patients seen, the successful outcome of the visit—whatever that means—remains intangible.

Students, often living in the fearful paralysis of their own incompetence, can be so focused on their performance that they "fail" to realize the power of their pastoral compassion as being sufficient unto the day. I'll return to my childhood again to provide an illustration. I was 13 years old when I picked up the circular saw for the first time. I had watched Dad for years cutting boards using this essential carpenter's tool. He made it look so easy and I thought, "I don't think I can do it that easily, but maybe I'm ready." He set me up with a marked board to cut a straight line. I picked up the heavy tool in my small hands, placed the wobbly saw on the board and began to rip through the board showing a jagged mess. The more I cut, the bigger mess I made, until I knew I had destroyed the board. Dad didn't seem too phased by my cut and simply said, "We can use that board somewhere else. Don't worry about it. Just get another board and try again." My competence didn't begin at that moment, but my courage in trusting his gentle teaching with me did begin. I simply felt his okayness with my mistakes in order for me to learn. In retrospect, I could risk the mistake because he had communicated that was the only path to learn how to do the job better.

The question for students, and any one of us for that matter, has to do with what they risk when they enter the pastoral encounter. They certainly risk rejection, dismissal, toleration, or condescending disdain. In addition to the fear of judgment and isolation from those he/she is trying to provide care for, he/she also risks receiving judgment and isolation from the peer group if brought in for consultation. The CPE community and the individual supervisor is subject to the same ambiguity as any other human experience. The difference, hopefully, resides in the community or group's decision to remain in relationship despite the ambiguity. As pastoral supervisors, we guide students in helping them identify the process of their control as they are in relationship. This includes how they protect themselves from the feelings of anxiety in tension with the content of their behavior. Certainly a goal as a pastoral supervisor is to help students by enabling them to name the anxieties that hinder their function in ministry. This encourages students to identify for themselves their own stories so that they will be able to evaluate their own ministry formation.

Painful learning for students takes place as they provide ministry to patients/clients/parishioners who are faced with pain, suffering, and death, as well as to the family and staff who provide for their care. My second year residency and supervisory residency took place at Children's Medical Center in Dallas where feelings of helplessness are confronted daily. Students questioned issues of adequacy as they struggled with the theodicy issues of childhood suffering. This represented a painful yet teachable moment for students, as well as myself. Part of the offering of grace in the face of failure with students happened here. I attempted to bring focus for the students as they experienced their teachable moments and to assist them in embracing more fully the hope of their gifts that they bring to ministry even in the middle of the ambiguity.

One example of this was seen in D, a Southern Baptist student whose learning issues of pastoral authority sometimes limited his ministry. He was called on to provide pastoral care to a family grieving the death of their child. He wondered about his competency with the family because of denominational and ethnic differences. This was evidenced in his ongoing struggle of speaking up or shutting down when emotions began to run high. I kept the focus of supervision on his ministry with the family. I asked him, "What was the family needing from you? How did you provide community for them? What would this have to do with your learning issues around pastoral authority and identity?" He began to reflect that the family relied on his presence to help direct them through the chaos and that he provided a "reminder of the Holy." Paradoxically, as he became more focused on his competency with the family, the less competent he felt. Theologically, you could say that D refused to die to self, pointing to an idolatrous worship of his own abilities and a rejection of God's creative grace. Despite his internal anxieties, he connected with them on a deeper, more transcendent level, dealing in the realm of the Spirit working in community with them, which was at the heart of his learning. The teachable moment for D was that in spite of himself, somehow God was sufficient.

It is such exciting moments, as with this student, that redeem and give hope to lean into the unknown despite these anxieties of inadequacy and fears of not being accepted. This is what helps me when I stand in the threat of being isolated or rejected; the life affirming response of courageously accepting and taking in the threat of not being, as Tillich would say, a courageously affirming self when everything else seems to scream to its contrary. Courage comes at a time, like hope, when I accept the presence of death and choose life anyway. Douglas John Hall reminds me:

> The suffering God—the God who yearns parentally towards creation; the God whose power expresses itself unexpectedly in the weakness of love . . . This, I believe, is not only a more profound image of God . . . it is also more accessible to the human spirit.

While at Children's Medical Center, the Pastoral Care Department provided an annual memorial service for the medical staff, nurses, and other care providers who needed an opportunity to express their accumulative grief. The following represents a "Litany of Hope" that I wrote for one of those services.

> Leader: O gracious God, we come to you because we recognize your love and care for us in the midst of this place that provides both safety and danger. It is painful to remember our loved ones and those we have cared for who have touched our lives and who have died. We remember not just their name now, but their face, their smile, and their story. At times we feel guilty in our helplessness—for not doing enough, for not knowing enough, for not stopping death. In our guilt and anger we come to you to be given comfort and to be reminded that you are with us in life and death. Gracious God, in your mercy . . .
> **People: Hear our prayer.**

Leader: O faithful God, we listened to our loved ones' and patients' hopes and prayers; we were pained by their suffering. There are times when we have blamed you for causing illness and we ask, "Why?" There are times we have bargained in our helplessness, promising to change. We know that not all of the news we hear or give is good, but we keep our hope and faith in you. Remind us that you do not take those we love as much as you receive them. We know that you are grieved with us when our family and friends have to suffer. O faithful God, in your mercy . . .
People: Hear our prayer.
Leader: O loving God, encourage us now as we come together remembering and celebrating the lives that have touched us. Bless our families represented here that we may be empowered by each other and that we may leave this place with a replenished spirit and determined will, but above all, that we may risk loving again as we give of ourselves to our friends, our families, and to our God. O loving God, in your mercy . . .
People: Hear our prayer.

There is something about "to risk loving again" that gets at the meaning of extending grace to others and ourselves when we experience what we sometimes define as failure. In pastoral care, death may not necessarily represent failure, but the pain involved in losing yet one more person to death with whom we have been in relationship. In pastoral supervision, grace in the face of failure is something we can experience as well as something experienced for those we are supervising.

CONFIDENCE IN THE LEARNER

I do, upon occasion, revisit my theory papers completed in the ACPE supervisory certification process, to evaluate how they have evolved or how I still operate within their perimeters.

Malcolm Knowles' theory of adult learning has been an ongoing helpful resource in my supervision of students. Knowles, Carl Jung, and Paul Tillich are great resources I utilize, particularly in trusting that the inward movement toward wholeness is God-given, whether the movement is conscious or unconscious. This inward movement is evidenced in Knowles' theory of a person's desire for wholeness and in their satisfaction concerning self-directed learning. This helps me understand how students learn and how any one of us participates in that learning. I'll briefly outline Knowles' primary components of adult learning that I still find helpful in my supervision of students: 1) Adults need to know why they need to know something before learning it because they become more self-invested, 2) Adults have a self-concept of being responsible for their choices, 3) The role of the adult's life experience is the central resource. For example, the life experience and learning needs of a 24 year-old African American male who recently graduated from seminary will vary from the experience and expectations of a 50 year-old Caucasian female who never attended seminary, 4) The adult's orientation to learning is task-oriented or problem-centered, meaning the arena of learning is how the adult perceives and responds to the problem affecting his/her life situation, 5) The most powerful motivating factor for adults is not external, but internal—that is, the desire for satisfaction, self esteem, and wholeness.[8]

Students considering a CPE program, and even long after they have arrived, will say on some level of awareness, "I need experience in ministry to help me practically in my pastoral formation and identity." The process of their anxiety is seen in the kinds of content questions that are asked, which have to do with curriculum, on-call schedules, or patient/client/congregant encounters. Underlying these anxiety questions is the unasked question of trust. "Can I trust you or others with myself?" "Will you do me right?" The deeper, sometimes more pertinent, questions that may go unasked are, "Am I trustworthy in ministry?" "Am I up for this challenge?" "Am I out of my comfort zone and skill set?" Malcolm Knowles reported that mutual trust is essential for learning to take place, which, ultimately, helps them trust in God's competence.

I also have the awareness that whatever lofty pursuit of wholeness the student is on, their resistance to change is equally great. We have witnessed the most motivated of students continue to resist their own movement toward more differentiated functioning because it means a change of behavior, paradigm, or a change of relationship with others. While in consultation with a more seasoned supervisor as I prepared to meet the Certification Commission for ACPE supervisor, a nagging theme of my tendency to over-teach continued to present itself. After several sessions of bringing student vignettes in for consultation, this experienced supervisor finally said, "You know, Mark, I trust that you will continue to do this behavior in one form or another. My hope is that you will be a little less satisfied with yourself the next time you do it!" I translated this to be his statement of trust in me that I would know the timing better than anyone else when my need to over-teach had reached its limit and I would begin to experiment with other methodologies in the moment.

The role in pastoral supervision is not too far from parenting, as we model for students our own passion for ministry, our ability to improvise in the face of impasse, extending grace in the face of failure, and confidence that in the final analysis it is the learner who will walk on his/her own two legs.

NOTES

1. Sidney Rosen, *My Voice Will Go With You: The Teaching Tales of Milton H. Erickson, M.D.* (New York: W.W. Norton and Company, 1991).

2. Studer Group, *Service Excellence Teams Manual* (The Studer Group), 2.

3. Edwin Friedman, *Generation to Generation* (New York: The Guilford Press, 1985), 2-3.

4. Samuel Wells, *The Drama of Christian Ethics* (Grand Rapids, IA: Brazos Press, 2004), 11.

5. Malcolm Knowles, *The Adult Learner: A Neglected Species* (Houston: Gulf Publishing Company, 1990), 57-63.

6. William McElvaney, *The People of God in Ministry* (Nashville: Abingdon, 1981), 57.

7. Walter Wangerin, *Ragman and Other Cries of Faith* (San Francisco: Harper-Collins, 2004), 108.

8. Malcolm Knowles, *Op. cit.*, 63.

CHAPTER TWO

Reflecting Theologically

Mildred Best

Reflecting theologically is a way of living, a way of being. It is a way of ever being sensitive to the "Other" beyond which we can sometimes see, hear, taste, smell, or touch using our natural senses. It requires us to become aware of another element beyond ourselves that defines who we are and what we are. Reflecting theologically reminds us of our unique calling as pastors, chaplains, and spiritual caregivers—a claim that is unique to our calling and vocation. It is what separates us from the social worker and psychologist, in that reflecting theologically can be said to be innate to our profession and calling.

REFLECTING THEOLOGICALLY DEFINED

Reflecting theologically can be defined as an effort to apply a theological understanding of our relationship to self, others, and God to any aspect of what it means to be a creature created in the image of God, *imago Dei*. It is the recognition that all of life is intertwined and one aspect of the story relates to and builds on the other.

The story of God in creation, the communal story, and its relationship to the individual all provide an understanding and definition of reflecting theologically. It raises questions such as "What does this situation have to do with God?" More fully, "How does the divine love of God permeate our relationships with one another?" It is using the resources at our disposal to understand what is going on in our relationships. It helps us to understand that there is a higher, ontological dimension of our existence. It requires imagination and an under-standing of storytelling.

Reflecting theologically can be applied to many areas of our existence. As an African-American woman, I have found it impossible to view myself as a human being without reflecting on God's movement in history with regard to the Africans brought to the Americas in chains—slaves from which I am a descen-dent. That God story has been informed and reflected upon from a scrip-tural/biblical standpoint, including the story of the Israelites in bondage in Egypt and God's movement in history toward liberation. This reflection upon a greater human story of our existence, as well as our current stories, can be used as a resource from many ethnic viewpoints.[1]

One definition of theological reflection is as follows: "Theological reflec-tion is a self-conscious, intentional act in which one seeks to know God and be known by God so that one can love God and others as God loves."[2]

REFLECTING THEOLOGICALLY WITH PARISHIONERS

Reflecting theologically occurs in churches and other ministry settings some-times in a natural, spontaneous manner. What is proposed in this chapter is a greater need to be intentional about reflecting theologically in our churches and other ministry settings. Possibilities are inevitable and far ranging. How are we intentional about encouraging and teaching our youth, students, and others for whom we supervise and teach to reflect theologically? How do we make sure reflecting theologically provides an impetus to our pastoral care? This chapter will attempt to examine reflecting theologically as the core, the essence, even the soul of our ministries with youth groups, students, laypersons, professional chaplains, and other spiritual caregivers concerned about a holistic view of min-istry and caring for the soul.

Reflecting theologically is also an avenue for helping our parishioners and, in particular, our youth "be in the world, but not of the world." It can provide an opportunity for youth who cannot hide from the outside influences of a pop cul-ture that focuses much on self—a narcissistic culture. Reflecting theologically can help youth frame a right perspective from their religious standpoint by teaching them to reflect theologically on the aspects of our culture that do more harm than good when "love thy neighbor as thyself" seems not to exist from a communal, relational standpoint.

For example, in focusing on morality, reflecting theologically has been used with youth who love to listen to rap music. As a youth superintendent in Sunday school, I invited youth to reflect theologically after listening to a rap song that had negative lyrics. With seminary youth (parents enrolled in seminary) several sessions were held, inviting the youth to reflect theologically on a popular movie. It is apparent that reflecting theologically can occur in an intentional way in many venues. Being intentional about reflecting theologically is akin to the philosophical concept of "habit taking."[3]

My experience of being intentional about reflecting theologically occurred during my seminary years in which I asked a youth group whose parents were seminarians to reflect theologically on the movie entitled *Dirty Dancing*. I selected this movie because I discovered that the youth were having a contest as to who could watch it the most. One young man boasted 20 times.

In order to explain reflecting theologically to a group between the ages of 12 and 14, I started with the explanation that all stories are about God, whether God is mentioned or not. I used the biblical story of the prodigal son as an example of a story that is about God, yet God is not mentioned. We applied this same concept to the movie. Students were shown selected portions of the movie and were asked to complete a simple form with the headings: *What in the story draws the characters closer to God?* and *What in the story draws the characters away from God?* Interestingly enough, most of the youth made notes regarding the relationships of the characters and the characters behavior toward each other. Genuine friendship and authentic caring of others were named as those things that draw the characters closer to God. Of course, those behaviors in the story in which people did harm to one another either emotionally or physically were noted as the things that draw us away from God. The youth had a lively discussion while making some connections to what they had learned in church and the Bible about loving one another. Youth were then asked to go home and use the same form while watching their favorite sitcom or television show. All of the young people did the assignment using shows such as *Star Trek: The Next Generation*. This appeared to be a very simple elementary way to teach reflecting theologically, yet it was effective. Of course, as with many approaches, there is a downside. For example, a church deacon that worked with me and our church youth group stated, "Mildred, you make me sick. Ever since you taught the youth about reflecting theologically, I cannot enjoy a decent movie without asking myself during the movie, 'What does this have to do with God?'"

REFLECTING THEOLOGICALLY ON CONTEMPORARY THEMES

Barth once said that doing theology is the Bible in one hand and the newspaper in the other. I found this approach helpful when asked in a class to reflect theologically on articles from the Wall Street Journal. One such article that caught my attention, for example, had to do with the cheap wines that were being sold sometimes under different labels by reputable fine wine companies. The article acknowledged that these cheap wines with higher sugar content were more addictive and caused more damage to the physical, mental, and emotional health of individuals, especially those who were prone to the disease of alcoholism. From a theological standpoint, this was a justice theme and a lack of concern for the least of these. This brings me to resources for doing theological reflection.

Reflecting Theologically and Clinical Pastoral Education

Reflecting theologically is the essence of what we do in Clinical Pastoral Education. It clearly distinguishes us from other helping professions. As clinical pastoral educators and supervisors, it keeps us from losing our soul in terms of our unique contribution to the helping professions from pastoral and spiritual perspectives. I find that in my work, incorporating theological reflection is an important element in the CPE model. Reflecting theologically becomes a significant component of pastoral formation, pastoral competence, and pastoral reflection.

In a didactic on theological reflection, students are encouraged to develop their own working definition of theological reflection as a group. From there, the focus is on resources for theological reflection and a final activity in which these resources are applied to a short narrative for level I CPE students.

The didactic on theological reflection for level II CPE students is a two-part presentation. In session one, students are asked to read the article entitled *The Discipline and Habit of Theological Reflection* as preparation. Students explore the definition of theological reflection and ascertain how reflecting theologically is similar to and yet different from analysis and meditation. Lastly, a typology is used as the group explores resources for doing theological reflection. Resources include scripture and other sacred text, various theologies such as narrative, liberation, womanist or feminist, and orthodox theology to mention a few.

In session two, students are asked to each bring a verbatim (dialogue only) that has been presented and critiqued previously. In this session, students reflect on the encounter strictly from theological perspectives using resources developed and articulated from the previous didactic. Other students are asked not to critique the verbatim a second time, but dialogue about the theology based upon their own theological perspective or applying some of the resources for theological reflection. In this respect, three steps for reflecting theologically are introduced to the students which are as follows: 1) What is theology? 2) What is reflection? and 3) What is theological reflection? In addition, a process for theological reflection is provided with steps and guiding questions. The eight steps are as follows: 1) Select the encounter, 2) Narrate the encounter, 3) Select a theological approach for the reflection, 4) Analyze the encounter in terms of the chosen approach, 5) Note surprises, 6) Make a theological statement,[4] 7) Design a pastoral care plan, and 8) Articulate in an oral presentation, written statement, or prayer (preferably to a peer group) what happened between you and God in the theological reflection.[5]

PASTORAL IDENTITY

Focus on pastoral identity, with a focus on narrative and the importance of story—personal story, communal story, and the story of the relationship with God—is essential.

> To be a person is to have a story. Without my story, I have no identity. I do not know who I am, or what I am about. If you have no story, how do you know where you're going; and if you're going somewhere, how will you know when you get there?[6]

In a seminar on the topic of pastoral formation and identity, the above quote is used to set the stage to dialogue about our personal narrative. The question that Jesus asked one of the disciples, "Who do you say that I am?" is used at the beginning of a dialogue among the group on the influences in their personal narratives. On the board, columns are placed with the names of each participant listed vertically. This usually is done in a small group. Horizontal columns consist of the following questions: 1) What messages did you receive from your family of origin about who you are? 2) What messages did you receive from your church or community of faith about who you are? 3) Who do you say that you are? 4) What scriptures and/or sacred readings inform who you are? and 5) What metaphors come to mind that shape your pastoral identity and who you are as a pastor? Questions are asked one at a time and each person is given an opportunity to respond. The presenter writes the responses in the appropriate columns.

CPE students have found this to be a helpful exercise, especially at level I. The peer group also comments on patterns and theological threads they gather from snippets of their personal stories for all to see. This is but a small example of how reflecting theologically can be applied to personal narratives as they inform pastoral identity and formation.

One way of reflecting theologically is to ask students to select a spiritual assessment tool that resonates with them. However, before using this tool as an instrument in pastoral care, they are asked to first use a tool such as Pruyser's, Fitchett's, Ramsay's, or others' and write a spiritual self-assessment. This results in students finding another avenue of reflecting theologically in terms of pastoral identity and formation.

A resource for Clinical Pastoral Education level II students is the theological integration paper. This idea was a result of my experience in writing the CPE theory papers. The purpose is to begin the initial phase of helping students to integrate their theology in this pastoral care context as informed by their personal narrative.

REFLECTING THEOLOGICALLY IN THE CULTURAL CONTEXT

When helping students to prepare the theological integration paper, I use my own story to discuss my pastoral theology of way making that informs my supervision, my pastoral care, and my life's view of how I experience God in my personal narrative and the communal narrative. For example, I am aware that African-American folk religion has greatly shaped my religious heritage, which is prevalent in black religion. Dwight Hopkins explored the image of God as Way Maker in his book, *Shoes That Fit Our Feet: Sources for a Constructive Black Theology*. These images include God as Creator Way Maker, Co-Laboring Way Maker, and Way Maker Deliver. The image of God as Way Maker is consistent with my pastoral theology of shepherding. God as Creator Way Maker, for me, was an indicator of the equality of human beings. It was in the Baptist church as a child that I was first introduced to the image of God as Way Maker in an often heard phrase during testimony services: "God can make a way out of no way. God is a Way Maker."[7]

Cultural context with regards to reflecting theologically is important in supervising students. One student I supervised from a war-torn country was well aware that the war in her country informed her theology and her understanding of pastoral care. Family members had died or were either under persecution as such. To leave out this experience while reflecting theologically would be to ignore what has shaped her so profoundly and has enabled her to understand the role of use of self in pastoral care.

CONCLUSION

Remembering all that shapes who and what we are, as influenced by our theological understandings in a familial and cultural context, is one way in which theological reflection can truly become a *habit* and a *discipline*. It is recognizing our individuality, but also the sociopolitical nature of the larger community and the ways God moves in our current history making. Martin Luther King once said, "We are caught in an inescapable network of mutuality, tied into a single garment of destiny. Whatever affects one directly affects all indirectly. We are made to live together because of the inter-related structure of reality."[8] Reflecting theologically keeps us honest and thoughtful as to the interrelatedness of all creatures, creation, and the Creator.

NOTES

1. Susan Brooks Thistlethwaite and Mary Potter Engel, eds., *Lift Every Voice: Constructing Christian Theologies from the Underside* (Maryknoll, NY: Orbis Books, 2004).

2. Heather A. Warren, Joan L. Murray, and Mildred M. Best, "The Discipline and Habit of Theological Reflection," *Journal of Religion and Health* (Volume 41, No. 4, 2002), 323-331.

3. Justus Buchler, ed., *Philosophical Writings of Peirce* (New York: Dover Publications, Inc., 1950) 359.

4. Heather A. Warren, Joan L. Murray, and Mildred M. Best, *Op. cit.*

5. *Ibid.*

6. William J. Bausch, *Storytelling and Imagination* (Mystic, CT: Twenty-Third Publications, 1986), 171.

7. Mildred Best, *A Pastoral Theology of Way Making*, Unpublished paper, 1996.

8. Katie Cannon, *Black Womanist Ethics* (Eugene, OR: Wipf and Stock Publishers, 1988), 177.

CHAPTER THREE

Pastoral Supervision and Field Education

Carrie Doehring

> Students come to seminary already formed by a variety of experiences with family, congregation, school, work, and the significant relationships in each. Later, the congregations that clergy serve in the years during and following formal theological education act as a forge or furnace of ongoing education and formation for ministry. An especially crucial point in this development is the transition from the relative safety of seminary to the fire of responsible congregational leadership, as the learning that takes place in the midst of intense experiences becomes embodied in the pastor who communicates God's judgment and grace, forgiveness and blessing.[1]

Field education provides a pivotal experience of embodied learning, as students venture out from the seminary culture of critical thinking and step into the roles of ministry in congregational and organizational settings. The formative learning through enactment that takes place in field education can be likened to a dramatic performance. As the curtain rises at the beginning of a supervised ministry experience, the student appears onstage as a pastor or rabbi, chaplain, counselor, or staff member in a nonprofit organization. The setting and the actors for this drama are provided by the supervised ministry site, which may be a community of faith, hospital, hospice, counseling center, or nonprofit organization. Performing the roles of leading worship, preaching, engaging in pastoral care conversations, and planning and teaching in religious education—sometimes for the first time—challenges students to embody learning, such that their tone of voice, body language, and ways of being present and relating all begin to communicate what they are learning in their theological studies.

In many ways, the drama of field education is most like an ongoing rehearsal where the supervisor and student, along with members of the lay committee, regularly step off the stage, and become co-directors of the drama. Additional opportunities to stop the action and reflect together are provided in the seminary setting, in seminars where peers and faculty often discuss systemic analyses of ministry settings, engage in theological reflection, and prepare and present cumulative integrative papers. Supervision provides a space for reflecting on the ways in which students' theological education is forming and transforming them, and more or less equipping them to step into ministerial roles. By paying special attention to the gaps between what they learn in theological studies and how they perform their roles and the challenging moments when students fall short of embodying the theology they are learning, students will be able to craft performances that are more and more authentic to their ministerial identities and the ecclesial or organization contexts in which their ministry will be practiced.

> Sustained experience in actual practice of pastoral ministry somehow takes all that one is and all that one has learned and is learning and refashions it in such a way that the many forces and dynamics working in and through one increasingly gain coherence and are mobilized for the sake of creative and intelligent pastoral leadership. Deep engagement in pastoral ministry itself, in other words, has a powerfully formative effect.[2]

In the process of supervision, the other players, no matter how seasoned and experienced they are, will co-create their roles in new ways and a unique community of mutual learning and formation will come into being for the duration of the supervised ministry experience.

The notion of field education as performance may, at first glance, seem to overemphasize the professional training that is part of preparation for ministry, rather than the historical understanding of ministry as an office of the church in which "the pastoral leader stands as the inheritor and communicator of the church's tradition that stretches back to the first Apostles."[3] In addition, the professional model of ministry, with field education as the stage on which students practice the performance of this role, may seem to diminish the importance of a student's call or vocation, as that which essentially equips them to pursue ministry. These three models of ministry—as an office, profession, and calling—have defined Christian ministry in different ways at different historical periods. In comparing these models of ministry as an office, a profession, and a calling, it is striking that the authority inherent in the role of minister is conferred in different ways. When ministry is seen as an office, the church authorizes the candidate's induction into this office. When ministry is seen as a profession, it is the seminary that provides the academic and some of the professional credentials for ministry. When ministry is understood as a calling, it is the spiritual gifts and inward calling of the candidate along with the affirmation provided by the community and church that makes someone a minister. Given that field education falls within the purview of theological education, it is more likely that it will emphasize the model of ministry as profession, especially when student ministry is described as an opportunity to rehearse and perform the roles of ministry.

These models of ministry are best understood as complementary; each important in different ecclesial and seminary contexts and at different stages in the lifelong learning that is part of ministry. For many people, the model of ministry as calling is more prominent at the early stages of the journey toward ordained ministry, in the recognition of gifts, and the inward calling that initially focus on the person as potential pastor. H. Richard Niebuhr delineates three kinds of call that are all part of the model of ministry as calling: 1) the providential call of having "the talents necessary for the work of the office," 2) the secret call, which is "that inner persuasion or experience whereby a person feels . . . directly summoned or invited by God to take up the work of ministry," and 3) the ecclesial call that comes from the community of faith and the institution of the church.[4] Within religious traditions emphasizing the office of ministry, the ecclesial confirmation of one's call comes before theological education. This is often the case, for example, in Roman Catholic and Orthodox traditions. Similarly, when the call is experienced within and confirmed by a denomination prior to seminary, students often seek seminaries that will acculturate them within the traditions of their denomination and help them meet the professional qualifications set by their denomination.

Within communities of faith that have the authority to ordain their own clergy, the initial emphasis is often on the providential call, especially as gifts for ministry are identified early on by one's family and community. The secret call may emerge in the form of an intense transformative experience and may be demonstrated in the form of testimonials or sermons in which the gift for evangelism is demonstrated within the community. In such contexts, the predominant model of ministry is one of calling rather than profession or office. Indeed, a graduate degree may not be required for ordination since the emphasis is on the formation of the minister within the community of faith rather than within a seminary or school of theology.

For people who describe themselves as spiritual seekers, a calling towards a spiritual vocation rather than a specifically clerical vocation often propels them into religious studies as undergraduates and graduate programs in theological studies. Such seekers experience a calling, but often without ecclesial confirmation. This is especially the case for spiritual seekers who did not grow up in a religious tradition or who have left their childhood traditions and are searching for a new spiritual home. They come to theological education in order to explore their spiritual calling and professionally equip themselves in ways similar to doctors and lawyers. In a sense, they look to the seminary to provide an affirmation of this calling, before finding a church home and seeking affirmation from an ecclesial judicatory body.

While there is an overlap between models of ministry as calling and profession at the beginning of theological studies, the model of ministry as profession often dominates the experience of theological education for students in graduate degree programs. The interlocking features of theological education—

> critical thinking and personal appropriation of historical, contemporary, religious and secular knowledges . . . , contextual analysis and global perspectives . . . , interfaith and other forms of cross-cultural and intercultural exposure, [and] practical skills for particular ministries[5]—

all come together in field education. Field education provides a practicum or internship in which one draws upon all that one has learned in order to perform as a professional in a training setting that provides oversight. As such, field education often plays an important role in helping students discern whether or not the roles of ministry suit them. In addition, evaluations by supervisors, lay committees, and seminary-based seminars of peers and faculty provide a form of endorsement of the student's calling, sometimes even the initial endorsement for students who have not yet found a spiritual home in which their calling can be realized. The evaluation in field education of students' vocation or calling, as well as their suitability for the profession of ministry, may propel spiritual seekers toward ecclesial affirmation of their call or toward alternate ways of living out their vocation outside of congregational ministry. In the last phase of their formal theological education, as students move toward ordination they are often evaluated by ecclesial committees in terms of all three models of ministry: whether they meet the professional qualifications for ordination within their denomination, whether their call is authentic and affirmed, and whether they can adequately fulfill the office of ministry as defined by their particular religious traditions.

Field education within the context of theological studies, as I have argued, usually emphasizes the model of ministry as profession. However, when performance is understood as a means of enacting theology, then the performance inherent in field education offers a window through which students and supervisors can reflect on whether students are learning to inhabit a ministerial identity by participating in practices as "the bearers and creators . . . of living principles of hope and obligation."[6] Their practices bring to light the theology they embody through their actions. Supervision creates a relational space for collaborative reflection on the lived practice of theology, providing an opportunity to "know in action by reflecting upon practice."[7] Coming at the juncture between formal theological education and full fledged ministry, field education provides a space for collaborative reflections on how "the practices of life and ministry not only reveal faith, but also embody and create faith."[8]

The metaphor of field education as performance need not, then, be limited to describing the professional enactment of the roles of student ministry. The notion of performance can more broadly describe a performative approach to theology, as has been articulated by Elaine Graham:

The proper focus of pastoral theology is not the pastoral agent or theological ethics or applied theology, but the pastoral *practice* of the faith-community itself. . . . The arena of Christian *praxis*—value-directed and value-laden action—is understood as the medium through which the Christian community embodies and enacts its fundamental vision of the Gospel. Theology is properly conceived as a performative discipline, in which the criterion of authenticity is deemed to be *orthopraxis*, or authentic transformatory action, rather than *orthodoxy* (right belief).[9]

In this sense, theology as a performative practice at the heart of field education ought to be continuous with the lifelong learning inherent in living out the vows which all Christians make at critical junctures in their lives, like baptism and confirmation, and for some, entering covenantal relationships and being ordained. The work of field education—reflecting upon the lived relational theology enacted in communities of faith—is the work of living in Christian community, and in this sense, field education is a natural extension of ministry that enhances the lifelong learning of all Christians. As John Patton argues, pastoral supervision is not only a form of professional education; when available to laity it can be a form of spiritual direction that helps lay members discern their gifts for lay ministry and live according to their religious values and beliefs.[10] Pastors can use what they learn in their role as field education supervisors to enhance their overall ministry, especially in helping members discern their spiritual gifts and live out their vocations.

In many ways, as I have noted, field education is part of the ordinary drama of living out or performing one's faith on a day to day basis. What distinguishes field education from this ordinary drama of Christian life are the structures that make it more like the intentional performances of a staged production with designated roles (that of student and supervisor), a director and producer (roles often shared by students, supervisors, and faculty), a script (the learning covenant), a theater (the field education site), a series of acts (the beginning, middle, and end) and evaluations, and an audience (the congregation and the seminary-based seminar). These common ingredients are what distinguish the learning within a field education experience from the lifelong learning inherent in Christian faith.

While these ingredients are common across almost all field education experiences, what actually happens within a supervised ministry experience—the narrative drama that unfolds—is unique. Staying with the comparison of field education to a dramatic performance, one could say that while all theatrical dramas have similar ingredients, the narratives that unfold can be as different from each other as Samuel Beckett's *Waiting for Godot* is different from Arthur Miller's *Death of a Salesman*. So, too, is the case in field education. Even when the seminary, site, supervisor, and seminar leaders are the same from one year to the next, the differences between one student and another make for remarkably different field education experiences. The highly contextual nature of supervised ministry experiences are shaped by many factors: the seminary's approach to theological education, the site's culture, organizational, ethical, and theological commitments, and the student's and supervisor's cultural and theological identities. These contextual factors make each supervised ministry experience unique. As I identify and elaborate the components common to pastoral supervision of field education, I will at moments provide illustrations of the extent to which context shapes these components.

Before I proceed further, I need to acknowledge how much my understanding of pastoral supervision and field education is shaped by my context. I teach at Iliff School of Theology, a theologically liberal protestant school located in Denver, Colorado. Many of Iliff's students are spiritual seekers drawn to the academic study of religion, who have a spiritual calling and are exploring whether the profession of ministry suits them and which tradition or denomination will be the best fit for them. Within this context, the models of ministry as profession and calling—especially providential and secret spiritual calling—predominate. The theoretical perspectives and practices most relevant to my experiences of pastoral supervision and field education come from theologically liberal pastoral theology, care and counseling, and practical theology. Rather than pretend to write universally applicable reflections on pastoral supervision and field education, I want to acknowledge at the outset that this chapter will be most relevant to readers who share similar theoretical and pastoral commitments.

Having described the ways in which field education 1) tests students' readiness for the profession of ministry, 2) clarifies the nature of their calling, 3) draws upon performative understandings of faith and theology, and 4) is part of the lifelong learning of Christians in communities of faith, I would like to explore in detail the key components of pastoral supervision of field education— how a trustworthy supervisory relationship needs to be established at the outset of field education, the need to formulate a learning covenant, and the need for ongoing theological reflection, self reflection, and evaluation.

ESTABLISHING A TRUSTWORTHY SUPERVISORY RELATIONSHIP

The process of reflecting upon the lived relational theology enacted by students takes place within supervisory relationships established between the student and the supervisor, lay committee, and seminary-based seminar. While the etymological meaning of the word supervision is oversight, Ward prefers the metaphor of "space" rather than "sight":

> The 'space of supervision' . . . becomes a space in which mutual learning occurs, a space of interaction and dialogue, a space where identities are formed and transformed, a space of interplay and experimentation . . . where both supervisor and reflective practitioner can experience safety and challenge so that growth and learning occurs.[11]

These supervisory relationships become the relational container that supports students as they step into ministerial roles and reflect upon the performative theology enacted in these roles.

In the beginning phase of field education, relationships based on trust need to be established in order for students to take the risks that inevitably occur when they become "so immersed in the human situation that they cannot fail to experience it as a predicament rather than a problem."[12] John Patton notes that when there is sufficient trust, both supervisors and students will resist the temptation to solve problems or "learn the right procedures"—instead, they will be able to experience problems "in a relation and move on, strengthened by that relationship, to minister in a situation where there is no clearly correct procedure."[13] Patton goes on to make this important distinction about the centrality of trusting supervisory relationships: "Pastoral supervision is pastoral, in its relational sense, because the supervisee needs not only what the supervisor knows, but he or she also needs the significant relationship that the supervisor may offer."[14] In the beginning phase of field education, supervisors and students can create a relational container by becoming aware of emotions, stressors, power dynamics, and relational boundaries.

EXAMINING MOTIVES AND FEELINGS AT THE OUTSET OF FIELD EDUCATION

As supervisors and students begin the process of establishing a relationship of trust, it is important that they each think carefully about their reasons for doing field education. Sometimes on-site congregational supervisors invite students into the culture of their congregation out of mixed motives. They may want to give the gift of mentorship, in memory of those who mentored them. They may be lonely and want a companion-apprentice. They may grudgingly step in to supervise a student with difficulties, sure in the knowledge that their pastoral counseling skills will equip them to manage a challenging supervisory relationship. I admit to being guilty of some of these motives. One of the most subtle and challenging motives I have experienced is when I want a student to fulfill my ideal of a supervisee. When it doesn't work out, I'm surprised by the intensity of my reactions. Being able to identify and process these feelings both psychologically and spiritually can help supervisors invest more freely in establishing a relational container in which supervision can take place.

Students undertaking field education are likely to experience a range of expectations and feelings, some of which may arise from the authority conferred on them as student ministers and the power differentials created by this role. They may be apprehensive about whether they will be able to assume the mantle of being a student minister and wear it gracefully. They may have some ambivalence about assuming the pastoral authority inherent in a student minister's role, or they may feel uneasy about the power differential created by the supervisor's authority and evaluative role.

Some stressors may be related to students' ambivalence about field education. If they have previous professional experiences similar to field education, they may feel resentful about being cast in a beginner's role and having to invest the time, energy, and tuition dollars necessary for training in the profession of ministry. Some who come out of traditions emphasizing the call rather than professional model of ministry may feel as through the strength of their call lessens their need for professional training in the arts of ministry. Spiritual seekers may over-invest in field education, wanting the supervisor to be an inexhaustible mentor and wanting the congregation or placement to be the ideal faith community, chaplaincy program, hospice, or nonprofit organization. If they have not yet identified their spiritual calling with a particular tradition or denomination, they may want field education to be an experience that affirms their call and sets them on the course toward ordination.

Supervisors and students need to have the psychological and spiritual resources to identify these motivations and feelings, process these feelings in appropriate supportive and collegial relationships, and cope positively with the stress of beginning a field education experience. Supervisors can invite students to identify their motivations and feelings, by asking open-ended questions (What is it like to begin this field education? How do you feel about beginning?), listening non-defensively to hopes, fears, longings, resentment, and ambivalence, and affirming students for taking this next step in their educational, professional, and spiritual development.

MONITORING POWER DYNAMICS AND RELATIONAL BOUNDARIES

One-on-one helping relationships that evoke memories of formative relationships can sometimes generate surprisingly intense emotional and relational dynamics. Given the power differential inherent in supervisory relationships, supervisors need to attend to relational dynamics that may make them want to disengage emotionally from supervisees or become emotionally fused with them by forming friendships or taking them under their wings in overly protective or directive ways. These relational dynamics can push supervisors towards acting in overpowering ways or towards feeling overpowered by students' learning or relational needs.[15]

Given the needs that some students bring into their vocations, as well as the tendency of some to idealize or belittle their supervisors, it should be no surprise that even supervisors who have received specialized training as pastoral counselors will need, first and foremost, to attend to whether this supervisory relationship is experienced as safe by the supervisee. Safety can be established by monitoring relational boundaries and power dynamics, ensuring that there is an appropriate degree of give and take that empowers students to be both proactive in and receptive to the learning process. Paying attention to relational boundaries that allow for an appropriate degree of emotional separation and connection can help supervisors maintain an empathic response to students. Supervisors can also pay attention to how well students can maintain relational connections with care seekers by stepping into the shoes of care seekers while maintaining a degree of separation that helps students gain perspective. Being able to evaluate a student's capacity for empathy at the outset of the learning experience will help supervisors and students formulate realistic learning goals.

While monitoring relational boundaries and power dynamics is essential for establishing any helping or supervisory relationship, it can be especially challenging in supervising field education in communities of faith. If off-site supervisors make on-site visits to ministry settings, there may be social occasions, like shared meals, included in the visit. I had an occasion, for example, as one of the seminary-based seminar leaders, to do an on-site congregational visit to hear a student preach in Steamboat Springs, Colorado, a four hour trip from Denver where I teach. The visit necessitated an overnight stay, and there were several occasions for shared meals with the student minister and her husband. On these social occasions, I needed to remember that I was always in my supervisory role; the more enjoyable the visit, the harder it is to remember this responsibility. On the other hand, when the supervisory relationship is strained, or when students do poorly or are stressed, it is important to use these social occasions as opportunities to defuse a charged atmosphere, to practice simple kindness and courtesy. During an extended on-site visit, supervisors need to make sure there is time and opportunity for them to unwind, go "off duty," take care of their own needs, and debrief, if necessary.

The requirement that supervisors remember that they are always in their helping and evaluative role is even more challenging for on-site supervisors, especially in smaller congregational settings which function as extended families. Such congregations often have ministries of training student ministers, if they have relied on students to help fill their pulpits, run the youth program or church school, or visit the elderly. In small or rural congregations, students may be billeted with church members and supervising clergy may have offices in their homes. Even when the need to rely on each other puts supervisor and supervisee temporarily in learning moments that stretch professional roles, supervisors can use such moments as opportunities to talk about how to monitor relational boundaries and power dynamics in extended family congregations that may evoke family of origin issues. Such circumstances can provide opportunities to talk about maintaining appropriate relational boundaries in order for students to recognize when they are on or off duty, how to separate work from their private lives, and the particular challenges of being married or single, gay or straight, and with or without children in settings where one is continually in the public eye as a student minister.

In addition, supervisors need to assess at the outset of a supervisory relationship whether there is a "good enough" fit between their social identities and their supervisees'. The more aspects of their social identities are similar— socioeconomic class, ethnicity, citizenship, sexual orientation, gender, age, religion—the more comfortable the initial fit will be and the more likely supervisors will make assumptions about similarities, and at least initially, experience more of a sense of connection in which the differences are less apparent. When aspects of the supervisee's social identity are unfamiliar to supervisors, the more likely they will experience a sense of separation and potential disengagement from the supervisees, and the harder they will need to work at the outset, in order to build a bridge between the world they inhabit and the supervisee's world.

When supervisors have had a range of supervisory experiences, from relationships in which there was a lot of commonality at the outset to supervisory relationships which began with nothing much in common between themselves and their supervisee, they will be more sanguine about the possibilities for connection, growth, and challenges in any supervisory relationship. When supervisors and supervisees take the time at the outset of field education to tell each other aspects of their vocational and faith stories, they can begin to appreciate the uniqueness of the religious and spiritual worlds they each inhabit. The concept of "religious world" proposed by William Paden, a comparative scholar of religious studies, is a helpful way to describe each person's religious faith as a habitat, "a system of language and practice that organizes the world in terms of what is deemed sacred."[16] Paden notes how:

> useful, synthesizing, and far-reaching the concept of 'world' is as an organizing category for the study of religion. 'World' is not just a philosophical abstraction . . . In more human experiential terms, it is an actual habitat, a lived environment, a place . . . [17]

When supervisors appreciate that "within a single tradition like Christianity, there are thousands of religious worlds"[18] they will be more intentional about building bridges between the uniqueness of their religious world and that of their supervisees.[19]

In addition to sharing aspects of their call or faith narratives, supervisors and supervisees may find it helpful to do their cultural genograms,[20] an exercise in which they identify 1) familial patterns related to religion, ethnicity, and social class, 2) important familial and historical events that affected these patterns, 3) family values, sources of pride and shame, and 4) the ethnic and religious sources informing these values. They can compare their genograms in order to identify ways in which cultural and religious values might predispose them to prejudge each other in favorable and unfavorable ways. For example, a student who experiences financial stress and a family history of financial anxiety may initially feel estranged from a supervisor or community of faith who are affluent and appear to be without financial worries. Comparing cultural genograms introduces ways of talking about the importance of social identity in shaping pastoral identity, and the value in identifying and having sometimes difficult conversations about power imbalances created by differences in social identity.

As these reflections on establishing a supervisory relationship illustrate, supervisors need to pay attention to building an alliance at the outset of field education and during moments when the supervisory relationship is disrupted to ensure that there is a relational container for the challenging psychological and spiritual work of immersing oneself in field education. Building a relational container is the process that takes place in the opening weeks of field education and one of the earliest tasks that occur within this relational container is negotiating the learning covenant.

FORMULATING A LEARNING COVENANT

Learning covenants need to include the practicalities of supervision (how often, how long, where, when the session can be interrupted or rescheduled, and the supervisor's availability), boundaries (confidentiality, the focus on the student in ministry and not on the student's personal life apart of ministry), the need to build and foster a working alliance, and establishing the flow of each session (and the student's responsibility for setting the agenda). Formulating and keeping track of learning covenants encourage supervisees to be, first of all, proactive in defining their learning and secondly, interactive in articulating the learning that is possible within the context of their field education sites and seminaries. For students seeking ordination or certification, learning covenants formulated in field education are part of vocational covenants they make with ordaining and certifying organizations. They are also part of the formation process at the heart of theological education and the lifelong learning at the heart of being a person of faith. This ongoing rather than fixed understanding of formation is captured in the notion of lifelong learning: "Instead of a formed identity as the end result of a training process, lifelong learning is about transforming and performing the living traditions of ministry in today's church and society."[21] The more students can appreciate how their spiritual calling, theological education, field experiences of professional of ministry, graduation, and ordination are intertwined, the more they will be able to be proactive in weaving formative and learning experiences together in the narratives they articulate within various circles of accountability, such as seminary, ecclesial ordination committees, and field education. When relationships of trust and accountability become containers for growth in seminaries, ecclesial ordination committees, and field education, students will experience what it is like to co-create their faith and vocational narratives within these relational webs of life. Conversely, when trust is not established or when it is broken or violated, learning will be constricted and it will be challenging for supervisors and ordaining or certifying committees to assess growth and readiness for ministry.

Ideally, past experiences of vocational discernment and evaluation can inform the formulation of the learning covenant. For example, if students' seminary experiences include testing, vocational counseling, and guidance, and if their ordination or certification process similarly includes vocational discernment and psychological assessment, these learning and evaluative experiences can inform their formulation of learning goals. If students are seeking ordination or certification, then they can bring the seminary's standards for completion of field education into dialogue with their ecclesial and/or professional associations' standards for ordination or certification. The more students can set their personal and vocational learning goals within overarching goals for the field education program, their degree program, and their certifying/ordaining organization, the more integrated and authentic their learning will be.

ONGOING THEOLOGICAL REFLECTION: BRIDGING THE GAPS

When trustworthy supervisory relationships have been established and learning covenant formulated, students can engage in the theological reflection that is at the heart of field education. As I noted earlier, the performance inherent in field education offers a window through which students and supervisors can theologically reflect on how students are learning to inhabit a ministerial identity by participating in practices as "the bearers and creators . . . of living principles of hope and obligation."[22] Given the gaps between the language of religious faith expressed within the community of faith and the language of theological studies used in seminaries, engaging in such reflections is challenging. Several distinctions are helpful for reflecting upon this gap: first, second, and third order religious language,[23] embedded and deliberative theology,[24] theological literacy and fluency,[25] and premodern, modern, and postmodern approaches to religious knowledge.[26] I will describe these distinctions and then elaborate how they can be used in supervision to reflect on the theology enacted within field education sites.

FIRST ORDER AND SECOND ORDER RELIGIOUS LANGUAGE

The distinction between first order and second order religious language, along with a similar distinction between embedded and deliberative theology, provide a framework for helping students connect what they learn in theological studies with the language of faith implicitly and explicitly expressed and enacted within field education sites. Theodore Jennings describes first order religious language as expressions of religious faith, like the language used in communal worship, individual prayers, hymns, and creedal statements.[27] Second order religious language uses theological perspectives to reflect upon first order religious language. Such theological perspectives may be learned through informal or formal theological education. Informal theological education is often available within communities of faith through religious education, denominational resources like study guides that discuss controversial issues, and bible studies that draw upon biblical critical methods. Sermons often provide a form of ongoing informal theological education that helps congregants make connections between the bible and their lives. In these venues for informal theological education, clergy and lay leaders draw upon second order religious language to help people explore their religious faith.

The curriculum of formal theological education provides students with an array of second order religious languages: comparative religious studies, biblical critical methods and biblical theology, historical and systematic theology, theological ethics, and practical theologies like pastoral theology, homiletics, and liturgical studies. Depending on the culture of the seminary, students may or may not have an opportunity to move back and forth between the first order language of their religious faith and the second order language of religious and theological studies. Students often experience a crisis of faith in their first year when the second order languages they are learning make them question the faith that propelled them into seminary. First year seminars exploring their call and vocation can help them bridge the gap between their first order language of religious faith and the second order forms of theological reflection they are learning. Field education offers further challenges, of finding ways to use second order religious language in reflecting upon the lived theologies enacted in religious practices.

THEOLOGICAL LITERACY AND THEOLOGICAL FLUENCY

Understanding the distinction between theological literacy and fluency[28] can help students and supervisors talk about the challenges of drawing upon the various second order religious languages students are learning in seminary as they formulate first order religious statements in preaching, worship leadership, pastoral care, and religious education. Academic studies help students become more theologically literate in using these various theological perspectives— comparative studies, biblical critical methods, historical and systematic theology, ethical studies, and practical theology—in their reading and writing, but may not challenge them to become fluent in the sense of being so familiar with these second order language that they are able to use them in first order expressions of religious faith. Students become fluent when they "inhabit" their theology as a faith perspective that they can instinctively use to understand and respond to the spiritual and psychological needs of others.[29] Much fruitful reflection can take place when students and supervisors pay attention to the gap between the lived theology performed in religious practices and the second order forms of theological reflection that students are learning to inhabit and use in fluent and natural ways.

EMBEDDED AND DELIBERATIVE THEOLOGY

Another way of talking about the differences between first and second order language is in terms of the differences between embedded and deliberative theology. In their book, *How to Think Theologically,* Stone and Duke define embedded theology as "the implicit theology that [people of faith] live out in their everyday lives," and they note that "some of us find it easy to articulate the embedded theology that we carry with us. But many do not."[30] Embedded theologies are those precritical and often unexamined beliefs and practices that have become a habitual part of people's worldview and practices. People may not even be aware of their embedded theology until they experience an existential crisis or decentering experience that disrupts their world in ways similar to an earthquake, causing deep layers of sometimes unconscious beliefs to come to the surface. Such moments provide opportunities to excavate these beliefs and decide whether such embedded theologies are still relevant and meaningful, especially in terms of helping people connect with a sense of the sacred and make sense of what is happening.

This process of examining embedded theology engages people in the work of deliberative theology, which Stone and Duke describe as "the understanding of faith that emerges from a process of carefully reflecting upon embedded theological convictions . . . Deliberative theology *carries us forward* when our embedded theology proves inadequate."[31] Embedded theologies use first order religious language that is often precritical to express but not interpret the ways people connect with a sense of the sacred. Deliberative theology draws upon informal and formal theological education to use second order religious language in order to interpret and deliberate over embedded theologies. Field education challenges students to become fluent in using the theological languages they are learning in seminary in the practices of faith and to reflect upon the disjuncture between the embedded theologies they may spontaneously express and the deliberative theologies that they are learning to inhabit in the process of theological education and formation.

THIRD ORDER RELIGIOUS LANGUAGE FOR REFLECTING ON THEOLOGICAL METHODS

An additional distinction that Jennings makes among first, second, and third order ways of talking about religious faith[32] can provide opportunities for students and supervisors to look at the underlying assumptions inherent in the theological perspectives they are learning in seminary and putting into practice in field education. Third order religious language examines the theological method being using to relate theoretical perspectives in psychology and theology to the practices of faith. Third order reflections allow students and supervisors to compare and contrast methodologies, like, for example, the various biblical critical methods that can be used to interpret scripture. Being able to talk about methodology requires a level of sophistication that may or may not be available in students' theological education. For example, students exposed to postmodern approaches to religious knowledge in their theological education will be more able to engage questions about methodology; such approaches offer ways of talking about basic assumptions about what is known, how knowledge is accumulated, and the ways in which knowledge is socially constructed.

Several recent texts offer accessible ways for supervisors and students to explore questions of methodology, particularly methods for connecting the second order languages of religious and theological studies with the first order language of faith practices. Charles Scalise[33] presents five models used throughout history that connect theology and ministry: 1) correlational models that bring the questions and answers of theology and the social sciences into dialogue with existential questions and answers, 2) contextual models that begin with the complexity of lived experience and move inductively to exploring the theologies that emerge out of these experiences, 3) narrative models that link the stories of persons, families, and communities with the narratives of faith found in scripture, 4) performance models that look at how theologies are enacted in the practices of individuals and communities, especially in the use of the arts in worship, and 5) regulative models that look at doctrine as the deep grammar of religious faith. After exploring and illustrating each model, Scalise offers a critical evaluation of each.

A similar text useful for engaging in third order methodological reflections is *Theological Reflection: Methods* written by Elaine Graham, Heather Walton, and Frances Ward.[34] They describe seven methods of theological reflection, providing historical examples and then listing the pros and cons of each method. They arrive at these methods by surveying historical and contemporary practices of theological reflection. Supervisors and students can use Graham et al.'s descriptions to think about their own style of theological reflection, the styles used in their theological education, and the styles used within the congregation. The first method they describe, "theology by heart," is used extensively in field education supervision, Clinical Pastoral Education, pastoral counseling, and spiritual direction:

> God is experienced as immanent, personal and intimate, speaking through the interiority of human experience. Records of such experience—journaling, autobiography, psychotherapeutic accounts of self—are vehicles of theological reflection and construction.[35]

In a companion volume entitled *Theological Reflection: Sources*, Graham et al.[36] offer excerpts from historical and contemporary texts that illustrate each method. In illustrating "theology by heart" they draw upon the writings of Augustine, Thomas Merton, C.S. Lewis, and Anne Dillard.

Another method, useful for highlighting differences between theologically conservative and progressive traditions in theological reflection is described by Graham et al. as "telling God's story." This method emphasizes the bible as "canonical." Theologian Karl Barth used to describe how Christian identity is rooted in the foundational stories of the bible often in opposition to popular culture, in contexts that are seen as fragmenting identity and threatening truth with cultural relativism. Theologians Hans Frei, George Lindbeck, Alistair McIntyre, and Stanley Hauerwas are identified with this method of theological reflection. In describing the drawbacks of this method, Graham et al.[37] note that the Christian tradition, which is believed to have an unchanging deep grammar, is, in fact, radically plural. Further, "while some canonical narrative theologians seek to engage fully with the postmodern challenge, others are nostalgic for a premodern world in which the Christian narrative provided the predominant epistemological framework for society."[38]

The last three methods they describe are relevant in seminaries and field education sites using liberal theological perspectives. The method they identify as "speaking of God in public" brings theological and religious perspectives into dialogue with scientific, artistic, socioeconomic perspectives in order to construct new religious and theological propositions, which in a postmodern approach are understood as contextual and provisional. This method, called the revised correlational method, has been used extensively in liberal pastoral theology, for example, in correlating Tillich with psychodynamic models of personality. A problem with this use of the correlational method is that it focuses on the individual and not on larger social systems.

Another method identified by Graham et al. as "theology in action" that is used within liberation theologies addresses this problem. "The starting point of this method of theological reflection has... never been abstract speculation on timeless truths"[39]—rather, theology begins with concrete experiential knowledge and asks questions about transformative praxis that liberates people from oppression. This theological method is relevant in field education sites doing ministry with those who are marginalized because of gender, race, social class, sexual orientation, or disabilities.

The final method they examine, which they call "theology in the vernacular" has great potential for doing theological reflection in field education sites in nonprofit organizations like shelters for those experiencing homelessness or intimate partner violence, residential care facilities, and hospice organizations. This method pays attention to the local theologies that can be constructed from everyday language, the symbols of ordinary people, and popular culture. It works well in settings where people pull together a syncretistic faith which blends aspects of material, ethnic, and religious culture in idiosyncratic ways.

This discussion of methods of theological reflection highlights how helpful it can be for supervisors and students to engage in third order reflections on the gap or the differences between theological methods used in a seminary context and in the field education site. Such discussions help supervisors and students evaluate the theological "fit" at the outset of a supervised ministry experience so that differences can be taken into account. Consider, for example, the potential conflicts between a supervisor who has developed an intercultural approach to ministry in multicultural and inter-religious contexts, and who uses a "theology in the vernacular" and a student who has been formed in a more conserving theological tradition, who uses a canonical approach. Potential supervisors and students need to be able to identify and talk about these differences in the preliminary stage of assessing whether a site will provide a viable learning environment. Third order reflections on methodology explored in Scalise and Graham, Walton, and Ward provide ways to explore similarities and differences in theological method.

THE TRIFOCAL LENS OF ASSESSING THE RELEVANCE OF PREMODERN, MODERN, AND POSTMODERN APPROACHES TO RELIGIOUS KNOWLEDGE

A final framework that can help students and supervisors talk about the gap between the first order language of religious practices and the second and third order theological and methodological reflections learned in seminary is the metaphor of the trifocal lens for assessing when premodern, modern, and post-modern approaches to religious knowledge are most relevant.[40] I liken the use of first order language or pre-reflective embedded theology to the ways Christian faith traditions were experienced in premodern times, when, after the third century, Christian women and men lived within a world where their faith was continuous with all other aspects of their culture. They did not need to interpret their faith or think critically about it because second order language was left in the hands of those in religious authority. It may be simplistic to equate premodern and precritical expressions of religious belief, since there was a great deal of critical reflection and religious plurality occurring during this historical period. Nonetheless, looking back we often nostalgically envision premodernity as a time in which religious authorities constructed doctrinal and liturgical uniformity that relieved the laity of any responsibility for critical reflection on their faith or practices.

Using the metaphor of a trifocal lens, students can use the lens of premodern approaches to religious knowledge to assess whether people are yearning for an immediate sense of God's presence or a sense of the sacred, in a precritical way similar to how God was experienced in the premodern traditions of Christianity. Students can use a modern or critical lens to see whether people are ready or need to interpret religious experience using a variety of theoretical perspectives, like biblical critical perspectives. Modern approaches to religious knowledge were formulated in reaction to premodern approaches that gave primary authority for interpretation to the Roman Catholic Church. The Christian Reformation shifted interpretive responsibility from the communal or corporate frame of the church to the individual, who, drawing upon the Enlightenment approaches to knowledge, used reason to approach the bible and make sense of it. When members of faith traditions are ready to turn to the Hebrew Bible or New Testament for help in meaning-making, they can be encouraged to think critically about how this source of authority can help them make sense of their lives. For those experiencing health crises, modern medical knowledge, often available on the internet, helps them understand what is happening physically to them. In the long term process of helping people with meaning-making, students can assess when people are ready to use a postmodern lens to appreciate the contextual and provisional nature of knowledge, including knowledge of God. This postmodern lens brings into view the importance of intrinsically meaningful religious experiences that emerge from the particular cultural, communal, and family narratives.

The challenge for field education students is discerning which lens is the most relevant or meaningful in any given situation. For many students, a postmodern lens is predominantly used in the academic study of religion and in theological and religious studies. A modern lens is often used in seminaries, particularly in biblical critical studies, and also in denominational debates over controversial issues like the ordination of gay and lesbian persons in committed relationships. A precritical or premodern lens predominates in communities of faith, especially during the experiences of worship. Students in field education often face the challenge of how to draw upon the modern and postmodern approaches to religion that they learn in seminary, in their supervised ministry with people of faith, who are likely to experience religion in precritical or premodern ways.

Students face a similar challenge when they are assessed for ordination. Some members of ordination committees want candidates to demonstrate that they can whole-heartedly use first order language in demonstrating their adherence to the core doctrines of their tradition, as if their use of second order language to explain their interpretation of these doctrines will make them less able to relate to the precritical first order language of their congregants. Other members of the committee will question any reliance on first order language, and will only want to hear how candidates are able to interpret their faith in intellectually sophisticated ways. Given that such committees usually represent the diverse theological stances within the geographical region of a denomination, students will almost inevitably be caught in the gaps between premodern, modern, and postmodern approaches to religious knowledge. Field education provides a unique opportunity to experience these gaps and become more adept at using second and third order religious language to talk about theological differences.

ONGOING SELF REFLECTION AND EVALUATION

Integrating the learning and formation experiences occurring in one's field education, seminary, and denomination can a daunting task. As the preceding discussion of theological reflection illustrates, students must learn to navigate the gaps between seminary and field education, especially in being able to use first order religious language with all of the theological fluency and sophistication they've gained through their theological education. Besides engaging in theological reflection on moments of ministry to others, such reflection can also be brought to bear upon moments when a student's performance of his or her vocation and theology either comes together in ways that confirm his or her calling or comes apart, often through an encounter with difference or otherness. Such encounters may decenter students in ways that stretch and challenge their theologies, and especially the theology of their vocation or calling. As Ward notes, "much of the learning that is formative of self and identity will be, as a result of the engagement with alterity or difference, an engagement that is at the heart of ministry. To dialogue well with difference is perhaps one of the most important skills for a minister in today's world."[41] Learning how to reflect theologically on decentering encounters with otherness within the space created by trustworthy supervisory and peer relationships is at the heart of the lifelong learning essential to both ministry and religious faith. Such learning will foster a "sense of identity that is dialogical, willing to share oneself with others and to be open to the (sometimes radical) otherness, or 'alterity,' of different viewpoints."[42]

The ability to self-reflect, particularly on experiences of otherness, can be greatly enhanced when students build a portfolio in which they can track, among other things, how encounters with otherness affect their sense of self and theology. Portfolios may include learning covenants, journal entries, reflections on critical incidents, verbatim accounts of and reflection on pastoral care conversations, sermons, educational programs, and annotated bibliographies that help them understand and explore their experiences. Portfolios can provide a space to experiment with different ways of encountering and theologically understanding otherness.

How one theologically understands decentering encounters with difference will depend upon which theological method is most relevant and meaningful to students. Students in more theologically conservative traditions will likely favor the canonical narrative method described by Graham et al. or the regulative model described by Scalise. Using such methods, they will reflect upon how the deep grammar of their religious identities reflects the deep grammar of their religious tradition. The challenge in this method will be respecting the radical plurality inherent in religious traditions—this means acknowledging, as Paden suggests,[43] that each person's religious world is in some ways unique.

Students relying more on progressive or postmodern theologies may find the "theology-in-action" or "theology in the vernacular" methods described by Graham et al. more relevant for theologically reflecting on decentering encounters with difference that challenge identity. The difficulty they face may be in finding the underlying connections between their contextual theologies and the theologies represented within their denominations. The more adept students become at using several methods for reflecting upon critical incidents concerning difference, the more they will be able to build bridges between their religious world and the religious worlds of those to whom they minister and those evaluating their vocation.

Students and supervisors can benefit from using the concept of performative theology to develop self evaluations based on a dynamic rather than fixed understanding of models of ministry as call and ministry as office. Students' understandings of the providential call experienced in their gifts for ministry and the secret call that has often propelled them into theological studies, as well as their experience of an ecclesial call, will obviously be reconstructed, sometimes in radical ways, through the process of field education. The more trustworthy the supervisory relationship is and the more students can be both proactive and interactive in formulating learning goals that help them explore their call, the more they will be able to experience new theological ways of understanding their call as dynamic rather than fixed, especially through decentering encounters with difference.

The concept of performative theology also offers a dynamic understanding of the office of ministry. Students using field education to prepare for ordination can reflect on the theologies of the office of ministry enacted at their field education sites and within the cultures of their denominations, especially as candidates are evaluated for ordination. Being able to use a performative theological understanding of the office of ministry may help students better appreciate the particular theologies of the office of ministry that may arise through the unique group dynamics that occur during interviews. Learning how to reflect upon theology as performative in the self evaluations that are part of field education and the evaluations that are part of ordination will help students envision their ministries as profession, calling, and office in dynamic ways, especially when they encounter difference.

CONCLUDING THOUGHTS

Pastoral supervision of field education offers a trustworthy relationship in which supervisors and students can dialogically engage profound questions of how theology is enacted in the practices of ministry. As I have illustrated, being able to pay attention to the gaps between theologies learned within the seminary and theologies enacted in faith practices will equip students for lifelong learning and help them navigate decentering moments when they encounter difference, not only within pastoral relationship at their field site, but also within the supervisory relationship, and in the process of discerning their vocation and seeking ordination. Being able to reflect theologically on these encounters with difference will allow them to be lifelong learners who can build bridges between their religious world and the religious worlds of all those they encounter in their ministry.

NOTES

1. Christian Scharen, "Learning Ministry Over Time: Embodying Practical Wisdom," in Dorothy C. Bass and Craig Dykstra, eds., *For Life Abundant: Practical Theology, Theological Education, and Christian Ministry* (Grand Rapids, MI: Eerdmans, 2008), 265-266.

2. Dorothy C. Bass and Craig Dykstra, eds., *For Life Abundant: Practical Theology, Theological Education and Christian Ministry* (Grand Rapids, MI: Eerdmans, 2008), 47.

3. Jackson W. Carroll, *God's Potters: Pastoral Leadership and the Shaping of Congregations* (Grand Rapids, MI: Eerdmans, 2006), 17.

4. H. Richard Niebuhr, *The Purpose of the Church and its Ministry* (New York: Harper & Row, 1957), 64.

5. Larry Kent Graham and Jason C. Whitehead, "The Role of Pastoral Theology in Theological Education for the Formation of Pastoral Counselors," *American Journal of Pastoral Counseling* (8, No. ¾, 2006), 15.

6. Elaine L. Graham, *Transforming Practice: Pastoral Theology in an Age of Uncertainty* (New York: Mowbray, 1996), 111.

7. Frances Ward, *Lifelong Learning: Theological Education and Supervision* (London: SCM Press, 2005), 3.

8. *Ibid.*, 17.

9. Elaine L. Graham, *Op. cit.*, 7.

10. John H. Patton, "Supervision, Pastoral," *Dictionary of Pastoral Care and Counseling*, expanded edition with cd-rom, Rodney J. Hunter, ed. (Nashville: Abingdon Press, 2005), 1239-1243.

11. Frances Ward, *Op. cit.*, 87- 88.

12. John H. Patton, *Op. cit.*, 1241.

13. *Ibid.*

14. *Ibid.*

15. Carrie Doehring, *Taking Care: Monitoring Power Dynamics and Relational Boundaries in Pastoral Care and Counseling* (Nashville: Abingdon Press, 1995).

16. William E. Paden, *Religious Worlds: The Comparative Study of Religion* (Boston: Beacon Press, 1994), 10.

17. *Ibid.*, viii.

18. *Ibid.*

19. Carrie Doehring, "Theological Accountability: The Hallmark of Pastoral Counseling," Compass 1 (forthcoming).

20. Kenneth V. Hardy and Tracey Laszoffy, "The Cultural Genogram: Key to Training
Culturally Competent Family Therapists," *Journal of Marital and Family Therapy* (21, No. 3, 1995), 227-237.

21. Frances Ward, *Op. cit.*, 17.

22. Elaine L. Graham, *Op. cit.*, 111.

23. Theodore W. Jennings, "Pastoral Theological Methodology," *Dictionary of Pastoral Care and Counseling*, expanded edition with cd-rom, Rodney J. Hunter, ed. (Nashville: Abingdon Press, 2005), 862-864.

24. Howard W. Stone and James O. Duke, *How to Think Theologically* (Minneapolis: Augsburg Fortress Press, 2006).

25. Carrie Doehring, "Theological Literacy and Fluency in a New Millennium: A Pastoral Theological Perspective," in *Theological Literacy for the Twenty-First Century*, Rodney L. Petersen with Nancy M. Rourke, eds. (Grand Rapids, MI: Eerdmans, 2002), 311-324.

26. Carrie Doehring, *The Practice of Pastoral Care: A Postmodern Approach* (Louisville, KY: Westminster John Knox Press, 2006).

27. Theodore W. Jennings, *Op. cit.*

28. Carrie Doehring, "Theological Literacy and Fluency," *Op. cit.*

29. *Ibid.*, 311.

30. Howard W. Stone and James O. Duke, *Op. cit.*, 13-14.

31. *Ibid.*, 16, 18.

32. Theodore W. Jennings, *Op. cit.*

33. Charles Scalise, *Bridging the Gap: Connecting What You Learned in Seminary with What You Find in the Congregation* (Nashville: Abingdon Press, 2003).

34. Elaine Graham, Heather Walton, and Frances Ward, *Theological Reflection: Methods* (London: SCM Press, 2005).

35. *Ibid.*, 13.

36. Elaine Graham, Heather Walton, and Frances Ward, *Theological Reflection: Sources* (London: SCM Press, 2007).

37. *Ibid.*

38. *Ibid.*, 106.

39. *Ibid.*, 170.

40. Carrie Doehring, *The Practice of Pastoral Care, Op. cit.*

41. Frances Ward, *Op. cit.*, 103.
42. *Ibid.*, 17.
43. William E. Paden, *Op. cit.*, viii.

CHAPTER FOUR

A Theological Anthropology for Transformational Education

If pastoral care and counseling and spiritual guidance and caring are dependent upon anything, they are dependent upon an adequate assessment of the spiritual and developmental needs of others. In my view, assessment lies at the heart of professional spiritual caring. Assessment is first and foremost the art of "beholding the other." Learning to see an individual for the unique creature that he or she is in the world takes practice and it requires some theory. Learning how to determine what Carol Wise called "meeting the person at their point of need" requires understanding what that need is. Wise reminds us of this about pastoral assessment:

> The concern of the pastor is for the quality of the life, the inner condition. But he must not jump to conclusions or generalize about this. His task is to help the person deal with his actual condition as he experiences it. This means he must deal with the symptoms the person presents as indications of deeper issues. He must make an evaluation of the person and his experiences. He is not interested in labeling people. He is interested in understanding them.[1]

A central component to understanding the person in front of you is the ability to take the information about that individual and place it in a context. Understanding the individual must be held within a larger understanding of how people form and how they relate to the Divine. In short, I believe spiritual care providers need to have a developed and understood theological anthropology. Without this, it is as if having all of the notes of a song placed in front of you with no ability to discern how they fit together.

This chapter outlines a theological anthropology that we teach in the third unit of our ACPE residency. It is modeled upon the writing of James Loder, who was, until the time of his death, the Mary D. Synnott Professor of the Philosophy of Christian Education at Princeton Theological Seminary. Although he does not explicitly claim this as anthropology, I believe he outlines a process that is encountered time and time again in all aspects of ministry, but particularly within the acute care medical center. It is a way of understanding how the particular individual engages in a process of meaning-making and creates a world in which to live. It is a lens by which spiritual care provider may "behold" all of the details of an individual life and place it into context of spiritual and religious dynamics.

Loder's pastoral theology is located more broadly in the existential phenomenological theology based on the thought of Husseral, Heidegger, Kierkegaard, Tillich, MacQuarrie, and others. A key concept to this type of thinking is that the individual is the "meaning-maker" of reality. Thus, humans are not born into a reality in which they then function. Rather, humans make meaning of the events and construct "worlds" from a rich and diverse tapestry of experiences, with each individual bringing her or his subjectivity to the event of interpretation. This thoroughgoing postmodern understanding leaves the interpretive act of the individual as the locus of being human. Thus, Sartre's old saying "existence precedes essence" is made true. How the individual interprets through culture, body, history, and more creates the reality in which they live. As meaning-makers of our world, we construct worlds or worldviews that match our experiences. Constructivism, the belief that we create the world of reality from our interpretations of experience, is gaining increased attention in the postmodern world. Pamela Cooper-White says:

> Constructivism rejects the notion that any reality exists outside the framework of some mental construct or theory. Objectivity is impossible because reality is shaped by the interaction between observer and observed. Reality, finally for constructivists, does not exist in any a priori sense but is literally created by interaction. Relativism replaces realism in this paradigm, as there is no fixed point of observation. Knowledge is approximated through hermeneutical and dialectical methods of inquiry, but there is no final truth, only consensus views which emerge from local, particular, experiences-near constructions, and these are therefore always open to transformation.[2]

We make sense of our experience and construct lenses by which to understand those experiences. Through a variety of experiences, individuals construct a sense of what the world is like and how it can have meaning for them. These experiences are located in distinct identifiable areas and facilitate the stuff out of which an individual makes meaning. Loder proposes looking at the human experience, and thus human meaning-making, from four distinct sectors: Embodiment, the Self, the Void, and the Holy. In each of these sectors the human experience is illuminated and delineated.

MEANING-MAKING THROUGH EMBODIMENT

Human beings are bodily creatures. Our understanding of others, God, ourselves, and our environment are all perceived through our senses. We are creatures embedded in the physical reality of body. God breathed into our bodies life, soul, or spirit. Our body, that physical "world" of flesh and bones, arteries, nerve endings, and neuro-pathways is our first and primary way of being. This body encompasses all of our senses, and consequently, our perceptions of the world. The physical reality of body is our primary sense of being. Central to the shared experience of humanity is that we experience everything with and through a body. The human experience begins with body. We move and breathe and have our being primarily and originally from within the context of body. Loder says:

> In the beginning is the body, the only entity we know from the inside and outside simultaneously and spontaneously. Early in life we "take in" all we can and we "get into" all we can; we have an innate restless desire to know things both inside and outside. Especially if the "objects" we encounter are people, we take in and indwell them as if it were a matter of life and death—because it is.[3]

Western thought—more accurately white, male western thought—historically has separated the body from any sense of spirit, numena, or intellect. This kind of splitting violates the uniqueness of the human creature and allows us to imagine a very different kind of creature and creator. Embodiment is seen as the unity of spirit and body. This means all of the hard-wired elements of the body such as genetic material, physical imitations and gifts, etc.

> With sucking mouth and clutching hand, though gazing eyes and harkening ears, and though myriad tactile perceptions of the skin, we take in and indwell, holding and molding everything to suit the structure, activity, sensitivity, and corporate model of the body.[4]

Being body as well as spirit creates the primary experience of tension between freedom and responsible freedom. Being body means that we are limited—limited by time and space. As an infant, we are dependent upon the care and nurture of our mother. As body, we feel the raw pain of hunger and the soothing comfort of food and supporting arms. As body, we experience the joy and delight of mother's face and the terror of her absence. As young children, it's again as body that we experience the exhilaration of completing new tasks, and the pain of skinned knees and wounded sense of self.

Because our human being is experienced as body, we become increasingly aware of time, another limitation calling for responsible being. As creatures with body, we experience the passing of days, the rushing of years, all leading to the inevitable reality of all bodies—death itself. Sickness and death are perhaps the greatest reminders of our nature as body. Through the death of body, whether that is in the form of Alzheimer's, the slow deterioration of personality, or the sudden loss of life, we are confronted with our limitations and desire to control. Through body we are constantly reminded that we are human.

But human interactions cannot be reduced simply to a physical dimension. This leads Carolyn Gratton to speak of our "second body"—that of our individual culture, our particular gender, sexual orientation, and other aspects that effect the way we understand the world.[5] Each person creates her own "worldview" in continual exchange between physical body and a cultural second body. The worlds of the *compesino* priest in El Salvador, a black Baptist preacher in the southern United States, and a white chaplain at a medical center are very different worlds. From within our second body, we begin to "see" the world. Our second cultural body is as dear and defining to us as is our own physical body. Thus, physical and social realities such as ethnicity, gender, age, physical challenges, etc., all affect the way a person understands herself in the world. Loder sees body as more than just the physicality of the skin and organs. He also sees embodiment as the social world in which we are born. Yet, as much as we are a physical body, there is also that part of ourselves that has intentions for that body. There is that part of being human that animates the body. As much as we are body, we are also self.

HUMAN BEING AS SELF

Human being is not limited to body or even cultural body. For within each of us is the one who says "I." As much as I identify myself with my body, there is another part of me that knows another reality. The "I" is the one who knows what is beyond the body.[6] Loder quotes the neurologist Wilder Penfield and his studies on brain injured patients. When Penfield would stimulate some part of the brain, a corresponding part of the patient's body would move. What made Penfield and Loder curious was the patient's response: ". . . when Penfield touched a part of the brain that made the subject move a limb or recall a particular childhood experience, the subject would respond, 'You did that, I didn't.'" What was striking to Penfield was not only the memory tapes, but the "I." Loder speaks of the self's transcendence as the second dimension of human "being."

The self, or the "I" of the individual, is the part of the person who creates and recreates his world: "Men differ not just because they select different objects or facts from the common world, but because they see different worlds; their perspectives have been formed from highly individual experiences."[7] Through the use of symbolic representation we become the creators of our own world, or we become meaning-makers. To be a "meaning-maker" is to be a creature that brings meaning to the phenomena of life. To call oneself human is at the same time to call oneself the one who forms the world into meaningful existence. We are indeed responders and creators of our own worldview. "The second dimension is 'the self' that transcends the embodiment of being human in order to repeatedly recompose its 'world' . . . this is 'the knower'; the self is embodied in the lived world and at the same time stands outside it."[8]

Yet human selfhood is not simply self-reflection, nor is it simply organizing phenomenon of the world. To be a self is also to be in self-other relations. This is best captured in the language of Martin Buber of "I-Thou." To be a self is to be in relationship with some other self. When this relationship is sufficient to allow for reflection of the self through the eyes of another, Loder, following Buber, calls this "I-Thou." Hence, to be a self is to be related to others. It is only from within the complex web of relationships that the self is able to form. The self is then free to engage the world as the initiator of action. The self is the part of the human that responds to freedom in its multiplicity of forms. The self then, is transcendent and uses symbols as the primary way of creating meaning in the "lived world" of body and second body. It is also created within the constellation of other selves and is not isolated from them. I believe the self is spirit. As such, the self is radically open to the Mysterious Other.

The relationship of body and spirit establishes the primary tension between finitude and transcendence. The human condition speaks of the relationship between existence and essence. Paul Tillich describes this tension as "estrangement." Tillich describes this existential reality saying, "Man as he exists is not what he essentially is and ought to be. He is estranged from his true being."[9] The self as spirit is constantly seeking to ground its own being in the Source of all being. It is the self that cries out for God. It is the self which as Loder says, "... as spirit may function reflectively or function as conscience, but its identity is with being-itself."[10] I will speak more of that a bit later. The third dimension of human experience is the "void."

HUMAN BEING AND THE VOID

The existential reality of non-being is the third dimension of being human. The reality of non-being is a central aspect of the human situation. Loder calls this the void. From the earliest unanswered cry as an infant, the void becomes a part of living. Called by many names and known through many experiences, several metaphors elucidate the void "non-being, death, loneliness, emptiness, shame, and the demonic."[11] In each of these realities, the sense of self is separated from the Source of Being. The void is the inevitable threat of non-being. It is from within the reality of our own limited life span that the void looms near. The void threatens throughout the life span. It can be found when pride in the self is the center of life's meaning or when death or disease threaten the created lived world we call "normal." The void is present when job loss becomes a reality or when the day-to-day arrangements that keep a marriage working are threatened.

The power of this third dimension of human existence leads most of us to construct "worlds" within which the void has no part. These created "worlds" may rest upon financial success, addiction to substances, or the endless cycle of sin-repentance-forgiveness. Creating a world where the void has no power is both an illusion and a necessity. To live daily in the presence of the reality of the void requires courage and faith:

> The void is more vast than death, but death is the definitive metaphor; "nothing" in itself is ultimately unthinkable, but death, shrouding all of our lived "worlds," gives us our clearest picture of nothing. Although its origin for experience is in the self's inability to be itself, the sense of void goes far beyond this in society, culture, time, and the universe, so that consciously we dread to include it in our "worlds."[12]

In the effective pastoral encounter, students and pastors walk with the patient as he or she encounters the void of accident, trauma, disease, or grief. It is the relationship itself which helps the patient or family member tolerate the sometimes immense anxiety and fear which accompanies an encounter with the void. As the patient "hands" some of that anxiety to the chaplain, she holds those deep feelings, allowing the patient to begin a process of meaning-making to his or her perception of non-being. In a similar manner, the student or chaplain brings into the supervisory relationship her or his unique and genuine encounter with the void as it was experienced with the patient. I believe it is within the void that we begin to hear the voice of and look upon the face of the Holy Other. It is from facing our demons that we begin to hear the redemptive call of God. Thus, the task is not to prevent the student/pastor/chaplain from moving into the void—rather it is the supervisory task to move with the student, allowing for the continued presence of God to be heard, felt, and seen as the student engages in meaning-making.

The void is presented primarily by the limit of body—death as non-being. It is from within the reality of our own limited life span that the void looms near. But the void is encountered throughout life. Again Loder says, "Void is the ultimate aim of all proximate forms of nothingness; the implicit aim of conflict, absence, loneliness, and death is void."[13] The despair often reported by people in the postmodern era is not simply loneliness or anxiety. Many people feel the profound effect of the void described as "emptiness."[14] The power of this third dimension of human existence leads most of us to construct "worlds" within which the void has no part. But this is only a means in which to live daily in its presence. Again,

> the void is more vast than death, but death is the definitive metaphor; "nothing" in itself is ultimately unthinkable, but death, shrouding all our lived "worlds," gives us our clearest picture of nothing. Although its origin for experience is in the self's inability to be itself, the sense of void goes far beyond this in society,

culture, time and the universe, so that consciously we dread to include it in our "worlds."[15]

When encountering the void, the temptation of the self is to cling to a false world where the void has no meaning. In so doing, the self creates and perpetuates a world where it is deceived and is the deceiver. This process separates the self from its source of true identity, The Source of All Being. When the self is presented with the awesomeness of the void, it may ground itself in some other form of power which ultimately cannot sustain it. Loder describes the void by saying:

> I prefer to speak of void with the implication that nothingness, or negation of being, is not beyond experience; indeed, it is part of the uniqueness of human being that negation is meaningfully included in the composition of our "lived worlds" and in our sense of self.[16]

As humans confront the powerful reality of the void, we encounter the always more powerful reality that we are not alone and that we are indeed accepted. To live in the presence of the void is to be filled with the awful reality of non-being and separation from the Source of All Being. Living in separation from the Source is not bearable for humans. Thus, it leads to various forms of living incomplete with pain, isolation, emptiness, and more. Yet we are always called and being called by the Holy Other into relationship. This brings up the fourth dimension of human being: the Holy—the breaking in of transformation. The void can only be understood in its reciprocal relationship with the Holy. The void—breaking into the lived world of human being—brings with it a process which is transformational, a process that leads to the Holy.

THE SELF, TRANSFORMATION, AND THE HOLY

To wrestle honestly with the void will always bring about the reality of transformation, the Holy. The Holy—the fourth dimension of being human—is always present, providing a transforming reality in the presence of the void:

> We continue to live precisely because in the center of the self, for all of its potential perversity, we experience again and again the reversal of those influences that invite despair and drive toward void. Kierkegaard repeatedly insisted with bewildering brilliance that the faces of the void become the faces of God.[17]

As we experience the void in its profound despair, we become increasingly aware that we are not only three-dimensional beings, but that we do in fact experience grace, love, acceptance, justice, and more. In the presence of the void, we cannot remain unchanged. In accepting the depth of the threat of non-being, we find the very source of transformation. In the midst of winter, we find an invincible summer. In the brokenness of communion bread, we find a source of forgiveness. In the cross of humiliation and death, there is the transformation from the void to the Holy. Thus, as much as the void lifts up our alienation, at the same time it speaks the words of transformation. Christ indeed descended into hell.

The art of pastoral care is an art that enables another to move from the surface of life to the inward depth filled with its uncertainty, painful truth, and liberating possibility. I believe that when a person is invited to look at the truth of the void, grounded and surrounded in a relationship of trust and confidence, that they are able to move toward a position of "letting be." When a patient is facing their own death, we call it acceptance when they have reached a position of "letting be." This is far from surrender. It is nothing like denial. It is the profound realization that by facing the void, we find the face of God. Pastors who choose not to look at the void in their own life often feel unable to help their patients or parishioners face the void in their life. Thus, a trusted guide is one who has journeyed toward the deep center of the self. The trusted pastoral care provider is the one who has considered and considers the void in his or her own life and, thus, knows that it is not only pain that will be found in the encounter with the void, it is also intimately the Holy Other who will be found. Pastoral supervision is such a process. It is an ongoing, courageous conversation.

The Holy brings with it "new being." The nature of Being is most dramatically demonstrated to us in relationships which "let be" or "let flourish." In my Christian faith, this is the form of love that Christ demonstrated to us. The life and death of Jesus speaks of a God who is seeking to "let flourish." Jesus based his relationships with others in the depth of his understanding God to be one who "lets flourish."

> Jesus is the one who establishes relationships in the ground of Being. Jesus, the one who made Being known to us, engaged in a way of relating which "lets flourish." The level on which Jesus interacted with people forced them to focus on his deepest identity and their own . . . The encounter moved through words and actions to their secret source, two people personally present to one another. In this situation divine reality, whom Schillebeeck once called the transcendent third in every relationship, also appears.[18]

In the presence of the Holy, experiencing a love which "lets flourish" the self finds the opportunity to ground itself in the Source of All Being. Grounding itself in the Source of All Being, the self no longer need create a world of denial where the void does not exist. The fear that comes with letting go of the self's defenses, risking the overpowering pain of the void, is accepted in the love that the self ultimately seeks. In the presence of the love that "lets flourish," the self finds itself known by the Knower, challenging the attempt to ground the self in anything else. In the presence of the Holy Other, we find the acceptance of ourselves that enables us to live with the ambiguity and tensions that characterize the human condition. In the presence of the Holy One, we realize that life is indeed a mystery and we find with wonderful amazement, that we are a part of that mystery.

SUPERVISION AND THE PATTERN OF TRANSFORMATIVE LEARNING

Thus far I have outlined a particular view of pastoral care and supervision that is grounded in an equally particular view of the human person. My hope at this juncture is to elaborate how this understanding of the human person and the human condition might translate to pastoral supervision to increase pastoral effectiveness in the provision of spiritual care.

Humans seek to experience their world as meaningful (meaning-makers) and then to experience themselves as having mastery in that world. The process of making meaning and acquiring competence is what I call learning. Competence, at least as seen in light of Loder's theological viewpoint, is partially understood as becoming a particular kind of person for others—namely someone who is able to live in a world where the void has a transforming role that leads to authentic living characterized by a self grounded in the Source of All Being. In order to assist pastors and students to become such a person, we as supervisors must be attentive to the movement of the spirit as it guides us to and through the void to what Loder called *the transforming moment*. How do we do this?

Adults learn as they begin to challenge their ways of knowing in the world. That is, we begin to learn when the worlds created by our established meaning-making process are experienced as inadequate or meaningless. Our meaning-making process, as outlined above, are characterized by our culture, gender, sexual orientation, life experiences, educational opportunities, etc. As we seek to become competent in our chosen work, we encounter aspects of our lived world that are inadequate to explain the current situation. When this happens, the void appears again, bringing with it the potential of shame, doubt, fear, and ultimately, the threat of non-being. For the adult learner, this is the beginning of transformation.

Loder outlines a five-step process that identifies the process of what he calls convictional knowing, although I believe it is more clearly articulated by the educational theories of Jack Mezirow in his book, *Transformative Dimension of Adult Learning*.[19] Before moving to transformative learning theory, I want to say another word about the process of meaning-making.

Constructivist theories of learning believe we formulate decisions based upon a particular set of cultural expectations and experiences—a particular symbolic and linguistic reality. That is,

> as adult learners, we are caught in our own histories. However good we are at making sense of our experiences, we all have to start with what we have been

given and operate within horizons set by ways of seeing and understanding that we have acquired through prior learning.[20]

These "understandings" that lead to particular ways of "seeing" are called meaning perspectives. Meaning perspectives are critical to education because they are the deeply embedded ways of seeing by which we make sense of our environment. Meaning perspectives, or habits of expectation, are the models we use to guide our decisions that lead to actions and behavior. They are the stuff of how we choose.

> Meaning perspectives provide us with criteria for judging or evaluating right and wrong, bad and good, beautiful and ugly, true and false, appropriate and inappropriate . . . when our meaning perspectives are inadequate to explain facets of our experience, we are faced with areas or dimensions of apparent meaninglessness.[21]

Our meaning perspectives serve as the "lions at the gate of awareness," providing form to the multiple inputs of our senses. Meaning perspectives are the unconscious determinants of what we attend to, acting as a regulator of what receives our focus.

Students begin confronting their meaning perspectives about the nature and process of education when they are asked to create learning goals, taking responsibility for their own learning. Or again, when they find pastoral conversations are more difficult than they assumed, based upon reading a book that included verbatim material. Meaning perspectives are challenged when the "good-hearted conversation" with a patient or church member is experienced as unhelpful and the student begins to wonder why.

These habits of expectation or meaning perspectives are deeply influenced by our parents (or by their handed down meaning perspectives), culture (or by their handed down meaning perspectives), and more. Our meaning perspectives may be distorted, false, limiting, or inadequate. Transformative education seeks to provide "different meaning perspectives that offer new ways of responding to a situation,"[22] and "negation or transformation of inadequate, false, distorted, or limited meaning perspectives."[23] Learning, then, is acquiring the ability to reflect upon our habits of expectation (cognitive and affective), compare them to current needs and contexts, and change them if necessary. This process is fundamentally transformative.

In the supervisory process, adults learn as they begin to challenge their ways of knowing in the world. The learning process begins or deepens when a particular meaning perspective or habit of expectation fails to sufficiently inform the learner about a particular situation. Our basic response to inadequate meaning perspectives is to become anxious, so "we trade off awareness for avoidance of anxiety when new experiences are inconsistent with our habits of expectation, which can result in areas of meaninglessness."[24] In short, we resist learning in order to avoid anxiety that comes with awareness, and we begin to learn when the anxiety stemming from inadequate meaning perspectives becomes too great. Balancing the student's anxiety with their increasing ability for self-reflection is a central task of supervision. What is crucial in this process, and at times missed by adult education theorists, is that not only does the student experience an increase in anxiety, they may also experience the void and the concomitant threat of non-being. As students begin to encounter the depths of pain and suffering present in ministry situations, they soon realize that they are unprepared to work with people at this depth. Their current situation does not match their own expectations and conflict ensues. The pastoral student finds he is unable to make sense of the situation and anxiety increases. If the student is able to hold or tolerate the anxiety long enough, he will begin a process of reflection focused upon his own meaning perspective.

What is crucial in this educational process is the role of reflecting upon the relationship of decisions, actions, feelings, and beliefs. As this transformation learning process begins, it will move through a series of identifiable steps or stages resulting in another action based upon completed reflection at various levels. The steps of this process are as follows: 1) Interpretation: A conflict occurs in a concrete experience which does not fit into the pre-existing meaning perspective. This may stem from a cognitive assessment or arise as an uncomfortable or unexpected feeling. Anxiety usually follows. Loder says, "Conflict initiates the knowing response, and the more one cares about the conflict, the more powerful will be the knowing event." The nature of this conflict can be quite uncomfortable. 2) Scanning: This stage is characterized by a process of searching for possible solutions, dissecting errors, following hunches, moving intuitively forward. The scanning phase often involves questioning previous meaning perspectives that may impinge or provide some sense of meaning to the original conflict. 3) Propositional Construal: Formulating a representation of the experience based upon beliefs (meaning perspectives), feelings, thoughts, and observations. This may focus upon the patient, upon the student, or upon both. A verbatim from a pastoral visit can be seen as a propositional construal. This is the attempt to represent what the "problem" is. 4) Reflection: Examining the previous steps at various levels. First, in reflective learning, the student reflects at the level of content (observations and facts). This may sound like, "Well, the problem was that I stood too far from the door when I introduced myself. That's why the visit did not go well." Secondly, the reflection occurs at the level of meaning. Here you may hear students say, "I was anxious, so I left when they said they were getting ready to leave." Linking the levels of reflection so that the focus of reflection increasingly moves to greater reflection on the meaning perspective is crucial to move to the next phase. 5) Imaginative Insight: A sudden and usually unexpected new way of looking at the situation. This is often a consolidation of several previously unrelated propositional construals. This is the "ah-ha" or the "I never realized that before" moment. Imaginative insight is experienced very much like reframing. 6) Reinterpretation: The process of integrating the results of the imaginative insight into the existing internal framework of the individual. Here, the new insight is integrated with previous meaning perspectives. 7) Remembering: Recognizing new situations and recalling the results of this process when confronted with similar situations. 8) Action: Acting upon the results of the transformative learning process.

The student moves through this process again and again in pastoral supervision. Conflict and the anxiety that arises when a student's meaning perspective does not match their current experiences is the initial experience in learning. In order for the student to feel as though he can bring his feelings of anxiety and conflict to supervision, he must feel or experience the warmth and trust of the supervisory relationship. Trust is a prerequisite to moving further into the reflective process.

When the student begins to bring to supervision the anxiety and deep feelings she feels in working with patients or congregation members, she moves into the process of reflection. In this stage of learning, the student and supervisor explore the "caring relationship" of the student and the patient. This will include reflection upon the process of the student's care for the patient and the content of the student's professional work. It may also include reflection on how the student's care is experienced by others, such as in formal and intentional group work like IPR. As relationships deepen and the student begins to experience the supervisor's care and trusts the interventions of the supervisor made over time, the student may begin to reflect at a deeper level—the level of meaning perspectives. This would include reflection upon the student's habits of expectation. Reflection at this level is quite anxiety-producing. The student must know that she is in a supervisory relationship and in an educational system capable of containing high levels of anxiety.

During this stage of learning, the student may be challenging deeply held patterns of belief about himself, the nature of his pastoral identity, what it means to care for others, the nature of suffering, and how he understands the providence of God, etc. Attending to the student's affective self is crucial at this stage in their learning. Strong emotions of grief, anger, shame, and more are consistent with the process of reflection at the level of meaning perspectives. Supportive pastoral care and attention to necessary referral to other supportive professionals is also important.

Imaginative insight and interpretation are the next phases of experiential learning. As the student's reflection moves to deeper levels and as she continues to experience the supportive and confrontive surrounding provided by the supervisor, peers, and others, the student experiences new insights about her pastoral care or pastoral identity. Affirmation of the student for their creativity and risking new ways of approaching their patient care is required. The integration of these insights prepares the student to care for patients differently, using new insights to increase the depth of their care for others. Acting upon these new insights and awareness increases the professional care of the student.

CONCLUSION

My hope for this chapter was to provide a way of looking at the human experience that enables pastoral supervision to be grounded in a process that took seriously the dimensions of the lived experience. This theological anthropology allows the supervisor to focus both upon the meaning-making structures of the individual student and upon the meaning-making structures of the patient or congregation member. It is an anthropology that allows for the depth of religious conviction, while at the same time is focused upon discernable learning patterns. Pastoral supervision requires us not only to teach our students how to behold the other and to meet them at their point of need, it also demands we provide the same care to our students.

NOTES

1. Carol Wise, *Pastoral Psychotherapy* (London: Jason Aronson, 1983), 81.
2. Pamela Cooper-White, *Shared Wisdom* (Minneapolis: Fortress Press, 2004), 44.
3. James Loder, *The Transforming Moment* (Colorado Springs: Helmers and Howard, 1989), 71.
4. *Ibid.*, 72.
5. Carolyn Gratton, *The Art of Spiritual Guidance* (New York: Cross Roads, 1993), 56.
6. James Loder, *Op. cit.*, 75.
7. Stanley Hauerwas, *Vision and Virtue* (Notre Dame, IN: Notre Dame University Press, 1981), 30.
8. James Loder, *Op. cit.*, 80.
9. Paul Tillich, *The Depth of Existence in the Shaking of Foundations* (New York: Scribner's Press, 1948), 62.
10. James Loder, *Op. cit.*, 80.
11. *Ibid.*, 84.
12. *Ibid.*, 84-85.
13. *Ibid.*, 81.
14. Donald Capps, *Pastoral Care: A Thematic Approach* (Eugene, OR: Wipf & Stock Publishers, 2003).
15. James Loder, *Op. cit.*, 84-85.
16. *Ibid.*, 81.
17. *Ibid.*, 85.
18. John Shea, *An Experience Named Spirit* (Chicago: The Thomas More Press, 1983), 27.
19. Jack Mezirow, *Transformative Dimensions of Adult Learning* (San Francisco: Jossey-Bass, 1991).
20. *Ibid.*, 1.
21. *Ibid.*, 44.
22. *Ibid.*, 56.
23. *Ibid.*, 62.
24. *Ibid.*, 63.

Chapter Five

Teología de conjunto: Not Just for Latinas/os Anymore

Francis Rivers Meza

> "At the heart of Latino/a theology we find a practice of doing theology jointly and in dialogue." Luis G. Pedraja, Teología: An Introduction to Hispanic Theology

CPE supervisors certified by ACPE, Inc. and working at North Carolina Baptist Hospital have, for the past several years, organized an end-of-the year retreat for participants in the year-long residency program. The retreat takes place away from the hospital. Summer interns cover the on-call pager and residents' clinical areas for the day, so dress at the retreat is casual and the mood relaxed. As a further sign of administrative support, the Department of Chaplaincy and Pastoral Care provides morning snacks and lunch for participants. These steps facilitate a reflection process focused on the transitions that characterize the end of a year-long residency. In effect, the retreat encourages residents to be mindful of their leave-taking and intentional about the closure process.

Over the course of the past three years, supervisors have given the retreat a distinctive structure. During the morning, participants share in a time of centering. This year, the practice consisted of a reading and discussion of the Gospel passage from the Common Lectionary for the previous Sunday. After a break, the group undertakes a 90-minute session of tai chi chuan. The leader of the session, a community member and friend of the department models a series of qigong during which members of the group channel strength, healing, and blessing toward one another.

After lunch, the residents make presentations following guidelines provided by supervisors prior to the retreat. Each of the residents shares two objects—one symbolizing the year that is drawing to a close and the other symbolizing plans, dreams, and challenges that lie ahead. The presenter explains the significance of the symbols chosen then places the objects on a table in the center of the room. (Memorable this year were the shoes that one resident placed on the table as a symbol of her journey to fit into a sense of pastoral identity and the ice scraper that another resident chose as symbolic of his struggle to discern his vocational path.) After each presentation, the group asks questions and offers comments. By the end of the process, the table has become a sort of makeshift altar. This sharing of stories marks the culmination of the retreat. Having the rest of the day off, participants gather their belongings, say goodbye, and head home.

Supervisors drew upon two sources to design the structure for the afternoon portion of the retreat. First was the hymn "Come, Thou Font of Every Blessing," which recalls Jacob's dream at Bethel (Genesis 28:10-22) and is a longstanding favorite of students, supervisors, and staff in the department. In the Biblical text, Jacob utilizes an object from everyday life (the stone he had used as a pillow) to fashion a symbol of his encounter with God. The second source was Paolo Freire's notion of "the cognizable object"—that is, an object or metaphor from a situation or even with which people are familiar and in which they are personally involved.[1]

TEOLOGÍA DE CONJUNTO

This type of reflection resembles what Latina/o theologians have come to call *teología de conjunto*. According to Orlando Espín and Miguel Díaz, teología de conjunto "is the process whereby a group of theologians gathers in order to do theology *jointly*. Hence, the 'product' ultimately belongs to the community and not to any one individual scholar."[2]

In fact, a significant portion of the texts of Latina/o theology exist as anthologies that reflect dialogue and collaboration among scholars. In this sense, teología de conjunto is a reaction against standard Western academic norms. In the words of Justo González,

> Western theology—especially that which takes place in academic circles—has long suffered from an exaggerated individualism. Theologians, like medieval knights, joust with one another while their peers cheer from the stands where they occupy places of honor and the plebes look at the contest from a distance—if they look at all.[3]

Latina/o theologians have sought a different model, one that underscores the importance of doing theology jointly.

Teología de conjunto also has a second meaning, one that González introduces through his reference to "the *plebes*." Not only are Latina/o theologians interested in collaborating with one another, they wish to be immersed in "the

reality and faith of the people among whom the theologians live and work."[4]
According to Espín, this aspect of doing theology jointly (i.e. of understanding
theology as the reflection and work of the community as a whole) has been one
of the most significant accomplishments of Latina/o theology.

> Our theology has been sensitive to popular expressions of the Christian faith.
> . . . We have tried to step behind the external expressions of faith (some of
> which might not be pleasing to our understanding of Christianity) and there lis-
> ten to the faith of everyday Latinas/os, not by pretending that Christianity could
> somehow exist without expression, but by not equating the former with the lat-
> ter. Why and how Latinas/os believe are not idle questions in and for theology.
> Indeed, to understand how Latinas/os "construct" what they hold to be real and
> good and important is crucial to the Latina/o theological movement. The first
> twenty years began the process of study of popular religion and the incorpora-
> tion of social scientific interlocutors into our theological dialogue—both in a
> clear and conscious attempt at listening to our people, recognizing in our com-
> munities' life and faith a source for our theology.[5]

The import of this approach is to shift the focus of theological inquiry from propositional truths about God to the religious practices, symbols, and rituals of
communities and individuals. Evidence of the extent to which Latina/o theologians have internalized this shift is the definition of theology that Jesse Miranda
offers. Theology, he writes, is not (or is not only) discourse about God, but
rather "the orderly presentation of the experience, belief, and understanding of
God."[6] Here we draw near to the subjective expressivity that took place during
the afternoon of the retreat. Here too, perhaps, consideration of the insights of
Latina/o theology can shed additional light on the design of educational structures that promote the art of theological reflection and further pastoral development.

Latina/o theologians are not naïve about the challenges that their adopted
task entails. Complexities abound in the process of "stepping behind the external
expressions of faith," gathering in as unbiased a manner as possible what one
sees, and using this material as a source of theology. Accordingly, Latina/o theology has drawn on methodologies developed by anthropologists and social scientists in order to address these challenges with conscious intentionality.[7] A further complication is the fact that grassroots expressions of faith are innovative
and often have emerged in resistance to practices of the institutional church.
Theologians can feel uneasy, therefore, when confronted with behavior and beliefs that do not coincide with established Christian doctrine or denominational
standards. Adding to the difficulty is the fact that both the Tridentine Catholicism established in Latin America during the Colonial Period and the Protestant
theology that reached the continent during the nineteenth century were deeply
suspicious of popular religious expression. Acknowledging this tension, Justo
González concludes that an insistence on the official and authoritative teaching

of the institutional church has caused theologians and church leaders to ignore or discount as mere superstition the variety of faith expressions among Latinas/os.[8]

Tensions of this type are not unfamiliar in Clinical Pastoral Education. Ten years after having been certified as an associate supervisor by ACPE, Inc., I still remember a difficult interaction that I had with a student during my training. Whatever may have been taking place in the relationship at a dynamic level, the student and I got stuck while trying to accomplish a task. I had asked her and her peers to write a reflection on their respective faith journeys. This particular student was in the midst of the ordination process with a mainline Protestant denomination and presented the statement of faith she had written for the examinations committee. I complimented her on the clarity and conciseness with which she expounded doctrine, but noted that I had difficulty seeing her or hearing her voice in what she had written. She found my comments hurtful and became angry. Eventually, we worked through the feelings that this exchange caused. In retrospect, I wonder to what extent the student and I had different understandings of the assigned task and why it was that we had no vocabulary with which to bridge these differences.

A central issue at stake in such misunderstandings is the role of revelation in the theological process. In an influential article, María Pilar Aquino states succinctly the perspective of Latina/o theology:

> The theological significance of daily life as source and locus of U.S. Latino/a theology is grounded in the fact that it is here where the real life of real people unfolds and where God's revelation occurs. We have no other place but *lo cotidiano* [the everyday] to welcome the living Word of God or to respond to it in faith.[9]

This statement dovetails with the emphasis that teología de conjunto places on the need for theology and theologians to pay close attention to the lived reality and religious practices of everyday people. "Theology," writes Nora O. Lozano-Díaz, "needs to be grounded in a specific context where a particular group of people—a community—can recognize it, relate to it, welcome it, and be challenged by it."[10] Also notable is the way in which the assumption that revelation occurs in *lo cotidiano* implies that revelation occurs in a multitude of places and under a variety of guises. In fact, the pioneering works of Latina/o theology emphasize the importance of contextualization. "Revelation," wrote Orlando Costas in 1982, "comes to specific peoples in concrete situations by means of particular cultural symbols and categories."[11]

The fact that Aquino is Roman Catholic and Lozano-Díaz and Costas are Protestant testifies to the ecumenical nature of Latina/o theology. Also apparent is the way in which Latino/a theologians have transformed and made their own concepts traditionally associated with European and Latin American theologies. An understanding of revelation as "contextual," for example, has roots in the theological ferment that began in the Latin American Catholic Church during the 1950s and came of age in the aftermath of Vatican II. Recalling this period,

Leonardo Boff describes it as a time during which a shift occurred in the church's center of gravity: "From a position of ecclesiocentrism, the Church has slowly moved to a 'mundocentrism.'"[12] Likewise, Stephen Bevans notes that "in theology written before the Second Vatican Council, revelation was conceived largely in terms of propositional truth." Gradually, a different understanding emerged. Revelation came to be "conceived as the offer of God's very self to men and women by means of concrete actions and symbols in history and in individuals' daily life."[13]

Within the realm of Protestant theology, the importance that Latino/a theologians attribute to the religious practices and beliefs of Latinas/os is most reminiscent of the viewpoint of Friedrich Schleiermacher.[14] Interestingly, Schleiermacher in his later work, most notably *The Christian Faith*, argued that a systematic theology had no need of the concept of revelation, since revelation could be subsumed within the category of Christology. This perspective differs significantly from the description of revelation that he put forward in the first edition of *On Religion: Speeches to Its Cultured Despisers*.[15] In this earlier work, he allows for variation in the experience of revelation due to peculiarities or differences among its recipients. According to Schleiermacher, "Every original and new intuition of the universe" is a revelation.

> All intuition proceeds from an influence of the intuited on the one who intuits, from an original and independent action of the former, which is then grasped, apprehended, and conceived by the latter according to one's own nature.[16]

Revelation occurs at the initiative of the universe. Intuition is merely a response, albeit a necessary one, to such activity. Human beings cannot generate revelation but they must "grasp," "apprehend," and "conceive" what is intuited. Moreover, people experience and understand revelation differently, according to their nature.

Latina/o theologians have drawn upon both these insights (that persons intuit revelation differently and that revelation occurs in daily life) to orient their work. In one of the groundbreaking works of Latina/o theology, Virgilio Elizondo underscored the fact that Jesus was a *mestizo*, a person of mixed ethnic heritage who did not fit into either the Roman or Jewish culture of his day. This interpretation of the Incarnation, which Elizondo dubbed "the Galilean Principle," arose from and was meaningful to the Mexican American community to which Elizondo belonged.[17]

Other Latina/o theologians have built upon and expanded Elizondo's work. Roberto Goizueta and Jeanette Rodríguez turned their attention to imagery and rituals that were part of everyday life for many Latinas/os. Rather than assume that they knew ahead of time the significance of participating in a *quinceañera* celebration (the traditional party that a family hosts when a daughter turns 15 years-old) or of Mexican-American women's devotion to *la Virgen de Guadalupe*, Goizuetta and Rodríguez allowed these events and symbols to raise questions about the ways in which Latinas/os construct their faith.[18] Likewise, Elizabeth Conde-Frazier, noting that expressions of Latina/o Protestant spirituality tend to be linguistic and word-centered, highlighted the ways in which *testimonios* (religious testimony shared as part of the worship service) were a conduit for "the people's theology" and constituted "a meaning-making ritual of the people seeking and sharing together a process of understanding God's mystery and grace in their lives."[19]

A new generation of Latina/o theologians has followed this line of inquiry and is exploring the question of how and why it is that Latinas/os know what they know. At issue is the right of Latinas/os to interpret their own experience, thereby gaining not only in self-understanding, but also in their ability to assess the significance and value of the Christian faith and tradition in relation to the lived experience of Latinas/os. In the words of Nancy Pineda-Madrid,

> If we understand "religious knowledge [to be] the product of our interpretive response to our experiences [and] not some absolutely certain grasp of divinely revealed truth," then what Latinas come to "know" from their experience is fundamental to the very possibility of religious knowledge.[20]

Anita de Luna offers a pithy summary of the viewpoint that Latina/o theologians have sought to articulate that "spirituality is mediated through lived experience, and experience is contextualized in culture."[21] Against this backdrop, Latina/o religious educators increasingly recognize the importance of sharing one's story as a way not only to articulate personal experience, but also as a creative expression of a larger cultural or religious heritage. Referring to narratives that serve this function, Hosffman Ospino has coined the term "sacred/popular stories," which he defines as "stories that are born out of people's everyday experience as they articulate the effects of God's presence in their lives within a particular socio-historical and cultural context." The sharing of such stories has "the potential of inspiring believers to understand, embrace, and live their faith with conviction and faithfulness."[22]

The inherent revelatory significance of sacred/popular stories hinges on their relevance to the daily experience of the narrator and his or her community.

> *Lo cotidiano* is a privileged reality where life unfolds with all its lights and shadows. It is a world shaped by the day-to-day decisions that people make individually and communally. It is the realm where believers enter in relationship with the divine, where God takes the initiative to disclose the divine self, and humanity weighs in freedom and in hope that self-disclosure.[23]

In order for sacred/popular stories to fulfill their revelatory potential, however, interpretation must take place. The theologian and religious educator have a role to play in this process, but he or she must be engaged in and in dialogue with the lives of the people telling the stories. A methodological assumption underlies this form of religious education: the interpretation that the narrator and his or her community draw from the experience of being a culturally and socially located human being in relationship with God is a privileged source of theology.

Reflecting upon the significance of the "base church communities" in the emergence and development of liberation theology, Leonard Boff recalls that among its many meanings, the word base "refers to a pedagogical process that works 'from the bottom up' in which the authorities and the teachers listen to the people, discuss with them the pilgrim journey of the Church, and supervise the implementation of decisions made jointly with them."[24] In similar fashion, Elizabeth Conde-Frazier recalls Mary Elizabeth Moore's definition of teaching as "an act of walking with, acting with, remembering with, and constructing meaning with people in a learning community."[25] Despite the difficulties inherent in such a process, Latina/o theologians and religious educators influenced by them remain committed to the task of listening closely to the religious experience of their communities and maintaining a dialogue over the interpretation of sacred/popular stories.

Conclusion

The sharing of objects and stories that took place during the end-of-the-year retreat at North Carolina Baptist Hospital fits within this pattern of attending patiently but purposefully as communities grasp, share, and interpret stories of revelation. At one level, the purpose of the retreat was straightforward—to encourage residents to be mindful of their leave-taking and intentional about the closure process. At a deeper level, the choosing and sharing of objects reminded residents of the agency that comes with being narrators of their own stories and members of a community willing to notice and interpret the everyday sights, sounds, and objects of revelation. As a piece of the puzzle of pastoral formation, events like the retreat remind participants of the value of listening to the stories of patients and church members with the same degree of attention. Reflection of this type serves to underscore the fact that teología de conjunto is not just for Latinas/os anymore.

Notes

1. Paolo Freire, *Pedagogy of the Oppressed*, Myra Bergman Ramos, trans. (New York: The Seabury Press, 1970), 106-107.

2. Orlando O. Espín and Miguel H. Díaz, eds., *From the Heart of Our People: Latino/a Explorations in Catholic Systematic Theology* (Maryknoll, NY: Orbis Books, 1999), 263. For an account of why "doing theology jointly" has been important to Latina/o theologians, see José David Rodríguez and Loida I. Martell-Otero, eds., *Teología en Conjunto: A Collaborative Hispanic Protestant Theology* (Louisville, KY: Westminster John Knox Press, 1997), 1-8 and more recently, María Pilar Aquino, Daisy L. Machado, and Jeanette Rodríguez, eds., *A Reader in Latina Feminist Theology: Religion and Justice* (Austin, TX: University of Texas Press, 2002), xvii. Indicative of the diversity of thought that exists among Latina/o theologians, a younger generation of

scholars has put forward a critique of the practice of teología de conjunto. See, for example, Benjamín Valentín, "Oye, Y Ahora Que?/Say, Now What? Prospective Lines of Development for U.S. Hispanic/Latino/a Theology," in *New Horizons in Hispanic/Latino(a) Theology*, Benjamín Valentín, ed. (Cleveland: The Pilgrim Press, 2003), 114-18 and Michelle Gonzales, "Latino/a Theology: Doing Theology *Latinamente*," *Dialog* 41, (Spring 2002): 70.

3. Justo L. González, *Mañana: Christian Theology from a Hispanic Perspective* (Nashville: Abingdon Press, 1990), 29. This quote is from the section of the book, pp. 28-30, in which González introduces the notion of "Fuenteovejuna Theology" (i.e., "a theology of the believing and practicing community.") Luis G. Pedraja, *Teología: An Introduction to Hispanic Theology* (Nashville: Abingdon Press, 2003), 85 (fn 8) sees "Fuenteovejuna Theology" as the seminal concept that give rise to the practice of teología de conjunto.

4. Orlando O. Espín and Miguel H. Díaz, *Op. cit.* Ada María Isasis-Díaz and Yolanda Tarango, *Hispanic Women: Prophetic Voice in the Church* (San Francisco: Harper & Row, 1988), ix, offer a clear statement of this commitment on the part of Latina/o theologians. "Doing theology is a communal process. We do theology because of, for, and with other Hispanic women with whom we participate in the struggle for liberation. Those with whom we engage in the struggle are our primary community of accountability. We begin to elaborate in this book has to be clear to them, make sense to them, be valid for them."

5. Orlando O. Espín, "The State of U.S. Latina/o Theology: An Understanding," in *Hispanic Christian Thought at the Dawn of the 21st Century: Apuntes in Honor of Justo L. González*, Alvin Padilla, Roberto Goizueta, and Eldin Villafañe, eds. (Nashville: Abingdon Press, 2005), 102. For an overview of the process by which a variety of theologians have come to regard the communities in which they live as a source of theology, see Robert J. Schreiter, *Constructing Local Theologies* (Maryknoll, NY: Orbis Books, 1985), 1-21, especially 16-20.

6. Jesse Miranda, "Latina/o Theology: Shibboleth or Sibboleth? A New Accent in Theology," in *Hispanic Christian Thought at the Dawn of the 21st Century: Apuntes in Honor of Justo L. González*, Alvin Padilla, Roberto Goizueta, and Eldin Villafañe, eds. (Nashville: Abingdon Press, 2005), 227. For a helpful overview of the tasks of theology, see Luis G. Pedraja, *Op. cit.*, 51-54.

7. The most well-known example is the use that Ada María Isasi-Díaz has made of ethnography to explore the lived experience of Latinas. See *En La Lucha: A Hispanic Women's Liberation Theology* (Minneapolis, MN: Fortress Press, 1993), 62-79. See also Gastón Espinosa, "Methodological Reflections on Social Science Research on Latino Religions," in *Rethinking Latino(a) Religion and Identity*, Miguel A. de La Torre and Gastón Espinosa, eds. (Cleveland: The Pilgrim Press, 2006), 13-45.

8. Justo L. González, "Reinventing Dogmatics: A Footnote from a Reinvented Protestant," in *From the Heart of Our People: Latino/a Explorations in Catholic Systematic Theology*, Orlando O. Espín and Miguel H. Díaz, eds. (Maryknoll, NY: Orbis Books, 1999), 217-29. For additional reflection by González on the ways in which Latina/o theologians can work within the tension that exists between grassroots expressions of faith and doctrines of institutional churches, see Anthony B. Pinn and Benjamín Valentín, eds., "Scripture, Tradition, Experience and Imagination," in *The Ties That Bind: African American and Hispanic American/Latino/a Theologies in Dialogue* (New York: Continuum, 2001), 61-73. The literature on grassroots religious practices that emerged in Latin America in the aftermath of the Conquest is enormous. For an introduction to the topic,

see Inga Clendinnin, *Ambivalent Conquest: Maya and Spaniard in Yucatan, 1517-1570* (New York: Cambridge University Press, 1987) and Louise M. Burkhart, *Holy Wednesday: A Nahua Drama from Early Colonial Mexico* (Philadelphia: University of Pennsylvania Press, 1996). On the marginalization experienced by Latinas/os in the mainline churches, see Virgilio P. Elizondo, foreword to *Mañana: Christian Theology from a Hispanic Perspective* by Justo L. González (Nashville: Abingdon Press, 1990), 9-20; John P. Rossing, "Mestizaje and Marginality: A Hispanic American Theology," *Theology Today* 45 (October 1988), 293-304; José David Rodríguez, "De 'apuntes' a 'esbozo:' diez años de reflexión," *Apuntes* 10 (Winter 1990), 75-83; and Gloria Inéz Loya, "Pathways to a *Mestiza* Feminist Theology," in *A Reader in Latina Feminist Theology: Religion and Justice*, María Pilar Aquino, Daisy L. Machado, and Jeanette Rodríguez, eds. (Austin, TX: University of Texas Press, 2002), 217-40.

9. María Pilar Aquino, "Theological Method in U.S. Latino/a Theology: Toward an Intercultural Theology for the Third Millenium," in *From the Heart of Our People: Latino/a Explorations in Catholic Systematic Theology*, Orlando O. Espín and Miguel H. Díaz, eds. (Maryknoll, NY: Orbis Books, 1999), 39. For additional background on *lo cotidiano* and its role in Latina/o theology, see Michelle Gonzales, *Op. cit.*, 67-68; and Ada María Isasi-Días, "Lo Cotidiano: A Key Element of Mujerista Theology," *Journal of Hispanic/Latino Theology* 10 (August 2002), 5-17.

10. Nora O. Lazona-Díaz, "Ignored Virgin or Unaware Women: A Mexican-American Protestant Reflection on the Virgin of Guadalupe," in *A Reader in Latina Feminist Theology: Religion and Justice*, María Pilar Aquino, Daisy L. Machado, and Jeanette Rodríguez, eds. (Austin, TX: University of Texas Press, 2002), 204.

11. Orlando E. Costas, *Christ Outside the Gate: Mission Beyond Christendom* (Maryknoll, NY: Orbis Books, 1982), 5. Luis G. Pedraja, *Op. cit.*, 14, reminds us that the corollary of an insistence on the centrality of context in the process of revelation is an acknowledgment of the fact that Latina/a theology is but one of "the multitude of theological voices that helps us understand, interpret, and live out our Christian faith."

12. Leonardo Boff, "Theology of Liberation: Creative Acceptance of Vatican II from the Viewpoint of the Poor," in *When Theology Listens to the Poor*, Robert R. Barr, trans. (San Francisco: Harper & Row, Publishers, 1988), 3. For an overview of the relationship between liberation theology and U.S. Hispanic/Latino theology, see Gilbert R. Cadena, "The Social Location of Liberation Theology: From Latin America to the United States," in *Hispanic/Latino Theology: Challenge and Promise*, Ada María Isasi-Díaz and Fernando F. Segovia, eds. (Minneapolis: Fortress Press, 1996), 167-182.

13. Stephen B. Bevans, *Models of Contextual Theology* (Maryknoll, NY: Orbis Books, revised edition, 2002), 13. For an extended discussion of the understanding of revelation that emerged during and after the Second Vatican Council, see Miguel H. Díaz, *On Being Human: U.S. Hispanic and Rahnerian Perspectives* (Maryknoll, NY: Orbis Books, 2001), 111-40.

14. Friedrich Schleiermacher, *The Christian Faith*, H.R. Macintosh and J.S. Stewart, eds. (Edinburgh: T. & T. Clark, 1928), 3-18.

15. Walter E. Wyman, Jr., "Revelation and the Doctrine of Faith: Historical Revelation within the Limits of Historical Consciousness," *The Journal of Religion* 78 (January 1998); 38-63, especially 41-51. According to Wyman, "The shift in conceptuality from intuition in the first edition of the *Speeches* to feeling in *The Christian Faith* is a classic problem in Schleiermacher interpretation."

16. Friedrich Schleiermacher, *On Religion: Speeches to Its Cultured Despisers* (1799), trans., from the 1st edition by Richard Crouter (Cambridge: Cambridge Univer-

66   Teología de conjunto

sity Press, 1988), 104. Wyman, points out that locating revelation in intuition, or as we might say in religious experience, leaves "a large role for the human imagination in the dynamics of revelation, for however uniform the action of the universe may be, human interpretation will inevitably differ. Thus, in the nature of the case, revelation is received in plural forms."

17. Virgilio Elizondo, *Galilean Journey: The Mexican-American Promise* (Maryknoll, NY: Orbis Books, 1983), 47-88. Orlando Espín, "The God of the Vanquished: Foundations for a Latino Spirituality," in *The Faith of the People: Theological Reflections on Popular Catholicism* (Maryknoll, NY: Orbis Books, 1997), 17-18, points out that "what we might correctly sense about God through the human experience of Jesus is not just what revelation might make possible, but also and more basically what our culture—in and through its complexity—might allow us to sense."

18. Roberto S. Goizueta, "Fiesta: Life in the Subjective," in *From the Heart of Our People: Latino/a Explorations in Catholic Systematic Theology*, Orlando O. Espin and Miguel H. Diaz, eds. (Maryknoll: NY: Orbis Books, 1999), 84-99; Jeanette Rodríguez, *Op. cit.*

19. Elizabeth Conde-Frazier, "Doing Theology," *Common Ground Journal* 1 (Spring 2004), 5-6. On the similarities and differences between Roman Catholic and Protestant expressions of popular religion, see Luis G. Pedraja, *Op. cit.*, 80-83; and Lozano-Díaz, "Ignored Virgin or Unaware Women," 205-209. However, see also Edwin David Aponte, "Metaphysical Blending in Latino/a Botánicas in Dallas," in *Rethinking Latino(a) Religion and Identity*, Miguel A. de La Torre and Gastón Espinosa, eds. (Cleveland: The Pilgrim Press, 2006), 46-68, on the dangers of imposing preconceived categories of interpretation on the spiritual practices of Latinas/os.

20. Nancy Pineda-Madrid, "Notes Toward a Chicana Feminist Epistemology (and Why It Is Important for Latina Feminist Theologies)," in *A Reader in Latina Feminist Theology: Religion and Justice*, ed. María Pilar Aquino, Daisy L. Machado, and Jeanette Rodríguez (Austin, TX: University of Texas Press, 2002), 261.

21. Anita de Luna, *Faith Formation and Popular Religion: Lessons from the Tejano Experience* (Lanham, MD: Rowman & Littlefield, 2002), 38.

22. Hosffman Ospino, "Unveiling the Human and the Divine: The Revelatory Power of Popular Religiosity Narratives in Christian Education," *Religious Education* 102 (Summer 2007), 329, 337. See also Elizabeth Conde-Frazier, "Religious Education in an Immigrant Community: A Case Study," in *Hispanic Christian Thought at the Dawn of the 21st Century: Apuntes in Honor of Justo L. González*, Alvin Padilla, Roberto Goizueta, and Eldin Villafañe, eds. (Nashville: Abingdon Press, 2005), 187-200.

23. Hosffman Ospino, *Op. cit.*, 330.

24. Leonardo Boff, *Op. cit.*, 26. Elsewhere, Boff has argued that an integral liberation theology, in whichever cultural context it may arise, has "a variety of accents." Among the accents that he identifies is that of "the people as agent of their own liberation." See Leonardo Boff and Clodovis Boff, *Salvation and Liberation: In Search of a Balance Between Faith and Politics* (Maryknoll, NY: Orbis Books, 1988), 24-25. According to Christopher D. Tirres, "U.S. Hispanic theology has articulated especially well... the idea of the people as *agent* [original emphasis] of their own liberation." See Tirres, "'Liberation' in the Latino(a) Context: Retrospect and Prospect," in *New Horizons in Hispanic/Latino(a) Theology*, Benjamín Valentín, ed. (Cleveland: The Pilgrim Press, 2003), 149-50.

25. Mary Elizabeth Moore, *Teaching as a Sacramental Act* (Cleveland: The Pilgrim Press, 2004), 13, quoted in Elizabeth Conde-Frazier, "Participatory Action Research: Practical Theology for Social Justice," *Religious Education* 101 (Summer 2006), 321.

CHAPTER SIX

Postmodern Theologies and Supervision

Timothy Thorstenson

A recent anecdote in the New York Times illustrates well the experience of postmodern life in America today. It is the story of an older gentleman with Alzheimer's, voting in the Democratic primary in the presidential race. The primary allows early voting, and the old man turns up every day at the voting center to cast his ballot. A carefully dressed widower with lots of time, he retains a strong sense of civic pride and social commitment, and he holds dearly to his dignity even as his losses now include his own capacities to order his world meaningfully. Yet he senses the importance of this election and so daily he tries to cast his vote. Friendly locals go through the motion of looking up his name, gently saying, "No, you voted two weeks back. Well done, sir. Thank you and rest easy."[1]

THE EVOLUTION OF MODERNITY

We struggle today to order our world meaningfully as our social arrangements continue to evolve and become more complex, driven by the rapid advances in technology and development on the one hand, and by the dissolution of the familiar on the other. Yet we "sense the importance" of current events in our world and want desperately to influence them positively, even as the fabric of our meaning frameworks has frayed and split. Many would note that, using the ancient metaphor, we have been "wandering in the wilderness" these last 40 years, and it is a current question whether or not we are finally approaching a promised land.

Forty years ago, I was an 18 year-old idealist ready to leave high school and enter a brave, new world. It was a powerful, frightening, and exciting time. The British Invasion in music hinted that we might be on the verge of becoming a broader, more global community. Racism, poverty, and war were being challenged in protest after protest. A renewed social consciousness was emerging. Civil and human rights were being advanced. But at the same time, the Cold War was increasing in tension as the nuclear arms race ramped up, the political parties in America were beginning to polarize, and the gap between the wealthiest and the poorest Americans began to widen, reflecting the decline of our inner cities and deepening social unrest. It was the best of times; it was the worst of times.

And then Martin Luther King and Bobby Kennedy, who had embodied so much hope for so many, were killed in what some historians now recognize as the real day the music died, as the true beginning of the postmodern era, as the moment we lost our way in our exodus from the despair of the Holocaust and the Great Wars of the first half of the century. The modern era, which had grown out of the Industrialized Revolution of the late nineteenth century, had been characterized by the struggle of good vs. evil and of freedom vs. tyranny, of *progress* and the rapid advances of science, of the effort to shift the benefits of economic development to the many rather than just the few. But as the old adage says, "What the gods want to destroy, they give forty years of success." And indeed, with the assassinations of King and Kennedy and others, with what Paul Erlich described back then as the "population bomb" and its projected effects on international development and resource use, with the rise of religious fundamentalism both abroad and within our own borders, and with growing American hegemony around the world, it is not surprising that change was in the wind and a new era of human consciousness was dawning.

This "change," introduced in part by Viktor Frankl's seminal work *Man's Search for Meaning*, along with the works of Tillich and Niebuhr, recast in both personal and social terms our emergence from the darkness of the Holocaust as both hopeful and necessary, as a struggle for identity and fulfillment that would only come through the evolution of consciousness itself and a new understanding of the divine energy of God. The only question was whether it would lead the human community to greater wisdom or to self-destruction. And after 40 years of tremendous advances and success accompanied by painful social and religious disintegration, the question still remains.

As human experience changed, so did theological expression. The paternalism inherent in neo-orthodoxy was challenged by the rise of feminism and a renewed emphasis on "the social gospel." Einsteinian theories, the exploration of space, and the scientific embrace of evolution as a constant in the universe were giving rise to *process* thought, perceived as threatening by the established church. The historical-critical method of scriptural study was beginning to deconstruct the predominant atonement theories in contemporary Christian expression, and mysticism and Eastern thought were emerging as powerful and attractive influences, shaping a new spiritual consciousness in the West. Each strand contributes today to the rise of what is being called the "new universe story" that is transforming the way we imagine and think about God and the way we see and engage our world and human community.

THE DECLINE OF THEISM

Humans have been worshipping gods since the beginning. It is a maxim that we define ourselves in part by our attempts to define that which is beyond us, that from which we have been born, that which is wholly "other" than us. In the Western world, that has taken on the form of the theistic "sky" God—the one who created our world and directs our destinies from beyond us or from "above" us. Our conceptualizations of that creative, divine force evolved over four millennia, from Abraham's jealous and all-powerful Yahweh, to the God of love of the New Testament embodied in the man-god Jesus. And in the course of that evolution, we defined ourselves as ones less than God, indeed as sinful and in need of God's redemption to set us right. Great religions grew up around these powerful frameworks for making meaning and for finding identity and "place" in the world.

But even as human consciousness began to discern the divine energy at work in the world and in the human heart and found it to be life-giving, human history also reflects how such conceptualizations morphed into expressions of oppression and control. As theism was gradually constructed to form and maintain commonly held beliefs, the beliefs themselves became dogmatized in order to shape like-minded communities and be self-sustaining. It is one of the mysteries of human life that we seem to struggle with that which is "known" but yet beyond our understanding, and instead we gravitate toward concreteness. When what we are trying to make communicable is beyond our ability to conceptualize, we seem to be at risk of ordering things in ways that run contrary to our experience, and that constrict rather than set free. In the West, as the great religions of Christianity and Judaism grew up, they were accompanied by patriarchy and hierarchy within and perceived as threats to one another without. And while at their best, they served and supported and created a spiritual grounding point for those within a tradition, so did they generate suspicion in other traditions. The vitriolic language and violent discrimination of Christian to Jew and Protestant to Catholic (and vice-versa) during the Middle Ages along with the Reformation/Counter Reformation served as a precursor to the Holocaust and the struggles of the modern era to come, laying the foundations for the schisms and distrust experienced within and between religions and even nations still today. Only recently has serious dialogue among differing religious groups begun to lead to deepened understanding, trust, and cooperation.

Theism at its inception replaced a nature-based understanding of the divine, giving rise to the concept of the "supremacy of man"—of humankind having dominion over the world while being subject to a Divine Being who is apart from nature. God was no longer seen as "in" nature, as in the pre-Christian goddess or tribal religions, but as "above" nature and Nature itself was de-divinized. Thomas Aquinas taught 750 years ago that the wise governor ordinarily governs by delegation to competent subordinates. In Aquinas' articulation of Theism and Nature, God's ordinary providence governs by means of the regularities ("laws") built into nature. To be faithful was to honor the natural law and the creator-God who set it all in motion.

Today, it appears we may be coming full circle, with a growing conceptualization in the postmodern theologies, both inside and outside the church, that God is not only *in* the natural order, but that God indeed *is* the natural order—its energy, its life force, its very soul.

THE RISE OF POSTMODERN THEOLOGIES

We are currently in the midst of a major paradigm shift theologically, spiritually, culturally, and socially. We are witnessing the deconstruction of traditional pre-enlightenment religious thought and we may even be experiencing the front end of the disestablishment of the Church as we have come to know it. This is a postmodern reality, meaning that we are coming to comprehend the limits of human progress, the evolutionary dynamics at work in the cosmos, and the rapidly growing threat to our environment and to our very existence. We are moving from our premodern expressions of religion that were founded on the belief that God could be captured through sacred texts, rituals, and spiritual experiences, through the modern understanding of critical methodologies and psychological theories, to the postmodern recognition that all knowledge about God and truth to this point has been provisional and socially constructed. We have learned that religious meaning more often arises out of heterogeneous social and moral contextual narratives than out of commonly held religious beliefs and practices. And we are learning that scientific exploration and imagination, rather than religious belief, may in fact be the primary pathway to enlightenment and understanding. Finally, the gap between faith and science may be closing.

It is a shift that is both troubling and hopeful. It is troubling because of the slowly growing sense that the traditionally dominant triumphalist and deliverance theologies, born originally out of enslavement experiences and social oppression, were long ago co-opted and distorted by institutions of power. It is troubling because we are seeing that the reformers' attempts to deepen personal and communal spirituality while heightening a sense of freedom and intimacy with God were also grounded in myths arising from our inability to see beyond our immediate circumstances. And it is troubling because of our growing sense that even our contextual theologies, emphasizing God's transcendence and the transformation of the human heart that deepens the common good—such as the liberation theologies "from below" that emerged out of the struggle for justice in Central America—are inadequate to speak to our current circumstances and the threat of annihilation. And it is troubling because it prompts a certain reorientation that is threatening to our traditional frameworks for making meaning. To deconstruct the beliefs that have shaped our history in such a way is painful.

Yet it is so hopeful at the same time. When Galileo peered into his newly developed telescope and began to discern our place in the universe, and when Einstein recognized the relationship of light and energy and mass, and when Watson, Crick, and Franklin recognized the structure of the gene and the potential to unlock the genetic code and all that might mean, everything changed. The emphasis was no longer on what God had done but on what God is at work *doing*. Now theologians and scientists both became engaged in exploring potential and possibility and an unfolding and open future. Determinism gave way to freedom of choice which, in turn, gave rise to the recognition that all things are constantly changing and evolving and that we may even play a role in creating reality itself.

PROCESS THEOLOGY

Sally McFague has written that "the picture of reality coming to us from contemporary science is so attractive to theology that we would be fools not to use it."[2] Alfred North Whitehead was among the first to embrace this new "picture of reality" and to seek to frame it as the expression of God.

For Whitehead, process thought is based on the scientific conclusion that all reality is energy. Everything—God, ourselves, our world, our "spirits"—is energy at its quantum level, with subatomic particles constantly moving, constantly creating and being recreated, ever-flowing, and changing. The scientific discovery that matter is energy and that energy is matter changed how we understood the processes of creation and evolution. And the discovery that reality actually changes when electrons collide *and* a new electron is created in addition (Whitehead's famous maxim that *the many become one and are increased by one*) led to the recognition that every moment contains the potential for new possibilities to emerge as a result. And the more recent discovery that any such electrons *remain in relationship* (what George Ellis has termed "kenosis") even after being split out of an atom, even across unlimited time and space, suggests that the possibilities are oriented toward maintaining relationship come what may, toward building up life rather than breaking it down. Whitehead called this *the attraction of ideals*, and extrapolated that all of reality is in God's sphere of influence and that the future is open, filled with redemptive potential; ours for the co-creating.

In process theology, the world is made up of energy "events," where the dynamic flow of energy creates all that is, and all that *is* is constantly being recreated. Indeed, everything is always *in process*. And the "aim" or impulse or purpose behind the energy flow comes from God, who brings together energy events in response to our needs and desires, providing an "inrush" of data and feeling that creates influence and shapes the unfolding of the future.

This is a *relational* theology, where individual events arise out of God's relationship with us, a relationship that does not end merely by us splitting ourselves away from God, just as electrons from the same atom maintain relationship despite their at times violent separations. God is in relationship with us as the source of the "aim" of the energy and as the one who knows all potentialities. God chooses the best possible potential for us and offers it (as feeling, intuition, discernment) as the initial aim. This is God as transcendent creator—the one who calls creative moments into being and who invites relationship. We respond or not. We are free to co-create or to turn away. But with every unfolding moment, God offers the next aim—"feeling" the outcome of every occasion, constantly seeking our fullest potential, always aiming for maximum intensity of feeling and the grandest expression of beauty possible.

It is a theology where God's power is regarded as persuasive rather than coercive. As opposed to the theist image of the lawmaker sky-god, or the deist image of the clockmaker, this is an image of God where God's power lies in the dynamic attraction of ideals within relationship, where God is always calling us in, always creating new possibilities. In fact, Whitehead would say that this is the fullest expression of love: that God remains "intimately" involved with us in all feelings and events, integrating all experiences, giving rise to new aims, wanting us to become the best that we can become. God genuinely loves us and provides the aims as well as the desire that we know well-being and harmony and fullness of life.

It is consistent then, in process theology, to claim that God is not off in the distant sky "apart" from us somehow, but that we in fact are "in" God as God is in us and in all things. As it is written, "God . . . is not far from each one of us. For 'in God we live and move and have our being . . . for we too are God's offspring'" (the Acts of the Apostles 17:27-28).

DECONSTRUCTING THE TRADITION

Process theology was a radical departure from neo-orthodoxy, which had attempted to integrate *into* the tradition new insights gained from the historical-critical approach to scriptural studies. Now the tradition itself was being transformed, the quest for the historical Jesus was well underway, and the true meaning of his death and resurrection for contemporary faith was being fully engaged.

It has led to the growing recognition in the postmodern era that theism is in decline. The question facing the church—and the culture that was founded, in part, on expectations of conformity to theistic creeds and constructs—is whether or not it can let go of what John Shelby Spong has called "the coping mechanism of theistic religion"[3] and embrace the growing self-consciousness that would enable us to relate openly and deeply to that in which our being is grounded and that which is part of who we are and yet somehow more than who we are. To do so would be to look to the teachings of Jesus and to frame the

Christ story as a calling to a higher order of being and as a personal engagement that empowers the courage to be. Could it be that Jesus revealed the divine through his call to follow the "way" of love and reverence for all and how he embodied that way of being in his own life, knowing fully well where it would lead him? Could it be that the theological meaning of the crucifixion is that it exposed our response to that call to a self-sacrificing and *giving* life—that is, that it revealed our resistance to life in God? We "could not endure either the vision or the maturity to which he called us, and he would not compromise his vision, so we killed him."[4] Far from the theistic story of God sacrificing his own son to atone for our sins, this is a story of love transforming abusive power and of self-sacrifice as the way to fullness with God. As our consciousness has evolved, we have come to see the evolution of the story as well, and that the call to live into the realm of God—a call which for Jesus was spoken in life and fully revealed through his death—is a call that generates a profound sense of "recognition" of God's intent for all humanity. This becomes the true Easter story: breaking the bonds of spiritual death to live fully in God and to have God live fully in us, *in life*, and in that which is before and beyond life. "To enhance life, to enhance love, to enhance being is to do the work of God's realm. This is the work Jesus was about."[5]

This changes everything. The modern era and the theistic tradition led to the inevitability of meaninglessness. The concepts handed down from previous generations have simply not been adequate to stem the proliferation of alienation and spiritual confusion in the face of growing complexity and threat. And perhaps alienation from self has been the greatest cost, exposed by growing psychological and spiritual illness. Today in the United States, one in four adults uses antidepressant medication in an effort to alter their brain chemistry, skewed by repeated insults to self-esteem. Suicide is epidemic. Eating disorders in our adolescents have emerged as a new expression of the struggle for meaning, as the addictive dynamics of older generations have been driven down to our young. And the communities that have traditionally given us the grounding and the support to cope and adapt with change are rapidly changing themselves with troubling trends of fostering exclusivity rather than generativity and self-giving love. Finding the "way" to fullness in God may be a more crucial question than ever before.

QUANTUM THEOLOGY AND THE NEW UNIVERSE STORY

As the scientific field of physics began to explore and theorize about quantum mechanics under Albert Einstein, the conclusions being reached began to reshape how we think about divine energy and reality. Quantum mechanics attempts to explore and understand the "organic fields of energy" at every level of the universe. As discoveries were made about the nature of light and energy, as the subatomic world began to open up through application of theory to discoverable data, and as the universe began to be understood as dynamic, expanding, and ever-evolving, so were concepts of God changing.

Building on process theology, quantum theology emerged as an expression of the new universe story. That story grows out of continuing discovery about creation itself, about the Big Bang and the birth of the cosmos, about the laws of gravity and the speed of light and the theories of relativity, and about the existence of the invisible dark matter and dark energy that shape the ongoing evolution of all things. Extrapolating from quantum mechanics, theologians began to conclude that built in to the story is a certain *intentionality* toward life. Things had to work "just so" in order for life to emerge. And the quickly-dawning realization than such processes are at work throughout the universe—a universe far larger than ever imagined in earlier centuries—changed the paradigm radically. Now God was no longer solely concerned with us but with all things, no longer a sky-God but now a universe-God, no longer a *personal* God but now a transcendent *and* imminent experience of loving energy, dynamically present at every level of existence, moving intentionally, offering an experience of redemption that becomes profoundly personal *as it is experienced*. In this new vision, God creates all things, is in all things, and imbues all things with energy; God is known in the heavens and known as well in the quanta particles that serve as the building blocks of all that is. And we are only beginning to comprehend, through our evolving consciousness, what this means.

In her book *Radical Amazement*, Judy Cannato reflects on this story and on the emergence of Life. She references that moment three billion years ago when a simple primitive cell mutated and began to capture light from the sun in the process of photosynthesis. She notes how the tiny chlorophyll molecules were imbued with photons of solar energy, which enabled them to convert that energy into food (sugar) for themselves, drawing in molecules of water and carbon dioxide, while emitting new oxygen molecules into the emerging atmosphere. The earth began to "receive" the sunlight so freely given, and utilize it in a new way, resulting in Life. We have since learned that the sun converts four million tons of its mass into energy in the form of light *every second*, never to be recaptured, given as energy to feed the universe—and as a result, we live. And there are trillions of suns and billions of galaxies.

Karl Rahner has called this radiating light one continuous act of grace, and "God's self-communication" an outpouring of the very being of God that not only permeates but maintains all life. In this story, the Incarnation is understood as the breaking through of God's Light into human consciousness. Through Jesus and his deep discernment of the realm of God, we became enlightened in a way never before experienced. It was an evolutionary leap, prompted by God's gracious intentionality. In a parallel process to photons and chlorophyll birthing Life itself, Jesus was able to "absorb" the radiance of God in a way that transformed Jesus himself and all who were in his presence, birthing a new level of consciousness about the divine intent and providing a new framework for living meaningfully.

The theories of quantum mechanics are helping us to begin to recognize that we are all connected, all a part of a cosmogenesis that continues to unfold over eons, that acknowledges evolution as a creative process urged on from within and without by the very Spirit of God. It recognizes that through the human species, the consciousness of the cosmos is itself evolving, and that all is intended to enhance life and love.

It may be, in fact, that it is our growing consciousness that is the essential component of co-creating the future with God, of bringing into being a new reality or of discerning what many in the field understand to be alternative realities. Such is the divine mystery unfolding before us, a mystery that invites us into a new and deeper spirituality that holds the promise of fullness of life in God.

RAMIFICATIONS FOR SUPERVISION

Things have changed radically in my generation. These last 58 years are, without doubt, the most exciting and the most threatening in all of human history. The realization of human potential has moved forward by leaps and bounds. The rapid advances in medicine, technology, and agriculture have improved the quality and length of life for millions of people. The development of the computer has expanded access to knowledge exponentially and connected us into a global community.

But all is not well. We have not yet succeeded as a species to embrace our potential for wisdom. Self-interest dominates the effort to promote the common good. More people suffer from economic and health disparities than ever. Wars and terrorism are driven by tribal and religious differences throughout the underdeveloped world. And most importantly, we are rapidly degrading our environment and facing potentially severe consequences, even our own annihilation. Yet the world powers continue to posture as competitors and consumers rather than collaborators. We have not yet embraced the evolution of our own consciousness and human potential.

The same may be said for the field of supervision. When I was a student, supervision was just emerging in the field of theological studies as a legitimate enterprise. Academic centers, charged with preparing students for ministry, were beginning to recognize the growing complexity of the profession of ministry and were realizing that clinical training and skill building would help students learn how to work effectively with people in pain and crisis without getting in their own way. It became the place where theology and psychology could work together to deepen understanding of the human condition and even to enhance the process of meaning-making, both for the student and for the client.

It was not a refined process, however. There were no uniform expected outcomes. There was little emphasis on personal spirituality. The concept of the integration of person, experience, theology, and professional expression was as yet undefined. And the process of supervision was anything but transparent. Nonetheless, the processes of direct engagement of the person and reflection on experience in a group of peers made for powerful, if vulnerable, learning. We began to unlock and slowly understand the dynamics of human behavior, and how to tend to them with compassion. And we began to learn how to bring our religious traditions to bear in the face of life's crises in meaningful and comforting ways. It was a very *modern* expression of ministry.

The challenge was that many of us already emulated *postmodern* thinking, searching for depth and insight and both personal and social transformation. I quickly learned that what I was being given was not enough to enter meaningfully into the brokenness of life. I was up until that point an observer rather than a participant, paralleling my experience of supervision, which prided itself in remaining objective and disengaged. My felt inadequacy was also paralleled by critical projections of supervisors who themselves were unable to engage meaningfully. There was much to be learned all around.

Today we are in the midst of a radical shift even within the field of spiritual care, where we are moving from tradition-based methodologies that primarily supported belief systems and the rituals of faith, to true postmodern professionalism that prompts the processes of change and transformation through both presence and prophetic engagement. It has become a field that is inclusive of all religious perspectives—driven by the growing pluralism of religious faiths and spiritual insights, grounded in those spiritual themes that are common to all humanity, and oriented toward empowering adaptive behaviors and generating the hope and courage to live fully and meaningfully. Supervision has become the primary process for facilitating personal integration among those studying to become practitioners in the field, recognizing that the essential component of effective spiritual care is mastery of one's own process for adaptation and meaning-making. Supervision, therefore, is transformational in nature, shaping the experience of the student to, first of all, synthesize their painful experiences of life with their theologies into a meaningful whole and then to draw from that spiritual framework to generate a parallel experience in their clients and patients.

No longer a disengaged and objective process, supervision in the postmodern era is a deeply engaged and reflective process of looking *with* the student at their own process of becoming, noting the barriers and pitfalls as well as the movement and opportunities, generating a deepening desire to live with depth of feeling in the realm of the divine. At the same time, the student is asked to consider the parallel processes of their patients or clients and how they might in turn aid them in *their* processes of becoming. Tending to such parallels in spiritual care while reflecting on both personal and clinical experiences has become the primary methodology for effective supervision today.

The deconstruction of the Christian tradition and of the Christ story is perhaps accomplishing what centuries of preaching and teaching from within the tradition were only able to do in part. And that is prompting the student to rethink the metaphorical and symbolic meanings inherent in the scriptural stories, letting go of basic, literal/historical interpretations, and entering personally into the experience of divine revelation and communication. A key task of supervision today is to expand that reflective spiritual practice and prompt deepened meditation on the revelation itself. This is spiritual supervision at its best, supporting the student to engage the creation story and the Christ story from a new vantage point, one that moves the student forward to exploring divine revelation *intimately*, a process intended to soften the heart and deepen compassion, to enhance feeling and shape direction. The student who is so supported and directed begins to speak out of the depths, honestly and with deep commitment— the hallmarks of effective spiritual care. When the process unfolds in meaningful ways for the student, the process of providing spiritual care unfolds in meaningful ways for the patient as well.

ENGAGED SUPERVISION

Process and quantum theologies start at the heart of the matter. In the new model of supervision and in light of the postmodern theologies, we begin at the center and not at the fringe. We do not wait for the student to stumble in their experimentation. Instead, we impart an understanding of the basic principles of spiritual care, teaching *essence*, but avoiding focusing on details. We reveal and disclose. We teach not content but process, not data but insight, not knowledge but wisdom. When the essence is perceived, the student is ready to hear what is necessary to expand the perception. Supervision becomes a dance, teaching movement and flow, pointing out the direction and intent, gently noting the disharmonies when the steps are out of sync.

"Every lesson is the first lesson; every time we dance, we do it for the first time."[6] This does not imply that the student forgets what was taught and experienced earlier. Rather, it suggests that every lesson is a first lesson, that something new emerges in the reflection and that another piece is fit into the integrative puzzle. Supervision, then, is characterized by a quality of enthusiasm, the linguistic root of which lies in the concept of infusing God, *entheos*, the process of together experiencing the divine intent. So both process and intent are crucial in supervision.

So what is intended when we sit down with a group of students? Process thought states that all aims are oriented toward realizing potential, that God provides the aim and that the potential is approached co-creatively. So it is in supervision. We provide the aim, seeing the potentialities, and invite the student into mutual exploration and co-creativity, seeking to realize the highest potential possible through an emotional investment in the student's journey of becoming. Life (and professional effectiveness in spiritual care) gets actualized as choices are made and as the student "owns" the learning, adapting their skills or assumptions to the process of becoming someone new. Supervision is an engaged process of naming, confronting, generating, and co-creating.

But what of the student who resists—that is, who is not yet able to risk losing the security of the tradition or of the academic model? Engaged supervision frames the resistance as normal and natural and names it simply as a barrier to the process of becoming. Far from the misconceived notion that we are to let the student be (which, understood from this perspective, is lost in their experience of not-yet-knowing), effective supervision goes to the heart of the matter and wonders with the student about the need for the resistance. Such compassionate and direct engagement allows the student the opportunity to begin to integrate the previous life experiences that may have laid the seeds of the current resistance to entering courageously into a fuller life.

And what of conflict in the group? Again, a common misconception in supervision is to allow conflict to be explored, trusting that the student(s) will learn about how to move through conflict to resolution and be empowered. In an engaged model of supervision, the conflict is named early, and the participants are asked to reflect on what prompted their expressions or may have given rise to their feelings. If the work of the divine in life is to move all things toward harmony and community and if the work of spiritual care is to connect with that divine energy and realign ourselves and our patients toward that harmony even in the face of life's brokenness, then the supervisor might be mindful to co-create the unfolding future through direct engagement at the center of things, naming the heart of the matter and inviting the students to turn to the aims of God.

In its fullest sense, the aim of supervision is to prompt *enlightenment* in the student and to equip the student to prompt enlightenment in the patient. By "enlightenment," I mean the mindful awareness and integration of the universal sacred values and the aims and promises of God. But more than merely being mindful of the values of love and justice, of mercy and reconciliation, of community and healing, the process of supervision generates in the student the desire for congruent expression of those values, for authenticity, for truth-telling, for intensity of feeling and harmony and fullness of life. As the students "leans" into such enlightenment, the dance of supervision develops greater flow and beauty.

Engagement generates more than was present previously. Energy expands. The next moment is co-created and mutually held. As a new electron is created when an atom is engaged by a photon, so is a new experience, a new insight, a new understanding created when a student is similarly engaged. "And behold, I will make all things new . . . (Revelations 21:5)."

Process and quantum theologies put their emphases on relational engagement and co-creativity. In supervision, the process hinges on engaged validation, energized reflection, and naming the barriers. The days of the supervisor being silent and objective and critical are dimming, replaced in this new model by a commitment to shine light into the darkness out of love and self-sacrifice, out of a commitment to empower and generate new potential. As the sun converts its own mass into light energy to create and sustain Life, so we give energy to the process of insight and integration that gives rise to courage and hope. Engaged supervision is an evocative, consciousness-raising flow of energy that will enhance life not only for the student but, in turn, for the patient as well. And the many become one and are increased by one.

LESSONS LEARNED

I have come to embrace the inherent promise of the new universe story, that all things are being made new, and that life is being deepened and sustained by a creative divine energy that is manifest and expressed in movement and rhythm and flow. This pulsating resonance vibrates throughout time and eternity, energizing me and all things within the cosmos. This "expanding horizon of divine belonging" is the context in which I experience revelation and leads me to the knowledge that I am already in God. The freedom to choose my own destiny is grounded in my deepening awareness of the aims of God and the invitation to co-create the unfolding future. And so the spiritual journey becomes one of opening up new horizons of love and understanding and community, not by ignoring or bypassing the darkness and pain of life but precisely by taking it in, learning from it, ultimately integrating it as a source of wisdom and hope.

Supervision is collaborative, integrative education. It is a dance of energy and commitment where presence and intent serve the flow of personal and professional development. It engages the pain and the resistance to pain; it validates the struggle and generates the desire to learn. It raises consciousness and it prompts mindfulness. It expands horizons. And it is a powerful privilege.

NOTES

1. Alan Gurganus, New York Times, *Op. ed.*, May 1, 2008.

2. Sally McFague, *Models of God: Theology for an Ecological, Nuclear Age* (Philadelphia: Fortress Press, 1987).

3. John Shelby Spong, *A New Christianity for a New World* (New York: Harper, 2001), 54.

4. *Ibid*, 211.

5. *Ibid*, 229.

6. Gary Zukav, *The Dancing Wu Li Masters: An Overview of the New Physics* (New York: Perennial Classics, 2001), 9.

CHAPTER SEVEN

From Object to Subject: Pastoral Supervision as an Intersubjective Activity

William DeLong

From the moment Einstein proclaimed that reality was dependent upon the vantage point of the observer, modern thought was propelled down the path of subjectivity. Although the idea is older and has been debated longer in philosophy, subjective *vs.* objective realities is again a hot topic in most modern areas of intellectual inquiry. Scientific methodology, once thought to be the arbitrator of "facts," is now well-known to be a subjective inquiry filled with unexamined assumptions, beliefs, and value laden decisions.[1] Postmodern society is requiring us to consider new ways of teaching and learning pastoral care. Postmodernism, now an often used and misunderstood word, is, I believe, characterized by a set of beliefs that feature, at least in part, the following:

1) the disbelief in any ultimate reliability in knowledge or truth,
2) the disbelief in being able to "discover" the essential nature of an object,
3) the doubt regarding unity, understood as sharing a common language, ethos, and
4) the denial of the transcendence of norms and values.[2]

Central to this understanding is the focus upon the subjectivity of an individual and her or his ability to discern truth. This is aptly captured in the phrase "perception is reality." The "turn to the subjective" inherent in postmodern thought is seen in pastoral supervision by the gradual shifting of supervisory models presented for certification in the Association for Clinical Pastoral Education (ACPE), as well as in recent publications on supervision that opt for a more systemic approach.[3] Theories that rely on objectivity are giving way to newer approaches that recognize the subjective system present in the supervisory encounter.[4] To adapt Winnicott's well-known phrase, "there is no such thing as a supervisor." Intersubjective theory challenges supervisors of pastoral care and counseling to consider how the supervisor's internal patterns of organization effect the supervision of pastors and pastoral psychotherapists.

In order to show how objectivity is embedded in analytic theory, in this chapter I briefly review the development of two processes in psychoanalytic theory: transference/countertransference and interpretation. As we follow the development and theoretical shifts in each, we see the movement from objective to subjective perspectives. This historical review of psychoanalytic theory is important, given that most of the early theorists of pastoral care and counseling were trained in the classical model. Objectivity lies embedded in the heart of the pastoral care movement.[5]

This chapter presents intersubjective theory as a practical model for pastoral supervision. The intersubjective approach, rooted in the Self Psychology of Heinz Kohut and elaborated on by Robert Stolorow and his colleagues, provides a framework for pastoral supervision in both individual and group work that challenges objective ways of seeing.

I believe intersubjective theory remains compatible with many of the historical and theological values of pastoral supervision, especially as they emerged in the tradition of Clinical Pastoral Education (CPE).[6] I believe intersubjective theory avoids many of the pitfalls of objectivity inherent in classical understandings of psychoanalytic theory and provides a more congruent, accurate, and ethical model for pastoral supervision. Thus, this chapter will primarily review psychoanalytic theory and practice. I conclude the chapter by pointing to some of the theological and educational implications this approach has for training pastors.

My hope for this chapter and my purpose in presenting the intersubjective approach is to encourage readers to reflect upon how the values and myths of objectivity are embedded into our theology, personality, and educational theories. I hope to help us re-examine how objectivity affects the practice of pastoral supervision and ultimately the pastoral care provided parishioners, patients, and pastoral counseling clients.

A second hope for this chapter is to continue the dialogue about the nature of pastoral supervision. I hope to wade into what one author has described in analytic supervision as "residual worries from the teach-treat controversy."[7] Along with a core curriculum, didactics, and providing direct pastoral care, individual and group supervision is a critical part of the formation process for professional pastoral care providers. Intersubjective theory provides a needed balance between legitimate concerns about not analyzing pastoral care students and the under-use of in-depth psychoanalytic theory in supervision. My attempt then, is to hold to the truth that "supervision is more than teaching and less than treatment."[8]

FROM OBJECT TO SUBJECT

The nature of the analytic relationship always has been a part of analytic theory. How the therapeutic alliance forms and the role of the analyst in helping that alliance is a significant part of any analytic theory.

As early as 1912, Freud was articulating abstinence and neutrality as the proper stance for psychoanalysis. In no doubt due to his medical and neurological training, Freud's theory was grounded in the prevailing enthusiasm of modern science and its believed ability to ascertain and describe facts. Freud's metapsychology, seen in his instinctual drive theory, satisfied Freud's need to adhere to his belief in scientific positivism.[9] [10] Freud's "rule of abstinence" served to ensure the role of objectivity in the analytic relationship. Closely allied to the rule of abstinence and considered by most to be an essential part of analytic neutrality is Freud's recommendation that the analyst "should be opaque to his patients and, like a mirror, should show them nothing but what is shown to him."[11] Because of this, Freud spoke very little about countertransference (recorded only four times according to the index to the *Standard Edition*) and believed it to be the neurotic transference of the analyst to the patient.[12] Countertransference, thought Freud, is a result of the analyst's unanalyzed neuroses and pathology requiring supervision and personal analysis.

A central and early dissenting voice emerges in the 1930s in the person of Sandor Ferenczi. Derived from his clinical experimentations, Ferenczi's developing theory leads him to different conclusions than his mentor. In particular, and important in my argument in this chapter, is Ferenczi's claim that it is not interpretation that leads to healing but the quality of the relationship between the therapist and the patient. Ferenczi is also concerned with how the analyst contributes to the therapeutic relationship. Ferenczi stresses 1) the ways in which what the analyst provides to the patient differs from what the patient has experienced in the past, 2) the analyst's love for the patient, and 3) the importance of reducing impediments in the analyst to understanding and connecting emotionally with the patient.[13] In this student of Freud, we can already hear the initial questions concerning the role of objectivity in the therapeutic process.

Melanie Klein, viewing transference from her object relations perspective, focuses on working with transference as a "total situation."[14] In her paper "The Origins of Transference," Klein articulates the relationship of transference with internal and external objects. She makes the historical move toward understanding transference as a part of the dynamic relationship between ego and object, as well as patient and analyst. Klein feels the relationship exists through the process of transference and interpretation of defense mechanisms. Although Klein maintains a classical understanding of countertransference, she points the way to viewing transference as a two-way street:

The psychoanalytic procedure consists in selecting the most urgent aspects of the material and interpreting them with precision. The patient's reactions and subsequent associations amount to further material which has to be analyzed in the same way. . . . I was determined not to modify my technique and to interpret in the usual way, even deep anxiety situations as they came up and the corresponding defenses.[15]

Soon, however, analysts begin considering their affective responses to patients from a broader perspective. As the analyst's reaction to the patient continues to receive attention, the "objectivity" and hence the interpretive power of the analyst also comes into questions.

Followers of Klein and the British object relations school begin to focus upon the relationship of the patient and analyst as the crucial dynamic of healing. This leads to increased investigation of countertransference. Heimann presents a pivotal paper in 1950. Heimann, a follower of Klein, investigates the role of the analyst's feelings in the therapeutic encounter:

The analyst's emotional response to his patient within the analytic situation represents one of the most important tools for his work. The analyst's countertransference is an instrument of research into the patient's unconscious.[16]

Heimann's counter to Freud's notion of objective neutrality brings with it a new way to view the analytic stance. Using the emotional states of the analyst as a tool continues to be a fundamental premise in British object relation theory, especially in the development of projective identification.

Analysis, then, begins to be thought of as the subtle interplay of transference and countertransference, within the relationship of therapist and patient. This trend in analytic thinking is most clearly voiced by D.W. Winnicott.

Central to Winnicott's technique is the role of the patient as the one with insight. The role of interpretation by the analyst takes the back seat to the responsibility for establishing and maintaining accurate relating. Winnicott believes interpretation can hinder the process of analysis: "I think I interpret mainly to let the patient know the limits of my understanding. The principle is that it is the patient and only the patient who has the answers."[17] With the publication in 1947 of his paper "Hate in the Countertransference," analysis focuses on the affective states of both the therapist and the patient. Interpretation as a function of the therapist's objective knowing is increasingly questioned. The emerging theory sees interpretation as a subset of the analyst's organizing principle, a central tenent of intersubjective theory. The analytic system of patient and analyst, not transference interpretation, is being recast as a primary tool for understanding and healing.

Another dramatic shift takes place with the publication of Heinz Kohut's paper, "Introspection, Empathy, and Psychoanalysis," presented at the International Psychoanalytic Association in 1957. In this paper, Kohut further extends the role of the subjective in the therapeutic relationship and established what is now known as self psychology.

HEINZ KOHUT AND SELF PSYCHOLOGY

Heinz Kohut was working with narcissistic patients that many thought were beyond the help of analysis. Many see his Self Psychology as an important paradigm shift from classical psychoanalysis primarily because of his reformulation of transference and his commitment to empathy as a clinical method.[18] Empathy is the centerpiece of Kohut's theory. Empathy is not conceived as a feeling, but rather a method that allows the therapist to enter the subjective inner world of the patient. He cites the example of a tall man to describe what he meant by "vicarious introspection."

> Only when we think ourselves into his place, only when we, by vicarious introspection, begin to feel his unusual size as if it were our own and thus revive inner experiences in which we had been unusual or conspicuous, only then do we begin to appreciate the meaning that the usual size may have for this person and only then have we observed a psychological fact.[19]

Kohut believes that the only way one can know the inner world of another person (mind or psychology) is through the use of "vicarious introspection." Alternating the use of terms between "empathy" and "vicarious introspection," Kohut limits the material he believes relevant to psychoanalytic work to that which could be observed through vicarious introspection.

> Only a phenomenon that we can attempt to observe by introspection or by empathy with another's introspection may be called psychological. A phenomenon is "somatic," "behavioristic," or "social" if our methods of observation do not predominantly include introspection and empathy. We may thus repeat the earlier definition in the form of an explicit statement: we designate phenomena as mental, psychic, or psychological if our mode of observation includes introspection and empathy as an essential constituent.[20]

By limiting the nature of what can be considered psychological, Kohut recasts the psychoanalytic task as a subjective enterprise. Objectivity, as conceived in classical theory, prevents the therapist from using empathy or from taking an "experience near" approach to the patient. Kohut and later intersubjective theorists insist that the limit and boundary of the psychoanalytic process be defined by the use of vicarious introspection. With this shift, Kohut places subjectivity at the heart of the healing relationship. For it is the therapist's ability to empathetically attune to the client that creates and maintains healing.

> By embracing empathy as his method, Kohut rejected the classical analytic primacy of insight through interpretation. He favored the empathic side in the running battle between cognitive insight and empathic responding in the history

of psychoanalysis, a conflict which can be discerned first in the thinking of Freud where insight and empathy were two separate strands.[21]

With the analytic primacy of insight through transference interpretation shifting to empathy and vicarious introspection, Kohut paved the way for further speculation on the role of the analyst in the subjective or intersubjective realm of the analytic encounter. At the same time, he redefines the understanding and use of transference, again in opposition to classical understanding. For Kohut, cure in analysis is achieved by working empathically with the transference and reinstituting the developmental process.

TRANSFERENCE AND COUNTERTRANSFERENCE IN SELF PSYCHOLOGY

Kohut believes that transference is not simply the repetition of the past activated by the "blank slate" of the therapist. Rather, he sees transference as a manifestation of developmental longings surfacing in the climate of empathy. Following the work of object relations theorists,[22] I believe Kohut sees the need of the self to have objects to which it could relate. Kohut saw the self relating to these objects as part of the self.

Selfobjects are objects which we experience as part of our self; the expected control over them is, therefore, closer to the concept of the control which a grown-up expects to have over his own body and mind than to the concept of the control which he expects to have over others.[23]

Selfobjects are objects (other selves) that provide a sense of well being for the self. In a carefully crafted paragraph in his book, *How Does Analysis Cure?*, Kohut explained the selfobject:

> Throughout his life, a person will experience himself as a cohesive harmonious firm unit in time and space, connected with his past and pointing meaningfully into a creative-productive future, but only as long as, at each stage in his life, he experiences certain representatives of his human surrounding as joyfully responding to him, as available to him as sources of idealized strength and calmness, as being silently present but in essence like him, and, at any rate, able to grasp his inner life more or less accurately so that their responses are attuned to his needs and allow him to grasp their inner life when he is in need of such sustenance.[24]

Kohut, then, sees selfobject transference as a reactivation of a developmental process that relies on selfobjects. Therapy consists of the self utilizing the empathic presence of the therapist to continue a thwarted or "derailed" developmental process of self formation, not a shift from primary narcissism to object love.

> . . . Developmental moves of normal psychological life must be seen in the changing nature of the relationships between the self and its selfobjects—not as

a replacement of selfobjects by love objects, not as a move from narcissism to object love.[25]

Kohut's emphasis on the relational aspects of the formation and maintenance of the self leads him to practice psychotherapy in a relational way. When this is combined with his method of observation—empathy—one sees a dramatic shift in the role and function of the therapist as a subjective presence in the clinical environment. Kohut accepts the subjectivity of the therapist as an essential part of the therapeutic equation. Kohut pushed the limits of subjectivity by acknowledging what he called the "I-You experience":

> Whereas self psychology holds that the application of these two separate frames of reference makes a significant contribution to our ability to explain human experiences in health and in disease, we also realize that there are occasions when the "I-You" experience is most fruitfully approached within a frame of reference that dispenses with this conceptual separation. We believe furthermore, that the mutual influence of the two intertwining sets of experiences, on upon the other, deserves intensive study.[26]

Through the realization of an experience near methodology, and the application of a model of transference that utilizes the subjective reality of the therapist, Kohut paved the way for a theoretical approach that fully utilizes the subjective nature of both patient and therapist. Kohut recasts the neurotic quality of the transference from the classical understanding of a repetition of the past and the "false connection" to a developmental process that is being reactivated through the narcissistic selfobject transference. Kohut's concept of the narcissistic transference focuses more upon the absence of a needed developmental experience than upon the projection of the patient's prior experience to the analyst. Kohut takes the step toward understanding transference as an indication of the patient's internal organization of their sense of self. This shift makes transference a key to understanding the developmental strivings of patients encountered in psychoanalysis. The further development of Kohut's theory is left to the intersubjective theorists, principally through the thinking of Robert Stolorow, James Atwood, and Bernard Brandchaft. A more detailed review of their psychoanalytic theory allows us to see the implications of subjectivity for education and theology.

INTERSUBJECTIVE THEORY

Thus far we see how countertransference and the subjective role of the therapist gradually shifts from the initial classical model of abstinence to the work of Heinz Kohut and Self Psychology's understanding of vicarious introspection. In the work of Robert Stolorow and others, we now see how transference, countertransference, and subjectivity of both the analyst and patient is given primary importance as an intersubjective system.

Intersubjective theory is the name given to a framework devised by Robert Stolorow and colleagues. He describes it as,

> a broad methodological and epistemological perspective that I believe can encompass and synthesize the contributions of both self psychology and object relations theory to the understanding of the therapeutic process.[27]

The analytic process, as defined by intersubjective theory, is "the unfolding, exploration, illumination, and transformation of the patient's subjective world."[28] The most critical theoretical shift made by intersubjective theory, at least for the purposes of this chapter, is the definition of transference as organizing principle and the reciprocal nature of the intersubjective field.

TRANSFERENCE AS ORGANIZING PRINCIPLE

As we have seen, transference is understood in psychoanalytic theory in many different ways. Initially, Breuer and Freud described transference as a "false connection" perceived by the analyst as a "distortion." It has also been conceived as regression, displacement, projection, and distortion.[29] Stolorow and Atwood seek to recast transference into an intersubjective perspective. They do this by conceiving of transference as "organizing principle." Instead of the false connection leading to a distortion as perceived by the objective analyst, they see transference "as the expression of a universal psychological striving to organize experience and construct meanings."[30] Transference then refers to:

> . . . all the ways in which the patient's experience of the analytic relationship is shaped by his own psychological structures—by the distinctive, archaically rooted configurations of self and object that unconsciously organize his subjective universe.[31]

The commitment to vicarious introspection requires transference to be understood from a subjective standpoint. The attempt of the patient to communicate to the analyst how he or she goes about making meaning in the world is communicated through transference.

> The idea that the transference constitutes the distortion of reality by the patient leads to the corollary that the therapist avoids contaminating the therapy so that the patient can see his or her own distortion more clearly. Such a view of transference places the whole burden of change on the patient, lowers the chances that a therapeutic milieu can foster growth and development, and turns the therapeutic relationship into a hostile one. All this implies that the therapist's organizing principles play no role in the therapy whatsoever. This view is based on the illusion that the therapist can invariably be objective and neutral, and abstain from instinctual gratification in order to be a truly blank screen. Such a stance is as undesirable to maintain as it is to achieve.[32]

By viewing transference as organizing principle, the myth of objectivity is denied and replaced by a subjective, "experience-near" perspective. Instead of a false connection understood by uncontaminated interpretation, transference is seen as the patient's expression of the organizing principles that guide the inner life of the self. Instead of forcing the patient to "renounce his infantile wishes toward the therapist," transference as organizing principle is to be included as a statement of the self's need for selfobject relations necessary for reinstatement of a derailed development process.

Another significant shift in viewing transference through intersubjective theory occurs with the conception of countertransference. Countertransference is simply seen as the analyst's organizing activity. Countertransference is no longer viewed as something that must be accommodated or cured. Rather, intersubjective theory defines countertransference as a part of the analytic process.

> Such a definition accepts countertransference as an inevitable fact in itself neither good nor bad. It does not view countertransference as a dangerous computer virus that has to be eradicated as quickly as possible to make the mental apparatus, the computer, function without error. Both transference and countertransference are necessary components of the configurations of self and object, or self and selfobject, that take place within the therapeutic milieu, which Stolorow and his colleagues have termed the intersubjective context.[33]

THE INTERSUBJECTIVE SYSTEM

As one can see, transference and countertransference are seen as the individual's organizing principle within the analytic relationship. Each then, the patient and the analyst, create the intersubjective field in which psychoanalysis takes place. The intersubjective field, created and maintained by a sustained empathic inquiry, allows the analyst to comprehend the meaning of the inner world of the patient. In this intersubjective field, there is no single objective viewpoint.

> What, from our intersubjective perspective, constitutes the essence of a therapeutic alliance? It is surely not the bond formed by the patient's commitment to follow the insights of the analyst. In our view the foundations of a therapeutic alliance are established by the analyst's commitment to seek consistently to comprehend the meaning of the patient's expressions, his affect states, and most centrally, the impact of the analyst from a perspective within rather than outside the patient's subjective frame of reference. We have referred to this positioning as the stance of "sustained empathic inquiry." Let no one believe that this commitment is an easy one to fulfill—it is frequently like feeling the sand giving way under one's psychological footing. Seeing himself and the world consistently through the eyes of another can pose serious threats to the analyst's personal reality and sense of self, much as the patient must feel threatened when his experience is treated as a distortion of reality.[34]

The analytic relationship, then, rests not upon a presumed stance of objective knowing. Rather, each person enters the relationship with a whole host of beliefs, attitudes, awareness, and more. That is, each enters the relationship as a subjective enterprise based on one's organizing principles. Stolorow and colleagues describe it this way:

> We do not believe that the analyst possesses any "objective" knowledge of the patient's life or of human development and human psychological functioning. What the analyst possesses is a subjective frame of reference of his own, deriving from a multiplicity of sources and formative experiences, through which he attempts to organize the analytic data into a set of coherent themes and interrelationships. The analyst's frame of reference must not be elevated to the status of objective fact. Indeed, it is essential that analysts continually strive to expand their reflective awareness of their own unconscious organizing principles, including especially those enshrined in their "objective knowledge and theories," so that the impact of these principles on the analytic process can be recognized and itself become a focus of analytic investigation.[35]

Conceptualizing pastoral supervision as in intersubjective process has many advantages to it—primarily because the myth of objectivity is replaced by a reciprocal system of mutual and equal subjective organizing principles. Pastoral supervision benefits from this kind of model because of its sense of equality (mutuality), its abandonment of objective ways of knowing, and its increased capacity to explore with a student how their central organizing principles affect their understanding of themselves as a person and pastor.

PASTORAL SUPERVISION AND INTERSUBJECTIVITY

We have seen how objectivity permeates the theory and practice of psychotherapy. And we see how that sets up a unique relationship based upon the "objective knowing" of the analyst. The same is true in education theory.

Parker Palmer shows how objectivity creates similar problems. Palmer, working from his perspective as a college teacher and educational theorist, believes objectivity distances the knower from the known, isolates us from ourselves, and separates us from the web of relationships he calls community.

As education takes place, particularly in graduate level education, the student is expected to learn from the one who knows all of the facts about a given topic. Palmer believes this is occasioned by objectivity,

> . . . because conventional education neglects the inner reality of teacher and students for the sake of reality "out there," the heart of the knowing self is never held up for inspection, never given a chance to be known. The ideal of objectivism is the knower as a "blank slate," receiving the unadulterated imprint of whatever facts are floating around. The aim of objectivism is to eliminate all elements of subjectivity, all biases and preconceptions, so that our knowledge can become purely empirical. For the sake of objectivity, our inner realities are factored out of the knowledge equation.[36]

If this sounds familiar to the reader, he or she is seeing the power that objective perspectives have in western thought. Pastoral supervision, at least as it is undertaken in ACPE, seeks to address this by the final step in the supervisory certification process. The primary focus in certification as a CPE supervisor is to "demonstrate the use of self as the primary teaching tool" (*Standards, Certification Manual,* ACPE). Hawkins and Shohet describe this process of mutual knowing in their third and final stages of development in the supervisory process. That process is characterized by an increase ability of the supervisee to view their work as "process-in-context-centered." The focus then becomes, "How do processes interpenetrate?"[37]

I believe, then, that intersubjective theory provides a psychological and epistemological framework by which supervisors may utilize their sense of self as the primary means by which the student will learn. Intersubjective theory seeks for both supervisor and student to be known within the supervisory encounter. And the object of their knowing is a mutually influenced system created by the intersubjective field comprised of two organizing principles. By recasting the neurotic transference to organizing principle, supervision can focus upon what transformation theory calls "meaning perspectives."

> Meaning perspectives provide us with criteria for judging or evaluating right and wrong, bad and good, beautiful and ugly, true and false, appropriate and inappropriate . . . when our meaning perspectives are inadequate to explain facets of our experience, we are faced with areas or dimensions of apparent meaninglessness.[38]

Jack Mezirow describes these perspectives as the "lions at the gates of awareness." That is, they are the principles and perspective to which we turn in order to make meaning of our world. A cohesive supervisory theory that utilized the intersubjective approach would encounter the meaning perspectives of a student through what we have called organizing principles. In either instance, the supervisor would encounter the principles the student used to make meaning out of her and his experience. Learning, then, is also reframed away from the conflict model inherent in classical theory to a relational model formulated on intersubjective learning.

In similar fashion, theology has been throwing off the shackles of objectivity. In the liberation theologies of Central and Latin America, context or subjectivity is seen as the starting place for theologizing. The use of hermeneutics and phenomenology as frameworks for theology have helped us to begin our theologizing from where people live out their lives together. No longer are we beginning theology from somewhere "out there." Rather, theology is beginning to seek a subjective perspective so that it becomes context sensitive. The inherent inequality found in objectivity (analyst knowing, patient distorting; supervisor knowing, student distorting) is being replaced by a subjectivity that seeks to honor the equality of each person's experience or journey. Paul Tillich speaks of this as mutuality:

The same is true of other person to person encounters. The other person is a stranger, but a stranger only in disguise. Actually, he is an estranged part of one's self. Therefore one's own humanity can be realized only in reunion with him—a reunion which is also decisive for the realization of his humanity. In the horizontal line this leads to two possible but equally ambiguous solutions: the effort to overcome the split between the subject and object in a person-to-person encounter (whereby each person is both subject and object) either by surrendering one's self to the other one or by taking the other one into self's self . . . neither surrender nor subjection are adequate means of reaching the other one.[39]

One could argue here that Tillich, in speaking of the "estranged part of one's self" is speaking about selfobject needs as articulated by Kohut. Intersubjective theory provides an alternative to the struggle of surrender or subjection. Through the intersubjective field, both supervisor and student participate in the mutual unfolding and illumination of the student's organizing principles. In this way, the student is engaged in a relationship based on a mutual understanding of equality freed from the archaic concepts of objectivity, neurotic transference, and distortion.

CONCLUDING THOUGHTS

I argue in this chapter for what I believe is a necessary shift in pastoral supervision. First, I show that concepts of objectivity are embedded in the psychological, educational, and theological theories we use to inform our supervision and that those concepts, by creating a relationship based on hierarchy and assume structures of power, force students into a position of subjection by accepting the "interpretations" provided in the supervisory relationship. Finally, I argue that intersubjective theory provides a framework by which supervisors may begin to rid themselves of the myths of objectivity, thereby creating a supervisory alliance based upon mutuality and characterized by an experience near, empathic approach. In so doing, we more accurately use ourselves as the primary teaching tool and create a supervisory environment that is based upon the subjective reality of each, both supervisor and student.

This chapter was originally published in *The Journal of Pastoral Care and Counseling* (Vol. 56, No. 1, Spring 2002) and is used with permission.

NOTES

1. Thomas Kuhn, *The Structure of Scientific Revolutions* (Chicago: University of Chicago Press, 1962.) See my response to Larry Dossey about prayer in Larry Vande-Creek, ed., *Scientific and Pastoral Perspectives on Intercessory Prayer* (New York: Haworth Press, 1998).

2. Ryan LaMothe, "Challenges of Faith: Transitional Objects, Faith, and Postmodernity," *The Journal of Pastoral Care* (Vol. 6, 1999), 255-267.

3. George Fitchett, "A Coherent Theory of Education Relevant for CPE," *Journal of Supervision and Training in Ministry*, (Vol. 6, 1983).

4. Paul Hawkins and Robert Shohet, *Supervision in the Helping Professions* (Buckingham, UK: Open University Press, 1989).

5. Scott Olbert, "Between Pastor and People: An Intersubjective Perspective," Unpublished manuscript, 16.

6. Joan Hemenway, *Inside the Circle* (Atlanta: Journal of Pastoral Care Publications, 1998).

7. Jean-Paul Pegeron, "Supervision as an Analytic Experience," *Psychoanalytic Quarterly*, (Vol. LXV, 1996), 693.

8. A.J. Solnit, "Learning from Psychoanalytic Supervision," *International Journal of Psycholoanalysis*, (Vol. 51, 1970), 359-362.

9. Ronald Lee and J. Colby Martin, *Psychotherapy After Kohut* (Hillsdale, NJ: The Analytic Press, 1991), 57.

10. Peter Gay, Freud, *A Life for Our Time* (New York: W.W. Norton, 1988).

11. Robert Stolorow and George Atwood, "Deconstructing the Myth of the Neutral Analyst: An Alternative from Intersubjective Systems Theory," *Psychoanalytic Quarterly*, (Vol. LXVI, 1997,) 435.

12. R.D. Hinshelwood, "Countertransference," *The International Journal of Psychoanalysis*, (Vol. 90, 1999), 797.

13. Donna Orange, *Emotional Understanding: Studies in Psychoanalytic Epistemology* (New York: The Guilford Press, 1995), 161.

14. Melanie Klein, "The Origins of Transference" in David E. Scharff, ed., *Object Relations Theory and Practice* (Northdale, NJ: Jason Aronson, 1997).

15. Melanie Klein, *Narrative of a Child Analysis* (New York: Basic Books, 1961), 12-13.

16. P. Heinman, as quoted in R.D. Hinshelwood, *Op. cit.*, 798.

17. *Ibid.*, 806.

18. Ronald Lee and J. Colby Martin, *Op. cit.*, 1.

19. Heinz Kohut, "Introspection, Empathy, and Psychoanalysis," in Paul Ornstein, ed., *The Search for the Self* (New York: International Universities Press, 1978).

20. Heinz Kohut, *Ibid.*

21. Ronald Lee and J. Colby Martin, *Op. cit.*, 108.

22. In particular, the work of Fairbain and Guntrip, as well as Winnicott and others. See Ronald Lee and J. Colby Martin, *Ibid.*

23. *Ibid.*, 167.

24. Heinz Kohut, *How Does Analysis Cure?* (Chicago: University of Chicago Press, 1984), 52.

25. *Ibid.*, 52.

26. *Ibid.*, 53.

27. Robert Stolorow, "An Intersubjective View of the Therapeutic Process," *Bulletin of the Menninger Clinic* (Vol. 57, No. 4, 1993), 450.

28. Robert Stolorow and George Atwood, *Op. cit.*, 442.

29. Ronald Lee and J. Colby Martin, *Op. cit.*, 225.

30. Robert Stolorow, Bernard Bradchaft, and George Atwood, *Psychoanalytic Treatment: An Intersubjective Approach* (Hillsdale, NJ: The Analytic Press, 1987), 37.

31. Ronald Lee and J. Colby Martin, *Op. cit.* 231.

32. *Ibid.*, 230.

33. *Ibid.*, 229.

34. Bernard Brandchaft and Robert Stolorow, "Varieties of Therapeutic Alliance" in Jerome Winer, ed., *The Annual of Psychoanalysis*, Vol. 18 (Hillsdale, NJ: The Analytic Press, 1990), 8.

35. Robert Stolorow, Bernard Bradchaft, and George Atwood, *Op. cit.*, 6.

36. Parker Palmer, *To Know As We are Known* (New York: Harper & Row, 1983), 35.

37. Paul Hawkins and Robert Shohet, *Supervision in the Helping Professions* (Philadelphia: Open University, 1989), 52.

38. Jack Mezirow, *Transformative Dimensions of Adult Learning* (San Francisco: Jossey-Bass, 1991), 44.

39. Paul Tillich, *Systematic Theology* (Chicago: University of Chicago Press, Vol. 3, 1963), 261.

CHAPTER EIGHT

Power and the Supervisory Relationship

M.C. Ward

But Moses said to God, "If I come to the Israelites and say to them, 'The God of your ancestors has sent me to you,' and they ask me, 'What is his name?' what shall I say to them?" God said to Moses, "I AM WHO I AM." He said further, "Thus you shall say to the Israelites, 'I AM has sent me to you.'"—Genesis 3:13-14

Jesus went on with his disciples to the villages of Caesarea Phillipi; and on the way he asked his disciples, "Who do people say that I am?" And they answered him, "John the Baptist; and others, Elijah; and still others, one of the prophets." He asked them, "But who do you say that I am?" Peter answered him, "You are the Messiah." And he sternly ordered them not to tell anyone about him. —Mark 8:27-30

INTRODUCTION

As a woman, mother, and priest, and as this particular woman, mother, and priest, I experience the world from a place of both power and powerlessness. Growing up on U.S. military bases in Cold War Europe as the daughter of a World War II-refugee mother and a soldier father, I saw myself as one who was relatively powerless in a world characterized by the constant struggle between good and evil. In that worldview, to speak truth to power openly and directly—that is, to show one's true self—was, at best, likely to get one reprimanded and, at worst, to get one killed, to be shamed verbally, or abandoned emotionally.

Better to take pride in using what power one did have manipulatively than to be humiliated by one's ultimate powerlessness. As an adult, I have moved into up-per-middle-class, educated, predominantly European-American circles that al-low me to have expectations for my life that are far removed from the struggles that characterize the lives of many of the people I live around, work with, and minister to. Nonetheless, I continue to carry the worldview of my childhood inside me, making it easy for me to make assumptions about others' power and misuse my own. Better to give my power away than feel guilty for having it. In my experience then, power versus powerlessness is not a simple either/or propo-sition.

Moreover, the ambiguity of power extends beyond my personal experience. As an Episcopal priest, I am part of the Anglican Communion, a fellowship that, even as I write this chapter, is in the throes of a power struggle that brings into question some of the communion's most basic principles and, indeed, may threaten its very existence. Much of the current struggle arises from a commit-ment to and vision for a fellowship based on shared authority rather than a strict hierarchy, dominated either by a single cleric or by the congregation. This makes things far more complicated than if there were a clear chain of com-mand—but, in my view, far more consistent with the uncertainties and com-plexities of real life, especially in the midst of illness, grief, and crisis. It is this ambiguity that also characterizes many pastoral supervisory relationships, as lay people and clergy alike on all levels often come to learn in uncomfortable, if not downright painful, ways. Again, as I began writing this chapter, my summer Clinical Pastoral Education interns were practically begging me to tell them my expectations so that they could live up to them—in much the same way that I myself have practically begged certification committees to just tell me what they are looking for. In both instances, the message is the same: tell me who you want me to be—tell me who I am—and I will be that person.

At its heart, I believe this pastoral identity question is a struggle between external power and internal authority, and the supervisory relationship is often the place where the struggle plays out. Clinical Pastoral Education and, indeed, many formation and ordination processes, correctly spend so much time on pas-toral identity formation precisely because a clear sense of one's pastoral identity is the source of pastoral authority. I must know who I am if I would know and claim the power of the one who sent me.

In my own experience, claiming and blessing my identity has been a life-long struggle that only has come to real fruition in the context of my vocational journey. I know myself primarily as "Mollie," my family's nickname for me, which created significant confusion when I began school since my birth and baptismal certificates identify me as "Mary Christine Ward." "Mary" was my paternal grandmother and "Christine" is my own mother. When as a small child I behaved contrary to my family's expectations, my German godmother tagged me *böse Christine*, or "mean Christine," the message being that I (Mollie) dis-appeared when I misbehaved. As I began my professional career as a journalist,

I thought to resolve the Mary-Mollie confusion by using the byline "M.C. Ward," only to encounter assumptions that I was trying to disguise my gender. When I married and chose to keep my own last name rather than taking my husband's, my parents expressed anxiety that people might think I was "living in sin." At age 35, the same year I began my CPE residency, I finally asked my bishop to say, and bless, *all* of my names—Mary Christine Mollie Ward—when he called on God to make me, first, a deacon and, later, a priest in God's Church.

I am reminded of the time I spent as a Peace Corps volunteer in the Dominican Republic, where my husband and I lived along the Haitian border. In a region where Vodun spiritual traditions stood alongside Christian traditions and where the memory of political dictatorship was fresh, it was common practice for the *campesinos* that we lived and worked with to conceal their real names and instead use nicknames. As my husband and I sought to understand this pervasive custom, our Dominican colleagues explained that to know someone's real name gave one power over that person—power to control, power to betray—and was reserved only for one's most trusted relationships. The quotes that begin this chapter illustrate that this wariness is not limited to adherents of Vodun, for in the Judeo-Christian context; there is a longstanding relationship between identity and power. The power to name is often equated with power *over*. Being seen, *being known*, makes one vulnerable.

As I have come to recognize and embrace both my power and my powerlessness as part of who I am and, I believe, part of the God in whose image I am created, I have come to heal the dualistic split of my upbringing that sees power as a zero-sum game. One of my goals in the supervisory relationship is neither to lord over my students nor to be lorded over, but rather to offer a third option—what I call mutual vulnerability. In doing so, I believe that I assist my students in healing some of the splits that seem to characterize many traditional views of power and authority.

MUTUAL VULNERABILITY AS THE IMAGO DEI

Paradoxical though it may sound, if knowledge is power, then self-knowledge, and by extension self-disclosure, is omnipotence. I begin with the idea that God's real power is derived from vulnerability rather than might—that mutual vulnerability is the divine identity in whose image we are created: the *imago Dei*. As I attempt to live and move and have my being in authentic relationship with God, neighbor, and self, I base my supervisory work on the idea that God risks God's self to be in authentic relationship with us, and that each of us is similarly called to risk self in order to be in authentic relationship with God and one another. My understanding of this God is as one who values not only the good of the community, but also the inherent goodness of each person and who images this risk-taking throughout the history of God's interactions with Humanity. As Creator, God endows Humanity with free will and, in doing so, risks the rejection of God's self: a self that glories not in blind obedience or empty praise, but in authenticity and integrity. As Christ, God experiences our incarnate humanity and risks being known for who God is: a self that is most powerful in its vulnerability. And as Holy Spirit, God establishes relationship between self and Other and risks transformation—of self as well as Other.

On a theological level, I experience this mutual vulnerability as most fully expressed in the concept of a Triune God. Even as I write the word "triune" it is with a sense of irony. In using "triune" rather than the more traditional "trinity" I consciously claim the mystery of understanding God as a tri-unity rather than simply a trinity or a unity. I also owe my interest in this distinction and its roots to many conversations, and often heated arguments, with my seminary systematic theology and ethics professor. In the relationship with this professor, I not only experienced the affirmation of my ideas but, too, the devastation of being silenced and shamed. From that dialogue, as painful as it was legendary among my seminary classmates, emerged much of my need to move beyond a dualistic view of God and to discover a third way of being.

As I contemplate that which I experience as a Triune God, I am drawn to the language of theologians as diverse as St. Augustine of Hippo and the Episcopal priest Carter Heyward, who offer images of God that are less like a group of persons than a group of relationships. Augustine, for example, describes God as the lover, the beloved, and the love between them[1] while Heyward writes of:

> 1) She who, from the beginning, has been the source of all loving, dying, and letting go throughout and beyond the cosmos;
> 2) He who—at the same time, in every moment—is embodied through us in our fur and paws, our hands and hearts;
> 3) The same Holy Spirit connecting our lives, celebrations, and griefs to those of persons and creatures in all times and places, strengthening us through the real presence of those who've gone before and those who will come after us.[2]

Being able to bring together two such diverse theologians represents for me a healing of a split, a stand both for and against the denominational milieu in which I find myself. Some 400 years after the articulation of what came to be known as the three-legged stool that supports the Anglican understanding of faith,[3] the Episcopal Church in which I was raised and find my spiritual home continues to be wracked by battles over the primacy of scripture, tradition, or reason. Both Augustine and Heyward, at times, have been painted as heretics by their opposition, and yet both help me to find words and images to enrich and express my theology—a theology that neither accepts without reason the "orthodoxy" of a literal interpretation of scripture, nor breaks ties with a tradition that continues to be life-giving to me.

In contemplating the Triune God, I also am drawn to the Russian iconographer Andrei Rublev's image of the "Old Testament Trinity," which portrays the Genesis 18 story of Abraham's three divine visitors at table under the oaks of Mamre. The Roman Catholic monk Henri Nouwen describes the icon this way:

"As we place ourselves in front of the icon in prayer, we come to experience a gentle invitation to participate in the intimate conversation that is taking place among the three divine angels and to join them around the table."[4] In the icon, none of the figures is subordinated to either of the others, and yet each of them is self-differentiated. They draw near to one another, but their faces are fully visible. Their circle—and the possibility of relationship—is not closed to us. In sitting around Abraham's table, they accept his hospitality and the risk that this might incur an obligation. The obligation at risk here is not a contractual or material one but a covenantal and relational one—that is, that in accepting the openness of another, one is obliged to be similarly authentic.

With the image of a Triune God as foundational, two other important images under-gird my understanding of mutual vulnerability: the integration of Christ as fully Human and fully Divine, and the Mother-Child relationship. The Christ language prevents me from splitting off the parts of myself or another that make me uncomfortable or anxious, while the Mother-Child image reminds me of the inter-connectedness of the supervisory relationship. An important part of my spiritual journey has been the understanding that I can be both "Mother Mollie—the priest" and "Mollie—Fiona and Ian's Mama" and that neither of those parts of myself needs to be set aside in favor of the other. Caring for my parishioners (students and patients, as well as congregants) does not require denying the nurturer in me, and I have encountered outward signs of inner grace in even the most basic care that I give my children. This understanding has helped me to broaden both my view of the priestly vocation and role as a CPE supervisor, and, insofar as my pastoral identity embodies these relationships for my students, my supervisory work is as sacramental as celebrating baptism and communion.

As a Christian and a priest, the priestly image of the second of the Triune circle of relationships resonates most deeply with me. In the person of Jesus of Nazareth—the great High Priest who closes the gap between Human and Divine—I experience the Christ as the embodiment of the kind of relationship of mutual vulnerability that invites us to a feast where Human and Divine can sit at the same table without pretense or shame. God's interaction with Humans is an invitation to a place where the vulnerability of God and the sliver of the Divine in the Human soul can meet, where "there is no in between," to use Dame Julian of Norwich's phrase. In the supervisory context, my encounters with Jack, an intern struggling hard to articulate his spiritual identity, underscored the importance of integrating both the human and divine natures of Christ. Not yet 25 years old, Jack had moved from one denomination to the next trying to make sense of what he perceived as a mutually exclusive call to ordained ministry and authentic manhood. He seemed intent on splitting the human and divine natures of Christ, leaving himself without a way to embrace both the human and the divine in himself or others. My supervision of Jack focused on encouraging him to find ways of relating to God, himself, and others that were not "either/or" but "both/and," inviting him to image a "third way" of being.

For it is my belief that God interacts with Humanity by *being* human and in being so, dares us to *be* divine. As God *experiences* Godself as Jesus, the Human carpenter from Nazareth, and as we *experience* ourselves as the Body of Christ, the hands and feet of the Risen One, the gap "between" Divine and Human is closed. In that shared relationship of being, not *doing*, God and Humanity connect. As they connect, a relationship is established between beings who are inherently relational, who have no existence outside of relationship. Such beings, to exist, must put their relationship first. They must be willing to risk self for the sake of being in relationship because only in doing so can they encounter what is truly precious and life-giving to and in each other. Thus, God not only gives us the power to reject God, as we do from our first fumbling attempts to differentiate ourselves,[5] but continues to risk by letting God's authentic (i.e. relational, vulnerable) self be known to us in the person of Jesus of Nazareth and "the least of these" who share in his vulnerability. We human beings take a risk and make ourselves vulnerable when we open ourselves to the "sliver of the divine," a sliver that may cut us as easily as it may inspire us. Either of us might be wounded, but the honesty that goes along with the risk-taking, the willingness to hold the relationship higher than false security, is what establishes the relationship in the first place.

Heyward speaks of right—what I would call "authentic" relationship—as being mutual relationship,[6] and I find kinship here in my own understanding of the   Mother-Child   relationship   and,   by   extension,   the priestly/pastoral/supervisory relationship. From at least the moment of our physical creation, each of us is in relationship whether we are aware of it or not, and the mutuality of relationship is evident from before we are fully knit together[7] in the womb. What pregnant woman has not been admonished to take care of herself because in doing so she is taking care of the child she carries? Even before the moment of conception, the impact of environmental factors can be a developmental factor, and I believe these dynamics are not just physical but emotional and spiritual as well.

Drawing from my own very human experiences as both child and mother, I am aware that not every mother-child relationship is "ideal," but I maintain that this "flawed" nature actually supports the metaphor rather than undermines it. I have learned painfully that I cannot automatically expect the kind of hospitality that Abraham extended to the angels of the Lord. Growing up as a member of a military family that moved every few years left me often feeling rather lonely and out of place. In my faith community, I find reason for both pride and shame: one of my first conscious attractions to the Episcopal Church was comfort in the familiarity of the liturgy no matter where I went; an ongoing grief for me is the well-earned reputation of the denomination as an exclusive club. More recently, as a woman, I have encountered the sexism of male-dominated vocations. While the visit of the "three angels of the Lord" to Abraham at Mamre—and Abraham's intimate relationship with God—is a core story for me, I also am aware that as Abraham's visitors continue their journey, they travel to Sodom, where they encounter Abraham's nephew Lot, who also extends hospitality to them.[8] In this story, however, the vulnerability of both Lot and the divine visitors becomes apparent as Lot's neighbors seek to abuse them. This relationship stuff is risky business, apparently. It is also messy business that rarely produces clear victims and perpetrators, as the sordid epilogue of Lot's daughters illustrates.

And, yet, I still believe we are called to live into our creation—that is, to be open to authentic relationship through mutual vulnerability. The goal of the transformation that I am trying to effect in supervision is authentic relationship—relationship that allows each person to be in covenant both to oneself and to the other. Thus, my idea of transformation is not becoming what one is *not* but becoming *aware of* and *blessing*, what one *is*—past and present, as well as future. Saint Paul touches on this idea in his letter to the Ephesians: "For we are what he has made us, created in Christ Jesus for good works, which God prepared beforehand to be our way of life." (2:10) So does British psychoanalyst D.W. Winnicott in his idea of the "good enough" mother.[9] The idea is that we are good by our very nature—not by anything we do but *simply by being true to ourselves*. I am convinced that "sinfulness" (that is, separation from God) isn't our *nature* at all. Rather, sinfulness is *not* being true to our nature—our nature as relational and vulnerable beings created in the image of a relational and vulnerable God. A life of sin involves a conscious choice to do or, as the words of the Confession say, to leave undone.[10] The good life, on the other hand, is a state of being and we are "good" simply by merit of our existence—as relational, vulnerable beings.

ASYMMETRICAL POWER RELATIONSHIPS EXIST

Nonetheless, it would be phony to assert that it is possible to create supervisory relationships where power and authority are always perfectly balanced. Like it or not, asymmetry exists, formally and informally, in any pastoral care setting, including supervisory work. For example, I was called recently to participate in an ethics consultation regarding a patient at our hospital. In the midst of several days of discussion, I became increasingly aware that staff and family members were listening to what I had to say not because of any formal decisional capacity (at our hospital, members of the ethics triage team only make recommendations), but because of the moral authority I carried as a chaplain. Moreover, there were times when I used that authority to move into an overtly guiding mode, such as when I bluntly told the patient's ex-wife that she needed to stop interrupting if she wanted the information that was being offered at a family meeting. In that instance, I had the power to give or withhold the information. The reality is that the chaplain can get up and walk out of the room in ways that the bedridden patient cannot. The reality is that the supervisor chooses whether to grant credit for a CPE unit. The reality is that the certification committee chooses whether to grant candidacy or supervisor status. The reality is that some people have more power than others, no matter how much they believe in colle-giality, shared authority, and collaboration.

While the reality of the power differential is not limited specifically to su-pervision or the formation of clergy, it certainly is highlighted as students seek to claim and bless their pastoral identity, and it is here that theoretical flexibility rather than absolutism allows the supervisor to vulnerably draw on a number of theories for guidance. Family systems theory, for example, reminds me that role-playing, alliances, communication triangles, and secret-keeping are all ways that groups develop to cope with, support, and sometimes challenge the "power" of a system. Thus, when my students tacitly elect a "spokesperson" to complain to me about onerous clinical expectations, I begin to wonder what the students are trying to learn about themselves in order to claim their own power. I allow my-self to wonder if I am invested in empowering my students or in maintaining my own power. I urge them to be curious about how they can take more initiative to attend to self-care and the internal obstacles to doing so. Object relations theory asserts that the person who engages in power projective identification dynamics is one who at heart sees him or herself as fearfully power*less*. Remembering this allows me to find compassion for the students whose insistence that they have nothing to learn, or whose demeaning comments leave me feeling incompetent and powerless myself. Allowing them to affect me and sharing with them the impact that they have on me empowers them by inviting them to begin to won-der about who they are in the world.

Moreover, it is unhelpful to assume that simply attempting to do away with power asymmetry is the goal in every instance. I was ordained to the priesthood around the same time I began to question, both in terms of theodicy and in terms of human beings as *imago Dei*, the idea of an omnipotent God. Yet there I was, Sunday after Sunday, leading my congregation in prayer to the "Almighty and everliving God" or the "God of all power, Ruler of the Universe."[11] It was only when I came to see the need of many of my congregants to idealize God that I let go of my (unempathic) desire to disabuse them of that notion. I'm reminded of several conversations I had during my residency in which a peer and I con-trasted our views of God. My fellow resident, an African-American, spoke of a fatherly God who is mightier than the dominant power structures of the world she lives in, while I, a European-American, tended to yearn for a more compan-ionable relationship with a God whom I could relate to as a friend. In deciding that neither of us needed to destroy the other's experience of God, we were able to explore not only our respective understandings of the Holy but also our true selves. In the language of self psychology, my peer's idealizing need for an "Almighty God" was not better or worse than my own twinship need for a God who could walk beside me in solidarity. Moreover, as I began to consider our spirituality in terms of basic human needs rather than from the standpoint of spiritual superiority, I realized that there are times in my life as well when I seek out a "greater power." When my child is the unresponsive patient in the emergency room, I am absolutely looking for a God who is almighty enough to wake her up.

Furthermore, it is at these times that I am not so much seeking a God who is powerful over me as a God who is powerful *on my behalf*. Ideally, the supervisor/chaplain/pastoral caregiver—for the principle holds true throughout the system—is looking for ways to empower the less powerful. But there are times, such as when a physician is berating a group of nurses and other staff trying frantically to revive a patient, that the chaplain must use his or her pastoral authority to intervene. Some months ago, I celebrated the Eucharist at a parish that had never had a woman presider before, as one of my brother priests noted just prior to the service. (No pressure there.) In the middle of the service, the music director drew me aside to inquire which musical setting of the Lord's Prayer I wanted to use—the traditional or the modern? At that question I suddenly realized that he was expecting that I would be chanting the communion prayers. Being a somewhat less formal liturgist and not a gifted vocalist, I suggested that he pick whichever setting he preferred for the corporately sung prayers, but added that I would be saying, not singing, the rest of them. "Why on earth not?!" he asked sharply. "Because I'm the celebrant and it's my decision," I replied evenly. The music director smiled broadly, declared, "I like a woman who knows her power!" and went on without further interruption. At that moment, both of us had needed me to assert my power and take charge.

MUTUAL VULNERABILITY: MOVEMENT FROM HEAD TO HEART

Just as pastoral care takes place in the gritty, messy experiences of life, it is primarily on the emotional and spiritual plane rather than simply the intellectual level that authentic—and transformative—supervisory relationships operate. I encountered this most vividly in my experience supervising Sean, one of my most challenging interns so far, whose wariness made him deeply suspicious of peers and supervisor. Rather than approaching him on an authoritarian level or engaging him in heady arguments, I tried to let him know how I *felt* about his behavior. Of course, this required some vulnerability on my part—a willingness to let down my defenses and let him see the me that he could hurt—but each time I took this risk, each time I put the relationship ahead of my own comfort, he seemed more willing to let down some of his own defenses. In creating an environment in which he could do so, I believe I modeled for him a different and far more trustworthy picture of relationship, one that is constant as well as open to the other.

When I approach my patients and students on a heady level, our relationships are often characterized by mistrust and intellectual sparring. But when I approach them on a feeling level, I allow them to see my most authentic (i.e. vulnerable, undefended) self and create an atmosphere in which they also can be authentic. This was the case with Sean. The more I tried to convince him intellectually that he shouldn't mistrust the group or me—the more I used my relative power in a hostile way—the more defended he became. But when I began to approach him on a vulnerable level—letting him know that not only the group and I had been hurt by him, but that I grieved the injury he was doing to himself—he began to lower his defenses, talking and weeping about his own sense of betrayal. As I opened my heart to him, he saw me at my most authentic—someone who valued him and our relationship enough to risk the possibility that my heart might be broken—and he received permission to be his most authentic.

I am also reminded of a process-group conversation with the first internship that I co-supervised. For some time, I had felt that the process-group sessions I led rarely moved to the emotional, inter-relational plane, but rather stayed on a very heady, disconnected level. This was borne out in the feedback I received from my training supervisor, who invited me to reflect on my own use of process-group sessions as an intern and resident. He suggested that the group might be encouraged to move to a feeling level if I were more vulnerable with them. One day, after struggling yet again with my role, I finally owned up to the group about feeling insecure and uncomfortable with my leadership, and then I took the risk of asking for feedback about how this admission made the group feel about me. Almost immediately the tone of the session changed. The group's feedback ranged from reassuring ("It just shows that you're human") to stinging ("If *you* don't know what the hell *you're* doing, I'm really in trouble!"), but it certainly could not be described as heady or disconnected! Just as in Rublev's image, my process-group experience created not a hierarchy that places God/Supervisor at the top and Humans/Interns at the bottom but a truly mutual relationship that allows each to be nourished—and, albeit, potentially hurt—by the other. It is on this vulnerable, feeling level that I believe that human beings are able to speak the language of God and that God is able to speak the language of human beings. It is on this vulnerable, feeling level that authentic relationship is created and transformation occurs.

SUPERVISOR AS THE MORE VULNERABLE PARTY

The greatest power a supervisor has is a willingness to function out of her places of greatest vulnerability. This first requires letting go of the idea that the supervisor is the "expert" or even the agenda-setter. Socrates referred to the educator as one who reminds rather than teaches. One commentator on the classical Greek philospher notes that:

> Philosophy, the love of wisdom, was for Socrates itself a sacred path, a holy quest—not a game to be taken lightly. He believed, or at least said he did, in the dialog *Meno*, in the reincarnation of an eternal soul which contained all knowledge. We unfortunately lose touch with that knowledge at every birth, and so we need to be reminded of what we already know (rather than learning something new). He said that he did not teach, but rather served, like his mother, as a midwife to truth that is already in us! Making use of questions and

answers to remind his students of knowledge is called maieutics (midwifery), or the Socratic method.[12]

Throughout the twentieth century, education theorists refined the role of the educator as a facilitator rather than an expert. Lindeman writes of "teachers who are also searchers after wisdom and not oracles . . ."[13] and Palmer writes that, "[b]y Christian understanding, truth is neither 'out there' nor 'in here,' but both. Truth is between us, in relationship . . ."[14] Thus, on a philosophical level, I believe that mutual vulnerability requires that a supervisor be willing to show his or her authentic self, and it begins in the subjective reality of a student's experience and learning style.

Ideally, it is the supervisor who is the more vulnerable member of the supervisor-student diad.[15] In my experience, when a relatively "powerful" person (like a chaplain or a supervisor) shows vulnerability to a relatively less-powerful person (like a patient or a student), it invites the less-powerful person to also show vulnerability. I remember an encounter in same-day surgery with a woman who was having a miscarriage. She told me her story rather matter-of-factly and with little emotion. I offered to pray with her and, as I did so, tears filled my eyes and began to roll down my cheeks. When she saw me weeping, she also began to weep. Another example is the IPR conversation I described earlier, in which I acknowledged my feelings of ineptitude. It was Sean, by far the most defended of the interns, who said my acknowledgement, rather than undermining my authority, only made me seem "human." Closely related to this is the way that a "powerful" person's acknowledgment of "weakness" can build trust rather than break it. I'm reminded of an individual supervision session when my own supervisor jumped to a conclusion about a rather vague but important statement I'd made only to realize that he'd misunderstood what I was trying to say. My own shame initially had kept me from speaking more directly and clearly, but my supervisor's admission that he'd broken empathy with me was what made me trust him enough to say what I really needed to say. Another time, in seminary, I confessed to a priest I greatly respected that I sometimes had doubts about God's existence. He simply said, "Me, too." That admission did much for my faith—in God as well as the priest. I realized that if this notable cleric and author could have doubts and still be a person of faith, so could I. Allowing myself to be vulnerable to another allows that person the freedom to accept or reject my love. When I do so, I act in the image of the God who showed vulnerability to me by giving me the capacity to accept or reject God's first love to me. It's also my declaration that relationship in and of itself is worth taking a risk for. If a relationship is worth taking a risk for, it follows that *I*, in and of myself, and *You*, in and of yourself, also are worth taking a risk for.

EMPOWERING THE TRUE SELF

Mutual vulnerability is a place of true power for both parties to the relationship, because a true self is an empowered self. It is the true self that is confident enough and self-aware enough to voice doubts, while it is the false self that is disempowered and in need of defense. Alice Miller aptly describes the true self as the "integrity" of the small child before it begins to defend itself in order to survive.[16] Scharff and Scharff write:

> Unempathic mothering can cause the baby to try to mold itself to its mother's needs, when its mother cannot respond flexibly to her baby. This leads to the infant's suppression of its 'true self' in favor of the development of a 'false self' that is apparently compliant, while the true self dwindles or is nourished secretly inside the self.[17]

Indeed, I have found a central task in supervisory work is letting my students see me for who I am, as a means both of creating safety and of modeling the authenticity necessary for their learning and empowerment.

For example, the students in one internship group seemed to struggle with expressing anger. One day, just minutes before a process-group session, I got a message that one of my supervisory training peers had abruptly postponed our plans to meet the following day. By the time I got to group, I was seething and consciously decided not to hide my petulance from the interns. Though several of them seemed surprised ("I didn't know that Mollie ever got angry"), my expression of anger seemed to mark a turning point for the group, which became much more daring in its own expression of feelings, both in the group and with patients and staff. In showing the group my authentic self—who could be as graceful to my grouchy side as to my pleasant side—I believe I helped them begin to catch glimpses of their own true selves.

As a supervisor, becoming aware of my true self and her needs has been crucial for my efforts to create a holding environment in which my students can recognize and bless their true selves. Further, I believe that mutually vulnerable relationships are the holding environment—indeed the womb—in which our true selves are created, re-created, and sustained. Kegan states this idea elegantly:

> Evolutionarily there is a sense in which the infant (and the person throughout life) climbs out of a psychological amniotic environment. Some part of that world in which the infant is embedded nourishes his gestation and assists in delivering him to a new evolutionary balance. I call that part the embeddedness culture, the most intimate of contexts out of which we repeatedly are recreated. I suggest that it serves at least three functions. It must hold on. It must let go. And it must stick around so that it can be reintegrated.[18]

In the language of family therapy, the aim of the holding environment is to "contain the emerging family anxiety so that the family has a place to hold it while they look at it and learn about it."[19] The creation of a holding environment not only allows a person's true self to emerge (or re-emerge, as the case may be), but it sets up the necessary condition for healing and learning to take place. I believe holding environments that allow for the emergence of true selves are created by those who, themselves, have been held. As the writer of the First Letter of John puts it, "We love because [God] first loved us" (5:19).

Even after a child is born, the parent ideally continues to create a holding environment as the child transitions from infancy to adulthood. In this holding environment, the parent helps the child to make sense of its world and develop means of experiencing the soothing relationship of the parent even when the parent is absent. CPE has been such a holding environment for me.

My own motherhood has coincided with much of my CPE journey, from internship through residency and supervisory training, and my children have provided me with a window on the earliest stages of human development. During my supervisory training, I attended a CPE regional conference with my husband and children. During some free time one afternoon, I spent a couple of hours with my children at the hotel swimming pool and I was struck by the contrast in their attitudes toward the water. As I held him loosely, my toddler son Ian floated on his back or his belly in what seemed like absolute relaxation, even after I once lost my grip and he momentarily slipped under the water. By contrast, my pre-school daughter Fiona anxiously clung to me and begged me to support her whenever I even suggested she try to float, though we were often in water shallow enough for her to stand. At just over two years of age, Ian seemed fearless—without the benefit of knowledge, he plunged blissfully from one experience to another. On the other hand, "brave" seemed the better word to describe five year-old Fiona—she entered the water trembling with fear but begged to return again and again. As their mother, it was my job to hold them both, loosely enough that they could breathe and splash, securely enough that they could relax and float. Eventually, I believe, this combination of breathing, relaxing, splashing, and floating will become swimming.

Although the parent-child relationship is for many people the first holding environment that they experience, holding environments are necessary for transformational learning and empowerment throughout the lifespan. Just as I see my primary job as a mother is to create a unique holding environment for each of my children as they grow into themselves as human beings, I see my job as priest, chaplain, and pastoral educator to be the creation of holding environments for my parishioners, patients, and students as they continue their process of becoming. In my view, the characters of holding environments differ primarily based on the unique development levels and issues of the various groups, but the broad principles are the same. As a priest and chaplain, I help patients negotiate the transitions of life, including birth, illness, and death, particularly through the sacrament of the pastoral relationship. As a pastoral educator, I help students transition into their pastoral identity, individually and as members of a group, particularly through the sacrament of the supervisory relationship. So, for example, in the first unit that I solo supervised, when my students began to negotiate authority by challenging what they had identified as the "power" of the system (i.e. me: the supervisor), some clung to me, some thrashed about and some seemed to bob along unaware of what was happening. As their supervisor, it was my job to hold all of them, loosely enough so that they could breathe and splash, securely enough so that they could relax and float. In the process, true selves began to emerge.

I believe that holding environments encourage the development of the true self in two main ways. One is by allowing people to make meaning of their experiences and relationships. Meaning-making is how we integrate our experiences into our lives—the "reflection" portion of the clinical model of learning. I believe that transference is a natural and significant part of the meaning-making process. Although classical theory views transference as a pathology to be overcome, intersubjective theorists see transference simply as one way people "organize" or make meaning of their experiences:

> From this perspective, transference is neither a regression to nor a displacement from the past, but rather an expression of the *continuing influence* of organizing principles and imagery that crystallized out of the patient's early formative experiences.[20]

However, because the holding environment is not the end in itself, the other way that it functions is to provide a place for people to craft means of soothing themselves when they inevitably encounter crisis. Self psychology would include among these "crises" moments of *optimal frustration*, which involves the inevitable empathic breaks that naturally occur in relationships:

> The vulnerable infant frequently requires the help of caregivers to meet his physical and psychological needs. Through the caregiver's intercession, the infant eventually learns to perform for himself the functions that previously he could not carry out—this process Kohut called *transmuting internalization*.[21]

The idea is that the mature person eventually is able to function outside the holding environment. Kohut refers to a selfobject as "that dimension of our experience of another person that relates to this person's shoring up of our self" and suggests that the development of personality is related to the meeting of three primary selfobject needs: mirroring, idealization, and twinship. If one or more of a person's selfobject needs is not met, the self-formation process (i.e. the maturation of narcissism from archaic to useful forms) is derailed, and the person spends his or her life trying to fill that need. In the view of self psychology, the therapeutic response to narcissistic wounding is to assist the person in meeting those needs.[22] Ideally, young children learn through ordinary experience that their parents not only don't cease to exist when they are absent, but that even when they are absent the children can draw on these internalized "selfobjects" to sustain them when they are uncertain or fearful. Even in adulthood, however, as people experience fragmentation of the self, either because of derailments in early childhood or situational stress as adults, they need a recharging, as it were, of their selfobject batteries.

Self-soothing—the ability to function outside the holding environment—must be the goal, after all, if empowerment is to happen, as I have learned through personal and professional experience. Throughout my childhood, even while flooding me with praise and attention for intellectual and artistic achievements, my family emphasized my basic helplessness and ineptitude concerning practical things. "Little Mollie couldn't possibly take care of herself" was the refrain. While I was pregnant with my first child, I told my mother and my closest sibling that I did not want them to visit for at least a week after the baby's birth. Although they both expressed hurt and anger, I had come to know enough about myself that if I started off motherhood allowing or accepting their need to "baby" me at a time when I was least confident and capable, "Little Mollie" would never mature into her true self. In creating for myself a holding environment, I allowed myself the chance to internalize a mothering one who was confident and competent enough to also be open to and accepting of help. Thus, and by contrast, just a day or two after my second child was born, I remember awakening from an afternoon nap, my son nestled in the crook of my arm, to the sound of my mother vacuuming downstairs. Rather than feeling anxiety about my mother's opinions about my standards of housekeeping, I found myself filled with an overwhelming sense of warmth and well-being. My true self could welcome my mother's visit in ways that "Little Mollie" never could. As supervisor, I need to constantly be asking myself, how does my intervention empower my student? Who does my intervention empower? How do I titrate my power sufficiently to empower the student? In the first CPE unit that I solo-supervised, the holding environment created with my students when they challenged my authority shortly after mid-unit served both purposes. By allowing them to voice their feelings without judgment or criticism, I fostered the holding environment. Educating them about the process of group development not only helped them to make meaning of their experiences but to develop means of soothing themselves the next time they encountered conflict.

CREATING THE HOLDING ENVIRONMENT

I believe there are three primary and interconnected ways in which a holding environment is created: empathy, mutuality, and curiosity.

Lee and Martin describe empathy as "a mode of gathering subjective data about another self through vicarious introspection. It is the process of exploring what another thinks and feels by placing oneself in another's shoes." In other words, empathy is the capacity to feel *with*, rather than to feel *for*.[23] Although I believe that human beings are hardwired to have the capacity to be empathically connected with one another, it is a rare person who emerges from childhood without scars from faulty attunement, and those scars in turn influence our capacity to be empathically attuned to others. Indeed, I believe that dominant patriarchal social and religious traditions, including my own, have created whole structures that inhibit the capacity for empathic attunement and create the possibility for abuse of power. I believe differentiation, rather than relationship, is what is learned. Stern describes babies' built-in capacity for attunement with their mothers and Beebe and Lachmann "call this capacity for mutual influencing . . . a precursor to empathy."[24] The work of Chodorow and Gilligan challenges the notion that a "feminine personality [that] comes to define itself in relation and connection to other people" is necessarily a problem, or that boys' separation of "their mothers from themselves, thus curtailing 'their primary love and sense of empathic tie'" is a universal norm, much less necessarily desirable.[25] Similarly, Lee and Martin note:

> The educational processes of Western culture are designed to replace this 'inferior' narcissistic capacity with unempathic forms of cognition that foster an objective, materialistic, and mechanical view of life. In Kohut's mature person, the primitive capacity for attunement has not been expunged but is transformed into vicarious introspection for appropriate utilization in adult personal relationships.[26]

The need for empathy is both universal and life-long, but, in contrast to the idea that empathy is synonymous with support and affirmation, I also believe empathy is always confrontational (literally, "with face") and is many times challenging and even uncomfortable, especially when considering power asymmetry. I attempt to establish empathy with my students by allowing them to experience me as someone who they can trust to tell it like I see it. This was particularly so with Henry, a student with the childhood trauma of discovering his alcoholic mother drowned in the bathtub. Henry's family and friends' response to his grief was to advise him essentially to "grin and bear it." He carried that advice with him into adulthood, consistently sporting an upbeat attitude and often reflecting on how the smiles of his patients made the stresses of his job worthwhile. Shortly after mid-unit, I confronted Henry about how his "happy face" attitude left his patients reluctant to disappoint him with unhappy feelings. This led to an increased awareness regarding what he came to see as a life-organizing principle of marching past, rather than through, grief. In confronting him, I refused to play along with his false self by putting a happy face on the visit itself. Instead, I was empathically attuned to him by looking his true self in the eye and seeing the little boy who needed a holding environment, not a happy face, to feel and explore his grief. In the language of self psychology Henry was narcissistically wounded by his unempathic childhood experiences, and I needed to re-establish empathy with him:

According to Freud, there is a totally narcissistic libido in the newborn, and as the infant becomes a child and then an adult, there is a shift toward all libido being invested in objects and none in the self. Using Freud's theory, the therapist tries to replace the patient's narcissism with object love, an aim Kohut thought not only difficult—if not impossible—but very undesirable. Kohut challenged the assumption that narcissism had to be eradicated. [27]

The second key ingredient to establishing a holding environment is mutuality, which starts with the understanding that there is no such thing as objectivity. Inevitably, just as two treasure-laden travelers meeting on a narrow rope bridge have to negotiate their conflicting needs, I bump into someone else, and we have to negotiate what happens next. In my experience as a child and younger adult, bumping into the other usually meant confronting two unappealing possibilities—either *I* would have to back across the bridge or jump into the stream, or, worse yet, the *other* would have to retreat or take a dive. The solution I typically found to this dilemma, particularly when the other looked like an elephant, was to transform myself into a mouse who nimbly dodged the feet of the oncoming traffic while sidestepping the abyss altogether. Whether dealing directly with my family members or with others whom I perceived to be victims of oppression and abuse, I avoided causing them even more pain by shielding them from the "pain" of my confrontation. While this seemed to secure my place on the bridge, it also ensured that I would have to leave my treasure behind and that eventually I forgot that I wasn't a mouse. In the context of an "intersubjective" milieu, authenticity requires me to acknowledge that I bring my own baggage—as well as insight—into any interaction, whether it is with my children, my patients, or my students. For example, when I found myself not only tuning Henry out when he went off on one of his lengthy tangents, but fearing to hurt his feelings by telling him so, I realized that I was responding to him in much the same way that I do to an elderly relative. Understanding that my subjective reality had an impact on his subjective reality as well as on the space between us, allowed us to create a holding environment in which to make more sense of our own relationship.

Mutuality also involves willingness to model risk-taking: I cannot ask of others what I am not willing to do myself. For example, in my first solo unit, I knew that my greatest anxiety centered on process-group sessions. But I also knew that owning my anxiety had established trust in the previous unit that I had co-supervised. So I decided to start off the first process-group session of the unit with a discussion of trust, and led the way by talking about that anxiety. One of the students, John, later told me that my willingness to share my anxiety directly prompted his willingness to trust the group with his own anxiety around trust issues. In turn, others in the group attributed their own risk-taking to John's openness.

The final significant ingredient to the creation of a holding environment is curiosity, which I see as essential to the healing of the good-bad object-splitting that characterizes early childhood and that follows many people into adulthood. Initially, of course, we are literally connected to our mothers and, object relations theory suggests, the newborn cannot even conceive of the mothering one as "other" to itself, much less as part of a relationship. Soon, however, the infant begins to differentiate, and the first attempts at this are to identify its experiences as "good" and "bad" (e.g. warmth versus cold, satiation versus hunger). As this splitting occurs the relatively powerless infant also is confronted with the reality that the relatively powerful mothering one—upon whom the infant is dependent for life itself—sometimes is experienced as "good" and sometimes as "bad." For example, sometimes the mothering one is able to respond quickly to the infant's needs, sometimes not. Although unsettling, the realization that "good" and "bad" not only exist within the mothering one but also within the child's own self is a move toward maturity. Ideally, splits begin to heal with the awareness that the "good enough" mother (and, by extension, the good-enough child) contains elements of both "good" and "bad." In my own story, good-bad splits are reawakened for me around issues of attention and competence. Being the center of attention was to be "loved" by my parents and "hated" by my siblings. Being competent meant being "loved" because of my achievements and being "hated" for attracting attention. Becoming a parent myself has forced me to admit that the difference between the "good guy" and "bad guy" (inside of me as well as my parents, siblings, and children) is rarely an either/or proposition. One morning, hearing screams from my children, I ran into the living room just in time to watch my son lunge with teeth bared at his bigger sister. "What's going on?" I asked as I separated them and Fiona tearfully acknowledged that she had just snatched a toy from Ian. It was startling to realize that, even in the midst of my horror at Ian's aggression, I wanted to cheer him on for asserting himself, and that, even though I was angry at Fiona's bullying, I wanted to protect her from injury. As I reflected on that mixture of emotions, I realized that I had begun to heal an important split.

Being curious rather than condemning, inquisitive rather than assuming, has been essential to creating a holding environment for my students. As suggested earlier, when integration does not take place early on, people develop defenses in order to survive. I see it as the supervisor's role to encourage exploration and understanding of these defenses with the aim of making the student a better pastoral caregiver. For example, my student John grew up with the idea that not having the "right" answer was to be condemned. John's father taught him that the way to the right answer was an orderly, linear progression and expressed frustration with John's more explorational thought processes, which John learned to condemn as illogical and rambling. Even though John achieved success and respect in his engineering career, he became frantic whenever he assumed he had given the wrong answer, no matter whether the information being sought was new to him or not. In fact, he frequently went far beyond expectations in his preparations, apparently to prevent being caught unaware. Nonetheless, the CPE internship was a new experience for him, and, inevitably, his growing edges began to show. So, in our first personal supervision session, John presented his learning covenant to me. When I suggested that goals he had listed as professional and skill-development sounded more like personal goals, he became visibly flustered—shuffling papers, eyes darting, stammering. He seemed wary when I called a time-out and asked him what he was feeling, and amazed when I invited him to be curious about what was happening, particularly about his anxiety itself. For the rest of the quarter, this curiosity was a theme for John and I believe it served him well as he reflected on his experiences—both affirming and challenging—with patients and peers.

CONCLUSION

In my experience, being deemed worthy of another's vulnerability and openness is profoundly healing and empowering, which, after all, is the point of pastoral care. Mutual vulnerability takes relationships to a feeling level, where people are empowered to be their most authentic selves and thus, more able to cope with the painful realities of life. Chaplain Dick Millspaugh writes of the importance of "a clear sense of an inner self" for one's ability to make sense of and cope with pain. Distinguishing between suffering (i.e. spiritual pain) and physical or emotional pain, he describes a woman experiencing the intense (physical) pain of childbirth but notes that "the degree that she suffers may be the degree to which she finds a purpose for which to endure or even embrace the pain," depending on the circumstances of her pregnancy and labor. Millspaugh links a "loss of self" to the breakdown in meaning-making that turns pain into suffering: "Anything that threatens one's existence or brings significant changes in one's relationships may result in the loss of one's 'is-ness' or sense of purpose and may readily be experienced as spiritual suffering."[28]

The lessons learned in CPE, or, more precisely, the authentic relationships that I have experienced, have helped me to create a holding environment as I have sought to claim my true self. My CPE internship in the summer of 2000 was for me in many ways a power struggle, a struggle to heal the split that said power is a zero sum game where I must choose to align myself with the powerless or the powerful. I continue to unpack the lessons of that summer even as I supervise my own CPE students and seek to empower them while not disempowering myself. At the end of my internship, however, I summed up my learning with the phrase "be more, do less," and I have come to see that this still characterizes the healthy place of power in the supervisory relationship. The reality is that both my greatest weakness and my greatest strength come from my identity as a vulnerable, relational being. I *am* created in the image of a God who loves me enough to let me walk away. I *am* created in the image of a God who loves me enough to be hurt by me. I *am* created in the image of a God who loves me enough to be transformed by me. The more that I obsess about my *doing*, the more likely I am to slip into abusing my power. On the other hand, when I focus on my *being*—that is, my identity as a vulnerable, relational being—I invite and, indeed, empower my students to greater self-awareness. I not only recognize and bless *my* relational, vulnerable, true self but also invite stu-

dents and patients to begin their own processes of healing and learning by recognizing and blessing them for what they are: precious children of God.

NOTES

1. Augustine, *On the Trinity*, Gareth B. Matthews and Stephen McKenna, eds.
(Cambridge, UK: Cambridge University Press, 2002), 22.

2. Carter Heyward, *Saving Jesus From Those Who Are Right* (Minneapolis: Fortress
Press, 1999), 74.

3. The Anglican divine Richard Hooker argues that faith must be based on scripture,
tradition, and reason. As articulated by further generations of Anglicans, an unequal emphasis on any of the three would produce a shaky faith in the same way that a three-
legged stool begins to wobble and tilt when the legs are uneven. See Richard Hooker, *The
Works of That Learned and Judicious Divine Mr. Richard Hooker*, arranged by Jon
Keble, 7th edition, revised by R.W. Church and F. Paget, (Oxford, UK: Clarendon Press,
1888), 3 Vols, http://oll.libertyfund.org/Home3/Book.php?recordID=0493.

4. Henri Nouwen, *Behold the Beauty of the Lord* (Notre Dame, IN: Ave Maria Press,
1996), 20.

5. I prefer this description over the traditional "fall" interpretation assigned to the
Genesis story.

6. Carter Heyward, *Op. cit.*, 20.

7. Psalm 139.

8. Genesis 19.

9. D.W. Winnicott, "On Transference," *Essential Papers on Transference*, ed. Aaron
H. Esman, M.D. (New York: New York University Press, 1990), 246.

10. *The Book of Common Prayer 1979* (New York: Oxford University Press, 1990),
41.

11. *Ibid.*, 363-370.

12. C. George Boeree, "The Ancient Greeks, Part Two: Socrates, Plato, and Aris-
totle," 2000, 16 January 2009, http://webspace.ship.edu/cgboer/athenians.html.

13. Quoted in Malcolm S. Knowles, Elwood F. Holton III, and Richard A. Swanson,
The Adult Learner, 6th edition (Burlington, MA: Elsevier Inc., 2005), 37-38.

14. Parker J. Palmer, *To Know As We Are Known* (San Francisco: Harper San Francisco, 1993), 55-56.

15. William R. DeLong, "Toward a Theological Understanding of Intersubjective
Self-Psychology or How Our Images of God Reveal Self-Object Longings," Behavioral
Health Continuing Education lecture given March 26, 2003 at BroMenn Regional Medi-
cal Center, Normal, Illinois.

16. Alice Miller, *The Drama of the Gifted Child: The Search for the True Self*, 2nd
edition (New York: Harper Collins Publishers, 1997), 2-7.

17. David E. Scharff and Jill Savage Scharff, *Object Relations Family Therapy*
(Northvale, NJ: Jason Aronson Inc., 1987), 45.

18. Robert Kegan, *The Evolving Self* (Cambridge, MA: Harvard University Press,
1982), 121.

19. David E. Scharff and Jill Savage Scharff, *Op. cit.*, 156.

20. Robert D. Stolorow, Bernard Brandchaft, and George E. Atwood, *Psychoanalytic Treatment: An Intersubjective Approach* (Hillsdale, NJ: The Analytic Press, 1987),
36.

21. Michael Franz Basch, "Are Selfobjects the Only Objects? Implications for Psychoanalytic Technique," *The Evolution of Self Psychology: Progress in Self Psychology Volume 7*, Arnold Goldberg, ed. (Hillsdale, NJ: The Analytic Press, 1991), 3-4.

22. Heinz Kohut, *How Does Analysis Cure*, Arnold Goldberg, ed. (Chicago: The University of Chicago Press, 1984), 49.

23. Ronald R. Lee and J. Colby Martin, *Psychotherapy after Kohut: A Textbook of Self Psychology* (Hillsdale, NJ: The Analytic Press, 1991), 123.

24. *Op. cit.*, 123.

25. Chodorow as quoted by Carol Gilligan, *In a Different Voice* (Cambridge, MA: Harvard University Press, 2003).

26. Ronald R. Lee and J. Colby Martin, *Op. cit.*, 123-124.

27. *Ibid.*, 122.

28. Dick Millspaugh, "Assessment and Response to Spiritual Pain: Part I." *Journal of Palliative Medicine* 8 (2005), 919-923.

CHAPTER NINE

Looking Toward the Future of Pastoral Supervision

Teresa Snorton

Those of us who live in the pastoral care world as practitioners and educators are so familiar with the concept of supervision, particularly as it is manifested in formal programs of Clinical Pastoral Education and other field education experiences, that we can assume everyone has that same familiarity. In reality, the larger world is just beginning to become acquainted with the pastoral/spiritual care world and its concept of supervision, largely because of a resurging interest in spirituality.

A traditional understanding of supervision has emerged in the field of pastoral care, reinforcing an assumed meaning and standard practice(s). Kenneth Pohly, author of *Transforming the Rough Places: The Ministry of Supervision*, borrows from psychotherapists William Mueller and Bill Kell to describe a "controlling supervisory model"[1] used in pastoral education. According to Pohly, pastoral supervision has a dual purpose: the utilization of professional skill and the development of professional identity, both of which must be based in "an empirical theology"[2] that transcends church, scripture, and other aspects of difference and focuses on the transcendent in all of life. An increasing emphasis on diversity and cultural awareness, as reflected in the 2005 Standards of the Association for Clinical Pastoral Education, Inc.,[3] is indicative of the field's struggle to continue to define pastoral supervision as the integration of self (skill/identity) with the practice of ministry in a changing world with diverse spiritual markers and reference points.

As we consider the future of pastoral supervision, it seems critical to look at some of the changing factors that impact pastoral care, pastoral education, and thus, pastoral supervision. A brief survey of these factors will be followed by a discussion of the ways supervision in the future might be different as a result of these trends and factors. Specifically, this chapter will consider the following: population growth and aging trends, globalization and international migration, urban shifts, technology, the redefinition of religion, spirituality and ministry, and finally, the reshaping of the meaning and role of education. Each needs to be attended to as we envision what it means to do pastoral care, how we educate and prepare for this ministry, and what it means to supervise that process. Finally, it is timely to then re-evaluate or at least restate the "controlling supervisory model" that reflects these trends.

THE TRENDS

Population growth and aging trends are both evident in national statistics as well as ACPE statistical databanks. The aging of the "baby boomer" generation has the attention of healthcare providers, as more and more "boomers" begin to utilize the system to cope with both chronic and acute conditions. Longevity brings with it an increased need for more caregivers, both in institutions and in family homes. Within the ACPE, we celebrate a steady increase in the number of students enrolled in CPE programs annually, but we struggle with the increasing number of programs that are without the required certified supervisory faculty because of retirements. At the present time, the ACPE is unable to keep the rate of retirement of supervisors balanced with a parallel certification of new supervisors.

Globalization and international migration is a second trend to note. The ACPE's emphasis on multicultural competence reflects a worldwide trend of increased migration and immigration. An increasing number of international and domestic students from a variety of cultural perspectives, social, and economic locations—not to mention religious and spiritual worldviews—challenge the previously unexamined assumptions about basic concepts such a "theology," "pastoral," and "ecclesiastical endorsement" that undergird the Clinical Pastoral Education curriculum. The need to examine language, curricula components, and teaching methodologies in acknowledgment of these differences is crucial. Globalization is also challenging the unspoken assumption that the western methodology of Clinical Pastoral Education is transferable to all cultures, as indigenous persons begin to give voice and definition to others ways of learning and of how to offer care. New partners are emerging as the concept of professional ministry is embraced across the globe.

Another trend is that of urban and economic shifts. Easy mobility means patients often seek the best care and not necessarily the closest care, even if it means traveling hundreds of miles. Insurance protocols also define who your caregiver will be, as healthcare networks give patients some, but not much, choice in whom they will see as their healthcare provider. The result of both is that care recipients often lack proximity to their family or community in times when they need support systems the most. The pastoral caregiver's role increases in importance to those who may feel isolated and without support. The supervision of pastoral persons learning the skill and ministry of presence must take this kind of trend into consideration. Additional social factors that change the landscape in which supervision is done include changes in the provision of healthcare (inpatient vs. outpatient, etc.) and the emerging justice issues that arise as access to healthcare and social service is increasingly being determined by "ability to pay." What additional skills are required for pastoral caregivers to speak prophetically to these public concerns? Do we begin to think of public theology as a "skill" to be taught in our supervision?

A fourth trend with undeniable impact is that of technology. The proliferation of technological advances, devices, and opportunities has shifted the "local marketplace" to a "global village." The demand for distance learning programs to accommodate both traditional and non-traditional students is unrelenting. In Clinical Pastoral Education, a methodology whose "controlling model" relies on face-to-face individual and group supervision and ministry, we ask ourselves, "Can it be done another way?" The rising popularity of chat rooms, member sites (i.e. Facebook, MySpace), and personal blogs physically distance persons from one another, while connecting them in new ways. How does this translate into Clinical Pastoral Education? Finally, in a global village where there are still wide economic disparities, the reliance on technology raises new questions about ethics, justice, and fair access to resources. Will education become another distinction between the classes, between the "haves" and the "have nots"?

In this changing world, we are further faced with redefinitions of ministry, religion, and spirituality. The changing role and demographics of denominations/faith groups, both mainline and new age, bring new kinds of "ministers" into the supervisory relationship.

An increasing number of lay or unordained persons now seek preparation for professional ministry in pastoral/spiritual care. An increasing number of persons come into Clinical Pastoral Education experiences as novices in their own faith traditions. The depth and breadth of their religious experience is narrow. Many also come with nontraditional degrees or theological studies from entities with which Clinical Pastoral Education has little experience, let alone the ability to determine if those students' theological education is equivalent to the historic Master of Divinity degree. Assessing readiness for learning and evaluating admissions practices that are inviting, rather than exclusive, are a must.

Finally, new kinds of relationships with denominations, faith groups, and seminaries wait to emerge as each struggles with decreasing members, wavering enrollments, and limited funding, in addition to all the diversity represented in today's student bodies.

A final trend to mention is that of the reshaping of the role and meaning of education. The previously mentioned use of technology, web-based education, and distance learning has changed what education means. Interestingly enough, the emergence of technology has also resurrected the notion of "vocational/technical" training as opposed to "academic" education that results in a degree. As such, the emphasis shifts to skill and competence versus the completion of a degree. In the midst of this shift, clinical pastoral supervisors continue to attempt to define the basic body of conceptual knowledge essential to one's ability to do theological reflection and to develop pastoral competence.

THREE WAYS TO THINK ABOUT THE FUTURE OF SUPERVISION

The "controlling supervisory model" in Clinical Pastoral Education has been moving towards teaching the utilization of professional skill and the development of professional identity. The field recognizes that both must be based in an "empirical theology" that transcends church, scripture, and other aspects of difference. The focus of ministry (and our supervision of it) shifts from those particularities to a more universal way of providing sound and relevant ministry based in an appreciation of the transcendent in all of life. This is a sharpening of the concept of "meeting people where they are," or having the *loci* of the pastoral care encounter revolve around the care receiver and his /her beliefs, values, and needs rather than those of the caregiver. How do the trends above call us to further sharpen how we craft and utilize supervision in skill and identity development along with full appreciation of the "other" and his/her religious and spiritual practices and beliefs?

    The future of pastoral supervision seems to be dependent on three concepts if it is to remain relevant in today's and tomorrow's world: transformational/adult learning as a central educational theory, cultural bridging as a central component of personality theory, and liberation as a central theological construct within the supervisory alliance. Educational theory, personality theory, and theology are the three categories of the current required theory papers for certification as an ACPE supervisor.[4] Their prominence in the process towards certification as a pastoral educator reveals the competencies one must possess in order to supervise others. Supervision is the ability to utilize theory educationally and professionally. Together these theories enable the supervisor to craft a personal "empirical theology" that weds the social and behavioral sciences with theology. The supervisor then teaches others this skill, an essential in providing care in a world that is changing daily.

    While many of our assumptions in Clinical Pastoral Education appear to be based in adult learning theory, it seems vital that our use of that general theory in working with current and future students (who are older, more experienced, and come to ministry as a second or third career, and representative of non-traditional faith groups) should place emphasis on the specific concepts of transformational learning. Transformative learning is understood as the process where adult learners critically examine their beliefs, assumptions, and values in light of acquiring new (emancipatory) knowledge and begin a process of personal and social changes. Transformative learning is manifested not only in new knowledge, insights, and awareness, but also in changed behaviors, perspectives, and worldviews.[5]

Transformative learning is distinguished from other forms of insight-oriented adult learning through its emphasis on changed behavior. Its learning schema demands content reflection, process reflection, as well as premise reflection. In the supervision of Clinical Pastoral Education, the urgency for relevant care requires the ability to elicit more than just awareness from our students. Using the verbatim as an illustration, students acquire skills in attending to content of pastoral conversations, reflecting on such content and self-evaluating the process(es) emergent in the encounter and in the presentation and discussion of the verbatim itself. However, transformational learning process also requires premise reflection. Using Mezirow's definitions, Patricia Cranton posits that premise reflection enables learners to identify meaning schemes, to recognize those that are invalid, undeveloped, or distorted, to revise those meaning schemes and to act on the revised belief.[6] The future of effective clinical pastoral supervision involves the subtle but crucial shift from an adult learning theory directed toward insight and awareness to one directed toward transformation.

While Clinical Pastoral Education is preparation for ministry, the care offered by the clinical learner must meet a basic level of competent care. The first step in supervision is in the pre-education stage of assessing and recognizing when students possess the prerequisite emotional and social maturity to engage in the tri-level reflection process and when they may be too wounded to utilize the transformative model. Admissions policies that are inclusive around issues of diversity must simultaneously accept applicants that meet standards of basic competence with the potential of cultivating enhanced skill and identity development. ACPE's emphasis on outcomes in clinical learning reflects the affirmation of Clinical Pastoral Education (and its supervision) as education and not as therapy for those who may have the desire for skill and identity development, but with real deficits in moving beyond initial content and process reflection. Potential students with personal barriers that may prevent their premise reflective skill development may not be the best candidates for CPE and supervisors must recognize these dynamics in the pre-admissions process. When thinking of transformation as the objective, rather than of insight or awareness as the objective, supervisors should be able to discern the applicant who can move into the intense transformational learning environment.

A second key concept for the future viability of pastoral supervision relates to the personality theory embedded within any specific supervisory practice. A credible theory for today's world of supervision must acknowledge cultural bridging as a part of formation of persons who seek to function in the multicultural context. At a number of levels, the pastoral context should always be understood as a multicultural one. Even in contexts that appear on the surface to be homogenous, a skilled care provider will recognize the ethnographic, demographic, and socioeconomic variables within any church, organization, institution, or community.

The skilled pastoral care provider[7] must develop a self-perception that is based in one's personal social and cultural location. The CPE student must know at the same time that his particularity is not universal. She must develop a sense of self that is developed and understood both within community and autonomously, and also understand those variables in others. When the individual is able to see his/her universality, and particularity alongside that of others, cultural bridging has occurred. Supervision will actively engage the student in assessing and monitoring his or her ability to do cultural bridging without anxiety and judgment. While this sounds simple, consider how the issues of race and ethnicity, for example, have such a painful history and impact in United States history, that cultural bridging around race is still a new and scary experience for many Americans. Many still have lessons of being socially and politically correct in their psyches that become barriers to addressing the real issues and needs in the practice of care and ministry, especially with culturally different persons. Supervision must be based in a personality theory that affirms cultural bridging as a vital and core developmental stage in the personal and professional formation process. Supervisors must wrestle with their own anxieties around cultural difference, privilege, racism, and all the other "isms." The supervisor sets the stage for the "teaching moment" by being able to identify, recognize, and speak to cultural dynamics operational in the student-patient, the student-peer, and the student-supervisor encounter.

Pastoral supervision must minimally know that how students learn and why they choose learn (motivation) are culturally acquired values. Clinical Pastoral Education is faced with owning the ways in which mono-cultural values inform, and perhaps dominate, our practice of supervision. For example, we value students who take appropriate initiative to do their pastoral work. Students with a cultural value of deference to the authority (supervisor) are often critiqued as "lacking a sense of personal authority." Cultural bridging resists this kind of assessment and, instead, places emphasis on how the student might utilize his culturally acquired values in pastoral practice, while at the same time learning other ways of being.

Another significant part of cultural bridging lies in the notion that culture also defines success and achievement. In addition, ACPE has its standards and outcomes and the local program has its success measures and performance standards as determined by the organizational culture. Three congruent or conflict sets of standards may be operative in the student's experience. The supervisor's role (as a cultural bridge) is to facilitate the student's reconciliation of all of those expectations to create real and relevant measures for him/herself. If the organizational culture (or pastoral care department's culture) does not embrace cultural bridging as an essential, it will be difficult for the supervisor to promote it as a value in the practice of ministry and supervision in that particular context. Essentially, this requires CPE supervisors to accept their role in cultural bridging in the institution and community. This bespeaks of the need for prophetic and public theology as a sub-skill within pastoral care. Finally, given the traditional ways in which pastoral education has been marketed, CPE still tends to involve disjunctive rather than serial socialization. Psychiatrist Ezra Griffiths[8] points out the liability of having training groups that have only "one" different (be it race, gender, ethnicity, sexual orientation) student in the group at a time. This kind of construct is disjunctive in that it generally calls for the one who is different to change to fit into the larger group, rather than force the underlying assumptions and values of the group to be questioned and examined. Supervision of a diverse group, rather than a group claiming to be diverse because of a limited presence of diversity, creates a learning environment open to a variety of values, learning styles, and worldviews.

In developing supervisory competence and the ability to supervise effectively, the following goals are non-negotiable. Supervisors must be able to: 1) understand the self and others as cultural living human documents, 2) articulate a theology, theory of personality, education and group theory that reflects an understanding of one's own culture and the culture of others, 3) develop the ability to supervise students individually and in groups with an awareness of the cultural dynamics that are operative, and 4) develop a CPE curriculum that reflects the cultural diversity of the institution or facility and the community. Veteran supervisors must reinvest in life-long learning around culture if this has not been a part of their standard practice. Supervisory education curricula must promote these goals explicitly and not assume the implicit learning that occurs when working with patients or students is enough. The inability to see and utilize cultural bridging as a part of the supervisory learning alliance will render supervision as an ineffective and inadequate teaching modality in the real world. The final concept that aspiring CPE supervisors must demonstrate through the theory writing process revolves around theology. Supervisory students are asked to articulate their theological position, including perspectives on creation, persons, suffering, and supervision. Supervisory students are often encouraged to write this paper first, before considering their educational and personality theories, so that it is the foundational position of all their theories. I have saved this as a last point because it may well be the most transformative aspect of present and future supervision. A theology based in liberation seems to fit with the controlling supervisory model's empirical theology. While much could be written about the various theologies that are implicit or assumed to be inherent in traditional pastoral supervision, liberation theology seems to point us to a future where the particularity of one's situation does not alter the ultimate goal for that person (or group or culture or community) to experience a sense of liberation from the oppressive forces—be they illness, trauma, economic need, relational distress, an "ism," and so forth.

Emmanuel Lartey[9] makes the case for understanding pastoral care as liberation because of the former's foundational action-reflection model. The objective of liberation theology is change. A wide variety of theorists and theologians have aptly defined the steps or stages of an active liberation theology. Lartey points to concrete experience (immersion), social analysis, and hermeneutical analysis as elements in common to pastoral care and liberation theology. Pastoral education utilizes these elements to aid care providers in their skill and identity development. Students are asked to take action, to immerse themselves in pastoral and ministry encounters. Those encounters must then be reflected on in terms of the personal and communal/cultural variables (social analysis). While the encounter may be one-on-one, clinical pastoral students are urged to see the extended family field, the cultural context, and the social systems in which the personal story occurs. Finally, clinical students are called to continue their reflection into the theological realm, what is the text—the text of their lives, their religion, their spirituality? What are the myths and legends operative in their interpretation of the current dilemma? What is the narrative[10] of their lives and how does the current situation enhance or alter that narrative?

In the same way that pastoral care is the praxis of liberation theology, so is pastoral supervision. Lartey writes "individual awareness interacts with group work and with collective symbolic action in a constant, synergic, and pastoral relationship which enables reflection, evaluation, and support continually to refresh and refine the process" [of liberation].[11] Lartey's pedagogy for pastoral education is echoed in Belle Hooks' notion of education as the practice of freedom. Hooks writes "making the classroom a democratic setting where everyone feels a responsibility to contribute is a central goal of transformative pedagogy."[12] Individual and group supervision that accepts the worldview of each student as valid for them, yet invites all to participate in the transformative learning process, is liberation. Through critique, feedback, and confrontation, students are liberated from the confines of an inherently limited set of personally-held values and experiences and introduced to a wide world of possibilities, options, and paradigms for doing ministry. Each student is also a teacher. The supervisor has expertise, but is not the only expert in a transformative/liberative supervisory relationship.

Supervision as liberation, particularly in a multicultural world shaped by technology and changing definitions and constant change, becomes the path to a more vibrant educative process in pastoral education. Seen this way, supervision is not the distribution of information, nor even the facilitation of a process. It is not simply reliant on theological constructs such as grace, reconciliation, and spiritual growth as the foundational basis for walking the educational journey with another. Hooks writes:

> Multiculturalism compels educators to recognize the narrow boundaries that have shaped the way knowledge is shared in the classroom. It forces us all to recognize our complicity in accepting and perpetuating biases of any kind. Students are eager to break through barriers to knowing. They are willing to surrender to the wonder of re-learning and learning ways of knowing that go against the grain. When we, as educators, allow our pedagogy to be radically changed by our recognition of a multicultural world, we can give students the

education they desire and deserve. We can teach in ways that transform consciousness, creating a climate of free expression that is the essence of a truly
liberal arts education.[13]

While Hooks is speaking to a different post-secondary learning context that is
academic, not clinical, the wisdom of her commitment to transforma-
tive/liberative education is clear and a relevant message for the future of pastoral
supervision.

Pastoral supervision cannot be grounded in the status quo—it cannot find its
vitality in mono-cultural values and measures. The future of pastoral supervision
engages the will to confront, challenge, and change any "controlling supervisory
models" that would have us deny the significance of the differences encountered
in students, patients, families, institutions, and communities. It demands that we
change models when they are oppressive. It calls us to be both selective and
inclusive. It requires embracing the known and the unknown with a definitive
gusto for action, change, and liberation.

NOTES

1. William Mueller and Bill L. Kell, *Coping with Conflict: Supervising Counselors
and Psychotherapists* (Englewood Cliffs, NJ: Prentice-Hall, 1972), 193.

2. Kenneth Pohly, *Transforming the Rough Places: The Ministry of Supervision*
(Dayton, OH: Whaleprints, 1993), 30, 52, 69.

3. ACPE Standards and Manuals for Professional Ethics, Accreditations, and Certification (Atlanta: ACPE, Inc., 2005), Standards 13-16.

4. *Ibid.*, Certification Manual, 19-22.

5. See Jack Mezirow, *Transformative Dimensions of Adult Learning* (San Francisco:
Jossey-Bass, 1991) for a more detailed description of transformative learning.

6. Patricia Cranton, *Professional Development as Transformative Learning: New
Perspectives for Teachers of Adults* (San Francisco: Jossey-Bass, 1996), 113.

7. See Derald W. Sue et al., *Counseling the Culturally Different: Theory and Practice*) New York: John Wiley and Sons, 1990), for a detailed description of the characteristics of the culturally competent care provider.

8. Ezra E. H. Griffith, M.D. and Andrea Delgado, M.D., "On the Professional Socialization of Black Residents in Psychiatry," *Journal of Medical Education* (1979) 54,
471.

9. Emmanuel Lartey, *In Living Color: An Intercultural Approach to Pastoral Care
and Counseling* (London: Cossel, 1997, revised 2002), 85-108.

10. See Edward Wimberly, *African-American Pastoral Care* (Nashville: Abingdon,
1991, revised 2008), 1-15 for discussion of a narrative approach to pastoral care.

11. Emmanuel Lartey, *Op. cit.*, 107.

12. Belle Hooks, *Teaching to Transgress: Education as the Practice of Freedom*
(New York: Routledge, 1994), 39.

13. *Ibid.*, 44.

CHAPTER TEN

Supervising in a Modern and Postmodern Age: The Need for an Integral Vision

Beth Burbank

Last year, I facilitated a theological reflection seminar that keyed in on the importance of historical experience in creating the context that informs an individual's perspective. Our Clinical Pastoral Education (CPE) group had been working together for weeks and had already established a bond of mutual trust and respect. This, despite the variety of faith perspectives that were represented in the group—from Pentecostal to Lutheran to Religious Science—the range of religious experience that is common in any CPE educational setting.

But I had a moment of vital insight during this particular seminar, as one young CPE student—in fact, the youngest in the group—reflected aloud on the major socio-political signifiers for her life. In her young lifetime, the memorable moments of great change revolved around the presidencies of Bill Clinton and George Bush. She had some vague memories of the U.S. entrance in the first Gulf War in 1990. And, most importantly and powerful for her, were the tragic events of September 11, 2001 and the suffering after Hurricane Katrina.

At the other end of the generational scale was a student who could remember vividly exactly where he had been when he heard the radio reports of the Japanese bombing of Pearl Harbor, Hawaii, and five years later, the news of the first nuclear attack on Hiroshima, Japan.

Then those who reached their majority in the years between—my generation—called out key pivotal moments: the Civil Rights marches in the early 1960s, the assassinations of President John F. Kennedy and Martin Luther King, and the protests against and end of the Vietnam War.

After each of us had recounted these moments, we marveled at how over the weeks prior we had been able to build intimacy and high levels of trust and cohesiveness as we witnessed the radical variance in perspectives among our group.

Let me acknowledge that I have been involved in Clinical Pastoral Education (CPE) since 1978, when I began my CPE residency. I have continued through supervisory training to practicing as a clinical pastoral educator to the present day. But as I have aged, one of the most obvious changes in the supervision of ministry students over the past 30 years have been cultural changes that have evolved and the way students identify themselves. A few years ago, I became conscious of the difference in the identifiers of my experience and those of my students. References that I habitually used in my teaching that had previously helped students relate to issues being discussed no longer connected. For younger students, the epochs that forged my worldview were no longer part of a socially shared experience, but the stuff to be studied in history textbooks.

In other CPE groups in recent years, students who self-identified as theologically liberal or theologically conservative (coming from mainline Christian denominations to Four Square Gospel or non-denominational institutions such as Oral Roberts University) also self identified with something new, identifying themselves as "postmodern." Gradually, I began to realize that my interior definitions for postmodernity were outdated. I saw myself as a part of the generation that forged a postmodern culture in the U.S. through the last 50 years, beginning with Civil Rights, Vietnam War, feminism, gay and lesbian liberation, recognition of multi-cultural perspectives, etc.

Yet here I was, encountering a new generation of students raised within a postmodern context, fully educated about the many perspectives and orientations that "had every right to exist," even if they didn't agree with them. In addition, I found that some of my younger students expressed a wisdom or point of view in their mid-20s that was similar to mine, but which had taken me decades to develop. Other colleagues mentioned that they depended upon supervising summer intern groups to stay abreast of new thinking and context in the academy. I began to ask myself: Did I really know how to supervise in this changed context? Was I genuinely respectful of each perspective brought to the group context? Was I able to understand and honor the starting point for each student in my programs?

It was at this point that a moment of clarity opened for me. I had undertaken a few years before the study of integral philosophy and the integral approach, based on the writings of Ken Wilber. Wilber's view—that our perception of every moment is informed not only by our current outlook, but also by the years (even centuries) of belief that thrive on as subtext—helped me to step back and view what it means to have a perspective that both transcends and includes the many varieties of religious experience that students are bringing to CPE today. We are now supervising students who, along with their patients and parishioners, are living in an increasingly complex world. Offering spiritual care in clinical settings that include the home, the hospital bedside, or in a message delivered from a pulpit means being in relationship with people who embody a widening variety of cultural perspectives. These cultural perspectives are not just ethnocentric nor gender specific, but include a complex mix of interior life embodying traditional, modern, and postmodern points of view. As these broad epochs have evolved and washed over the cultures of the Western world, those living in the midst of them have internalized aspects of new thinking or new values that characterize them. Each person's interior center of gravity in relation to these values influences what they need or are looking for from spiritual caregivers, including a vision for coming to terms with an increasingly complex world. It is a world that challenges their beliefs as well.

For the purposes of this chapter, I am primarily using broad historical definitions of modernity and postmodernity, following the work of Ken Wilber in *The Marriage of Sense and Soul.* Wilber describes modernity historically as the period of time known as the "Age of Reason and Revolution" by Durant that "had its roots in the Renaissance," came of age in the Enlightenment, and continues to influence us today. More specifically, modernity is defined by Habermas as the "differentiation of the cultural value spheres" of three strands—art, morals, and science—elements that were fused together in premodern culture. Differentiation of these value spheres allowed them to develop independently of one another. Using this definition, Wilber is able to honor what he calls the "good news" and the "bad news" of modernity. He refers to the good news of modernity as the values of Western Enlightenment of "equality, freedom, and justice" that gave rise to representational democracy, the concept of inalienable individual rights, the separation of church and state, the development of physical sciences, the abolishment of slavery, the growth of feminism, etc.[1]

But Wilber also identifies the bad news of modernity, referring to those areas where the differentiation of these cultural value spheres went "too far" into "dissociation or fragmentation." This is precisely what happened when empirical science overtook the other value spheres and laid claim to truth as being only that which can be objectively measured, or what Wilber calls "scientism."[2]

Wilber broadly sees postmodernity as any of the "major currents occurring in the wake of modernity—as a reaction against . . . or a counterbalance to modernity." He also gives a more technical definition of postmodernism: the currents that claim that "the world is not perceived, it is only interpreted. Different interpretations are equally valid [and socially constructed] ways of making sense of the world and thus no interpretation is intrinsically better than another."[3]

An Integral Approach

Since it was established, modern pastoral supervision has demanded of supervisors the ability to engage theological, psychological, and cultural differences of students, as well as to understand differences in how students learn. Spiritual supervisors need both the skills of entering into our students' worlds (empathy) and stepping back from our students' worlds (perspective) so that we can make observations and reflect with them the reality that they are experiencing. We become both a witness to the present moment and a player in the crucible that is the subject of learning.

Supervising in an age that is influenced by both modernism and postmodernism increasingly requires a larger vision. It demands a view of the whole that can encompass and embrace a "multi-perspectival" view of reality, something that goes beyond the traditional bounds of multicultural and multi-religious sensitivity. We need a view of reality that helps us see how the perspectives that our students inhabit—and inhabit contemporaneously—relate to one another. We need a view of reality that observes and assesses the deeper meanings of the conflicts between the various truth claims of individuals and groups in postmodern culture. Supervision can serve as a locator within that larger vision that helps us place ourselves and our students within these larger frameworks and develop the direction of spiritual leadership needed for our time.

The evidence of such meaning conflicts in postmodern culture is everywhere around us—the battles between fundamentalists and progressives, between creationists and subscribers to evolutionary science, those who rely on literal interpretation of scripture and others who accept traditions of continued revelation, and the conflicts within and among spheres of Muslim traditions, for example.

For this world, in short, we need to transcend or differentiate from postmodern perspectives to offer a wider vision of our world. We need an integral postmodern metaphysics whose span and depth can offer a place of unity for humankind and indeed all sentient beings and creation. This is a worldview in which "post-metaphysics replaces perceptions with perspectives."[4]

It is this type of integral vision that Ken Wilber, mystic and philosopher, has developed. Wilber is the most significant proponent of an integral theory that makes the claim that it "might be the first truly comprehensive world philosophy."[5] He started this journey studying biology and biochemistry, at which point he began a personal odyssey studying the world's wisdom traditions before moving into Western psychology, philosophy, sociology, and anthropology.[6] His philosophical journey has been accompanied all along the way with the practice of Zen and other forms of meditation and study under "numerous living lamas, gurus, and spiritual masters."[7] In that process, Wilber developed an integral vision that includes the wisdom and knowledge of both human *interior* and *exterior* experience. While his primary spiritual practice has been through Eastern mysticism, he has studied all of the world's religions. His developmental examples include serious attention to the Christian mystics and James Fowler's *Stages of Faith*.

As mentioned earlier, an integral vision requires stepping back far enough to get a vision of the whole. In a series of interviews (published in cd format), Wilber lays out his view from 40,000 feet above, creating a map for understanding reality, and how the many perspectives and articulations of exterior and interior experience fit together into a recognizable whole. He synthesizes knowledge from a wide variety of disciplines into a system structured with what he calls quadrants, levels, lines, states, and types. He relies heavily on the research and ideas of others who have studied different lines of individual and cultural development that he incorporates into his own thinking.

Wilber likes to incorporate everyone's reality. "Everybody is right . . . but everybody is not equally right," as he puts it—a reference to his view that every discipline, worldview, or intellectual position is "correct, but partial."[8] Or to put it simply, we are never finished in our understanding of the whole.

Put another way, Wilber's map is a compilation of what he calls the world's "growth technologies" or growth potentials, including spiritual and meditative paths and Western forms of growth and development. He includes the "essentials" of each discipline so that significant areas of exploration are not left out. He says, for example, that "Zen . . . has some very powerful, very positive [characteristics for growth, but] you won't find anything about working with the unconscious or working with the shadow" in that tradition.[9]

Wilber's map explores the evolution of consciousness in human beings as individuals and as a part of the larger cultures and systems in which we live. It is a way to both understand and organize the various "waves/stages" of emergence or growth in human history. The four quadrant overview "of universal development . . . shows how the evolution of culture is intimately connected with the evolution of biology, the evolution of individual consciousness, and the evolution of external structures of human society."[10] Wilber has been writing for 30 years about these ideas, so it poses a significant challenge to communicate in one chapter much of his thinking. This chapter is, of necessity, "one taste" of his thinking, illustrated by examples of pastoral supervision.

Before moving into the specifics of Wilber's system, some historical antecedents can help position the concept of integral philosophy. The Integral Worldview is influenced by the ideas of a number of philosophers who saw the importance of a "spiritual interpretation to the discoveries of evolutionary science" and the "pervasiveness of interiority," which is foundational to "integral philosophy's understanding of the interior universe."[11] Historical influences include Teilhard de Chardin, Alfred North Whitehead, Georg W.F. Hegel, Henri-Louis Bergson, Jean Gebser, Sri Aurobindo, and Jurgen Habermas. Other profound influences include the social sciences, especially developmental psychology through the work of James Mark Baldwin (consciousness evolves through universal cross-cultural stages of development), Jean Piaget (empirical confirmation of developmental stages of consciousness), and the research by other stage theorists Kohlberg, Gilligan, Gardner, Kegan, and Loevinger, among others. Also influential is the work of Abraham Maslow and his student and colleague, Clare W. Graves, whose work has been advanced in *Spiral Dynamics* by Don Beck and Christopher Cowan.[12]

WILBER'S MAP: QUADRANTS

Let's move now to a necessarily brief exposition of Ken Wilber's integral vision. After, we will examine the bearing this has on pastoral supervision.

Wilber equates the aforementioned distinctions of art, morals, and science with Plato's "the good" (morals), "the true" (science), and "the beautiful" (art). Wilber calls these "big three" perspectives "I," "we," and "it." He adds a fourth: "its"—the collective version of science or objective reality, a view of systems—to create a quadrant model.

Wilber's organizing principle is that all of reality falls into one of four quadrants or perspectives. On the left side are the interiors of things (consciousness) and on the right side are their exteriors (form). On the top are individuals and on the bottom are groups. These quadrants reflect the differing perspectives of any event.

I	It
Intentional	Behavioral
Self and Conscious	Brain and Organism
Subjective	Objective
Truthfulness	Truth
We	**Its**
Culture and Worldview	Social System and Environment
Intersubjective	Interobjective
Justice	Functional Fit
Cultural Fit	

Table 10.1

Any instance possesses an inside and outside, as well as an individual and collective dimension. The quadrants are variations of the first, second, and third person pronouns. My reality or "I" is located in the left hand upper quadrant. Our perspective, you and I, becomes "we" and is located on the lower left hand quadrant. On the right hand side is the objective perspective or "it," and the lower right becomes the collective or "its," which refers to systems. Another way Wilber describes these quadrants is the intentional (upper left - UL), behavioral (upper right - UR), cultural (lower left - LL), and social (lower right - LR). These provide a place from which to view the perspectives of things: subjective (upper left - UL), objective (upper right - UR), intersubjective (lower left - LL), and interobjective (lower right - LR).[13]

When we focus upon the interiors of experience, the individual exploration is found in the UL of his quadrant. This is where we explore the "I" of experience from the *inside* through insight, meditation, contemplation, and introspection, which Wilber sums up as phenomenology of experience. Students explore this interior experience in supervision as they share their feelings and reflect upon experiences of pastoral encounters. They may be asked to share personal stories or explore their own autobiographical geography, write verbatim reports of pastoral visits, or keep journals of their experiences.

We can also look at the individual experience from the *outside*, as well. This is where Wilber places disciplines that study the elemental nature of consciousness, including the work of developmental theorists, depth psychology, and spiritual teachers, among others.

In the LL area of the quadrant we look at what do things mean—how we develop mutual understanding. On the *inside* of this quadrant, Wilber places the "'we' interpretation," or hermeneutics. If you're looking at this "we" from the *outside* you might be a cultural anthropologist or ethnomethodologist.[14] This quadrant explores the context of the cultural community of a person. This is where I would locate most of the world's religious identity—what makes me a Buddhist, Muslim, Christian, etc. From the outside I might be able to observe practices or learn about the tenets from reading or conversation with a practitioner. From the inside it is the formation process of growing up within the tradition or becoming one with the tradition through many years of belonging.

The UR area of the quadrant concerns objective individual expression. This includes the physical form (brain and organism, neuronal pathways and biological systems) and behavioral aspects, actions, and expressions that we see or observe. The *inside* of this view Wilber terms "autopoiesis" (something that is self-structuring or self reproducing—he uses the example of cognitive science). The *outside* perspective is empiricism, behaviorism, and the physical sciences. The LR quadrant is the collective exterior experience—the social dimension of experience, including social and political structures—the environment and systems of communication between sentient beings. The *inside* LR view Wilber terms "social autopoiesis" and the *outside* perspective is systems theory.[15]

QUADRANTS AND PASTORAL SUPERVISION

Pastoral care, as it has traditionally been practiced, would be situated in Wilber's upper individual quadrants—caring for the individual and including both interior and exterior reality. Pastoral supervision, in turn, has focused upon the interior identity development of the student pastor and on growing observable skills. Practical reflection groups become settings where students test out their individual perspectives with one another. In pastoral care seminars, supervisors observe while one student shares his or her perspective about a specific incident, followed by another who does the same. The students are looking for places of connection and understanding or what it is we share in common (the "we" domain), as well as looking to challenge one another, to express their individual differences. The supervisor is aware of many more levels of meaning as the group processes their work together. The supervisor may observe or intuit the perspective of a third student in the group and what s/he is thinking about what the others are sharing, based upon prior knowledge of the third student, her cultural view, or perhaps noting the body language or other clues at hand. Or perhaps the supervisor is aware that a group pattern has evolved and one student often takes a particular role or perspective in the process (the developing group system in the "its" domain). The group process in the collective domains includes the perspectives of the hermeneutical understanding of the group and group systems perspective.

Pastoral supervisors try in many ways to help students reflect upon these same perspectives in their learning process; integrated spiritual care involves awareness of all of them. The chaplain or pastor who is with the family at the time of death and attending to the loss of a family member learns to differentiate the needs of various family members, to discover the unique culture of the family and the roles each individual member takes on, and to observe those who differentiate from the family norms. In modern ministry, some families are cohesive in their concept of God, while in others each member may approach religion and spirituality differently. The premodern idea of spiritual care, where a comforting prescription from a particular tradition can appeal to all those to whom you minister is often not an option, though some ministry students may begin there. Their intention is to be inclusive, yet they may be unconscious of the ways their ministry distances them from others.

Wilber's quadrant model is a way to examine "any occasion." For example, we might see a student whose church internship takes place in an inner city environment. Pastoral supervision could focus in the LR quadrant, on social needs and concerns in the community. Supervision might include exploring economic issues, violence, gang-related concerns in the neighborhood, or homelessness and how this particular church is responding to those issues. The LL quadrant supervisory issues might include how the student is integrating the ways in which his/her tradition and theology (Catholic, Lutheran, etc.) speaks to or discerns how one proceeds with those concerns. Other LL issues might include exploring the qualities of relationship that define that particular parish—the culture of the church or how the congregation understands the meaning of this ministry. Supervision in upper individual quadrants (subjective) might concern the student's own initial physical fears or discomfort in an unfamiliar environment and how s/he reflects psychologically, spiritually, or culturally upon the ministry experience. As the student integrates his experience in the setting, his definition of ministry and pastoral care might expand to programs that the church may offer (soup kitchen, tutoring, after school programs) and what the church's response should be to the policies of the larger political systems in which the parish is situated. A Wilber-based integral approach to supervision would also suggest a spiritual contemplative practice, such as daily prayer or devotions, *Lectio Divina*, or contemplative prayer that could help the student ground his practice and deepen his experience of pastoral presence in the ministry situation.

In a hospital pastoral care setting such as CPE, the student and supervisor explore the parallel process of the ministry visit and the student's own response to it. We look at ministry from the student's experience, perspective, and learning needs, as well as assess the pastoral encounter and patient needs. Using

Wilber's framework, the pastoral care needs of a particular patient may require that the student develop some understanding of the biological disease process (UR) and the treatment possibilities and decisions that the patient is facing. It means exploring the personal subjective feelings and issues with which the patient is dealing (UL) and the student's internal response to the patient. As the mutual relationship deepens (LL), an understanding of what care is needed develops between them, perhaps including an explicit covenant between them. In addition, the pastoral student may explore family issues, attitudes of family and friends toward the patient's illness, or cultural attitudes about the patient's disease. The student pastor may need to advocate for the patient in the hospital medical system (LR) or learn more about the interface of this particular patient with the health care system.

So in the first sense, quadrants can be used as a tool for analysis of pastoral care and supervision. They provide a map for supervisor and student to sort out the essence of the experience and its complexity. Wilber's quadrant model can help identify what sector of reality the sections of the verbatim learning tool are addressing, whose perspectives are being addressed, and what areas of examination are included or excluded. It can help the student examine pastoral care as an all quadrant affair. It can also help clarify what type of need a student is addressing in their learning goals.

When supervisors read prospective students' application materials we look for the ways in which students describe their experiences. Do they tell their life story concretely (UR) or are they able to reflect upon how their story has led to interior development of their sense of self, of interpersonal relationships, cognitive awareness, or emotional experience (UL)? Is the student able to talk about their emotional experience? Does the student perceive his or her story in a larger framework of meaning or history (LL, LR)?

QUADRANTS AND THE PROBLEM OF MODERNITY

The quadrant map is especially helpful in clarifying the larger picture of the problem of modernity, or what Wilber called the "bad news" of modernity—that point when the differentiation of the value spheres went too far, and science and spirituality became dissociated from one another. Following Huston Smith's work in comparative religions, Wilber describes the core human view of reality in premodern experience as expressions of the simple hierarchy of the:

> great chain of being . . . from matter to mind to body to soul to spirit . . . [more accurately described as] a series of nests within nests . . . [with a deep sense that] all beings and all levels were ultimately enfolded in the all pervasive and loving embrace of an ever present Spirit.[16]

Each new level added to what had been there before by transcending and including the previous level. Each level had a "specific branch of knowledge associated with it . . . physics studied matter, biology vital bodies or life, psychology and philosophy the mind, theology the soul and mysticism spirit."[17] But within this premodern worldview the value spheres or perspectives of art, morals, and science were fused so that a scientist like Galileo could be tried for heresy when his discoveries threatened the theological worldview of the church. Wilber argues that, as the individual self emerged from the role self in modernity and these value spheres became differentiated, some philosophers hoped that the various domains could develop simultaneously with the independent authority of their various truth claims contributing to the understanding of the whole. But as modernity progressed, these value spheres became dissociated from one another. Science "went too far," denying the existence of spirituality because it could not be proved with exterior methods. Modernity, taken over by "scientism" (the belief that there is no reality save that revealed by science), came to view reality or truth as only those things that you could measure or observe in the exterior domains. The knowledge of the left hand or interior domains was collapsed or "flattened into objective exterior processes." This created a "flatland" world, a world of surface and no depth.[18]

> The result is a scientific framework that is global in its reach and omnipresent in its information and communication networks, [but] forms a meaningless skeleton within which hundreds of sub-global, pre-modern religions create value and meaning for billions; and . . . science and religion each tend to deny significance, even reality, to the other. This . . . massive schism . . . in the internal organs of today's global culture . . . is exactly why many social analysts believe that if some sort of reconciliation between science and religion is not forthcoming, the future of humanity is at best, precarious.[19]

When the Clinical Pastoral Education movement was founded in the early part of the 20th century, it was in response to an earlier discussion of this flatland world regarding science, psychology, and religion. Anton Boisen attempted to address the divide of the interior experience in the theological endeavor within the medical setting. As a student of the psychology of religion, Boisen wanted to break down the walls between religion and medicine. He brought theological students into the clinic to learn through the case study method, listening to the patients' own expression of their experience (interior domains). Coining the term *living human documents*, he wanted students to "learn to read [them] as well as books," particularly those experiences of inner spiritual pain or human suffering.[20] He believed that certain (functional) psychotic experiences were attempts to resolve internal existential conflicts. He correlated his own experience with those of patients and believed that facing into these conflicts could result in personal transformation or personality integration. In his work with mental patients, he tried to help them "take the next step of freeing the divine from their idea of themselves so as to make possible a larger universe."[21] Boisen's approach would probably be seen by Wilber as an attempt to understand the role of illness in relation to transformation of consciousness. Boisen saw the clinic setting as an opportunity not only to empirically examine the human condition and religious experience, but as a place where theological students would be challenged to explore their own theology in light of the existential questions that arose through their experiences in the clinical setting.[22] Boisen continued to champion this emphasis in CPE even as he developed a growing concern that theological education in the clinic was becoming more focused upon psychological dynamics of students and pastoral skill development.

It is my experience that much of the educational focus of pastoral care and CPE today—with its emphasis on outcomes—focuses more upon skill development and pastoral identity than exploring the deeper existential meanings of human experience. In addition, the nature of the clinical environment is such that students must be oriented quickly to clinical protocols and the norms set by regulatory agencies. Expectation for pastoral documentation has grown in institutional settings and many of the reporting mechanisms are problem-centered. Modern pastors have had to become sophisticated about the medical care system in order to understand the complex issues that their parishioners face. Technology has brought both benefit and burden to the decision-making process in medical care, including the concept of brain death, and a growing responsibility on the individual and family to make end-of-life decisions. There may be an even greater focus in understanding the objective domains of reality in the CPE experience than ever before.

This flatland world continues to occupy a significant place in CPE group seminars. In addition to the above, students experience first-hand the ways in which spiritual care can be relegated to the sidelines until modern medicine feels it has nothing else to offer a patient. Students encounter the confrontation of the illness experience and the ways that modern western medicine contributes to a sense of the fragmentation of the person. Spiritual caregivers find themselves forming a bridge between these two worlds for patients and families. Chaplains express frustration when their work is devalued by colleagues from other disciplines who do not understand or grasp the depth or meaning of the ministry of presence and its corresponding "truth claims."

It is my contention that we can help our students evaluate the complex milieu in which they operate by applying Wilber's quadrant model and by facilitating their understanding of how to measure the truth claims in each of the four perspectives or domains of reality. Not just sympathy and cultural and social sensitivity, but worldview. Wilber explains that each quadrant of reality has its own criteria for "validating truth claims." My subjective reality is validated through the interpretation of the listener who is hearing me and is assessing what they are hearing, and whether they experience me as "sincere, truthful, or trustworthy."[23] The "truth claims" of interior experience cannot be measured by exterior criteria. Science may be able to measure brain wave patterns when a person is meditating, but is not able to evaluate the interior experience of the meditator. The UL or interior subjective domain measures validity as *truthfulness, sincerity, integrity,* and *trustworthiness.* The UR exterior objective measures truth through *observable measures using correspondence, representational,* or *propositional methods.* The LL or collective interior, intersubjective quadrant explores *justness, cultural fit, mutual understanding* or *rightness.* And the LR quadrant, the collective exterior or interobjective experience, is measured by *functional fit, systems theory, web,* and *social systems mesh.*[24]

The four quadrants express different aspects of the ways human beings understand and experience reality. If you reduce reality to any single quadrant, your experience is partial, not whole. An integral vision understands the importance of including all of these perspectives and their equal claims of validity. For true integration to take place, science must move beyond "narrow empiricism" and religion "must open its truth claims to direct verification."[25]

The response to this problem, Wilber says, is to integrate the "four faces of the kosmos" or the four quadrants of reality to integrate interior knowledge developed over thousands of years in the spiritual traditions, with scientific and developmental knowledge of the modern eras, or science and religion. This integration is the work of spirituality. But he says "spirituality must be able to stand up to scientific authority."[26]

The integral approach integrates at least three ways of knowing: the eye of flesh using sensory data (empiricism), the eye of mind using reason (rationalism), and the eye of contemplation—knowledge learned through intuition or spirit (mysticism).[27] Wilber says that to validate knowledge in any quadrant you need to follow these three "strands": 1) Instrumental injunction—if you want to know this, do this. 2) Intuitive apprehension—an immediate . . . or direct experience of the domain or data-apprehension . . . whether sensory, mental, or spiritual experience. 3) Communal confirmation (or rejection)—checking the results (data, the evidence) with others who have adequately completed the injunctive or apprehensive strands [or with a community of the adequate].[28] In a broad sense, these injunctions are at the core of a CPE program and the learning experience may involve all three strands of knowing. It is beyond the scope of this chapter to go into this in depth. But the CPE group becomes the container—the community of the adequate that goes through the experience together. Pastoral education students often talk about how difficult it is to explain their CPE experience with those who have not been through it.

WILBER'S MAP: LINES AND LEVELS

Today's societies are a mixture of premodern perspectives, modern perspectives, and what Wilber calls postmodern "rebellions" to the changes in our culture through the influence of modernity. One rebellion is a yearning to go back to a simpler time. Wilber says that this romanticism of the past obscures the reality that many of those values that moderns take for granted simply did not exist before, not to mention the many technological changes that have resulted in the maturing of science. Most romantics would not like to live in a world without antibiotics, for example.[29]

Central to understanding this cultural mix is to put it into the context of evolution. The integral approach affirms the understanding that human beings evolve along with all of the rest of creation. As human beings evolve biologically from early versions of our ancestors to who we are today, so do our interior selves. Interior consciousness grows along with evolution. New perspectives come into being as human consciousness grows. Modern human consciousness is the recipient of thousands of years of evolution. The integral approach shows how the evolutionary process is occurring simultaneously in all four domains of reality.

Lines or streams of development are central to understanding human reality. Wilber cites the work of Howard Gardner in bringing together the research that resulted in his concept of multiple intelligences. Gardner names seven or eight human intelligence streams that have strongly influenced educators' thinking about how individuals learn.

Many of Wilber's named interior developmental lines will be familiar to pastoral supervisors. Wilber claims that there are as many as 12 to 24 major lines of development in each of the four quadrants. Individual interior lines include cognitive, linguistic, kinesthetic, affective/emotional, self, interpersonal, moral, spiritual, and psychosexual—even psychological—defenses. These lines develop relatively independently from each other, though some are more dependent upon other lines. Some people have innate abilities in certain lines. Mozart, for example, was a genius in the musical line but not very developed emotionally. Lines can mature or atrophy in people depending upon culture, context, and individual focus. Wilber stresses that the streams of development that he includes in his integral map are not just nice theories, but are based on solid research. Some, like the cognitive line outlined by Piaget, have been replicated and validated in research done by many others across many cultures.[30] There are some principles or "tenets" that Wilber argues are common to the evolutionary process, whether biological, social, or interior. What follows is Wilber's description of this development process. But first, let's explain Wilber's concept of a *holon*. He uses the word holon to describe any reality. It is a concept meant to encompass a wide array of realities—things, people, ideas, matter, and processes. Holons have their own intrinsic wholeness and are made up of other holons. A holon is both whole in and of itself, and is a part of something greater. For example, an individual student is a holon, as is a seminar group, as is the seminary community, as is the context of the greater society upon which each of these rest.

Holons develop or *emerge* in an evolutionary sequence of consciousness. Each holon transcends and includes its predecessor, but the emerging holon cannot exist without its predecessor. The following sequence describes the emergence of physical matter: subatomic particles to atoms to molecules to polymers to cells and so on. A cell has greater *depth* (more levels of evolution) than an atom and less *span* (there are more atoms than cells). If you destroy a holon, you will destroy all the holons above it, but not below it. So, an atom can exist without a cell but if you destroy the atom the cell cannot exist. Simpler levels of development have greater *span* (there are more atoms than cells). More complex levels have greater *depth*. Holons have *interiority* and *exteriority* (as seen in the four quadrants). "The within of all things is consciousness, the without of things is form. . . . the within of things is depth, the without is surface"—or span. A human being is more complex and has more *depth* than the plant and animal life that support human existence. If you destroy life at any level, you will destroy "all of the levels above and none of those below." If collective humanity were to engage in a nuclear war, atoms and molecules would still exist even if the earth could no longer support complex life as it is currently known.[31]

Each stage of development is characterized by *differentiation* from what went before, *transcending and including* the earlier developmental stage and adding something new. In the process of evolution, a holon develops internally at the same time as it develops externally. Evolution has *directionality*. The development of a holon has been defined in science and religion "hierarchically—composed of enveloping nests of increasing embrace" (development that is envelopment). Size is not a relevant factor in looking at the growth of an interior holon. For example, "a symbol is not bigger than an image; an image is not bigger than an impulse." As a holon evolves, it moves toward increasing complexity, increasing *differentiation and integration*, increasing *organization and structure*, increasing *relative autonomy*, and Wilber says *increasing telos*. The greater the depth of a holon, the greater degree of consciousness.[32]

It is important to note that hierarchy in the context of evolution refers to a *growth hierarchy*, not hierarchies of dominance or suppression—that is, pathology. One has to pass through a particular stage or wave to get to the next stage. Or, as one of my students said, you have to be 15 before you can be 30 or 50, but you may still be able to remember what it felt like to be 15. Wilber uses the term *holarchy* to emphasize the idea that in integration each holon is embraced by a larger holon.

As we have noted, the within of all things is consciousness. The question of interior evolution becomes how do you measure the "altitude" of the various developmental lines? All of the lines "seem to be growing in the same direction of increasing complexity . . . or increasing consciousness." Wilber says that one "basic yardstick" is the cognitive line. "Growth in the cognitive line is necessary but not sufficient for growth in the other lines. . . . You have to be aware of something in order to act on it, feel it, identify with it, or need it."[33] But two people can be at the level of formal operational cognition (Piaget) and each embrace a different level in the values line (Graves) or be at different levels of moral development (Kohlberg). So, in addition to the cognitive line, there must be another altitude marker. Wilber then posits a "y-axis" of the "degree of consciousness itself: the more consciousness, the higher the altitude (subconscious to self-conscious to superconscious)." Consciousness used this way "is not itself a line, but the space in which lines arise. . . . it is the openness, the clearing in which phenomena arise and if those phenomena develop in stages they constitute a development line."[34]

The tenets listed above do not imply of human evolution that only continuous progressive improvement occurs. With more complexity there are both increasing possibilities and the greater possibility that something can go wrong as well as improve. "Each stage [of evolution] solves or diffuses certain problems of the previous stage and then adds new problems of its own."[35] Pathologies occur when things go wrong—as when differentiation goes too far into *dissociation*. With some evolutionary processes, instead of transcending and including, they can transcend and "repress, deny, or distort" earlier capacities. Higher structures can also be "hijacked by lower impulses"—rationalism made advanced technologies possible, but when employed by ethnocentric tribalism, it can result in ethnic cleansing such as Auschwitz and modern day Bosnia. The more complex a being, the more opportunity there is for pathology to exist in any of the four quadrants.[36]

THE EVOLUTION OF CULTURE AND ACCOMPANYING INTERIOR WORLDVIEWS

The four quadrant model follows the streams of evolution in all of the domains. As human beings evolved over time, so did their collective systems. The exterior social systems developed alongside modes of technology. Humans foraged to live and developed survival clans. Later, ethnic tribes formed and the horticultural era developed. Ethnic tribes developed into early nations and the agrarian age was born, eventually turning into corporate states and the industrial age, and so forth. Developing in parallel to these social systems were the interior meanings or shared values that correspond with them. Wilber follows Jean Gebser's evolution of cultural worldviews from archaic to magic to mythic to rational to integral, but breaks the later interior stages into rational/scientific to pluralist to integral to transpersonal. [37]

I'm now going to talk about one line of interior development, spiral dynamics, as it connects to the evaluation of postmodern worldviews within students. Spiral dynamics follows the development in individuals of internalized value systems that emerged alongside Gebser's worldviews. Each of these worldviews developed in response to the "life conditions" that humans faced in the environment. The first time each of these worldviews emerged, they were the *cutting edge* of culture. Today, we live in a complex society in which all of these worldviews co-exist—some none too happily.[38]

Spiral dynamics is based upon the research of Clare Graves. Graves gathered data about adult human development through interviews correlated with mind/brain research. The data surprised him. A student of Abraham Maslow, his research showed adult values that were expressive of "higher levels" of human organization than self-actualization. His "data supported the conclusion that [in] human nature . . . modes of being can ebb and flow. New ones can replace old ones, yet the old ones don't disappear. They still exist in us."[39] He developed the following constructs through his research: 1) Human nature is not static, nor is it finite. Human nature changes as the conditions of existence change, thus forging new systems. Yet, the older systems stay with us. 2) When a new system or level is activated, we change our psychology and rules for living to adapt to those new conditions. 3) We live in a potentially open system of values with an infinite number of modes of living available to us. There is no final state to which we all aspire. 4) An individual, company, or an entire society can respond positively only to those managerial principles, motivational appeals, educational formulas, or legal or ethical codes that are appropriate to the current level of human existence.[40]

Graves saw the "emergence of human systems" evolving through levels of increasing complexity as like going up a "spiral staircase." Later, after refining his thinking, he believed his data showed that people could be self-actualized within any particular worldview. He identified what he called first tier (existence) and second tier (being) value systems, believing that human beings were about to go through (in 1974) a momentous leap of human consciousness from first tier into second tier.[41]

Don Beck and Christopher Cowan have continued his work using the language of memes ("core intelligences that form systems and impact human behavior") to describe these value systems or worldviews. As human beings and cultures evolve, the earlier mindsets don't disappear but become a part of the internal fabric of the spiral within us. They classified the memes using a color scheme to make it easier to identify them. Ken Wilber identifies spiral dynamics as one of the many streams in the "great river" of development in interior consciousness and incorporates them into his quadrant model, changing the color scheme slightly to follow the arc of the rainbow. Graves described each of these "waves of existence" as evolving in a series of "nesting envelopment." Wilber says that each meme is a holarchy—a series of nests within nests of increasing embrace.[42]

Wilber notes that the language of levels and stages implies a solidity that is just not real in describing dynamic human beings and cultures. When you say someone's center of gravity is at a particular level of development, such as rational, it is based upon percentages of answers. In this case, a person's answers to research questions are 50% of the time related to rational worldview responses, 25% of the time pluralistic worldview responses, and 25% of the time traditional/conventional worldview responses. In addition, everyone born goes through the various developmental stages. Your worldview is dependent upon a number of factors beginning with your age and level of cognitive and self development. The center of gravity of the culture in which you live tends to "pull you up" as you develop. But if you begin to differentiate from the ideas or mindset of the culture within which you live, it tends to try to pull you back into its embrace.[43]

The worldviews or waves of the spiral are listed below. I adopt descriptive language from both Beck and Wilber and add Piaget's cognitive line of development in parenthesis.

First Tier Levels/Memes (Piaget)	Basic Motives (Where Found)
Beige (Sensorimotor)	*Survival Sense.* Level of basic survival. (First human societies, infants, shell shock.)
Purple (Preoperational, Symbolic)	*KinSpirits.* Safety and security. Magical, animistic thinking. Ethnic tribes. Spiritual exist in ancestors.
Red (Preoperational, Conceptual)	*PowerGods.* First emergence of self distinct from tribe. Impulsive, egocentric, heroic, feudal empires. (Terrible twos, rebellious youth, frontier mentality, street gangs.)
Blue (Concrete, Operational)	*TruthForce.* Conformist rule, purposeful, law and order, absolutist, rigid social hierarchies, paternalism. (Puritan America, patriotism, fundamentalism, Boy Scouts, codes of chivalry and honor.)
Orange (Formal, Operational)	*StriveDrive.* Scientific achievement, multiplistic, success and autonomy, self escapes herd mentality, competitive. (Enlightenment, Wall Street, trophy hunting, materialism, entrepreneurialism.)
Green (Pluralistic mind)	*Human/Bond.* Communitarian, relativistic, harmony, equality, ecological sensitivity, against hierarchy, pluralistic values, multiculturalism, social construction of reality, refresh spirituality. (Postmodernism, humanistic psychology, liberation theology, Greenpeace, ecofeminism, politically correct.)

Table 10.2

Second Tier Levels/Memes	
Yellow (Low vision-logic)	*Flex/Flow.* Flexible adaptation to change, integrative, systemic, natural hierarchies, spontaneity, functionality. Knowledge and competency supersede rank, power, status, or group.
Turquoise (High vision-logic)	*GlobalView.* Attention to whole-Earth dynamics, holistic, experiential, unites feeling with knowledge, synthesis, and renewal.

Table 10.3[44]

Beck emphasizes that spiral dynamics explores an adaptive system within people. These are not types of people. These are systems of thinking, approaching, and valuing *within* people that can change over time. They impact all of life's choices and can be healthy or unhealthy. As individuals grow they need enough of the structure of one level to effectively move to the next. Wilber notes that people in American (U.S.) culture tend to move through the first four waves by adolescence, where blue (conformist) is challenged by orange (individualistic, experimental). The research shows that most people will remain for years in the value system they have attained by their mid-twenties until mid-life (50's) when once again transformational change occurs.[45]

When I began supervising CPE, many students seem focused somewhere between the value systems of conformist Blue and differentiation or autonomy Orange. Students would come to mainline seminaries with a traditional theology, only to have it upended by exegesis, literary, or contextual criticism of scripture. A sense of loss of faith would ensue as they integrated this new knowledge into their faith perspective. A similar process would happen in CPE as they were confronted by the reality of people's suffering, with differences in cultural perspectives of their peers, or with an individual struggle with building pastoral identity involving issues of race, culture, gender, power, and authority.

It's not that the above related dynamics don't still occur. I simply recognize more levels of complexity in my student groups. As I said earlier, many students' self-identify as postmodern. Students who make such claims often express inclusion of other perspectives intellectually, but when exploring their pastoral care or peer relationships they are confronted with strong dissonant feelings about worldviews not like theirs.

Spiral dynamics is another lens for assessing the clashes within groups and to view the sub-groupings that develop. Two students who share strong Blue (absolutist) value systems but imbue it with different content may clash more strongly than students who approach issues from different worldviews. A recent student, a strong "Purple/Blue/Orange," carried herself with shamanic authority, was highly intuitive, had strong conventional faith, and was challenging her church's exclusion of women in ministry. There were times when the theological language of some of her Orange/Green (autonomous, relativistic, egalitarian) peers was incomprehensible to her, but she found them inspiring mentors for developing pastoral authority. At the same time, one of the characteristics of first tier systems is intolerance between these worldviews. We might say that we see this played out on the national stage in our election cycles between the "red states" and "blue states."

Individual students or groups have different centers of gravity in various worldviews. I have found it helpful to approach pastoral supervision with an understanding of these value systems and how they impact change and growth. Students are mixtures of these worldviews, of course, but I have found that if I correctly interpret a student's center of gravity, it helps me in developing a supervisory approach.

I spent two years supervising CPE in an army setting. I entered rather naively and approached the first group of students with the value system out of which I primarily operated—collegial, consensus-building, trying to get the group to establish their own contracts and norms. I was met with a good deal of resistance to the CPE process. When the next group arrived, I changed course and assumed the role of senior officer, essentially establishing clear guidelines of operation. This group was far more responsive to the process. Looking back upon this experience with the hindsight of spiral dynamics, I had approached the first group, who shared a strong Blue/Orange values system (absolut-ist/achievist/competitive), with a Green (relativistic/equality) supervisory strat-egy that simply did not connect with them.

An integral approach calls for the perspective of second tier (being) world-views. The view from the second tier is not competitive with the previously de-lineated value systems. First tier value systems often clash with one another. Green pluralists intellectually support all cultural views but think Orange is too materialistic or dislike the ideas of Blue. Blue does not respect Green's relativ-ism and Orange thinks Green is too naive. But in Yellow and Turquoise there is a radical shift in consciousness that is not fear-based and understands the value and necessity of each of the levels of the spiral. Second tier worldviews are ac-tively at work to support the contributions of each level of the spiral. Second tier value systems want to build the health of the various memes, understanding that each person needs to pass through healthy memes on their way up the spiral. Spiral dynamics asserts that when a new system is emerging, societies experi-ence disorganization and fragmentation. Yellow and Turquoise value systems are emerging out of the need in our time for a new perspective to respond to the complexity of today—a perspective which sees that all memes are actively func-tioning and in many cases clashing with each other, a perspective that integrates both science and spirituality.

CONCLUSIONS

As I said earlier, this chapter is "one taste" of the approach and philosophy of the integral vision of Ken Wilber. There is much that is, of necessity, left out. I did not venture into the areas of states of consciousness and how they overlap with the various structures of consciousness that have been central to this dis-cussion. Wilber talks about how both natural states and altered states or peak experiences of a temporary nature can occur to anyone at any age. These experi-ences are interpreted by people depending on where they lie in the spectrum of development or worldview.[46] Meditative and contemplative traditions have well established descriptors for these experiences. Transpersonal or higher states of consciousness can only become permanent traits with practice. Types—another lens in Wilber's integral map—refers to differences of gender and such typolo-gies as the Enneagram and Myers-Briggs. Types are horizontal categories in that they are different ways of describing aspects of identity at any level or wave of development.

The deep interior focus of Wilber's work is recognition of the spiritual crea-tive core of existence, the ground of being, the "is-ness" of things, the Great Nest of Being. This ground of being or spirit is the lure that draws evolution ever onward. Evolution is a process of growth that is an envelopment of previous stages or waves of being, transcending, differentiating, and including what went before.

Wilber's system of integrating reality has helped me to make sense of the complex world in which we and our students live and work. It has also given me a new lens with which to evaluate the worldviews that different students inhabit. It is a lens that supports the idea of verticality in development; that recognizes structures or waves of consciousness—"progressive and permanent milestones along the evolutionary path [of human] unfolding."[47] These structures or waves are one measure of consciousness, what Wilber calls the "altitude" of consciousness.

Proponents of integral philosophy assert that they are observing a new level or reality of consciousness that is emerging historically. Something is stirring in individuals and in the wider culture as a whole. Clare Graves asserted that what appears to be fragmentation in society is actually the beginning phase of this emerging consciousness in humans. Integral philosophers believe that this emerging integral worldview is in many ways the evolutionary equivalent of the emergence of the modernist worldview known as the Enlightenment.[48]

An integral map is helpful in exploring the ways of knowing—of empiricism, rationalism, and contemplation. These ways of knowing are all significant in an integral vision. Knowledge cannot be reduced to any one perspective of reality.

NOTES

1. Ken Wilber, *The Marriage of Sense and Soul: Integrating Science and Religion* (New York: Random House, 1998), Chapters 2-4. I am primarily using Wilber's own language and categories in describing his definitions of concepts throughout this paper. He, in turn, includes terminology from the many varied disciplines that he includes in his integral approach, since he is actively including research and ideas from a wide range of sources. I am attributing the language used primarily to Wilber, as he uses them in his own way in his system, and there are many antecedents with which I am not familiar.

2. *Ibid.* Chapter 2.

3. *Ibid.* Wilber evaluates a number of various responses to modernity and other definitions of postmodern thought. He corrects problems developed by what he says is a misreading of postmodern philosopher, Thomas Kuhn.

4. Ken Wilber, *Integral Spirituality: A Startling New Role for Religion in the Modern and Postmodern World* (Boston: Shambhala Publications, Inc., 2007), 42.

5. Ken Wilber, *The Integral Vision: A Very Short Introduction to the Revolutionary Integral Approach to Life, God, the Universe, and Everything* (Boston: Shambhala Publications, Inc., 2007), 84.

6. Brad Reynolds, *Embracing Reality: The Integral Vision of Ken Wilber* (New York: Penguin, 2004), 2-3.

7. *Ibid.*, 11.

8. Ken Wilber and Tammy Simon, *Kosmic Consciousness* (Sounds True, 2003). A series of ten cds that lay out Wilber's entire framework of reality. Wilber has developed his ideas over 30 years. In each of his published works, he expounds on different areas of

his thinking in depth. Later works often have a quick review of aspects of earlier published ideas as they are the foundation upon which his later work rests. His later work also corrects areas that were troubling in the earlier integration of different systems of thought. This conversation is a comprehensive and accessible introduction to his system of thinking up through 2003, creating a theoretical foundation for his recent work.

9. Bill Harris, *Mastering Eckhart Tolle's "The Power of Now"* (Beaverton, OR: Centerpointe Research Institute). Taken from a conversation published online as one of a class series. This class was intended to help people who viewed Oprah Winfrey's television series with Tolle, understand his teachings from various spiritual points of view.

10. Steve McIntosh, *Integral Consciousness and the Future of Evolution* (New York, NY: Continuum, 2007), 193.

11. *Ibid.*, 171.

12. *Ibid.*, 153-197. McIntosh gives an overview of the historical figures that have influenced the development of integral philosophy.

13. Ken Wilber, *Integral Spirituality, Op. cit.* The terminology used is taken from an overview of Wilber's quadrants model in the Introduction and Chapter 1.

14. *Ibid.*, 36.

15. *Ibid.*, 37.

16. Ken Wilber, *The Marriage of Sense and Soul, Op. cit.*, 6-9.

17. *Ibid.*, 6.

18. *Ibid.*, 56.

19. *Ibid.*, 4.

20. Anton Boisen, *The Exploration of the Inner World* (Philadelphia: University of Pennsylvania Press, 1937), 10.

21. *Ibid.*, 200.

22. Taken generally from *Ibid.* and Glenn H. Asquith, ed., *Vision From A Little Known Country; A Boisen Reader* (Decatur, GA: JPCP, 1992).

23. Ken Wilber, *The Eye of Spirit: An Integral Vision for a World Gone Slightly Mad* (Boston: Shambhala Publications, Inc., 1997), 13-15.

24. *Ibid.*, 20-29.

25. Ken Wilber, *The Marriage of Sense and Soul, Op. cit.*, 160-61.

26. *Ibid.*, 160-61.

27. Ken Wilber, *The Eye of Spirit, Op. cit.*, 84.

28. *Ibid.*, 85.

29. Ken Wilber, *The Marriage of Sense and Soul, Op. cit.* Wilber discusses three major "postmodern rebellions" to this flatland world. 1) In romanticism—we find the view that human beings need to get back to our original nature and rediscover our basic goodness. 2) The rebellion of idealism—the 19th century vision of transcendence saw that "cosmic and human history is most profoundly the evolution and development of spirit." 3) Postmodernism—an attempt to undermine science in its own foundations by recognizing that "interpretation was a feature and fabric of the universe"—took deconstruction to self-defeating extremes.

30. Ken Wilber and Tammy Simon, *Op. cit.*.

31. Ken Wilber, *Sex, Ecology, Spirituality: The Spirit of Evolution* (Boston: Shambhala Publications, Inc., 1995), Chapters 2-3.

32. *Ibid.*, Chapter 2.

33. Ken Wilber, *Integral Spirituality, Op. cit.*, 65.

34. *Ibid.*, 61-69.

35. Ken Wilber, *The Eye of Spirit, Op. cit.*, 73.

36. *Ibid.*, 73-76.

37. Ken Wilber, *The Integral Operating System,* Version 1.0, (Sounds True, 2005). Wilber has may charts in each of his publications outlining various parts of his integral system or integral map. These lines are taken from charts found in a version of his integral map called IOS Explorer included in a boxed set of cds and introductory materials.

38. Don Beck, *Spiral Dynamics Integral* (Sounds True, 2006). A lecture series on cd.

39. *Ibid.*

40. Don Beck and Christopher Cowan, *Spiral Dynamics: Mastering Values, Leadership, and Change* (Hoboken, NJ: Blackwell Publishing, Inc., 1996/2006), 29.

41. Don Beck, *Spiral Dynamics Integral, Op. cit.*

42. Ken Wilber, *Integral Psychology: Consciousness, Spirit, Psychology, Therapy* (Boston: Shambhala Publications, Inc., 2000), 47.

43. Ken Wilber and Tammy Simon, *Op.cit.*

44. Don Beck and Christopher Cowan, *Op. cit.*, 41 and Ken Wilber, *Integral Spirituality, Op. cit.*, 85 and Figure 2.4, 68 and Ken Wilber, *Integral Psychology, Op. cit.*, 47-53.

45. Don Beck, *Spiral Dynamics Integral, Op. cit.* and Ken Wilber, *Kosmic Consciousness, Op. cit.*

46. Ken Wilber, *Integral Spirituality, Op. cit.*, 88-93. Wilber has developed a model for examining the interface between levels of consciousness and states of consciousness or "the many faces of God" called the Wilber-Combs Lattice.

47. *Ibid.*, 7.

48. John McIntosh, *Op. cit.*, 2.

CHAPTER ELEVEN

Reconsidering Supervision as an Ethical Endeavor

David McCurdy

INTRODUCTION

In 1990, the *Journal of Supervision and Training* (JSTM) featured a symposium titled "Supervision and Training as an Ethical Endeavor." Symposium articles discussed ethical concerns arising in the supervision of pastoral counseling and Clinical Pastoral Education (CPE). Framing appropriate questions for ethical attention and analysis was a recurring theme of the symposium, which was described as an initial exploration of ethics in pastoral supervision.[1] Gender, sexual intimacy, authority/power dynamics, and related justice concerns were central concerns in several essays.[2] Conspicuously absent, especially by today's standards, was direct discussion of issues posed by racial, ethnic, and religious/spiritual diversity. Nor were issues in supervising seminary field education or spiritual direction yet on the ethical horizon.

Literature in related disciplines was recognizing ethical concerns arising in their clinical practice and supervision. The third edition of Corey et al.'s *Issues and Ethics in the Helping Professions*[3] had already appeared, although no symposium article referred to this now-standard cross-disciplinary work.

In this chapter, I will revisit supervision as an "ethical endeavor." Since 1990, professional organizations in pastoral or spiritual care (as chaplaincy is now widely known[4]) have shored up codes of professional ethics, tightened formal complaint processes, and collaborated to develop a common code of ethics.[5] Issues not addressed in the JSTM symposium, including forms of diversity noted above, have drawn considerable attention in codes of ethics and in certification and accreditation standards. "Ethics," i.e. professional ethics and/or other areas of ethical concern, is a required focus in curricula for supervisory education in the Association for Clinical Pastoral Education, Inc. (ACPE), the National Association of Catholic Chaplains (NACC), and the American Association of Pastoral Counselors (AAPC).

This chapter will focus primarily on supervision in CPE and, to a lesser extent, pastoral counseling. Professional organizations in both fields of supervision, especially ACPE, have given considerable attention to ethical concerns, and each field has developed standards for practice and certification that express widely held ethical perspectives. Moreover, professional organizations in chaplaincy have incorporated ethical concerns in their standards of competence and conduct for certification.[6]

This chapter will also consider some ethical concerns that arise in spiritual direction and theological field education (seminary-sponsored supervised ministry experiences). Supervision in these ministry contexts has become a focus of increased discussion since the early 1990s, and ethical concerns have been an ingredient of that discussion in JSTM (now *Reflective Practice: Formation and Supervision in Ministry*) and elsewhere.[7]

FRAMING THIS ETHICAL ENDEAVOR

Today it is relatively easy to identify a "laundry list" of ethical concerns that have emerged in supervision across the helping disciplines. *Issues and Ethics in the Helping Professions*, in particular, provides a broad survey of issues in fields of counseling and psychotherapy that significantly parallel pastoral care and pastoral counseling.

I will forgo an extensive laundry list discussion here. Rather, I will engage areas of ethics and supervision in which I believe a deeper analysis or different perspective may be helpful, and I will consider some fresh or previously unaddressed concerns.[8]

WHY ETHICS?

At the beginning, it is important to reflect on the nature of pastoral supervision's interest in ethics. Why do, or why should, we care about "ethics"? Are we most interested in finding a standard approach to issues that vex the field because they occur repeatedly, inflict reputational damage, and/or visit harm or injustice on vulnerable supervisees? The often overlapping concerns about boundary violations, abuse of power, and cultural insensitivity come to mind. Or do we seek to integrate overarching notions of justice, respect, care, and integrity in our practice and curricula? Both interests have their place. But the ethical interest of pastoral supervision—why we care about ethics—is broader and goes deeper than any list of recurring problems or set of key concepts.

Supervision's ethical interest begins with the purposes and outcomes of pastoral care and counseling, extends to values and virtues relevant to professional practice, and encompasses both negative and positive obligations of supervisors, programs, and the pastoral practitioners it seeks to form. Its scope includes ethical practice *in* supervision as well as ethical *content* that supervisors seek to communicate. It also extends to issues arising in the *contexts* that affect supervision's practice and outcomes.[9]

THE GOODS OF PASTORAL CARE, COUNSELING, AND SUPERVISION

The ethical interest of pastoral supervision is characterized in part by attention to ends, to hoped-for outcomes. The goods that supervision seeks are intertwined with goods that pastoral care and pastoral counseling seek for persons they serve. As medicine seeks to benefit the patient in terms of health, the pastoral care field seeks to benefit its various clients in the areas of psyche, spirit, and relational health.[10] Supervisors seek to equip supervisees to participate competently in this endeavor.

To take one specialty within pastoral care, Don Browning has proposed that pastoral counseling fosters "premoral goods" such as health, the "centrality of personhood," and recognition of "the goodness of emotions." While such goods are not "directly moral," they make for human flourishing and are generally to be promoted. The moral work of pastoral counseling is to help clients achieve these goods and to help "mediate" between them when they compete.[11] Some similar claims might be made about the aims and work of chaplaincy. Spiritual direction and pastoral ministry in the congregational settings of supervised field education may more strongly emphasize enabling faith or creating conditions for its enhancement.

It can be said that pastoral supervision seeks these goods indirectly by equipping supervisees to foster them in professional practice. But typically supervision also seeks similar goods for those being supervised. It attempts to nurture and stretch supervisees' own psyche, spirit, and relational health, and thereby to facilitate their use of the self in ministry. It does so both because supervisees are ends in themselves and because the integration of the pastoral and the personal is deemed vital to competent practice. Historically, CPE stressed *formation* of persons competent for ministry and their *liberation* from personal and cultural constraints that impeded their use of their personhood in ministry.[12] In spiritual direction, supervision can mean "looking into the well" of the supervisee's "inner experience" during his or her practice of spiritual direction[13] in order to enlarge the interior freedom that is a primary resource in helping directees.

Practitioners of pastoral care and supervision understand their pursuit of these goods as, in some sense, a professional obligation: if they *can* help a client or supervisee in areas or ways suggested here, there is a general sense that they *ought* to do so, all things being equal.[14] At the same time, there are ethical constraints on this obligation, including respect for students'/clients' autonomy and boundaries.

But what, really, is the nature and extent of the apparent obligation to pursue pastoral goods? It has been argued that humans' obligations are "dynamic"—they change as our abilities to realize or enable pre-moral and moral goods wax or wane.[15] By this logic, if the field of pastoral care and education grows more skilled at facilitating positive human development, responding to cultural or religious difference, or realizing justice, professional obligations in those areas grow as well.[16] Here, the ethical burden of supervision is proportionate to its positive possibilities: "can" implies "ought."[17]

VALUES AND VIRTUES INFORMING PRACTICE

Pastoral care and supervision has long celebrated each individual's unique personhood, in all its actual and potential richness.[18] This emphasis has been questioned in pointed criticism alleging culturally insensitive "individualism" in the field, especially CPE.[19] Yet the conviction that one's personhood is both a good in itself *and* the primary means of ministry has not diminished.[20] As a result, attention to the *kind of person* one is and seeks to become, and therefore to questions of virtue and character, attitudes and dispositions to act, has been central to pastoral care and supervision.

Historically, and especially in the "New England" understanding of CPE,[21] it was incumbent on the ministerial student to develop the relevant virtues and dispositions. The extent of this obligation was indeterminate, since competence could always be enhanced, and had in any case to be maintained. "Growth" was always possible, although minimal standards of competence could be established. Thus a de facto mixture of obligation and aspiration has always characterized CPE. An ethic that incorporates ideals and aspirations, and is not limited to duties and obligations—or to meeting standards—has long had a place here.

PRINCIPLES AND CODES

Recognition of gender, power, and justice issues and of supervisors' engagement in problematic sexual intimacy propelled a strengthened sense (from the 1980s on) that pastoral care professionals and supervisors must observe certain ethical constraints. It was not a giant leap from this precipitating awareness to a "laundry list" of specific issues, frequently ensconced in organizations' codes of professional ethics.

Today there is also a widespread recognition that the "do no harm" principle, long enshrined in medical practice, is crucial to ethical practice in pastoral care and supervision.[22] As in healthcare, which now stresses patient safety and avoiding medical error, there is greater recognition that pastoral care professionals can inflict harm, even if inadvertently, and that their various clients must be protected from that possibility.[23]

The sense of "ought" in pastoral care reaches well beyond obligations to avoid harm and eschew reprehensible conduct. But principles and codes aimed primarily at avoiding negative conduct and consequences are now a vital, seemingly indispensable part of the ethical landscape.

A "PRINCIPLES" FRAMEWORK

Tom Beauchamp and James Childress' widely used *Principles of Biomedical Ethics* sets forth four summary principles of biomedical ethics: respect for autonomy, nonmaleficence, beneficence, and justice.[24] This framework's success has spawned similar lists of principles in related fields. Pastoral supervisors may find it helpful to consider the following set of principles, adapted from a list developed by Peter Hawkins and Robin Shohet for supervisors in secular helping professions: 1) Balance between: appropriate responsibility for the work of the supervisee and respect for supervisee autonomy, due respect for the well-being and protection of the client and respect for client autonomy, 2) Action within the limits of one's competence, recognizing when to seek further help, 3) Faithfulness (fidelity) to explicit and implicit promises made, 4) Anti-oppressive practice, particularly in working with difference, and 5) Openness to challenge and feedback, and active commitment to ongoing learning. Hawkins and Shohet also commend the "do no harm" principle as an ethical baseline.[25]

Practicing these principles often emphasizes *refraining* from certain actions, such as inappropriate or unhelpful supervisory intrusion into the client-supervisee relationship or exceeding one's competence. But all or nearly all these principles also require *positive* steps to ensure their fulfillment. Besides avoiding prejudice and other pitfalls, "anti-oppressive practice" (discussed further below) requires proactive efforts to understand cultures, religions, and power dynamics in the context of justice and other values. Hospitals have discovered that doing no harm to patients requires positive (and extensive) programs to identify causes of medical error and design corrective processes.

Differences among the types of pastoral care and supervision will affect the relevance and application of these principles, which are most directly transferable to pastoral counseling and psychotherapy. The aims and the clients of spiritual direction, field education, and chaplaincies present different challenges and opportunities and these might suggest modified principles or additional ones.[26]

SPECIFIC ISSUES

Supervision in pastoral care and counseling has, broadly speaking, made significant strides in addressing major ethical concerns since the late 1980s. Boundary issues (sexual intimacy, dual relationships, multiple supervisory roles), cultural concerns (sensitivity and response to multiple forms of difference), justice and power dynamics (which infuse most of the issues already noted), supervisee rights (informed consent, confidentiality, non-exploitation), competence and oversight (acting within one's competence, protecting client welfare), and even professional organizations' processes (especially certification) have received considerable ethical attention. Organizations have developed enhanced codes of ethics, curricular materials, and ethics-related bibliographies to help supervisors and supervisory students learn about and address these issues.[27] In this section I will consider a selection of boundary issues, including some that involve sexuality and supervision, the "rights" of supervisees such as "informed consent," ethical approaches to cultural/diversity issues, and supervisory teaching about ethics.

SEXUAL AND NON-SEXUAL BOUNDARY CONCERNS

SEX IN SUPERVISORY RELATIONSHIPS: NO, BUT WHY NOT?

An extraordinary amount of attention has been given to questions of sexual intimacy between helping professionals and clients (past or present) and between supervisors and current or former students. These questions are a subset, and the one most discussed, of a group of problems classified as "boundary issues" or problems of "multiple" or "dual" relationships. One might think, with all this attention, that enough has been said about "sex and supervision," that the issues have been essentially resolved. Even so, in my judgment, lingering conceptual and practical ambiguities remain.

Professional organizations in both secular and religious helping professions have typically dealt with sexual boundary violations by promulgating codes of ethics that proscribe sexual intimacy with clients or supervisees, both present and past. This approach has become the received ethical orthodoxy in the professions and it is often defended as both legally necessary and reputationally prudent. It has been buttressed by tighter, more "consumer"-accessible organizational complaint processes and by more stringent sanctions, including public disclosure of misconduct findings and sanctions imposed.[28]

Occasional dissenting voices have questioned the absoluteness of the prohibitions or the strictness of the sanctions.[29] And some have disagreed with the prevailing rationale for prohibitions. Should supervisors avoid sexual intimacy because it unjustly abuses power with another who cannot truly consent and causes harm—the now-standard view—or rather, because it subverts the supervisory relationship (and its educational purpose), e.g., by transforming it into a peer relationship?[30]

Perhaps this lingering undercurrent of dissent or confusion is a reminder that prohibitions alone are never enough. For one thing, prohibitions housed in professional codes of ethics are the result of a political process within a professional group. To some, such an organizational "product" will always be suspect. Besides, some absolute prohibitions may be the reactive product of knee-jerk responses to publicized violations.[31] Thus, there is also a need continually to remind ourselves *why* professional prohibitions and restrictions exist, indeed to reconsider our rationale for establishing them.

Sex is a compelling and complex part of life, a force difficult to contain. In particular, the intensity of the interpersonal educational process in CPE lends itself to strong emotions and the potential development of intimate ties. It is striking to see how several articles in a 2001 symposium on sexual intimacy and supervision move, more than most literature on this subject, beyond prohibition alone to consider the positive meanings of sexual attraction both in itself and in the supervisory context.[32]

Respect for the power of eros, the insistency of sexual desire, and the energizing potential of awakened sexual feelings[33] serve as reminders not only that sexual intimacy is a premoral good, but that something is lost if we fail to recognize and engage its meaning and power. The positive potential of sexuality, even in a relationship of ostensible power disparity, leads some authors to hedge a bit on the absoluteness of the prohibition.[34] Even some who clearly favor a prohibition of sexual intimacy between supervisor and student lament the chilling effect, such as diminished freedom for personal touch, that such a prohibition can create.[35]

But there are also red flags in these discussions, reminders that sex is the riskiest of premoral goods. One author's question, posed amidst valuable theological commentary, suggests the issue: "How do I love my students and how do I show this in a way that is life-giving *for each of us*?"[36] The appeal to love and the recognition of mutuality are important and admirable factors, in supervision that seeks to be pastoral. And the hope that a supervisory relationship will be life-giving for all involved is, in itself, a worthy aspiration. But this way of construing the professional relationship can also leave the door open to a certain sense of entitlement: "The supervisory relationship *ought* to be life-giving— fulfilling to both of us in a way that *I too* can experience as life-giving."

That hope-become-expectation conceals a pitfall because it forgets a moral premise of the supervisory calling. Professional helping and teaching relationships are also relationships of renunciation. The professional renounces—gives up—some forms of personal gratification for the sake of a calling and for others' good. Surely this is true of pastoral care and pastoral supervision, where words like "sacrifice" and "the way of the cross" may be part of the vocabulary and love's expression is qualified by justice and even a notion of self-emptying.[37] Further, and especially for a professional belonging to and endorsed by a religious community, engagement in sexual intimacy with a supervisee may violate an existing personal covenant with a significant other (and may implicate the supervisor in a similar violation by the supervisee).[38]

DOING NO HARM

Not least, it is important to recall that in surveys of former clients or supervisees who engaged in sexual intimacy with therapists or supervisors, the overwhelming majority of those retrospectively surveyed reported a negative aftermath of the experience. More than 90% of former therapy clients in one survey had subsequent regrets and/or felt harmed.[39] In another survey, well over 80% of CPE students who were sexually intimate with a supervisor later considered the supervisor's actions to be misconduct, and "many" of them continued to experience "pain, confusion, guilt, and anger."[40] These findings suggest strongly that, *from the standpoint of outcomes*, supervisors who engage in sexual intimacy with students run *an indefensibly high risk of inflicting harm.*

This statistically overwhelming likelihood is not changed by the undeniable existence of exceptions: some students had no regrets, some found their sexual expression "mutual and enjoyable," a few eventually married the supervisor.[41] Yet this remains an instance in which the exceptions prove the rule. The statistics place the burden on the reflective professional to say why he or she is willing to run a demonstrated substantial risk of engendering harm. It is not just the prohibition (by external forces) that matters here, but the professional's own ethical commitment, searching reflection, and due regard for a predictable likelihood of harm to the supervisee. Such reflection might well begin with that old but still clinically—*and ethically*—important supervisory question, "Whose needs are being met?"[42]

CREATING LEARNING OPPORTUNITIES: A CONGREGATIONAL POSSIBILITY

The context and structure of supervised field education provides another possibility in some situations where sexual boundary issues can arise. Often, both a site ministry supervisor and the seminary's field education director facilitate student learning. If a student experiences pressure from a site supervisor to engage sexually and is able to discuss this dynamic with the field education director, the director may be able to help the student respond out of the student's own resources—such as existing relational skills, intuition, past experience—in a way that is not only self-protecting but empowering, and builds professional confidence.[43]

Despite this salutary presumption in favor of process learning, if the student feels "unsafe" in the ministry environment, a more direct intervention by the seminary representative may be called for.[44] In any case, the question of the seminary's institutional response to a site supervisor who engages in misconduct while acting as an agent of the seminary would need to be addressed.

NON-SEXUAL EXPLOITATION

Questions of "exploitation" not involving sexuality in pastoral supervision are often classified as another form of multiple-relationship problem (though it can be argued that they equally involve violations of students' rights. See "'Rights' and 'Responsibilities'" section below). In theological field education the question of exploitation can be raised, although the term is not often used, in light of the arrangement made between the seminary and the ministry setting (typically a congregation). The supervisor is normally accountable both to the seminary and to the congregation. The supervisee may or may not be paid, but in either case the supervisor and parish/congregation sometimes treat the supervisee primarily as a source of "field *work*" rather than as a field education *student*.

This attitude may be mitigated structurally if students are not dependent on field education sites for financial support and/or if seminaries fund the field education sites.[45] Such an arrangement can support the learning process by helping to ensure that the supervisee is not treated solely as a temporary worker in the church, but as one who is both minister and learner. It is worth noting that the tension students may experience between the roles of minister and student is not itself a sign of exploitation. This tension may be an important ingredient in learning, since pastors are continually subject to the pull between competing roles or obligations.[46] In CPE, issues ranging from the extent of students' work/time commitments to fees and payment schedules can reflect a conflict between supervisors' administrative roles and institutional relationships and their directly educational roles. Questions about "overworking" unpaid or low-paid students, particularly via "on-call" requirements in hospital CPE programs, have long been asked in the supervisory community, albeit with varying levels of conviction. Are students being "used" as unpaid help, at least partly to compensate for an institution's or department's inability or unwillingness to pay for fully trained chaplains? Or are students being similarly used to give full-time staff some relief from regular on-call duty? The short answer to these questions is, often enough, "yes." If so, is the arrangement exploitative?

If beginning trainees are unpaid, one can surely ask whether they are treated unjustly when significant pastoral service commitments are asked of them for no remuneration. The rejoinder might be that this is not exploitation but, rather, an opportunity to learn by immersion while simultaneously receiving quality supervision and paying little for it. It must be conceded that fees for CPE are generally quite low relative to other kinds of education. Less clear is how to weigh this reality against the service demands sometimes made of unpaid students. The fact that these long-standing practices are not unique to CPE or limited to supervised ministry settings does not legitimize them. But it does place them in a larger context where parallels with a broad range of unpaid student internships and/or modestly paid graduate assistantships or medical residencies may be relevant.[47]

On balance, do such arrangements—particularly unpaid ones—constitute injustice or rather, a fair trade-off between service or work demands and educational benefits? There seems to be no simple answer. CPE supervisors and centers commonly address the issue indirectly, within an "informed consent" process (see below), through advance disclosure of the program's service requirements. The tacit ethical assumption is that informing students of what will be asked of them permits them, as autonomous contractors, to decide whether they will accept the arrangement. It is further assumed that disclosure is an ingredient of respectful treatment and thus lends ethical acceptability to the situation. But disclosure of an unjust arrangement—if indeed it is unjust—does not remove the injustice, particularly if would-be supervisees bear the added external vulnerability of "having to" complete this training sooner or later. The fairness or justice issue may be mitigated but not resolved in this fashion.[48]

"RIGHTS" AND "RESPONSIBILITIES"

Accreditation standards for ethical practice in ACPE and other organizations now require programs and supervisors to provide a list of "rights and responsibilities" to program participants. Some or all supervisee "responsibilities" may be specific to the institution or setting; professional organizations rightly hesitate to stipulate responsibilities for supervisees who are not also their members.[49] The case is different with student/supervisee "rights," however. Professional organizations and the professional literature have proposed lists of supervisee rights, sometimes in tandem with parallel lists of client rights.[50] But the term "rights" in this context is ambiguous. Just what counts as a "right"? Is every assertion of a right legitimate?

Ethically, rights are serious moral claims a person or group can make on others.[51] Some rights obligate third parties (people or entities) to *do something for* a person (positive rights); other rights obligate third parties to *refrain from* some action affecting that person (negative rights). It is probably possible to frame all presumed institutional, programmatic, and supervisory obligations toward students as rights of the student. Some lists of supervisee rights come close to doing just that.

As *serious* moral claims, rights are distinct from *interests* and *desires*. Rights are claims about justice or fairness, or they assert that upholding particular claims and imposing corresponding obligations are vital to the well-being of persons and communities. Rights can serve to equalize the moral (and legal or socioeconomic) playing field by placing both strong and weak, those with more power and those with less, on equal footing. In the helping professions and supervisory practice, rights often specify what it means to show *respect* for clients and supervisees, and how those being served as clients or learners can expect to be treated as autonomous moral agents. Rights support expectations of fidelity as well as "anti-oppressive practice" in areas where the playing field has been, or still is, uneven.

Lists of supervisee rights sometimes fail to strike a balance between the general and the particular, the vague and the too-specific. Excessive detail and exhaustive lists may assuage legal or risk management fears. But, like the ubiquitous "privacy statements" of today's corporate America, these lists can also stupefy. They can sink into micromanagement, e.g., by prescribing a detailed list of elements that should be addressed in a first supervisory session.[52] Ironically, excessive specificity tends to weaken the very force of rights language, which has profound meanings enshrined in the U.S. Declaration of Independence and Bill of Rights, and in contemporary international declarations of human rights.[53]

The field of supervision and its professional organizations have a responsibility to avoid contributing to our society's rampant trivialization of rights language. In order to preserve and evoke its deeper meaning, rights statements should keep the overarching moral purpose of rights in mind, should *selectively* address concerns that matter substantially, and should permit actual fulfillment by supervisors and programs. The rights lists that exist today, whatever their shortcomings, probably constitute the substantial form of future iterations. But it remains important to ask what refinements can help them function with greater integrity and achieve their deeper purpose. One suggestion is to reframe some of the more detailed aspects of rights lists as "requirements"—obligations—the institution must meet,[54] or as "reasonable expectations" that supervisees may have. Fulfilling the requirements or meeting the expectations would remain a supervisory responsibility and would be so characterized. Such a change would keep supervisors and programs on the hook without diminishing the significance of rights.

"INFORMED CONSENT": WHAT AND HOW?

The ethics literature and statements of rights often espouse the obligation to provide supervisees with "informed consent." Typically, this admonition seems to mean that students' right to know should be respected by providing them adequate information about programs and processes, including individual supervisors' approaches to supervision. An in-depth effort to inform may, and probably should, include mention of the therapeutic or therapy-like aspects of the supervisory process (especially in CPE and pastoral counseling programs), along with assurance that in fact supervision will *not* be therapy and the boundary between the two will be preserved.[55]

The term "informed consent," however, suggests more than a right to know. It also poses the question of *consent* to supervised education in a particular setting and under specified conditions. Those who work in healthcare are familiar with an informed consent process in which the "informed" aspect is (or should be) integrally linked to "consent." Adequate information makes genuine consent possible. The information provided includes not only a description of *what* providers propose to do to help the patient, but also a projection of possible *effects* on the patient: anticipated benefits, risks of harm and, often, uncertainties.

Does "informed consent" to pastoral supervision provide equivalent forms of information, particularly when learning is likely to contain therapeutic or therapy-like aspects? Is an advance "benefits-burdens" assessment offered or facilitated by supervisors, or even possible for students? Information can be provided on outcomes that students tend to experience, on vocational or job prospects that may result upon completion of a program, and on the promising yet partial nature of process learning—including difficulties that may be encountered along the way—but, it is impossible to say everything in this regard.

And there are other complications. There are limits to the *descriptive* information that can be given or that supervisors may feel it wise to offer. One might, for instance, discuss supervisory style in a general way (and certainly model it in an interview or first supervisory meeting), but it is impossible to explain or anticipate everything that might happen in process education.[56] And telling too much up front could rob the supervisory process of effectiveness, since part of its power lies in a certain spontaneity and the supervisor's exercise of options in the moment.

Fortunately—for both supervisor and supervisee—"adequate" information does not mean full disclosure of all possible aspects of the process or its outcomes. In healthcare, the crux of informed consent is to provide *enough* information of the right kind(s) to enable well-considered decision making. Determining the parallel requirements for genuinely informed decision making in supervised education, perhaps especially in CPE, is still a practical and ethical challenge and opportunity for the field to address.

Finally, there is the question of consent itself. Logically, "consent" entails the possibility of refusal, of saying "no" to what is proposed. The old bugaboo of "required" CPE or other required ministry experiences may complicate this possibility. One requirement of informed consent in healthcare is that consent be truly voluntary—free and uncoerced. If students "have to" complete CPE for their seminary degree or as a prerequisite of ordination, how free are they to refuse and thus, to consent?

One might reply that in healthcare the illness often supplies its own "coercion" to undergo the treatment; the options are always forced to some extent. Moreover, whatever the status of the ostensible consent given in CPE and other supervised education, the dynamic created by the "requirement" issue is familiar to supervisors. Skillfully addressed, it can even become a fruitful part of the learning process.

How, then, can an admission and entry process empower supervisees to say a genuine yes (or no) to what supervised ministry programs and their supervisors seek to do and have to offer? To the extent that the potential power of supervised ministry experiences derives from or is associated with a level of risk (as through self-disclosure, confrontation, and evaluation),[57] the ethical challenge is to communicate this reality in an inviting yet realistic way that inspires trust. Especially when students feel vulnerable because of cultural, religious, and/or personal history factors, the ability to give genuine consent may matter a great deal, both viscerally and substantially. The experience of participating in a consent process that is more profound than perfunctory may even be novel, empowering, and energizing. Perhaps the ethical challenge of informed consent in pastoral supervision is not to clean up our language by reducing it to a right to know, but to find better ways of engaging in dialogue about what supervisors and programs are really "up to" and what it may mean existentially for prospective supervisees.[58]

Supervisees generally assume (and should be assured) that they can expect confidentiality, whether as a "right" or simply as a matter of course, in supervisory relationships. This requirement recognizes the quasi-therapeutic features of educational supervision in ministry and so parallels the norm of confidentiality in healthcare and psychotherapy. Supervisory confidentiality also recognizes the importance of supervisees' freedom to share and disclose information, feelings, and behavior. This freedom, deemed vital to the educational purpose of most forms of supervised ministry, depends on supervisees' trust that communication with supervisors will remain confidential. The norm of confidentiality typically involves an assumption that information about a client or supervisee "belongs" to that person in a property-like fashion because, like property, it is part of the person's privacy—indeed, an extension of the person.[59] Thus, confidentiality in supervision normally extends beyond the direct content of communication to records that describe and depend on that content. The widely accepted exceptions to confidentiality as non-disclosure are that the content of these communications may be released to others when the law requires the release—or, perhaps, merely when the law permits it[60]—or when the supervisee requests or permits it.

The question of disclosures to third parties such as seminaries and denominational bodies with a stake in students' learning experience is a common variant of the confidentiality question.[61] In CPE, the issue is typically one of what is done with the supervisor's evaluation after the training program is completed. When students "take" CPE for academic credit, use it to meet a graduation requirement, or complete it as a prerequisite for ordination or other judicatory authorization, disclosure of confidential information can become an issue.

Training programs typically address—or circumvent—the problem by ceding control of the evaluation to the student. The student may share it or not, at his or her discretion. This practice, however, may beg the question of what supervisors write in evaluations when they know, as they often do, that the seminary requires the student to submit the evaluation before credit is given. This issue overlaps with the "informed consent" issue. Students will likely be "informed" that they will "own" the evaluation after the program; it is less clear whether their "consent" to be evaluated will truly have a voluntary or uncoerced character, given seminary or judicatory requirements. This problem may be unavoidable, but deserves further reflection.

It has been suggested that supervisors create two evaluations: one for the student's eyes only and another, written in essentially descriptive terms, for institutional or judicatory consumption.[62] Another solution to the problem is for supervisors to write one evaluation, with the understanding (spoken or unspoken) that it will be more or less "generic"—unless, perhaps, there are "red flags" in the student's conduct or self-presentation that the supervisor feels compelled to share.[63] Specific nitty-gritty evaluative concerns might then be shared with the student personally, but not in writing.

One area where confidentiality seems vulnerable, at least within CPE, is the use of peer group session videotapes by supervisors for self-education or for review by others in consultative or certification roles. Students in ACPE programs are routinely asked to sign waivers permitting the use and sharing of these videotapes and written materials concerning the student. The waivers indicate that personally identifying information about the student will not be used unless the student signs the waiver. But they also indicate that students' "materials," including videotapes, may nonetheless be used pseudonymously if the student does not sign the waiver.[64] This latitude seems, oddly, to ignore the vulnerability of visibility: what could prevent a student shown in videotapes from being recognized on sight by any viewer who has seen or met the student?

DIFFERENCE AND ANTI-OPPRESSIVE PRACTICE

Responding to "diversity" has increasingly been an explicit theme in pastoral care since the 1980s. Perceptions of diversity issues and the language used to describe them—as well as desired outcomes of addressing them—have evolved over the years. Cultural sensitivity, cross-cultural awareness or communication, cultural competence, multiculturalism, and interculturality are among the concepts that have vied for normativity and/or been viewed as successive phases or levels of response to difference.[65]

Here I will adopt "difference" as an umbrella term spanning a wide spectrum of diversity.[66] Over the years, the range of categories recognized under the difference umbrella has expanded. Race, ethnicity, culture, language, age, gender, sexual orientation, disability, and religion constitute only a partial list, and some of these would not have been on every list 20 years ago. Much of substance and value has been written, both descriptively and normatively, about responding to difference in the helping professions and in pastoral care and supervision.[67] My principal aim here is to trace an ethical evolution in normative approaches to difference.

One of the most significant steps toward addressing difference helpfully has been a gradual and widespread recognition that any dominant culture is indeed a culture among others—one that *participates in* difference—and not a normative baseline in relation to which all difference is defined or judged. This recognition has affected the traditional, dominant subculture of supervision (racially "white," ethnically "Euro-American," in gendered terms "patriarchal," religiously "Christian").[68] The gradual turn to "cultural humility" as an aspiration for members of the dominant professional subculture has begun to transform consciousness and change conduct, albeit slowly and incompletely.[69] So, too, has broad adoption of interculturality as a normative framework to define outcomes that pastoral care, pastoral counseling, and pastoral supervision should seek in addressing difference.[70]

FROM "DO NO HARM" TO ANTI-OPPRESSIVE PRACTICE

If the "do no harm" principle is ethically fundamental to supervisory practice, early awareness of the need for more "sensitive" responses to cultural difference was a tacit expression of this principle. Calls for sensitivity to difference and efforts to "accommodate" it sought to minimize the immediate harms inflicted by insensitivity and disrespect. They also tended to assume and preserve the norms and power of the dominant culture. Further, in practice the need for greater sensitivity to difference was often acknowledged only after wrong was done and harm had ensued.

Gradually, the field of pastoral care and counseling and its supervisors realized that avoiding such harm required more than ad hoc situational recognition of the potential for (or the reality of) insensitivity, the disrespect it conveyed, and the harm it might inflict. Supervisors needed to take positive and proactive steps to understand cultures different from their own and anticipate issues and situations that might require informed, congruent responses to difference. It was not enough to *seek* to avoid harm or even to refrain from known harmful behaviors. As one author put it, "The potential to harm a client or supervisee is enormous when the practitioner does not understand his or her cultural world"— irrespective of the supervisor's good intentions.[71] Therefore, supervisors needed to educate themselves about the cultural world of supervisees. Personal empathy had also to be cultural empathy.[72]

The no-harm injunction could not be fulfilled, in other words, simply by *refraining* from certain known harmful behaviors. The principle of doing no harm was, in effect, evolving into a norm of *non-oppressive practice*. This norm served the larger principle of *justice* (by recognizing disparity of power) and also began to be associated with *competence* in supervision. Avoiding harm through active efforts to understand cultures—and to recognize the log one's own culture placed in one's eye—could serve "the urgent need for social justice in our multicultural society."[73] Put another way, avoiding harm in one's supervision meant becoming a moral agent who did not inflict or intensify the further injustice of oppression—a social and political reality that creeps insidiously into individual behavior, even that of well-meaning professionals.

The next step, ethically speaking, may be described as a further move from non-oppressive practice to what Hawkins and Shohet call *anti-oppressive practice*. Anti-oppressive practice is constituted by particular anti-oppressive practices that embody it. Among such practices are supervisors' active efforts to help supervisees recognize, attend to, and address "past and current oppressive experiences."[74] The ultimate purpose is to equip supervisees to attend to these issues with their various clients and, of course, to avoid *inflicting* harm in the process. But helping supervisees attend to *their own* experiences with oppression—on whichever side of the oppression they may have been—is clearly part of this process.

This approach is *anti*-oppressive because it seeks to heal wounds or, to put it politically, to counteract the *effects* of oppression. Such efforts also have a preventive component: equipping the person to recognize, cope with, resist, and/or otherwise creatively respond to oppressive structures and forces as these are encountered now and in the future. In this process, disparities of power are not only recognized, but addressed in both client and supervisory relationships for the client's/student's own sake and for the sake of learning. Supervisory virtues of courage (to broach these issues, for example) and openness—owning the authority of the supervisory role as a useful *instrument* for raising power questions[75]—can support this process.

But true anti-oppressive practice will also seek to address oppression at its root. For the pastoral care community and its supervisors, legislative or community advocacy has sometimes provided a "macro" avenue to address structural forms of oppression that inflict the wounds these professionals encounter in their daily practice.[76] At a "micro" level, supervisors who double as administrators or managers might facilitate "courageous conversations" about possible oppressive practices in their settings.[77] These supervisors might, in turn, capitalize on their activities and experience as both leaders and supervisors—a positive side of the "dual-role" phenomenon—to create educational opportunities in supervision (see "What We Teach").[78]

CONCERNS ABOUT EDUCATIONAL INTEGRITY

The relative success of supervisory efforts to exemplify and encourage anti-oppressive practice, especially in CPE programs and peer groups, has surfaced concerns about unintended consequences. One author suggests that *how* these efforts are carried out may threaten other educational and ethical values long prized in CPE. Have attempts to provide welcoming space and foster cross-cultural inclusiveness in CPE emphasized the "commonality" of diverse persons and groups and creation of a stable holding environment, at the expense of the constructive "confrontation" that has long characterized CPE?[79] This worry suggests a larger fear that CPE may lose or has lost, its integrity—its "voice"—as an educational process. In this scenario, creating a larger tent for a diverse population of persons and cultures might inadvertently be leading CPE to compromise its once-distinctive educational product.[80]

At its best, CPE as relational learning and process education has helped students learn from honest expression and exploration of difference, not least in the supervised tension of conflict and disagreement. Often it has been *through* that tension that the most powerful (and dearest-won) insights have emerged, leading students to new perspectives, skills, and inner strength. Can CPE still (or once again) have it both ways and not settle for less? Can the "voice" of CPE as a learning process find continued (or renewed) expression through confrontation and constructive—"transformative"—engagement[81] while retaining recent gains in openness, hospitality, and inclusion in its emerging multicultural reality?

Some might fear that raising such questions will jeopardize the hard-won progress toward anti-oppressive practice that has recently been made in CPE.[82] But perhaps progress in this area has been sufficiently internalized and consolidated to permit fruitful consideration of dissenting views and dissonant values. In the end, the CPE community will have to ascertain the aptness of these concerns and the wisdom of considering them seriously. Yet they may point the way to an ethically enhanced integration of "old" and "new" in CPE.

ANTI-OPPRESSIVE LEARNING OPPORTUNITIES: THE CONGREGATIONAL SETTING

Some specific opportunities in the field education context to instill anti-oppressive perspectives across cultures and develop a level of skill to act on them involve lesbian, gay, bisexual, and transgender (LGBT) persons and issues. Sometimes a LGBT ministry student enters a congregational context and the student's sexual orientation becomes a focus of congregational attention, perhaps a contentious issue the field supervisor is unprepared to address. Field education directors can provide resources to help site supervisors support LGBT students and enable their congregations to engage the students constructively.[83] Such situations may present unexpected opportunities for parishes to be not just "field ed" *settings*, but true "teaching parishes"[84] and *learning* parishes in the process.[85]

WHAT WE TEACH

As the preceding discussion suggests, "ethics and supervision" encompasses not only ethical *conduct* in the supervisory relationship and process, but also the ethical *content* that supervisors seek to convey. Undoubtedly the most effective "teaching" by supervisors is through the example they set and the behavior they model. There can, for example, be many opportunities for supervisors to exemplify anti-oppressive practice in their supervision. "Practice what you teach" and "walk the talk" are relevant slogans—conduct consistent with content matters. But so does the content itself. What ethical understandings and related practices do supervisors in CPE, pastoral counseling, theological field education, and spiritual direction want their students to "come away with"? What ethical content do they seek to instill didactically and/or by modeling?

These content questions encompass issues endemic to supervisory and clinical/ministerial practice itself and issues that are substantially a function of the *context* in which ministry takes place. The former issues are typically grouped under the heading "professional ethics" and a number of the professional laundry list issues named above are now identified subjects for specific teaching and curricular attention. Often it is now *expected* that supervisors and programs will address them. In AAPC, academic curricula required for certification at various levels are to include coursework that specifically addresses ethical issues.[86] An ACPE ethics curriculum for supervisory students has been developed and competence in the "understanding and application" of "professional and organizational ethics" is now an expectation for new supervisors.[87]

Issues more specific to particular ministry contexts, such as healthcare or congregational settings, often offer significant opportunities for supervisors to incorporate additional ethics-related content in their teaching. These issues often (maybe, always) overlap or interface with professional ethics concerns. What follows in this section is not a full listing—let alone a full discussion—of issues in either category, but it may suggest some avenues for further development.

CONFIDENTIALITY WITH CLIENTS

Pastoral counselors preparing for AAPC certification receive instruction, both academic and clinical, in ethical issues that commonly emerge in their setting. Not least of these is the need for confidentiality, which is continually in view. Supervisors are adjured to take seriously the confidentiality both of supervisees *and* of clients discussed in supervision.[88]

What may be overlooked, perhaps in all areas of supervised ministry, is a parallel between the confidentiality that supervisors owe to supervisees and the confidentiality that supervisees may owe their various clients. Supervisees' legitimate desire for confidentiality in the educational setting may provide an opportunity to reflect more deeply on *clients'* needs for and expectations of confidentiality. It could be asked, for example, whether some supervisee uses of clients' communication with them—particularly by chaplains (in various settings) or field education students—treat patients'/parishioners' communications as sensitively as supervisees themselves would desire from their supervisors and colleagues.

Confidentiality concerns can arise and be addressed in other ways. In the chaplaincy field, for example, a provocative recent article questions chaplains' access to patient records as purported members of the healthcare "team."[89] Read in tandem with many CPE students' clinical activities, this article could precipitate important reflection on confidentiality as well as the appropriate role of the chaplain and the chaplain's relationship to other healthcare team members. Supervisors might themselves reflect and invite students to reflect with them, on the rationale for and nature of spiritual care entries in the medical record. Are chaplains' charting different because of the nature of pastoral communications? The relationship among confidentiality, privileged communication, privacy, HIPAA privacy regulations, and the secrecy of the confessional could be part of this discussion,[90] along with standard concerns about exceptions to confidentiality (e.g., possible legal duties to report abuse).[91]

CONCERNS INHERENT IN VARIOUS MINISTRY CONTEXTS

In CPE and theological field education, there is a significant opportunity to teach about ethical concerns that reach beyond professional ethics and are pertinent to the specific ministry context. CPE programs in healthcare settings, for example, have a ready-made opportunity to identify and reflect on bioethical issues that students may see played out every day. Not least of these are concerns about care at the end of life, decision-making by others than the patient, and responding to cultural and religious difference in informed consent discussions and treatment decisions. The process model of education provides adaptable tools, such as verbatim write-ups and group case discussions, that can be co-opted to address these issues. Several articles in the CPE literature have suggested curricular models and educational options for approaching bioethical issues.[92]

In field education, ethical issues arising in congregational ministry could be considered both didactically and as they arise in students' ministerial practice. Field education directors would need to alert field supervisors to this curricular interest, and perhaps to provide or suggest relevant materials. Today's widely discussed concerns about boundaries, abuse, and the creation of safe space in congregations should probably be part of every curriculum.

It still seems that confidentiality questions specific to the congregational context often go unrecognized. Not only counseling or counseling-like encounters, but also parishioners' disclosure of personal information such as health problems and hospitalizations, can pose questions for supervisees. What, for example, may—or should not—be said about a parishioner's illness or life problems during the congregational petitions and intercessions in worship? The pastor's fiduciary responsibility as a steward or trustee of information[93] may be considered in relation to specific ministry instances the student is encountering. (Congregationally-oriented ministry students may also use the healthcare context, whether visiting ill congregants during field education or during a CPE unit in the hospital, to reflect on these issues.)

CONTEXTUAL ISSUES: ETHICS AROUND SUPERVISION

The issues considered in the previous section arise largely within pastoral and supervisory practice and/or in the specific ministry context where pastoral care and supervision take place. The issues discussed in this section concern institutional and organizational contexts, some macro and some micro, that affect supervision or its horizon of attention. These concerns might be said to constitute "ethics *around* supervision." They intertwine with issues considered earlier, as those discussions have suggested (e.g., issues addressed in organizational codes of ethics or those involving seminary-congregation relationships).

A number of these contextual concerns involve CPE. Some arise specifically in the administration of CPE programs; others reflect a local organizational context such as the institutions or agencies in which supervised education takes place.[94] Still others reflect issues in macro-organizational contexts, (e.g., concerns arising within professional accrediting or certifying bodies or in relationships between them).[95]

In approaching these issues, one premise alluded to earlier as a feature of anti-oppressive practice bears clear articulation here. Supervisors (and pastoral practitioners, generally) are well advised to cultivate a critical perspective on practices and statements of institutions and organizations with which they are associated. There is value in a capacity "to abandon the assumption that social structures, the state, healthcare organizations, church structures, and congregations are necessarily correct."[96] Nurturing a sense that things ethical are not always what they seem, as supervisors routinely do in other psychological, cultural, and spiritual matters, will enhance the educational repertoire and help students expand the virtuous professional inclination to look beneath the surface of appearances.

RECRUITING AND SELECTING STUDENTS

The process of recruiting and selecting students for CPE programs, especially for summer units of training, can present ethical challenges. In recruitment, competition between CPE programs in some areas is intense when multiple training programs have student "slots" to fill. Programs seek "critical mass" for their peer groups. Many, especially hospital programs, use summer students to enhance "coverage" in their spiritual care programs. These realities can raise some of the informed consent and exploitation concerns discussed earlier, as well as broader questions of respectful treatment in communication about programs. Is there, for example, "truth in advertising" about programs, their opportunities, and their requirements? Are costs, stipends (if any), and service demands disclosed and accurately represented? Certainly, principles that promote sound informed consent or right-to-know processes and non-exploitative practices should guide programs' and supervisors' approach to these concerns.

But there may also be inter-program questions such as integrity and fairness in relationships between CPE centers, programs, and supervisors when the number of potential students is limited and competition is high. Students often have multiple options for summer units of CPE. Like other consumers, they are likely to look for what they consider the best deal. Favorable start and end dates, lower fees, availability of stipends, minimal travel, the most or best perceived educational resources, reputational excellence, healthcare benefits, and favorable educational benefit/service demand ratios, may all play a role in students' choice of programs when multiple options are available. In a buyer's market, seminary students may be reluctant to "commit" according to centers' timetables for acceptance of invitations to enroll.

CPE programs and their sponsoring organizations have legitimate interests—needs and goals, informed by institutional missions—that rightly affect supervisors' decisions and actions. Integrity and respect for students' rights and interests, expressed through informed consent processes and non-exploitative practices, should take precedence over programs' self-interest in the event of an actual conflict.[97] Indeed, competition between centers can be salutary if it leads centers to upgrade programs and perhaps treat students more considerately. So long as programs' educational integrity and value for students is not compromised (e.g., by relaxing standards in order to attract students), such competition-generated programmatic changes can be a positive development.

Similarly, CPE centers and sponsoring institutions may pursue legitimate self-interest in competing with other centers for students. However, competing centers often recognize that it makes sense to cooperate. They may establish common schedules, deadlines, and practices for receiving applications, conducting interviews, extending invitations to preferred applicants, and expecting responses from invitees. Insofar as such collaboration helps them administer programs, does not operate to students' detriment, and even leads to program improvement, there seems little reason to criticize it.

If, however, competition is intense and centers are driven to compete "hard" by withholding information about their programs' calendars, engaging in deceptive practices with one another, or excluding certain competing centers from a collaborative arrangement, they may violate norms of integrity or somewhat more ambiguous expectations of collegiality. In particular, compromising fulfillment of accreditation standards—e.g, by shortening units to the bare minimum number of required hours—may raise the question of educational integrity if the sole rationale is to compete successfully for students. The structure of programs and arrangements with students should not undermine—indeed, should enhance—the reputation of CPE for *both* hospitality and rigor.

When it comes to student selection, especially in summer units of CPE, programs may feel pressured—by seminaries or by seminarians' limited opportunities to "take" required CPE units—to give open program slots to seminary students. But what about other applicants, such as local clergy? Is it fair, particularly if other applicants have arguably superior qualifications, to admit seminarians first?

The practice of preferring seminarians seems to be defensible, *so long as* this potential basis for admissions is made clear from the outset to all applicants. In light of the qualified but real legitimacy of program self-interest, as noted above, those who administer the program should have latitude to realize a range of values in student selection. Accommodating seminarians (and the desires of seminary stakeholders) can be a way of realizing these values. As long as programs and supervisors do not falsely claim that "merit selection" is a sole criterion of student acceptance, it seems reasonable and not unfair to select students in this fashion. What is necessary from an "informed consent" perspective is openness and truthful disclosure about the use of non-merit selection criteria. Non-seminarians may of course wish it were different, and may feel they have been denied a fair chance at participation in the program. Further, if it appears that no non-seminarians will be admitted because of a glut of acceptable semi-narian applicants, other applicants should be promptly apprised of this reality.

CERTIFYING COMPETENCE

Assuring supervisory competence through standards that establish minimum criteria of competence, and educating would-be supervisors to meet those criteria, is a major preoccupation of professional organizations in pastoral counseling and CPE.[98] In these organizations, perhaps in ACPE most of all, certification is a rite of passage marked by a series of specific, anxiety-producing rituals. Every CPE supervisor seems to have "war stories" and the remembered pain to prove them from his or her journey through the certification process. Few supervisors pass through unscathed, i.e., without being denied at least once in a committee appearance before a certifying body or delayed because a required theory paper did not "pass" its readers.

Certification raises ethical concerns because candidates can feel unfairly or disrespectfully treated, because certain boundaries are not always maintained, because failures of cultural sensitivity or understanding affect committee processes and decisions, and because certification processes are inherently situations of unequal power that may result in oppressive practice. These concerns are, in turn, questions of organizational as well as professional ethics because the certifying organizations are responsible for the ethical soundness of both standards and processes. Certification committees and their members, for example, are not independent agents but represent NACC, ACPE, or AAPC.

It is impossible here to discuss in detail the ethical nooks and crannies of certification, so I will concentrate on what I consider a few key dimensions of this process. First, certification as a pastoral supervisor has a significant and inescapable subjective component.[99] Even sensitive certification committee members with an evident capacity for self-criticism can perceive a committee process as fair and even hospitable to the candidate, while the candidate—whether or not successful in the appearance—offers a far different, much less affirming perspective on the same meeting.[100] Perceptions of fairness and respectfulness in committee processes may inevitably be characterized by such differences and there may be no clear way either to resolve the difference or to judge between the characterizations. The difference in roles (and numbers), and the power differential, between candidates and committees is surely an ingredient in this reality.

AAPC stands out among certifying organizations for apparent attempts to ameliorate negative dynamics associated with this power disparity (although it should be noted that AAPC recognizes and/or certifies pastoral counselors at multiple levels, not only pastoral counselors who supervise).[101] These mitigating efforts have included basing certification decisions more explicitly on approval of materials by committee members *prior* to the certification interview, identifying certification committee appearances as "consultations," and seeking to create a more hospitable tone for the interviews themselves.[102] For certifiable membership categories it is nevertheless true that, after the "consultation" interview with the candidate, certification committees make recommendations to grant or withhold certification.[103]

Second, ethical concerns about certification reach beyond what happens in committees or in the process of evaluating candidates' materials. Certification as a supervisor in pastoral counseling or CPE is typically a lengthy and arduous process. As one CPE supervisor put it, certification is "costly for [the] student and family, [and the] institution and needs to be supported and requires fortitude."[104] Much is required: not only the candidate's perseverance and commitment, but multiple forms of investment by many, often including the candidate's employer. To be justifiable, this investment must be "worth it," not only for its benefits to the candidate or other stakeholders, but also as a reasonable response to ethically defensible requirements imposed by the certifying organization.

Supervisory certification typically aims to protect supervisees from poor or harmful practice, establish a strong probability that the new supervisor will competently facilitate learning, fulfill regulatory requirements, bring a worthy new colleague into the profession's fold, and/or—indirectly—promote the good of and minimize harm to future ministry clients.[105] Certification establishes, or seeks to establish, abilities to practice consistent with a minimum threshold of competence. It cannot *guarantee* such competence in practice, let alone assure performance "over and above" the baseline, but it can serve a "gatekeeping" function as protector of this baseline.[106]

The fact that supervisors in CPE and pastoral counseling work in depth, even quasi-therapeutically, with supervisees and assist them to work in depth with others,[107] justifies a rigorous supervisory education process with rigorous standards of competence and a correspondingly rigorous process to certify competence. It does *not* justify excessive arduousness or a lengthier process than is necessary to achieve and verify this level of competence. Fortitude is a legitimate prerequisite of certification; heroism is not.

As for the process of certification, particularly in committee appearances, one CPE supervisor has sketched an "ethic of justice" appropriate to this process. This ethic begins with a norm of hospitality, reflecting a "hermeneutic of community" in contrast to older models characterized by a "hermeneutic of suspicion." Further, evaluation of candidates should consistently focus on what is relevant to *professional functioning* and should respect personal boundaries by avoiding undue attention to extraneous considerations. A related principle of respect for "various cultural and personality expressions" in assessing competence further supports the focus on professional functioning.[108]

This last norm may also be seen, however, as baseline guidance for *relational* treatment during the interview, not merely a criterion guiding evaluation itself. Indeed, this norm can and perhaps should extend beyond "respect," in the limited sense of "tolerance" or even "acceptance," to an active desire and effort to engage and understand the candidate's "cultural and personality expressions" and their potential positive role in the candidate's professional functioning.

In the real world, it may be inevitable that the certification process will sometimes be "painful and unfair."[109] Fortunately, reflection on the negative experiences and efforts to improve the process may bear redemptive fruit by reducing untoward impacts and strengthening the professional community.[110] But a redemptive outcome does not justify pain and unfairness, though it may mitigate one or both. And nothing can justify the unmitigated continuation of identifiable process problems that yield, even occasionally, injustice and disrespect in the certification ritual.

Even so, a complicating reality of "human nature" and the certification power dynamic should be acknowledged: it is generally easier for those who have "made it" to accept the process's shortcomings and to lack urgency about remediating it than it is for those are have not (yet) succeeded in it. It is true that pain and unfairness—and certainly perceptions of unfairness—in a subjective process so highly charged as certification cannot be eradicated like smallpox. These may have to be lived with, but never complacently—particularly by those who have successfully negotiated the certification process they now administer. "You shall not oppress a stranger; you know the heart of a stranger, for you were strangers in the land of Egypt" (Ex. 23:9 [RSV]).

WHY CAN'T OUR ORGANIZATIONS JUST GET ALONG?

Ethical concerns in the context surrounding supervision are also *inter*organizational. For many years there has been growing, and salutary, collaboration among organizations in the fields of pastoral care and supervision.[111] There has also been dissension and even fragmentation.[112] Given such (perhaps inevitable) vicissitudes, it is worthwhile to ask whether there are identifiable ethical requirements that should characterize relationships between these organizations. A situation drawn from recent interorganizational history within CPE offers some grist for reflection on this question.

In the late 1980s, the College of Pastoral Supervision and Psychotherapy (CPSP) was formed, in part as a reaction to perceived shortcomings of other organizations such as ACPE and AAPC. The relationship between CPSP and ACPE, in particular,[113] has been competitive and sometimes contentious over the years, although a number of CPE supervisors have held simultaneous membership, even dual certification, in CPSP and one or more of the other organizations.[114]

Recently, the tone of the ACPE-CPSP relationship has shifted from competitive/contentious to downright adversarial. In 2006, ACPE's board acted to prohibit ACPE-accredited CPE centers from offering units of CPE accredited by CPSP. At the request of its accrediting body, the board adopted the following motion:

MOTION #43: ACCREDITATION OF DUALLY ALIGNED (CPSP AND ACPE) CENTERS

Whereas, the Accreditation Commission has consistently received reports from students and seminaries of a lack of informed consent about the contrast of ACPE CPE and CPSP CPE;

And whereas, the Accreditation Commission has experienced a lack of consistent application of the program standards of CPSP CPE programs;

And whereas, the Accreditation Commission finds a lack of transparency with the organization of CPSP, its curriculum processes;

And whereas, the Accreditation Commission has received reports of ACPE CPE centers who hire CPE Supervisors who have membership in both organizations being dropped from the ACPE roster and offering only CPSP CPE after telling the hospital administration the CPSP CPE is "cheaper";

And whereas, the Accreditation Commission has received reports of students being offered both CPSP and ACPE units at the same time, but being told that the ACPE units are more expensive and therefore they would have to pay a higher tuition fee. The student is then given the choice of which they would like to be granted;

And whereas, the Accreditation Commission works diligently to uphold the standards required by the DOE accreditation. This is stated on the certificate we give to each ACPE CPE center. When an ACPE supervisor offers CPSP within the same center, it is the Accreditation Commission's belief that this gives the appearance that both organizations have the same rigorous process.

Therefore, the Accreditation Commission requests the ACPE, Inc., Board of Representatives to immediately establish a policy that no ACPE, Inc. accredited center can conduct units of CPSP CPE.

The motion:
Move that the ACPE, Inc. Board of Reps immediately establish a policy that no accredited ACPE, Inc. Center conduct units of CPSP CPE.[115]

Several reasons given for this action are substantial: 1) claims that deceptive practices misled students about which organization was accrediting a given unit of CPE and violated norms of "informed consent," 2) organizational failure by CPSP to oversee and enforce its accreditation standards consistently, 3) "reports" that some CPSP supervisors at dually accredited institutions acted to undermine and terminate the institution's affiliation with ACPE, and 4) alleged actions amounting to disloyalty and perhaps a certain duplicity by CPSP supervisors who persuaded students to enroll in CPSP units of CPE on the basis of lower cost.

The board also alleges a general failure of "transparency" by CPSP and a parasitic tendency of supervisors at dually accredited centers to use ACPE's reputation for quality, reflected by its hard-earned U.S. Department of Education (DOE) accreditation,[116] to legitimize CPSP programs. An underlying, pervasive complaint cited by ACPE leaders in a cover letter to supervisors was that the dual-accreditation relationships resulted in "concerns and confusions" and even "growing frustrations" for consumers of the CPE educational product, including seminaries and judicatories.[117] Following adoption of the prohibition, every ACPE center was required to "declare and report," over multiple official signatures, which accrediting organizations' brands of CPE it offered.[118]

Besides unseemliness,[119] one might ask, what is the ethical problem posed by this internecine conflict? The most significant concern may not lie in the organizations' failure to "play nice" or talk "adult-to-adult,"[120] preferable as one or the other might be, or even in the serious charges made by one organization against the other. Of course organizations' or their representatives' displays of disloyalty, duplicity, or disrespect, and their failure to uphold standards appear reprehensible. And one must believe that the spectacle of "religious" professional bodies duking it out has brought some disrepute to the field of pastoral supervision.[121] But the problem also lies in the impact that this organizational conflict and associated decisions and practices have on people and institutions served by and depending on the supervisory endeavor—all its "consumers" or, better, stakeholders. In particular, are some students poorly served or even harmed by organizations' conflict-driven actions, such as this ACPE board decision? Moreover, are seminaries, judicatories, and institutions that sponsor (even pay for) CPE hindered in their efforts to be educational partners for students' and learning's sake? Are they perhaps further confused, even alienated, by the interorganizational set-to? The ramifications of the conflict and any organizational action based on it must be carefully considered in light of these questions and potential impacts. Facile appeals to student welfare or stakeholder protection to justify sweeping decisions significantly affecting educational relationships—and stakeholder trust—do not suffice.

Finally, it should be asked whether professional organizations' decisions exemplify their publicly espoused ethical principles or codes and set the moral tone those principles aim to create. Has an organization used its power and authority in ethically nuanced ways that display integrity? To take the example at hand, the rationale justifying draconian measures and sanctions like those imposed by ACPE needs to be clear and well supported.

The language of the motion initiating the prohibition is, unfortunately, dubious in this regard. While the concerns it expresses seem well worth considering and investigating—and surely have a history not captured in any "whereas" clause—the rationale and the evidence it offers do not adequately support the restriction and the punitive measures that are enacted. A broad allegation of lack of "transparency," for example, seems flimsy grounds for specific action, however rooted the allegation may be in a history of frustration not articulated in the motion.

Similarly, the statement that the ACPE accrediting body has "experienced" inconsistency in CPSP's application of its standards accuses without demonstrating. In the end, it appears that ACPE leaders also felt the "frustrations" their board ascribed to CPE consumers—frustrations that may have resulted in a less than measured use of organizational power.

To be sure, the purported conduct of supervisors who play CPSP and ACPE accreditation against one another seems egregious. If verified, however, it might most obviously merit sanctions *against the individual supervisors* by one or both organizations. It would be indefensible for supervisors to resort to manipulative bait-and-switch tactics, whether with students or with institutions (even if the latter might be presumed to know better). ACPE should have some authority to take some action against offending supervisors who are both CPSP and ACPE certified if there is clear evidence of the misconduct in question.

In reality, the ACPE board might have unfairly penalized some supervisors (e.g., ACPE-only supervisors in dually accredited institutions offering both kinds of programs). Further, the procedural requirement that each center provide documentation of the brands of CPE it offers, over *three* signatures—including that of an advisory committee chair who may be a community volunteer—drags third parties into the internecine conflict while intimating a lack of trust in the integrity of other signatories (supervisor and administrator). Whatever the provocation, one might ask whether this action and the language justifying it are faithful to ACPE's espoused identity and values. Does this action, or its rationale, cast ACPE as an organization all members can take pride in, or one that institutions, seminaries, and judicatories should rely on for equanimity in judgment and decision making?

It is important to protect the integrity of educational processes, safeguard institutional and even governmental recognition, and—above all—protect students and assure "informed consent" in CPE. If, however, an organization teaches the importance of knowing how one's motivations and feelings affect pastoral practice then appears organizationally to act out of unmodulated frustration, the incongruity deserves notice, reflection, and perhaps some organizational soul-searching.

THE ETHICAL FUTURE

In recent years, ethics has been on the radar screen in pastoral supervision as never before. Unfortunately it remains true that much ethical attention is occasioned by and focused on problems involving blatant misconduct. But awareness of and nuanced response to issues posed by difference, power disparities, and multiple ministry contexts has also grown. There is no good reason to believe this trend will cease or diminish.

As for the future, I believe that two significant challenges (and, concurrently, significant opportunities) merit special attention. One is the continuing question of "prophetic" ministry in pastoral/spiritual care. What is appropriate participation by pastoral supervision in recognizing and addressing relevant prophetic issues? How do questions of social justice and ministry to vulnerable populations affected by injustice become better integrated in both pastoral care and pastoral supervision? The literature and the questions considered by Frances McWilliams continue to suggest significant points of departure.[122]

The second challenge and opportunity is the evolution of the field (profession?) of chaplaincy, particularly in healthcare—a field intimately tied to much pastoral supervision and a key professional grounding for many pastoral supervisors. Recent publications have proposed or attempted to describe an emerging understanding of healthcare chaplaincy. Pastoral supervision occurring in the healthcare setting and/or attempting to equip supervisees to become healthcare chaplains may be profoundly affected by the shift in the identity of chaplaincy that is proposed and/or under way. The ethical dimensions of this change are now receiving some attention; the ethical implications for supervision will surely deserve attention as well.[123]

NOTES

1. Chris R. Schlauch, "Functioning as an Ethicist in Pastoral Counseling," *Journal of Supervision and Training in Ministry* (12, 1990), 111-131 and Marie McCarthy and David B. McCurdy, "Introduction," *Journal of Supervision and Training and Ministry* (12, 1990), 106-110.

2. See especially Chris R. Schlauch, *Ibid.* and these articles, all of which also appeared in *Journal of Supervision and Training in Ministry* (12, 1990): Robert Cotton Fite, "Ethical Dimensions of Gender Issues in Supervision," 145-152; Kenneth R. Mitchell, "Ethical Issues in Supervision: Justice, Authority, Equality," 153-161; Karen Lebacqz and Ronald G. Barton, "Power, Intimacy, and Supervision," 162-169; John H. Weston, "Ethics in CPE: A Consumer's Report," 175-183; Terrill L. Gibson, "Justice in Pastoral Practice: The Inadequacies of Both the Legal and Ethical Models," 198-209; Beth Burbank, "Supervision: a Collegial Discernment Process," 210-212; and Dean Williams, "In Praise of Manipulation," 213-216.

3. The third edition was published in 1988. The most recent edition is Gerald Corey, Patrick Callanan, and Marianne Schneider Corey, *Issues and Ethics in the Helping Professions*, 7th ed. (Belmont, CA: Thompson Brooks/Cole, 2007).

4. For a consensus statement of several professional organizations on the meaning of spiritual care and the role of chaplains in providing such care, see Larry VandeCreek and Laurel Burton, eds., "A White Paper: Professional Chaplaincy—Its Role and Importance in Healthcare," *Journal of Pastoral Care* (55, No. 1, 2001), 81-97. For a critical appraisal of the terminological shift from "pastoral" to "spiritual" care, see Herbert Anderson's editorial "Spiritual Care: The Power of an Adjective," *Journal of Pastoral Care* (55, No. 5, Fall 2001), 233-237. "Spiritual care" may better convey respect for an interfaith and sometimes "non-religious" spiritual and cultural context. This term has its greatest currency in the chaplaincy field, where ministry typically occurs in interfaith and broadly "spiritual" contexts within settings such as hospital, the military, or correctional facilities.

CPE, in which some form of chaplaincy is usually the clinical ministry students under-take, has also adopted "spiritual care." In this chapter, however, I will generally refer to "pastoral care," "pastoral counseling," and "pastoral supervision" and will large reserve "spiritual care" for specific references to chaplaincy. Certainly "spiritual supervision" would be a nonsensical term. The pastoral counseling field has retained "pastoral" in its professional self-designation (and "spiritual counseling" would suggest a different focus in its ministry). The inclusion in this chapter's purview of theological field education, which takes place largely under Christian seminary auspices, is another consideration tipping the scales toward the use of "pastoral." "Pastoral care" retains the historical ter-minology of a movement and its original grounding in the Christian tradition, indeed "the one-on-one ministry of Jesus" (Joan Hemenway, "The Shifting of the Foundations: Ten Questions Concerning the Future of the Pastoral Care Movement," *Journal of Supervision and Training in Ministry* (20, 2000), 61.) Unfortunately, none of these terms serves as an adequate umbrella for spiritual direction, and I must beg the indulgence of readers with an interest or grounding in that field.

5. A pilot inter-organizational ethics complaint process has also been used jointly by ACPE and APC, http://www.acpe.edu/acroread/Joint_Ethics_Process.pdf.

6. Professional chaplaincy organizations have all adopted or adapted the *Common Code of Ethics for Chaplains, Pastoral Counselors, Pastoral Educators, and Students* (Council on Collaboration, 2004), http://www.professionalchaplains.org/uploadedFiles/pdf/common-code-ethics.pdf. The organizations expect chaplains they certify to be familiar with this code and abide by it.

7. See Maureen Conroy's *Looking into the Well: Supervision of Spiritual Direction* (Chicago: Loyola University Press, 1995), in which the author touches peripherally on ethical issues in supervising spiritual directors, and Dwight Judy, "Wisdom from the Desert: Qualifications for Supervisors of Spiritual Directors," *Journal of Supervision and Training in Ministry* (24, 2004) 70-82.

8. See also Peter Hawkins and Robin Shohet, *Supervision in the Helping Professions*, 3rd ed. (Maidenhead, UK: Open University Press, 2006) 54-55, 144-146.

9. It can even include an exploration of the scope of "ethics" itself, although I will not pursue that possibility here.

10. For a critical yet appreciative perspective, see Russel Stannard, "The Prayer Experiment: Does Prayer Work?" *Second Opinion* (No. 2, January 2000) 26-37.

11. Don S. Browning, "The Pastoral Counselor as Ethicist: What Difference Do We Make?" *Journal of Pastoral Care* (47, No. 6, 1988), 286. Browning's reference to "pre-moral goods" draws on the work of Louis S. Janssen's "Norms and Priorities in a Love Ethics," *Louvain Studies* (6, 1977), 207-238.

12. E. Brooks Holifield, "Ethical Assumptions of Clinical Pastoral Education," *Journal of Pastoral Care* (34, No. 1, March 1980) 39-53. One could argue that the "ethical assumptions" cited by Holifield largely concern what Browning calls premoral goods, and that it was the *conflicts* between those goods that posed the ethical questions for the CPE movement.

13. Mauren Conroy, *Op. cit.*, 13, 34.

14. This reality was noted in the introduction to the 1990 JSTM symposium (McCarthy and McCurdy, *Op. cit.*, 107). More recently, the Spiritual Care Collabora-tive's (formerly the Council on Collaboration) *Common Code of Ethics* seems to lend support to the idea that promoting such premoral and moral goods in an obligation of pastoral and educational practice in the pastoral field. It articulates the claim that code-congruent actions can "bring greater justice, compassion, and healing in the world."

15. Louis S. Janssen, *Op. cit.*, 213.

16. These examples also suggest that *recognizing* the impact of a phenomenon such as cultural difference may create an obligation at least to *try* to respond to it in a better way. Such moral resolve might precede the development or enhancement of our actual capacity to respond.

17. Frances McWilliam's survey of pastoral care literature calling CPE to be "prophetic" tacitly applies this norm to CPE. ("Voices Crying in the Wilderness: Prophetic Ministry in Clinical Pastoral Education," *Journal of Pastoral Care* (51, No. 1, 1997), 37-47.)

18. Robert Fuller, "Rediscovering the Laws of Spiritual Life: The Last Twenty Years of Supervision and Training in Ministry," *Journal of Supervision and Training in Ministry* (20, 2000), 19.

19. For a trenchant critique of CPE's "individualism," see Therese M. Becker, "Individualism and the Invisibility of Monoculturalism/Whiteness: Limits to Effective Clinical Pastoral Supervision," *Journal of Supervision and Training in Ministry* (22, 2002), 4-20.

20. Joan Hemenway, *Op. cit.*, 60.

21. The New England approach to CPE emphasized *formation*, reflecting in part on Richard Cabot's view of professional development as "growth." It implicitly stressed a set of formative values constituting criteria of competent ministry; cultivation of professional relevant virtues, and the overcoming of corresponding deficits of character that impeded competence. The development of these virtues and related capacities for ministry required considerable effort in a long-term process. Perhaps this mix of New England virtues was qualified by the New Yorkers' analytically driven sense that liberating the self to "be" competent was itself a de facto moral development process, since it freed the minister's personhood from the shackles of "moralism" with its needless, guilt-inducing "shoulds."

22. Peter Hawkins and Robin Shohet, *Op. cit.*, 55.

23. Robert Springer Loewy contend that chaplains may inflict harm through their handling of patient information, e.g. by not adhering to "strict confidentiality" and instead entering information gained through pastoral interaction into the medical record ("Healthcare and the Hospital Chaplain," *Medscape General Medicine* (9, No. 1, 2006), 59. Clearly, both in medicine and in pastoral care the prevailing norm of beneficence—doing something positive for those served—has not sufficed to protect those served from harm (of many sorts). Neither, for that matter, has the norm of love. Love is often understood, like beneficence, as imposing an obligation to "do good." But often this understanding has not recognized possible unintended consequences of our "goodness" nor yielded sufficient protection against them. Love not only does good things for others, according to the apostle Paul, but also (first of all?) "does no wrong to a neighbor" (Romans 13:10). Here "wrong" seems to encompass "harm."

24. Tom L. Beauchamp and James F. Childress, *Principles of Biomedical Ethics*, 6th edition, (New York: Oxford University Press, 2008), 12-13.

25. Peter Hawkins and Robin Shoshet, *Op. cit.*, 54-55. Their set of principles largely reflects ethical standards meant to guide direct work with clients; the authors adapt them slightly for the supervisory context.

26. It should be noted that Hawkins and Shoshet supplement their list of principles with a recommended case analysis framework for use when ethical concerns actually arise in practice (see pages 55, 144, 146; the case analysis framework is adapted from

Michael Carroll, *Counselling Supervision: Theory, Skills and Practice* [London: Cassells, 1996].)

27. Besides Corey et al., *Op. cit.*, readers may consult useful symposia in recent volumes of the *Journal of Supervision and Training in Ministry* on sexuality and supervision (Vol. 21 [2001]), multiculturality (Vol. 22 [2002]), and competence and certification (Vol. 24 [2004]).

28. It should be noted that both ACPE and NACC have recently sought to ground their approaches to misconduct in a "restorative justice" framework, which aims to repair harm and restore community rather than simply to punish. See Anne Underwood's paper, *Restorative Justice as a Model for the ACPE Ethics Process*, www.acpe.edu/ethics_anne.htm.

29. See Raymond J. Lawrence, "Cooking the Books," *Journal of Supervision and Training in Ministry* 21 (2001), 123f. See also Corey et al., *Op. cit.*, 206, 304 (although clearly they support an absolute prohibition on sexual relationships with current clients).

30. Raymond Lawrence, *Ibid.*, 122f.

31. Gerald Corey et al., *Op. cit.*, 206.

32. See Duane Parker, "Sexuality and Supervision: A Complex Issue," *Journal of Supervision and Training in Ministry* (21, 2001), 37-45; Denise G. Haines, "Desire, Intimacy, and Attraction: The Erotic Nature of CPE Supervision," *Journal of Supervision and Training in Ministry* (21, 2001), 46-65; and Patricia Davis, "Supervision and Sexuality," *Journal of Supervision and Training in Ministry* (21, 2001), 126-131.

33. See Denise G. Haines, *Ibid.*, passim, and Davis, *Ibid.*, 129f.

34. See, for example, Fitchett and Johnson's comments in their groundbreaking study of sexual conduct in CPE: George Fitchett and Marilyn Johnson, "Intimate Sexual Contact in the CPE Supervisor-Student Relationship," *Journal of Supervision and Training in Ministry* (21, 2001), 109.

35. Denise G. Haines, *Op. cit.*, 48.

36. Duane Parker, *Op. cit.*, 43.

37. Abraham Maslow appeals to renunciation when he describes the group leader's responsibility, in certain situations, to forgo an indulgent transparency: "'The good leader must keep his feelings to himself, let them burn out his own guts, and not seek the relief of catharting them to followers who cannot at that time be helped by an uncertain leader.'" ("Notes on Unstructured Groups at Lake Arrowhead," unpublished mimeograph, 1962, cited in Irvin D. Yalom, *The Theory and Practice of Group Psychotherapy*, 3rd edition (New York: Basic Books, 1985), 223.)

38. Patricia Davis, *Op. cit.*, 131n.

39. Gerald Corey et al., *Op. cit.*, 299.

40. George Fitchett and Marilyn Johnson, *Op. cit.*, 90.

41. *Ibid.*, 90, 92. Lawrence sees this last outcome as an ethically relevant counterpoint to the "politically-correct view" condemning intimate sexual contact between supervisor and student (121).

42. Gerald Corey et al., *Op. cit.*, 206. And this is not even to ask pragmatically what is in the prudent *supervisor's* professional self-interest. Some have disputed the premise that supervisees are in fact in a vulnerable role or in a more vulnerable position than the supervisor (see Raymond J. Lawrence, *Op. cit.*, 123f.)

43. Connie Kleingartner, "Maintaining Healthy Boundaries, *Journal of Supervision and Training in Ministry* (21, 2001), 80-82.

44. *Ibid.*, 82.

45. Jeffrey Mahan, "Problematic Supervision in Field Education," *Journal of Supervision and Training in Ministry* (17, 1996), 61. Mahan notes that, unfortunately, such structural solutions are often financially infeasible.

46. Robert T. O'Gorman, "Supervising within the Walls: Problematic Supervision in Ministerial Education," *Journal of Supervision and Training in Ministry* (17, 1996), 71f.

47. Given this commentary by the Ethics Commission, it is noteworthy that Harper's paper, also posted on the ACPE website with apparent organizational sanction, cites approvingly these anti-union comments by the National Right to Work Committee: "'While some students may have Marxist dreams that they are workers, rather than students, who will be in the vanguard of an economic revolution when the workers of the world unite, the fact remains that they are students and not employees and have little commonality of interest with most employees'" (Harper, *Interns*).

48. To its credit, the ACPE Professional Ethics Commission recognized the issue in an "exploitation" section of its *Sample Ethics Curriculum* and acknowledged a need for balance between "service" and students' "educational needs" in CPE programs. http://www.acpe.edu/pec_cirr.htm#exploit.

49. The 2005 *ACPE Accreditation Manual* recognizes this distinction in its guidance to accreditors for evaluating statements of student responsibilities (commentary on Standard 304.7; http//:www.acpe.edu/acroread/2005_accreditation_manual.pdf). I am grateful to Teresa Snorton of ACPE for noting this distinction (phone conversation, September 8, 2008), and also for forwarding examples of current statements of student rights.

50. Gerland Corey et al., *Op. cit.*, (352-354) reproduce a detailed "Supervisee's Bill of Rights" (Maria A. Giordano, Michael K. Altekruse, and Carolyn W. Kern [unpublished manuscript, 2000]).

51. Perhaps it should be added that rights are not only "serious" but *justified* claims that people or groups can make on other individuals or groups (Tom L. Beauchamp and James F. Childress, *Op. cit.*, 350).

52. Maria A. Giordano et al., cited in Gerald Corey et al., *Op. cit.*, 352.

53. It must be noted that the profound protections of the rights delineated in the founding United States documents were not extended to all the people of the new nation. Yet they could later be called upon as an unfulfilled promise and were so evoked by Martin Luther King, Jr., and others. Perhaps the most well known example of a statement of human rights is the 1948 *Universal Declaration of Human Rights*, www.un.org/Overview/rights.html.

54. Gerald Corey et al., *Op. cit.*, speak of "responsibilities," perhaps as an alternative to the "rights" list of Maria A. Giordano et al., *Op. cit.*, 354f.

55. See the "expectations of the supervisory relationship" in Maria A. Giordano et al., "Supervisee's Bill of Rights," in Gerald Corey et al., *Op. cit.*, 352.

56. This is true in practice despite a stated "specific right" of the CPE student to be "fully informed of the supervisor's approach," according to *Professional Ethics Resources for CPE Supervisory Education*, http://www.acpe.edu/pec2.htm.

57. Gerald Corey et al., *Op. cit.*, note this correlation particularly in their discussion of group work: "The fact that groups can be powerful catalysts for personal change means that they are also risky" (472). *Mutatis mutandis*, something similar can be said about the power—and the ethical significance—of supervisory relationships in CPE and other supervised ministry programs.

58. It is also important to recognize "consent" as, de facto, an ongoing process, and to acknowledge that students could have reservations about "going along with" a current or proposed supervisory tack that may not have been anticipated earlier (see Dean Wil-

liams, *Op. cit.*, 215f., for an excellent description of this ongoing process without specific recourse to "consent" language).

59. See D. Eugene Kraus, *Confidentiality in the United Church of Christ: Some Theological Reflections* (Cleveland: Parish Life and Leadership Ministry Team, United Church of Christ, 2002), 2.

60. An example is an Illinois statute that permits but does not require a physician to notify a spouse of the other spouse's positive HIV test result (410 ILCS 305/9).

61. This issue can be viewed as both a confidentiality issue and a multiple-relationship problem; only the confidentiality aspect is considered here.

62. Pamela D. Couture, "'If in a Safe Land You Fall Down'—Why Evaluations Cause So Much Turmoil and What Supervisors Can Do about It," *Journal of Supervision and Training in Ministry* (12, 1990), 196f.

63. Serge D. Castigliano, "Some Ethical Issues Concerning the Use of Evaluations by Seminaries and Religious Judicatories," *Journal of Supervision and Training in Ministry* (12, 1990), 186, 189.

64. Certification Commission, Association for Clinical Pastoral Education, Inc., *Certification Manual*, 2005, Appendix 5: "Consent Form," http://www.acpe.edu/acroread/2005_certification_manual.pdf. If there are other privacy protections for videotaped students, they are not apparent from the waiver itself or from the organization's accreditation standards. A related gap in confidentiality protections seems to exist in that an ACPE supervisor may export material from a student's "file" that mentions another member of the peer group into that peer's file (Accreditation Commission, *Accreditation Manual*, 2005, Appendix 12: "Guidelines for Student Records," http://www.acpe.edu/acroread/2005_accreditation_manual.pdf.

65. See Gerald Corey et al., *Op. cit.*, 113f., for a glossary of multicultural terminology.

66. In this usage I am following Peter Hawkins and Robin Shohet, *Op. cit.*

67. Peter Hawkins and Robin Shohet's chapter, "Supervision across Difference" (the chapter title appearing on page 104) is a readable effort, written from and largely for a British context, to flesh out the clinical and supervisory reality of "anti-oppressive practice." (Note that in the table of contents this chapter is titled "Working with Difference—Transcultural Supervision"). See also the *JSTM* symposium on multicultural supervision, (Vol. 22, 2002) and Gerald Corey et al., *Op. cit.*, Chapter 4.

68. Although today "race" is not recognized as a legitimate differentiating category by many, de facto it continues to be a functional difference category because it is so perceived, and significant consequences thus follow from its recognition.

69. It was, of course, not always so. I recall vividly some features of the "old" mindset from my experience as a CPE supervisor. When supervisors first began to see a significant influx of students from "other" cultures who did not speak English or share certain Euro-American cultural assumptions (let alone the cultural assumptions of the CPE ethos of the time), the issue was often framed (and felt) as how "we" would "have to accommodate" to "them" and, at the same time, how "we" might get "them" to understand and accept the norms of the CPE culture as "we" understood it. There was often also fascination with cultural difference, which could be attractive in its newness, and thus also openness to learn from it. Even so, the sense of "our" normativity tended to predominate.

70. Kathleen Greider has characterized "interculturality" as fully engaged cross-cultural communication in which intentional maintenance of difference and boundaries blends with "vibrant interrelatedness" and "day-to-day cooperation" (Kathleen J. Greider,

"From Multiculturalism to Interculturality: Demilitarizing the Border Between Personal and Social Dynamics Through Spiritual Receptivity," *Journal of Supervision and Training in Ministry*, (22, 2002), 40-58.)

71. K. Samuel Lee, "A Multicultural Vision for the Practice of Pastoral Supervision and Training," *Journal of Supervision and Training in Ministry* (20, 2000), 114.

72. At the same time is it important, as Peter Hawkins and Robin Shohet point out, for the supervisor *not* to assume that he or she has "understood" the culture of the supervisee (120).

73. K. Samuel Lee, *Op. cit.*, 113.

74. Peter Hawkins and Robin Shohet, *Op. cit.*, 222.

75. *Ibid.*, 111-113. The authors' discussion nicely situates classic "authority issues" in supervision within the dynamics of difference.

76. See Frances McWilliams', *Op. cit.*, impressive 1997 survey of "prophetic" articles from the 1970s to 1990s. Taken together, these articles suggest a still-neglected area of opportunity for education and ethical reflection within pastoral care and supervision, and a continuing need for an active Pastoral Care Network for Social Responsibility or similar entity.

77. This suggestion is in line with comments by Bruce Hartung, who also notes that simply recognizing the institution or organization is not by definition "right" in its perspectives and positions on issues is an important building-block of organizational awareness among pastoral care professionals (Bruce M. Hartung, "The Pastor/Chaplain/Counselor as Organizational Prophet: Reflections on the Role and Function of Pastoral Care in an Organization," *Caring Connections: An Inter-Lutheran Journal for Practitioners and Teachers of Pastoral Care and Counseling* (2, No. 1, Summer 2005), 11.

78. See, for example, Robin Brown-Haithco, "Standing on Holy Ground: The Vocation of Pastoral Supervision," *Journal of Supervision and Training in Ministry* (20, 2000), 103, who recounts a critical juncture in which, as leader of a department, she discovered that the ministry was both "*to* and *within*" the institution—*to* it as a "spiritual entity with a life force and energy." The author incorporated this spiritual and (I would say) ethical discovery into her practice of supervision. See also Bruce M. Hartung, *Op cit.*

79. Timothy A. Thorstenson, "The Stones Cry Out," *Journal of Pastoral Care & Counseling* (60, No. 5, Supplement 2006), 459. It appears that, in raising these questions, Thorstenson does not intend to denigrate or undermine the educational aim, articulated in the ACPE Supervisory CPE curriculum, of "insuring mutual respect for the dignity of persons in the small group process" ("Ethics Education in the Mid-Phase of Supervisory Education," in *Professional Ethics Resources for CPE Supervisory Education*, http://www.acpe.edu/pec2.htm.

80. See Timothy A. Thorstenson, *Op. cit.*, 463. Thorstenson's discussion does not expand his concern as broadly as my formulation here.

81. *Ibid.*, 462.

82. Might such questions be a propos, even if troubling, in other fields of supervised ministry as well?

83. This is the suggestion of Shelley Davis Finson, "Systematic Injustice of Heterosexism in Theological Education," *Journal of Supervision and Training in Ministry* (23, 2003), 95-107. Davis-Finson uses "LGB" rather than "LGBT."

84. Barbara Troxell, "Mutuality and Dialogue in Pastoral Supervision," *Journal of Supervision and Training in Ministry* (20, 2000), 203.

85. Similarly, congregations experiencing division and tension over LGBT issues, including ordination of LGBT persons, can provide a supervisory opportunity to help students pick up on congregants' attitudes and comments and develop options for response to their comments and concerns about LGBT persons and issues. Intentional efforts by field education programs and directors to provide appropriate ministry placements for LGBT students, and to assist field supervisors as needed in supervising the students and addressing congregational responses, can be helpful—and may be vital—to the success of such placements (Shelley Davis-Finson, *Op. cit.*, 102).

86. Among these, according to the AAPC *Membership Standards and Certification Manual*, are "ethical and legal issues," "consequences of prejudice, racism, and other forms of oppression," and the "ethics of professional identity" (Fairfax, VA: American Association of Pastoral Counselors, 2007), 72-73.

87. See Standards 318.6 and 319.1 in the ACPE *Standards Manual*, 2005, http://www.acpe.edu/acroread/2005_standards_manual.pdf. NACC standards touch lightly on central professional ethics issues, and the standards expect chaplain and supervisor conduct consistent with the NACC's code of ethics (which closely follows the *Common Code* of the Spiritual Care Collaborative), but the issues named are not a direct focus of standards for certification or of corresponding standards for accreditation established by the United States Conference of Catholic Bishops Commission on Certification and Accreditation. http://www.usccbcca.org/docs/CPE_Handbook_March_2008.pdf.

88. And pastoral counselors, including supervisees, have a responsibility to remind others—both peers and supervisors—who have access to their clients' information of the "importance" of treating that information confidentially (AAPC *Code of Ethics*, 1994, Principle IV.C, www.aapc.edu/ethics.cfm.)

89. Robert Springer Loewy and Loewy, "Healthcare and the Hospital Chaplain," *Hastings Center Report* (38, No. 6, November-December 2008), 15-33. A just-published set of articles—virtually a symposium—addresses the related question of whether or how hospital chaplaincy is a profession and how to "measure" its outcomes. This issue of the journal, which arrived too late to be given full consideration here, will surely be a resource for supervisors interested in ethical dimensions of chaplaincy and potential implications for supervisory theory and practice.

90. On confidentiality, privileged communication, and the secrecy of the confessional, see D. Eugene Kraus, *Confidentiality in the United Church of Christ, Op. cit.*

91. Potential ethical concerns about conducting spiritual assessments, which have become standard fare in chaplains' practice and spiritual care curricula, might also be considered. What could it mean, for instance, for a patient to give informed consent to a spiritual assessment? What dialogue about this question should chaplains have with patients?

92. Central articles in this literature are Scott W. Hinrichs and William Nelson, "Biomedical Ethics and Clinical Pastoral Education," *Journal of Pastoral Care* (39, No. 3, Fall 1985), 200-207; David B. McCurdy, "Clinical Bioethics Education in Clinical Pastoral Education," *Journal of Supervision and Training in Ministry* (14, 1992-1993), 3-20; and Martin L. Smith and Ronald K. Morgan, "Bioethics Education in a Clinical Pastoral Education Program," *Journal of Pastoral Care* (52, No. 4, Winter 1998), 377-387.

93. See "Stewards of Information, Stewards of Trust," *e-Ethics* (January 2003), 2 and D. Eugene Kraus, *Confidentiality in the United Church of Christ, Op. cit.*

94. One example is the question of what happens to a CPE program and commitments made to students in the event of a significant change in the institution, such as new leadership or financial shortfalls and loss of institutional support for the CPE program.

Regarding the latter, ACPE Standard 301.3 requires each CPE center to devise and share with students a written plan to keep commitments to students in such contingencies; it is not clear, however, that this standard functions as an effective deterrent to institutional program termination practices that result in harm to potential students.

95. Still other concerns grow out of relationships between programs and governmental entities, such as conformity to law and regulation and relationships of a supervisory program, a sponsoring institution, or a professional organization to government entities. In CPE, the Medicare pass-through that helps to fund the continued existence of many programs and labor law governing payment to stipended residents are two examples.

96. Bruce Hartung, *Op. cit.*, 11. This generalization can be extended to labor disputes as well. Both labor and management, including leadership in health and human service organizations, invariably paint union organizing situations in terms they hope will advance their interests. Supervisors in these situations may have an opportunity to address this dynamic as an ethically relevant phenomenon (see David B. McCurdy, "The Chaplain and Labor Relations," *Chaplaincy Today* (23, No. 1, Spring/Summer 2007), 3-10.

97. Leonard J. Weber, *Business Ethics in Healthcare: Beyond Compliance* (Bloomington, IN: Indiana University Press, 2001), 16-19.

98. This preoccupation certainly exists in ACPE, NACC, AAPC, and CPSP (which appends this motto to its organizational name: "A Certifying and Accrediting Community").

99. CPSP appears to make the inevitable subjective dimension a centerpiece of its standards for certification (Standard 240 in "Program Standards for Supervisory CPE," *The Standards of the College of Pastoral Supervision and Psychotherapy*, 2007, http://www.pastoralreport.com/THE_STANDARDS_2007PDF%20for%20web.pdf.

100. Stephen S. Ivy, "The ACPE Certification Review: An Alternative Model," *Journal of Supervision and Training in Ministry* (24, 2004), 18n.

101. See the personal-historical account by Werner Boos, "Personal Reflections on the Formation of a Pastoral Counseling Supervisor," *Journal of Supervision and Training in Ministry* (24, 2004), 44-52. It should be noted that AAPC recognizes and/or certifies pastoral counselors at multiple levels, including non-supervisory categories. Thus, the evolution in its approach to certification encompasses more than certification of pastoral counselors as supervisors.

102. See the AAPC *Membership Standards and Certification Manual* (January 2007), 29 and Appendix N, 83: "Interviews for all certified categories are non-evaluative, non-voting consultations to support the candidate's professional formation."

103. However, committee interviews for Diplomate status (the highest level of AAPC certification) are expressly described in the *Membership Standards and Certification Manual* as "consultative" only.

104. William R. DeLong, *Proceedings of the Summit on Supervisory Education*, (Burnsville, MN: North Central Region of the Association for Clinical Pastoral Education, Inc., 2007), 7.

105. Gerald Corey et al., *Op. cit.*, 339.

106. William R. DeLong, "Enduring Questions," *ACPE Newsletter of the North Central Region* (August 2006), 4.

107. On ethical concerns about maintaining a boundary between supervision and psychotherapy, see the exchange between N. Keith Little, "Supervision: Education or Therapy?" *Journal of Supervision and Training in Ministry* (19, 1998-1999), 147-159

and Stuart A. Plummer, "Response to Little," *Journal of Supervision and Training in Ministry* (19, 1998-1999), 160-162.

108. Stephen S. Ivy, *Op. cit.*, 11. See Warner Boos, *Op. cit.*, 36, regarding an apparent turn toward such a focus in AAPC's certification process.

109. William R. DeLong, "Enduring Questions," *Op. cit.*, 3.

110. *Ibid.* In this respect, efforts to improve the certification process might participate in the "restorative justice" that is the aim of current complaint processes in ACPE and NACC (see Anne Underwood, *Op. cit.*).

111. The spirit of collaboration is exemplified by the joint white paper on spiritual care and chaplaincy, and most recently by a joint code of ethics and a shared complaint process (*Ibid.*, 5).

112. See Charles Hall, *With Head and Heart: The Story of the Clinical Pastoral Education Movement* (JPCP Publications, 1992), and Stephen D. W. King, *Trust the Process: A History of Clinical Pastoral Education as Theological Education*, for the history of collaboration, its fits and starts, and conflict among the pastoral care and education organizations up to 1990.

113. In the sparring between the organizations, ACPE has been called the (essentially non-nurturing) "parent" of CPSP (Bonnie MacDougall Olson, "Building Transformative Community: Confronting Shame," *Pastoral Report: The Newsletter of CPSP*, July 17, 2007, http://www.pastoralreport.com/the_archives/2007/07/building_transf_1.html.)

114. In this regard, the rhetoric of some CPSP web publications seems to alternate between pugnacity, superiority, and victimization in relation to ACPE.

115. *ACPE – National: Notice of Important ACPE Board Motion*, www.maracpe.org/modules/news/article.php?storyid=38. "DOE" is the U.S. Department of Education.

116. *Recognition as an Accrediting Agency*, www.acpe.edu/recognit.htm.

117. *ACPE – National: Notice of Important ACPE Board Motion. Op. cit.*

118. Board of Representatives report, *ACPE Newsletter of the North Central Region*, December 2006, 7. ACPE centers may still be dually accredited to offer units jointly approved by ACPE and the Commission on Certification of the United States Conference of Catholic Bishops (USCCB/CCA).

119. The unseemliness was acknowledged by CPSP leaders James E. Gebhart and Raymond J. Lawrence in *A Report to Religious Judicatories and Seminaries on the Current Strife in the Clinical Pastoral Field*, May 25, 2007 http://professionalchaplaincy.blogspot.com/2007/05/report-to-religious-judicatories-and.html.

120. The phrase "adult-to-adult" appears in the Board of Representatives report, *ACPE Newsletter of the North Central Region* (December 2006), 7.

121. While noting the distastefulness of the spectacle, Gebhart and Lawrence also appear to capitalize on it in a bid for the moral high ground in this dispute (A Report to Religious Judicatories and Seminaries).

122. *Ibid.*, 17, 76.

123. Margaret Mohrmann's article may be of particular interest in its attempt to frame an ethical perspective on a changing understanding of chaplaincy from the outside (Margaret E. Mohrmann, "Ethical Grounding for a Profession of Hospital Chaplaincy," *Hastings Center Report* (38, No. 6, November-December 2008), 18-23.) The earlier discussion by Loren Townsend (*Op. cit.*, 95) raises some of the same questions from the vantage point of one immersed in the pastoral/spiritual care field.

CHAPTER TWELVE

Sexuality in Clinical Supervision

Gordon Hilsman

The elemental nature of sexual attraction and its persistent complexity as a major aspect of life that is both fulfilling and potentially destructive, make it a necessary and important topic in supervising pastoral care. Excellent clinical pastoral supervision can be defined as "objectively and creatively assisting the exploration and augmentation of the inner processes of a student's ministry relationships for the continuing development of pastoral identity and ministry excellence." In that context, the sexuality of both supervisor and student become significant matters in the process.[1]

The life project of sexual maturing—making sense of natural childhood sexual urges, awakening to full-blown adolescent churning, integrating emotional intimacy with sexual passion in adulthood, maturing to satisfying long-term generativity, and healing the inevitable wounds that occur along the way—invariably intersects with pastoral relationships, peer engagement, and supervisory interaction during periods of clinical preparation for self-reflective professional practice.

The two person configuration of human reproduction makes the topic even more complex. Men have finally been taught, in the last half of the twentieth century, that we see the sexual and relational world far differently than women. This chapter for example, is written with a man's body, one whose romantic involvements have been seen by others as normally spotty, but never abusive. How men and women who have been abused and assaulted perceive sexuality must be far different from my own views.[2]

One in four women and one in seven men,[3] and probably a larger percentages of those who present themselves for clinical supervision, have had the enormous vulnerability of their genitality and emotional tenderness used, abused, and treated with hostile disregard for human boundaries—as things rather than as people. The would-be supervisor who blindly works in blatant disregard of the effect such widespread abuse has had on students and patients alike fosters a specific brand of irresponsibility.

This writer became seriously engaged in the search for intimacy only in his mid-30s, after 20 years of pre-adolescent groping and yearning as a heterosexual, vowed celibate. My perspectives on intimate loving fairly glow relative to those seeing the sexual aspect of life as perpetually dangerous. One can assume that literally all of us peer similarly from one unique point of view, working to help one another heal, grow, learn, and together contribute to the evolution of love in all its forms—intimate, care giving, familial, befriending, and communal.

Anyone preparing to learn the art of supervision then, would do well to engage in some level of self-examination of the history and state of one's own sexual experience—painful, abusive, satisfying, developmental, confusing, enlightening, and/or repeatedly regretted—and one's conscious and unconscious stances, attitudes, and assumptions that have resulted. As the supervisor enters the group room or the individual supervisory consultation office (this one window) through which they need to peer together at times, will be only as clear as the supervisor's perspectives on sexuality in her/his own life on that day.

The setting for ministry in which clinical supervision is undertaken matters. Hospitals, for example, make people vulnerable in different ways than addiction treatment centers, mental health units, prisons, and parishes. Each presents its unique ways in which the sexual aspect of life can dramatically or subtly affect pastoral relationships and those who initiate them. Thorough familiarity with one's own setting for practicing this art increases the supervisor's alertness to including sexuality in the array of inner processes that may need processing in the educational process.

Early writing on clinical supervision in social work and psychology contains no developed treatment of sexuality as a component of supervisory practice and the supervisory relationship. Some classic treatments of psychotherapy deal significantly with sexual dynamics in the therapy relationship, but do not adapt them usefully to supervision. Mueller and Kell include a brief section on the confusing difference between nurturance and sexual attraction that can easily go unresolved between supervisor and student.[4] Kadushin merely mentions gender along with race and age as differences that tend to cause job-related issues for the supervisor.[5]

Sheehan's chapter on gender issues in Steere, instructive on sexual development and gender differentiation and healing, makes little reference to the supervisory relationship.[6] Transformational learning theory honors the complex processes by which people rework early experiences, including those that are sexually charged, in fashioning adult identity and constructing their own framework of knowledge.[7] The term "intersubjectivity" fully described by Cooper-White emphasizes the subtle and complex ways in which the inner experience and previous wounding of both supervisor and student deserve careful attention in psychotherapy and supervision.[8]

While considerable differences in integrating sexual perspectives into supervisory work remain among practitioners, six basic principles can be offered as a beginning.

SIX BASIC PRINCIPLES

SEXUALITY AS SPIRITUAL

Sexual experiences throughout a lifetime have powerful effects on the human spirit, and thus must be seen as eminently spiritual. Sexual energy serves to generate and energize intimate relationships, contributing significantly to the spirituality of virtually all persons. Perpetually mysterious in that it never becomes fully comprehensible but continues to unfold the deeper one enters it, experiences of sexual intimacy both wound and edify, validate and discourage, mature and stunt development. To a great degree, sexuality shapes our personalities and etches the corners of our souls. While the twentieth century spawned new helping professions that deal effectively with sexual problems of all sorts, the fact that sexually-intimate relationships seem created to buoy our human existence and forge the virtues of adult citizens, puts it clearly in the domain of pastoral care as well.[9]

SEXUALITY AS UBIQUITOUS

When the supervisor enters the consultation room, individual or group, she carries with her the keen awareness that sexual energy flows everywhere. Appraising ministry data from cognitive, behavioral, emotional, theological, and various conceptual perspectives can be inadequate without peering occasionally with an eye to how personal and bodily attractions are playing out between students, patients, authorities, other adjacent people, and the supervisor her/himself.

SEXUALITY AS DANGEROUS

The supervisor knows that nearly a third of the people seeking his clinical mentoring have been in some way sexually wounded and each carries the scars in uniquely painful and variously accessible ways. Re-victimizing unaware may be the greatest peril of taking on the supervisory task. Entering the room of unhealed personal injuries of any person's sexual house in the intricate process of clinical supervision must be done only with the greatest reverence for the sacred.

OBLIGATION

The sexuality perspective ought not to be avoided in the supervisory relationship, regardless of the peril. It is the supervisor's responsibility to manage her own attractions, revulsions, and love relation history in order to focus on the ministry and supervisory relationships involved. When the topic of sex is raised in the supervisory relationship in any way, it must be given serious consideration. It cries out for exploration. In many students' lives the clinical supervisor stands as a rare confidant regarding aspects of their lives they consider most private. Unconscious invitations to bring some collegial sense to current sexual questions and past events provide one theme of students' chosen interaction with a trusted supervisor.

PROFESSIONAL BOUNDARY REVERENCE

In addition to the danger of re-victimizing the abused, supervisors are obliged to maintain a professional distance with all students. Overt sexual engagement between supervisor and student so obscures objectivity that it violates the integrity of the relationship. The power differential between student and supervisor renders such a relationship an unethical arena for romance and sexual sorting. Even a hint of the supervisor's actual interest in romance or sexual engagement with a student makes it impossible to continue the clinical work. It immediately transforms the relationship from professional to personal, as the student will no longer see the supervisor as altruistically objective. Since one cannot supervise one's lover with any measure of objectivity, manifesting an attraction also distorts the supervisor's reverie. Only with powerful defensive inner maneuvering can the supervisor convince him/herself that adequate supervision is taking place when the relationship is continued. The fact that some known supervisors have married and thrived with their students for decades does not alter the reality that the beginnings of those relationships born during supervision were highly unethical and the likelihood that they would be minimally useful professionally once the attraction was made manifest.

SUPERVISORY AUTHENTICITY AND INTEGRITY

The supervisor who carries significant unhealed sexual wounding into the supervisory task limps into the work. The subtly homophobic or veiled misogynist is not ready to supervise with adequate efforts at objectivity. Neither is the woman quietly carrying similarly powerful hostility towards men, though no adjective yet describes her in a word. Just as operant addiction and psychopathology render a supervisor impaired, so must strongly negative sexual attitudes be viewed as potentially damaging to professional functioning.

Monitoring the field of clinical supervision and sanctioning practitioners who have fallen into this dysfunction is a shared responsibility. The supervisor her/himself carries a part of it. Local peer groups of supervisors hold another, and may need to bolster their courage to challenge and confront one another. Certification committees cannot excuse themselves from attention to these dynamics. And professional associations in the persons of their current leadership, take on significant accountability for facing rather than avoiding the messiness of conflict that can arise in matters of sexual bias as well as sexual exploitation.

Trainers of supervisors can refer for therapy or human sexuality education as part of the supervisory residency. They can also facilitate a process for supervisory students to familiarize themselves with their own sexual history and its unfinished issues that show themselves in the learning process.

SPECIFIC ISSUES

Issues that can arise in supervision regarding the sexuality of supervisor and student, while numerous, can be clustered for a single chapter into nine categories. Each of the issues presented below challenges a peer group, and can either impede or enrich the group intimacy. Each of them threatens the adequate functioning and even the integrity of both individual and group peer supervision. The vignettes that illustrate each issue clearly portray the uniqueness and charged nature of situations that arise with sexuality as a major component.

STUDENT ATTRACTION TO PATIENT

In processing a verbatim presentation in group supervision, single 26 year-old Jason has vaguely referred to a positive relationship he senses between him and a female intensive care patient. A peer eventually asks directly about his feelings for her. As he rummages awkwardly through his emotions, he becomes more boldly aware of a warm attraction he has towards her. Another peer notes that the written verbatim material, which includes a significant segment of interaction with the patient, discloses no likelihood that she shares any of the same feelings for him. In addition, this peer says she thinks she knows the patient was quite recently married. Embarrassed and enlightened, Jason is confronted with his naiveté about romance and seems to grow a bit in psychosexual development in processing his shame.

Attraction of a student chaplain to a patient in any configuration can provide a vivid educational experience. Events related to such attractions are common, almost universal, in the trusting context of open student reflection. Students flung into the intimacy of visiting hospital patients who are in bed, even in a semi-public situation, are easily attracted on a cellular level to the blatant erotic vulnerability of some. No matter how much previous academic and work-shop education on boundaries in pastoral care situations such students have re-ceived, the experiential situation can surprise and ambush the most well-meaning fledgling caregiver. Judgment-free supervisory assistance, within the unique situation presenting itself, offers perhaps the best scenario for fostering mature perspective and the fashioning of an ethical and pastoral identity.

Here is the opportunity for a student to consolidate the line between being sensitively pastoral and straying into the ethically errant. Seminary has taught him that under no circumstances is he to encourage sexual or romantic energy with parishioners. Are patients parishioners? Is this warm patter romance? Is he not fashioning his own identity as a man? Is there somebody to forbid his flirt-ing? Couldn't this warmth be facilitating the helping relationship? How does one differentiate between the nurturing warmth of the caregiver and the beckon-ing of romantic attraction?

An intricate aspect of supervisory work seeks to help a student separate the idealizing distortions of countertransference with a patient, from here and now romantic attraction to that patient. Indeed, actual romance and countertransference often cannot be distinguished from one another. We may be attracted to our wives and husbands due to the phenomenon of transference, and great romances can follow from that attraction.

But suggesting to the student that the patient may resemble a previously cherished person provides an alternative way of viewing the patient attraction situation. This student may be currently sorting potential lovers in his personal life. Helping him do so, in a context in which she/he can heal pockets of shame that impede the developmental process, is often a byproduct of supervisory rela-tionships. Doing so, while honoring the boundaries of ministry to vulnerable people, builds a pastoral identity that doesn't flinch in the face of attractive peo-ple.

When such explorative self-definition is brought into the supervisory peer group, there may be a need for the supervisor to not only facilitate the student's unfolding self-awareness by focusing peer feedback, but also to moderate peer teasing and subtle implications of superiority. The above student doesn't need more shame. He needs for his naiveté to transform into budding wisdom in the perpetually mysterious area of intimate relationship.

When a supervisor discovers that a student is indeed carrying on an actual romantic or sexual relationship with a person the student met as a patient or fam-ily member, the task differs. Indulging one's attraction to a person in a vulner-able life situation such as hospitalization immediately renders unavailable and inaccessible a portion of a student's self-awareness for supervisory exploration, adding to the normal range of resistances already operant. While that relation-ship may have the potential to live for decades in committed intimacy, it remains unethical. A supervisor's responsibility is to confront it in supervision. Is it a relationship of "consenting adults" or a caregiver misusing—intentionally or unconsciously—the power differential between patient and pastor for personal benefit? From a supervisory perspective, it must be treated as the latter. The supervisor's efforts to foster the student's development of a thorough understanding of the ethical and moral implications for continuing the relationship become imperative for the integrity of the program and the very field of Clinical Pastoral Education.

STUDENT SEXUAL MISCONDUCT

The management responsibility of clinical supervision includes overseeing the ethical nature of the student's ministry work. Questions that arise when a student can legitimately be accused of sexual harassment include: How can the supervisor use a student's inappropriate judgments and behavior as educational events while simultaneously curtailing the behavior? How can a willing interdisciplinary staff member be used in educational and management confrontation without violating confidence and/or damaging the supervisory relationship? What is the supervisor's responsibility to disclose to seminary or judicatory officials the transgressions of boundaries and apparently resilient resistance to learning what is necessary to function as a professional pastoral person?

> Joe is a married student from a Hispanic country. He is in his first unit of CPE and has been in this country for two years with his family. He is a pastor in the Seventh Day Adventist faith and served congregations in his home country for almost 20 years. He has been processing in individual and group supervision the possibility of divorcing his wife. The group has already brought to his attention his inability to be direct with the women in the group. Every time he addresses a woman in the group he stares at the floor. Joe has shared with his group some of the taboos and customs that he adheres to in his native culture regarding addressing women and how that is being challenged in both the group and clinical context. The supervisor receives a phone call from a nurse who is concerned about Joe's behavior on his floor assignment. She states that one of her fellow staff members is contemplating filing a sexual harassment complaint against Joe. The supervisor asks the staff member to describe the behavior and she states that every time Joe addresses her, he stares at her breasts. The complaint has not yet been made formally.

For Joe's sake, as well as the many people to whom he may minister in the future, he needs help in processing his sexual attitudes, his truncated self-awareness, and his behavior regarding women. Regardless of where this happens—in the group or in individual supervisory settings—the supervisor carries primary responsibility for it. Since that work has already begun in the group, continuing there while augmenting it individual sessions makes sense. Referral for therapeutic treatment can be seen as essential, to avoid group preoccupation with the juiciness of the issue and sabotage of the supervision in favor of "therapizing" Joe in unconscious or partially-conscious manipulative avoidance of the group supervisory work.

How the supervisor uses the complaining staff member can vary. A reasonable approach would be for the supervisor to hear firsthand what she experiences, rather than operate on hearsay. Confronting Joe with her feelings without including her in the supervisory encounter may suffice, but is not optimal. The "he says, she says" impasse can be avoided if the supervisory relationship carries enough trust to bring Joe into self-reflection without heavy defensiveness. Processing his thoughts and feelings in this complicated array of relationships and issues will optimally lead to motivation for his accepting a therapy referral. Indeed, referral can reasonably be considered in any case, regardless of his motivation and capacity to bring his behavior into professional boundaries. Failing that, the supervisor is confronted with responsibility to expel Joe from the program.

Does Joe's ethnic and cultural heritage matter? He is working in ministry in the complex conglomeration of cultures we call the United States, not in his own. He is not being trained in or for his native culture, but for this one, and any certification he seeks will authorize him to practice here. Understanding his heritage may be essential to treat him with respect and sensitivity, but educating him to work in this country's legal, ethical, religious, and cultural milieu remains the commitment of clinical pastoral supervision.

What and to whom does the supervisor disclose about the issue as (if) Joe finishes the educational program? Regardless of how well Joe seems to learn from the situation and heal, the supervisor has a responsibility to notify appropriate denominational officials of the peril in authorizing Joe's future ministry. Merely describing it in a written final evaluation will not be adequate, since that written document might not be shared by Joe as it could jeopardize his professional career. If he seems to make significant progress in maturing his psychosexual development through therapy and supervision, that improvement can be mentioned as well. But remaining silent about what is clearly verging on significant clergy sexual misconduct is neither fair to the church, nor ethical for public service, nor helpful to Joe himself.

STUDENT ATTRACTION TO SUPERVISOR

Sally is in her second unit of CPE and is a lesbian in a partnered relationship that has been on and off for the last couple of years. Sally is in a group with other lesbians and one in particular challenged her regarding her dressing "like a hetero." Sally has in the last year confessed her sexual orientation to her parents and the fact that she is living with her partner and contemplating marriage. Her brother and father will no longer speak to her, but her mother continues to talk with her on the phone. Sally is preparing for ordination, but in her denomination if she is actively engaging in "homosexual activity" she cannot be ordained. Her denomination seems to tolerate homosexuality as long as it is hid-

den. Sally states that she no longer wants to hide her sexual orientation. This
has become a point of contention at home as her partner chooses to hide her
sexual orientation. Sally also refuses to change denominations. In individual
supervision with her male supervisor, she confesses that she feels attracted to
him. Further along in the unit she tells him that she has fantasies of sexual intimacy with him and they recur almost nightly. By the end of the unit she tells
the supervisor that she has confessed this to her partner, who became jealous,
and now they are both considering separation.

While this situation presents itself as more complex than those easily envi-
sioned by the above subtitle, it illustrates the intricacy of supervising a student
admittedly and overtly attracted to the supervisor. This student's sexual confusion or emerging bisexual identity can be addressed to some degree in the supervisory relationship, but will also likely benefit from therapeutic intervention.

The supervisor's part in the education and healing processes includes giving
clear messages that he has no interest at all in a romantic or sexual relationship
with the student, providing direct feedback that her attraction and her confusing
feelings need therapeutic assistance for clarification, honoring the vulnerability
of the student's disclosed feelings and maintaining the peer group as a ministry
educational endeavor rather than support group or therapy.

The first three of these apply for virtually any manifested attraction of a
student to the supervisor, and the fourth is a perennial supervisory task. Being
clear about the absence of a supervisor's interest in a non-supervisory relationship gives a solid impression of safety and persistent integrity in the essential
trust of supervision. Expressing the possibility that the supervisor may change
his mind at any time sabotages the supervisory work completely. Distracted by
the possibility of romance, the student is confused and unable to remain open to
processing ministry data.

Direct feedback to the student that relational confusion needs therapeutic
processing offers her what she needs. It also clearly indicates that such transitional uncertainty is inadequate as a basis for clinical ministry and has to mature
into greater clarity. Listening to extensive details about the ongoing process of
identity formation hazards her assuming that, simply talking about it will suffice
for her adequate resolution. Since that is unlikely to be true, and even if it is, the
educational work will then not be done. A conservative, viable opinion would
require that the student be firmly referred to therapy, with communication to the
student's judicatory.

SUPERVISOR ATTRACTION TO STUDENT

The inherent intimacy of the supervisory relationship provides a perpetual arena
for the supervisor to be compelled by the personal attractiveness of students.
Commonly, if not inevitably, that situation is handled variously by seasoned
supervisors. One supervisor I know once commented about admissions inter-

views that, "If she's pretty, I simply don't accept her into the program. Too much hassle." Another male colleague, now deceased, always seemed to surround himself with physically attractive women. Some supervisors in between these extremes either disclose their attraction to the student or never do so.

The art of supervising a student to whom one is attracted is to allow the attraction to fuel the supervisor's careful attention to the student as a learner for his/her own flourishing as a minister.

Three common safeguards for the supervisor's integrity in working with students attractive to her/him must be mentioned. The first is to acknowledge the fact to a colleague or colleague peer group. Open processing, hazardous as it seems, helps keep perspective. Many who have lost careers crossing the line of romantic or sexual involvement with students have regretted not trusting peers in that exhilarating and mysterious space of romantic sorting in which the idealistic attraction is so easily misunderstood even by friends. What professional supervision programs teach all students is to seek consultation openly, courageously, and easily. That is the primary content of the initial unit of clinical ministry training. Certification as a supervisor ought not to negate that practice and the humility that allows it.

Secondly, there is a commitment to supervise an attractive student using the altruistic aspect of erotic affection that is always necessary for a love relationship to mature. Genuine care for the wellbeing of a lover transcends sexual attraction in a long-term romance, as the bloom eventually and inevitably comes off the rose. Accessing that aspect of romantic attraction compels a supervisor to think carefully about what supervisory approach will be best for the student as s/he learns and grows in pastoral competence.

Other practitioners will prefer to intentionally and repeatedly strive to see the student as sister or daughter rather than lover or wife. The altruistic care for people that motivates the practice of supervision is then enlisted to supersede the energy of eros. In either case, the sexual attraction is channeled into genuine care rather than self-gratifying indulgence.

That practice is only possible when the supervisor keeps clearly in mind "the line" between ethical practice and unethical engagement. That line can best be described as the moment a supervisor indicates in any way to a student that s/he may be interested in a romantic or sexual relationship with that student.[10] Crossing that line terminates the supervisory relationship. Seeking to continue the relationship only exacerbates the situation. The decision has been made to pursue a romance or sexual engagement which cannot coexist with clinical supervision. It is time to obtain immediate consultation and proceed with whatever unpleasant arrangements may be necessary to provide for the end of that professional relationship, whether the romance is pursued or not.

Romantic attraction naturally cries out for action, for avowing the attraction to the potential lover. As an attraction grows, a savvy student may intuit the romantic interest and even be mature enough to ask about it directly. To maintain authenticity in the relationship, it may be necessary for the supervisor to acknowledge the truth. If done so with a clear indication that the supervisor has no interest in pursuing a romantic or sexual relationship, the supervision may remain intact. In such a situation, attempted verbal denial violates authentic integrity and is likely to corrupt the credibility of the supervisory communication.

CATALYZING THERAPEUTIC ISSUES

> Forty-six year-old Monica, a candidate for Methodist ordination and a popular church pastoral care minister, disclosed early to her peers that she had engaged in years of therapy after having been raped in her own house when she was five years old. As she waits in a reception area for her fifth scheduled weekly individual supervisory session, the supervisor emerges from his office wondering why she hasn't arrived and is 10 minutes late. A bit flustered, she says she had found that when the door is closed she knows the supervisor isn't ready for the session. He points out that the door was indeed partially open. A week later she begins individual supervision with the statement, "It is amazing how one simple interaction can shake loose what years of therapy had only prepared me for." Her reflection after the door incident had taken her to the hallway outside the room where she was raped, frozen, not knowing what to do next. She said that since that supervisory intervention she had tried several things that she simply wouldn't have done before, recognizing and overcoming the feeling of facing a partially open door she dare not enter.

The highly emotional and interpersonal richness of a clinical training program tends to thrust therapeutic issues to the fore. For Monica, previous success with EMDR had brought her to the point of seeing herself standing in that hallway unfortunately precisely at the time she needed to terminate the therapy. She had been mystified for years why she stayed in a persistent, mostly joyless and sometimes abusive love relationship. Inertia and finances had kept her from continuing therapy at a later time. The supervisory event described above motivated her to continue therapy, promising to free her for greater depth in her love life, assertiveness in a mostly male peer group and improved pastoral significance in her patient care.

While the precipitating supervisory occurrence was not overtly sexual in nature, it prodded Monica's moving off a plateau and re-engaging her psychosexual development in her mid-40s. Attending to the course of that development as one theme in supervisory relationships stands as a productive responsibility and adds a useful dimension to supervision.

REDUCING MORALISTIC DUALISM

The history of Christianity (as well as Islam, Buddhism, Confucianism, and even to some degree the Hindu faith that spawned the 4th century classic Kama Sutra) features longstanding and deeply-rooted traditions of moralizing about sexuality for its dangerous and highly destructive power. A great deal of that dualistic truncating of the spiritual value and maturing potential of intimate loving remains and is perpetuated by religious regulation and rigid organizational structures. It is the role of clinical supervision to assist pastoral care students to explore their own areas of moralistic judgment and make mature decisions about the effectiveness and integrity of those attitudes as background for ministry practice.

> A 60 year-old married female, ordained, Independent Assemblies of God first unit hospice CPE resident enters the individual supervisory arena in the fourth week of the program, pulls her chair a little closer to the supervisor, and begins with, "There is something I need to talk about." She starts, "I went into this comatose man's room. I didn't know what to do, but I'd heard in orientation that if you breathe in tandem with a non-responsive patient it can calm him. So I started to breathe with this guy. Pretty soon I started getting aroused. It reminded me of some times with my husband and it stimulated me. I got scared." The supervisor responds, "How did you handle that?" "I left the room!" she said.

While the student's quick exit response was neither surprising nor any kind of pastoral failure, processing the student's feelings and thinking about herself in the situation can be fruitful. As the supervisor queried about the student's awareness of the reason for such charged energy about the event, she acknowledged that guilt was motivating her. Further exploration revealed that when the student had entered recovery from addiction many years ago, she had found the first stability in her abusive childhood life in an evangelical church and settled for the way a key pastoral figure taught about sex. As she was invited to focus on her own best thinking, she was stunned to find that she could think of no harm done by the pastoral event. Where was the evil? What is the difference between hurtful sex, tedious sex, preoccupying sex, and the glorious messiness of passionate, loving sex? If pastoral people are to assist parishioners in finding a mature perspective on their sexual experiences, they will do so more healthily if their own views are realistic, wholesome, and self-treasuring.

As this student grew increasingly disappointed with her dualistic, mostly unexamined sexual attitudes, she was able to expand them with reading and further supervisory conversations, both individual and group. She became more open to a renewed course of therapy.

INTER-PEER ATTRACTION

> Frank and Susan are in the same peer group. Susan's dynamic in the group is to please others. Frank is a Jesuit priest from West Africa. Frank invites Susan to have coffee with him. During this meeting he confesses to her that he loves her, wants to renounce his vows, and wants them to get married. Susan brings this up in individual supervision but refuses to do so in the group. In group times

the tension between Frank and Susan is strong and other group members notice and bring attention to it. The concern is met with resistance by both Frank and Susan.

Sexual or romantic attraction among members of a peer supervision group can be some of the most difficult to supervise. Preventing spouses or lovers from entering such a group together is optimal. The strength of collusion between lovers, as well as the acting out of their intimate conflicts, far too seriously exacerbates the inherently complex dynamics of peer supervision.

When group members fall in love with one another after a program has begun, however, there is little choice but to use the charged energy the best one can in the supervisory work. Expelling one or both is rarely justified. Keeping the observable dynamics between the partners as overt as possible and using the energy of attraction and conflict to foster direct feedback within the group may be the best initial supervisory tack.

In the above situation, however, one party may be enchanted while the other is disinterested. The supervisory task can then be seen as three-fold. First, can Susan be induced to explore her own feelings for Frank, whatever they are? If she is interested in Frank and available herself, she may choose to pursue the romance, which is the situation of lovers in the same group mentioned above. If she is not (yet) interested, a vigorous approach would be to insist that she raise the one-way attraction issue in the group or to bring the two students together in an extra three-person supervisory session to process the situation. Keeping the highly-charged emotions between these two peers covert amounts to powerful resistance in which the group unconsciously refuses to do process work, while the most obvious process is being ignored. Continuing avoidance of processing inhibits the group work by preoccupying the unconscious and some conscious processes that are crying out for perspective.

A less vigorous approach would be to refer her to a counseling venue in which she can clarify her own position relative to Frank. The supervisor can do some of this work, but to the degree to which it preoccupies the supervisory process, it could sabotage Susan's studenthood and learning.

Second, the supervisor needs to artfully draw Frank's attention to the need to find integrity in his life. Is this an infatuation he will regret when it ends his priestly career? Is it the beginning of a lasting romance? Is it the bungling "junior high" groping of a naïve, inexperienced, and confused celibate? How can this be done in the absence of Susan's willingness to deal with the issue? Perhaps by simply asking Frank about his feelings for Susan based on observations of the group dynamics. Even if he stonewalls, the issue will have been raised and brought closer to the surface. If and when he acknowledges his professional and relational confusion, the supervisor can either assist Frank's self-exploration in romance and celibacy or refer him to spiritual direction or therapy.

202 Sexuality in Clinical Supervision
Thirdly, it may be possible for the supervisor to raise the issue in the group through verbal observations of the dynamics between the two. At least one of these students, and perhaps both, is in need of verbal processing of their romantic attitudes, values, inclinations, and reticence. Can the peer group be such a place for them? Perhaps it could begin there. It might be instructive for their peers as well. It also might detract from the supervisory group work and supervisory care should be taken to see that it doesn't.

SEXUALITIES DIFFERENT FROM ONE'S OWN

When a heterosexual supervisor meets a student in some phase of making her/his orientation as gay, lesbian, or bisexual known fully to self and publicly, the challenge is again multi-faceted. The trust relationship of supervision naturally invites disclosure of delicate personal issues. The often confusing unfolding of awareness that one's sexual identity is different from the majority of one's childhood peers takes time and relational experience. It invariably includes considerable misunderstanding, perceived rejection, awkward embarrassment, and episodes of violence along the way. An astute supervisor who brings realistic perspective to most any student assertion can seem, to a person in the midst of "coming out," like a haven in that developmental process.

Again, the supervisory arena is not therapy. Nor is it equivalent to the advising and mentoring of a more experienced, similarly-oriented person, which may be a more effective arena for facilitating the process of coming out. Yet when the supervisor is a chosen trusted-one for support and clarification of one's budding sexual identity, facilitating the complex concerns regarding family members, friends, current group members, ecclesiastical authorities, and even former lovers can be a significant point of the coming out process. Indeed, assisting this process may legitimately be seen as ministry as much as it is therapy. As a major component of a person's pastoral identity, it is also supervisory.

The process of "coming out" or integrating one's counter-cultural sexuality into the fabric of one's life can be seen as taking place in six stages,[11] and a supervisor can well learn to recognize, validate, and facilitate progress in each one. Whatever work can be done on this issue with a student as related to patient pastoral relationships will likely be more easily integrative for the student. The stages proceed as: 1) Innocence—Growing up gay generally means having no place to feel at home. School, church, and the family all present emotionally dangerous territory. Frequently sensing that "something is not right" as a child, the GL person has nowhere to safely seek solace from ridicule, innuendo, rejection, and the episodes of violence that s/he rarely talks about, even when fully "out" later on. 2) Avoidance—Conscious and unconscious efforts to prove to oneself and everybody else that one is not gay can be vigorous and even exaggerated. The obsession to fit in as normal can last for years. Even an experienced supervisor may not recognize that hyper-masculinity or hyper-femininity for what it is. 3) Experimentation—As illustrated in that initial carried-away sexual groping in the tent on *Brokeback Mountain*,[12] engaging sexually for the very first time stands as one of the most exhilarating and scary events of a lifetime, and needs to be verbally shared, almost confessionally, somewhere, sometime. As in heterosexual falling-in-love or falling-in-lust, mystery has grabbed one by the genitals and thrust her/him to the ground. Who will be told? How will that glorious narrative be expressed, to whom, and when? 4) Identification—Once a gay person embraces her/his true orientation, the world seems to turn on being gay, and all aspects of life are colored by this new knowing and being. To be "real" seems to this student to require blatantly, rebelliously, angrily, and even flauntingly acting with oblivion to "safe-sex" common sense. A supervisor may truly assist a student in this stage to remember her/his own safety and not abandon self-care. 5) Integration—As the sense of what it is to live as gay falls into perspective, a student's sense of ministry can broaden beyond advocacy for the sexually-marginalized and fighting for the cause into awareness that people need ministry of all sorts, with the realization that this person is indeed gifted and called to provide some of that, in many situations. The discovery that one can preach on topics other than those related to sexual orientation, and that God has indeed been pushed to the sidelines of one's life, allows new and deeper theologizing. One is no longer defined by being gay, but continues to minister informed by that aspect of one's experience. Without supervisory guidance or mentoring of some pastoral kind, many gifted gays are lost from ministry and church membership in favor of such similar vocations as psychology and social work. The question, "Do I as a mature adult have a place in an organization ambivalent about my worth?" takes a central place in one's adult search for meaning and purpose. 6) Proclamation—Having grown through the coming out process, the person at this stage becomes a solid and credible voice for continued incorporation of gay and other sexually "different" individuals into the mainstream of society's primary functions. Having found and fashioned a treasured self, s/he can use that self to contribute to society and ministry with recognized and proven giftedness and dedication. Being gay becomes less about what you do with your genitals and more about long-lasting intimate relationships.

Gay people tend to repeatedly share the narrative of their coming out process just as supervisors and chaplains share the stories of their certification drama, AA members the pivotal process of their early recovery, and Jews the epic of the Exodus. Sensitivity to that need both honor the coming out process and continues to instruct heterosexual supervisors on a part of life they will never fully see. Each student disclosing a sexuality different from that of the supervisor is likely to provide that supervisor with learning of her/his own, if allowed to do so. As gay people age, things are changing in their world. Continually learning about different sexualities will remain a professional responsibility for an excellent supervisor for many years to come.

VOWED CELIBACY

Supervising students who are ritually and soulfully vowed to a life of celibacy requires several specific and simple skills. Honoring the sacredness of the vow remains a supervisor's ethical responsibility. Respecting the student's reticence to share with a sexually active person the intricacies and doubts of living celibate is too. The best mentor will relate to celibates with consistent acceptance rather than a representation of the impossibility of rigorous celibacy for ordinary people that the supervisor thinks is obvious. That kind of validation by a respected mentor is likely to prod continuing openness. Honest answers to the student's specific questions that the supervisor may think naïve can stretch a fledgling supervisor's maturity of practice.

> A 29 year-old Roman Catholic priest meets an earthy, 50-something African-American man on a renal dialysis ward who asks him, "Why the funny collar?" When the student responds with intellectualizing about the spiritual value of celibacy, the patient simply replies, "Well, you gotta either screw or masturbate, one or the other. Which one is you?" The priest enters individual supervision pouring out an account of his habit of rationalized masturbation and his fears of ending his dream of priestly vocation or even of eternal damnation for his inability to curtail autoeroticism, despite his solemn vow.

Men and women who have committed themselves to a life of celibacy differ considerably with one another on what "celibacy" means to them. A rigorously traditional person may consider all sexual pleasure to violate the vow while a more Christian humanistic celibate may excuse occasional autoerotic behavior to be normal and not at all sinful. In the case excerpt above, the student's brief but dramatic patient confrontation so derailed him from ministry interaction that only its implications for him could be immediately processed in supervision. He desperately needed to define what his vow actually meant to him. He would either deepen that spiritual commitment here or move toward abandoning it as unattainable as a lifestyle.

The supervisory stance with committed celibates includes an intentional reverence for the sacredness of the vow in the individual's spiritual makeup, its place in the individual's psychosexual development, and the sensitivity required to openly process that part of her/his life. While therapy or spiritual direction may be more appropriate practices for such processing, it can easily begin in the midst of a clinical education program in which openness defines the milieu.

Teasing out the student's meanings of vows, attitudes regarding sexuality, habits of dealing with sexual arousal, and the intertwining of vocational and personal issues inherent in facing adolescence later in life can be intricate work. It can also be most productive for the ongoing development and learning of celibate students.

The "I can tell this person anything" ambience so useful in a practicing chaplain can be difficult to emerge in one inexperienced in romantic and sexual relationships. But it is not impossible. It happens and it needs to be honored when it does. A small segment of society matures quite successfully without genital interpersonal relationships. An unconscious Protestant bias, or even an acknowledged opinion, that considers celibacy to be "unnatural" or unhealthy, skews that supervisor's ability to inspire confidence in a celibate student. At the same time, a celibate supervisor who neglects or even avoids sexual dynamics in ministry processing fails in one significant responsibility of a mentor.

CONCLUSION

As highly spiritual, perpetually mysterious, persistently operative, frequently dangerous, and often prompting troublesome interpersonal situations, human sexuality will remain a significant aspect of the supervisory work of many practitioners who are willing to incorporate it. Carefully seeking to use all major interpersonal processes in the supervisory exploration naturally includes occasionally viewing dynamics through the window of sexuality. The ethical perspective is simply not broad enough. Supervisory trainers, certifiers, association policy makers and committee leaders need to develop their own precise thinking about their roles relative to sexual issues in the field of pastoral supervision.

NOTES

1. Bill L. Kell and William J. Mueller, *Coping with Conflict* (New York: Appleton Century-Crofts: 1972), 99.

2. I am highly indebted to my wife Nancy Hilsman, to CPE supervisor Angelika Zollfrank, and other women for their helping to shape many of the perspectives in this article.

3. Department for Health and Human Services, Centers for Disease Control and Prevention, "Prevalence of Adverse Childhood Experiences," www.cdc.gov/nccdphp/ace/prevalence.htm.

4. *Ibid.*, 99-101.

5. Alfred Kadushin, *Supervision in Social Work* (New York: Columbia University Press, 1976).

6. Barbara Sheehan, "Gender Issues in Supervision," 222-235 in David A. Steere, ed., *The Supervision of Pastoral Care* (Westminister, UK: John Knox Press: 1989).

7. Mary Field Belenky and Ann V. Stanton, "Inequality, Development, and Connected Knowing," 71-102 in Jack Mezirow, *Learning as Transformation* (San Francisco: Jossey-Bass, 2000).

8. Pamela Cooper-White, *Many Voices: Pastoral Psychotherapy in Relational and Theological Perspective* (Minneapolis: Fortress Press, 2006).

9. Gordon Hilsman, *Intimate Spirituality: The Catholic Way of Love and Sex* (Lanham, MD: Sheed & Ward, 2007), 3-13.

10. This is a key teaching of Marie Fortune, M.Div., who has been training, writing, consulting, and blogging on clergy sexual misconduct and other sexual abuse issues since 1977 at the Faith Trust Institute in Seattle, WA, www.faithtrustinstitute.org.

11. See the unpublished ACPE theory position papers of Michael Hertz, ACPE Supervisor in Eugene, OR who has authorized this use of his material.

12. Alberta Film Entertainment's Oscar-winning best motion picture of 2005, *Brokeback Mountain*.

CHAPTER THIRTEEN

Expanding Dimensions of Spiritual Direction and Development

Scott McRae

I sat with my daughter in the car for her first excursion into the world of driving and was unnerved by a sudden realization: there are a staggering number of things to be learned if a person is to safely navigate more than a ton of metal, electronics, and fuel along streets and highways.

Sitting in the front seats for the first time, her eyes get big as she looks over the lights, buttons, levers, knobs, and numbers. Driving lesson #1 is a mental exercise like memorizing the state capitals. Lesson #2 involves both mind and body as she adjusts her seat, moves mirrors around, and then navigates the various steps that come with starting a car. Of course, the actual driving of the car requires even more of her. She will have to coordinate body (hands, feet, eyes, ears), mind (dashboard functions, driving rules, signs, and speed limits), and spirit (prayers are wise).

As she slowly presses on the gas to move the car for the first time, I stop her. "Ana, you're forgetting something." She realizes she needs to look around before she moves forward. Moving the car forward creates a shift in worlds—she moves from a world of "me" (radio, cd player, heat controls) into a world of "we" (other drivers, bikers, pedestrians, rules, and signs). She must quickly develop high-speed panoramic vision: scanning left and right, front and back, while stopped and while moving. There are mirrors to master so blind spots can be found. There are on-the-fly equations that must be solved as multiple cars meet at a single intersection. Most harrowing of all, is the necessary insanity of "putting the pedal to the metal" while looking backward and merging at high speed into unsympathetic traffic. Like life, learning to drive is difficult. It is all about expanding vision, awareness, and in no small measure, nerve.

LEARNING THE ART OF SPIRITUAL DIRECTION

The supervision of spiritual directors has many parallels with the supervision of a novice driver. The supervisor's task, whether working with drivers or spiritual directors, is to assist them in expanding their vision and their awareness. It involves helping them gain new capacities to increase the feeling of safety for them and others. It involves equipping them so they safely navigate increasingly complex people, relationships, or even traffic.

I approach the supervision of spiritual directors by equipping them—by expanding their dimensions of depth, width, and height. Similar to the new driver, this involves seeing into new worlds. We must learn to see more deeply into ourselves, into the "I."[1] This is the depth dimension. We must learn to see more broadly our relationships with others, into the "We." This relational dimension is referred to as width. And we must learn to see with a more expansive awareness into the transcendent realm, into the "Thou." This is the height dimension.[2] In the same way that a driver must develop and coordinate physical and mental capacities in order to drive safely, so too must a spiritual director develop and coordinate capacities related to depth, width, and height if they are to work effectively and safely with spiritual direction clients.

A fourth aspect that I call engaged presence is the underlying and generative ground of being that I believe is manifest when we arrive at genuine depth, width, and height experiences. Engaged presence is a capacity to be deeply attuned to the directee and it results when the depth, width, and height dimensions are working as one awareness. In short, this is the mode from which effective spiritual direction is practiced. I will present it as a way of being with another in a spiritual direction relationship that is fully open and present while being compassionately and prophetically engaged.

To proceed, I will begin with a description of what spiritual direction is for those who are unfamiliar with this practice. I will then speak to the issue of the changing context of religion and spirituality that both sets the stage for the unique challenges that are present for the spiritual director and suggests why its popularity is growing so significantly. I will briefly address the kinds of supervision that apply to spiritual direction and then move to a fuller description of the dimensions of depth, width, height, and engaged presence. I will identify capacities that are a part of each of these dimensions and why they are critical for developing spiritual directors. Associated curriculum components will also be identified. These dimensions and capacities provide a helpful framework for understanding the broader developmental issues related to the self and spirituality. I will address this developmental framework and then will offer some thoughts about the importance of developing the spiritual direction discipline and how it represents a prophetic response to and resource for our current religious and spiritual climate.

A WORD ABOUT SPIRITUAL DIRECTION

Spiritual direction is an ancient practice that occurs formally and informally in most religious and spiritual traditions. It is a relationship initiated by a person who seeks direction, guidance, or companioning in order to grow spiritually. The following statement captures well the motivation that leads many to seek spiritual direction and the kind of support that is needed from a spiritual director:

> Some of us long for a safe harbor to explore the deepest questions of our lives—questions about God, Spirit, Ultimate Reality, meaning, purpose, and calling. It is not therapy we are after, but something with a larger context. It isn't that we need to be fixed, but rather heard—held in a sacred space of unconditional love, and trusted to find our own deepest connection with Spirit. . . . It is more that we just need a place where we can be heard, where we can hear ourselves, and where someone will help us notice the movement of the Spirit within our ordinary lives and listen for the wisdom and guidance available within our own deep heart. We, like those early pilgrims, seek a soul-friend from whom we might receive a word, a gentle sweep of a hand suggesting a place to look, or a practice or a prayer to guide us on this, our most important journey.[3]

The spiritual director[4] assists directees in deepening their understanding and awareness of the spiritual dimensions of their daily lives by offering thoughts and wonderings, observations and questions, resources and spiritual practices. Along with the core capacities that I believe must be present for all spiritual directors (I will articulate these below), there also are sets of tools for exploration that will be unique to the individual spiritual director. These tools include but are not limited to conversation, silence, readings, poems, rituals, journaling, music, art, sand-play, toning, movement, dreams, meditation, and prayer. However, as William Creed notes in drawing upon the metaphor of ballroom dancing, there is more needed than a wide assortment of capacities, tools, or "dance steps":

> [The] ability to do the dance steps by itself does not make a good dancer. A good dancer does need to know the steps. But the key to dancing dwells in listening into the music, dancing to the music, and moving with the music together. Analogously, spiritual direction involves skills, but all the effort of listening and responding, noticing the verbal and non-verbal movements of the directee, do not make a good spiritual director. Directors need to know those skills. But the key is the Mystery where the divine and the human kiss. I believe that listening to the music of Mystery Incarnate and moving with that In-

carnate Mystery holds the supervisory conversation of spiritual directors and focuses it.[5]

After explaining what spiritual direction is, it is important to be clear about what it is not. Spiritual direction is not therapy or pastoral counseling.[6] Whereas therapy and pastoral care tend to be initiated due to the presence of a problem, spiritual direction is best initiated when there is a clear desire for spiritual growth and personal transformation. Walter Conn, speaking out of his Christian tradition, makes the distinction this way: "I specify pastoral counseling as dealing with particular problems (developmental and others) in a Christian's life, and spiritual direction as addressing a Christian's radical desire for ongoing development and conversion."[7] Given that therapy and pastoral care often are problem centered, they tend to have a narrower range of focus compared to the more expansive focus of spiritual direction. Or, to risk an oversimplification, it has been said that the task of therapy and pastoral care is to engage a problem in order to return to "normal," and that spiritual direction's task is to move us beyond "normal" and into our higher potentials and into greater wholeness.

THE CHANGING CONTEXT OF SPIRITUALITY

This deep yearning calls together the community of people that is the Spiritual Guidance and Leadership Program, a spiritual direction training program that I co-lead with three women.[8] A few people come into our program with clarity—they want training to become spiritual directors. Most come into our program as if lured by a force they don't understand. "I'm not sure why I am here" is a common refrain that is voiced during our first weekends together. There is a power, disquieting for most and exciting for some, that is present in the yearning that leads people into spiritual direction training or practice.

On a communal level, some people come into our program with active affiliations with a faith community. Most come into our program after cutting ties with their faith tradition. Some experienced their faith community as abusive, some found that they "just drifted away," and some are in a process of leaving a faith tradition that no longer feels relevant to the spiritual questions and journey they are experiencing. We are in the midst of a profound swirl of change in our spiritual and cultural worlds.[9] To state the obvious, we are in the midst of a great "unraveling" within many of our ecclesiastical, environmental, and social structures.

On the religious and spiritual front, we repeatedly hear people talk about how their traditional frameworks and belief systems lack the elasticity to accommodate the natural convergence of truths and practices that occur within an increasingly global context. The internet, massive bookstores, storefront yoga or meditation centers, and the prevalence of workshops and schools of spirituality all reflect and encourage an amazing "coming together" of people on this globe around spiritual, environmental, and communal issues. There is a vast spiritual smorgasbord available to all who can go online or to the big bookstores. As a result, we have reached a tipping point that makes the traditional institutions' call to "come back," at best ring hollow and at worst seem ridiculous. And yet, the going forward is lonely. I daresay that for most who find themselves on this path, they find themselves journeying alone. There is a pervasive vacuum that is present in the collective soul of this group of seekers, not to mention the combustion of terrorism and warfare occurring throughout the world that is generated, to a significant degree, by religious conflicts.

It is also true, I believe, that the religious traditions and their communities hold too much truth and wisdom to write them off as passé or as *the* problem. The vacuum will not be filled by each person filling their plate at a smorgasbord or by small groups establishing spiritual clubs or impromptu religions. Furthermore, as Leigh Eric Schmidt points out eloquently in his book, *Restless Souls*, seekers have been around for a long time and they have a rich tradition within our religious institutions.[10] All of this suggests that spiritual direction is a potent answer to the spiritual vacuum that is pervasive, but it is not the solution. What is certain is that spiritual direction is experienced by many as a refuge from the faith communities that feel irrelevant or that appear locked into inflexible dogmas and literalized mythologies. At the same time, spiritual direction can become a bridge to the religious traditions (again, because it is already a part of many of these traditions) and it can help people who feel at odds with their religious tradition, assisting them to integrate the best aspects of their faith tradition. If we are to ever move toward a solution to this current vacuum (and to the warring combustion) it must involve the religious traditions. And I believe these solutions require that religious communities gain the capacity to hold to the life-giving centers of their faith, and to reform, stretch, and honor the spiritual convergence that is upon us.[11]

It is my hope that the spiritual direction community can increasingly become a force that pulls religious communities toward a broader and more compassionate understanding of theology and spiritual expression. We need an intentionality that encourages a higher consciousness of self, others, and the Divine. We need clear expressions of appreciation for the rich spiritual diversity that surrounds us. It is my hope that the spiritual direction community can be a grounding influence in this "new age" of spiritual seeking so that the wisdom and the communities of our religious traditions can be claimed as an essential resource.

Spiritual direction is providing for many people a new form of spiritual community in the midst of this changing religious context. As a facilitator of spiritual development, spiritual direction is helping people broaden their frameworks of belief and experience to include this rich mixture of past tradition and expanding spirit. At the center of this spiritual resurgence is a process of prioritizing our personal experience with the Divine, enlarging our cosmologies to include the amazing discoveries of the Universe Story.[13] This new cosmology represents an alternative way of perceiving and understanding time and space. It weaves together and reorients religion, contemplative spirituality, physics, psychology, and ecology. But more than an intellectual theory, this cosmology views the universe itself as a material and spiritual vessel that holds us. The universe becomes a vast and very near source of love, energy, and mystery. I have found that when we feel its embrace, our consciousness is changed. We come to trust in the support and guidance of the Divine Creator who animates the universe, and we are empowered and made hopeful.

SPIRITUAL DIRECTION SUPERVISION

Given the complexity of the spiritual landscape described above, it is both challenging and crucial to provide supervision that equips people to function effectively. Spiritual directors today must be able to attend to the bewildering vacuums and the rising consciousness. Increasingly, we need spiritual directors who are adept in accompanying seekers and mainstream believers as they navigate these new spiritual landscapes. Moreover, if we need spiritual directors who can work with these complexities, then we need processes and programs that can equip spiritual directors for this unique journey and role.

When distinguishing the various types of supervision related to spiritual direction, generally they will fit into one of four categories:

	People in a Spiritual Direction Training Process	*People Professionally Practicing Spiritual Direction*
Individuals	The individual training of a spiritual director by a seasoned spiritual director. (This is rare.)	A spiritual director receives one-on-one supervision of their professional practice from a seasoned director.
Groups	Group spiritual direction training provided by a team of seasoned directors in an established program.	A seasoned director leads a supervision group for individuals who are practicing spiritual directors.

Table 13.1

While I have not researched this, it is my observation that the majority of spiritual directors are trained in programs that range from 10 to 25 participants. Most programs in the United States are rooted in the Christian tradition while honoring the religious and spiritual diversity in our changing culture. Most programs base their curriculum upon a mix of theological, spiritual, and psychological study. They emphasize ritual and community building, and they use some form of practicum in which participants are carefully supervised in their initial spiritual direction experiences.

Training programs usually provide certificates for their graduates because there is not an official certification process in spiritual direction. Therefore, there is no such thing as a "certified spiritual director," though unfortunately some present themselves as such. Spiritual Directors International is the professional organization for spiritual directors. They produce the journal *Presence,* are a web resource, offer a directory of spiritual directors who are members, and sponsor an annual conference. Once graduated, the "community standard" is that spiritual directors participate in supervision groups or receive supervision of their work from a seasoned spiritual director.

SPIRITUAL DIRECTION SUPERVISION: EXPANDING THE DIMENSIONS OF DEPTH, WIDTH, AND HEIGHT

Spiritual directors need to build capacities and expand their vision just like new drivers do. Depth, width, and height represent three dimensions that are essential to the work of spiritual direction. Each offers a unique range of vision. Each dimension has core capacities that are important for spiritual directors to acquire if they are to be fully effective as directors. To be sure, these three dimensions are interrelated and overlapping. It is common for spiritual directors to favor or be comfortable in one or two of these domains and to struggle with the other(s).

For example, it is common in our training program to work with people that are quite skilled at observing, listening to, and responding to others (width), but who are unaware of their feelings or inner assumptions (depth). Or, a more cerebral trainee may be well-read theologically and may have a dynamic prayer life (height), but struggles to engage other people (width). The work of spiritual direction requires that all three of these dimensions are developed and coordinated to some degree within the spiritual director. Accordingly, these same dimensions provide a framework for assessing and working with a spiritual direction client. In the material that follows, I will further define each of these dimensions and then speak to the basic capacities needed for effective spiritual direction.

DEPTH

Snowflakes, fingerprints, DNA, rocks—it is an amazing feature of our universe that, if you look closely enough, no two things are exactly alike. The Jesuit mystic and paleontologist, Pierre Teilhard de Chardin, went further and made the case that not only are no two things alike but each existing thing has a sacred center that imbues it with being and holiness.[15] As I am using the term, depth is that dimension that reflects our holy interiority. Just as every acorn holds the blueprint for an utterly unique oak tree, every self holds a blueprint that establishes our true nature and our essential self. I think of depth as both the process and the place for accessing this essential self. Depth is the dimension of the "I."

Typically, the deeper our awareness of our depth, the more grounded and alive we are. For we know ourselves better. The more conversant we are with our interiority, the more we know our place in the order of things.

The interior life is a place of the wild—uncivilized and predictable, giving us fevers, symptoms, and moments of impossible beauty. Yet within the appearance of chaos are both a richness and a deep level of orderliness. Like a national park, the interior world doesn't do anything—it is the treasure-house of life. It can't be strip-mined for our conscious purposes. The only request it makes of us is that we love it and in return it responds to our attention. To learn to attend well is to discover our place in the natural order: it brings an element of consistency and harmony to our lives and gives us a story about who we are. To learn to attend is a beginning. To learn to attend more and more deeply is the path itself.[16]

People typically seek out spiritual direction because, in some fashion, they are weary of living on the surface of their lives. There is a longing to access an authenticity that seems to be lying dormant. Lying within is a sense of incompleteness or deficiency related to a job or a relationship that may not fit, to a voice that is stifled within us, or a vision that has not yet coalesced. Accessing a client's depth dimension, therefore, becomes a primary task and resource for the spiritual director.

WIDTH

The journey into the depths of the self, however, is not an end in itself. Over time, to confine oneself to one's interior life becomes a bleak kind of existence. A self that is deepened with "essential" awareness, paradoxically, is best able to join another. The deeper we are able to engage our own interior lives the more likely we are able to engage deeply the interior of other human beings, of creation itself, and of the Divine. Walter Conn uses the concept of the "desiring self" to speak to the essential nature of width:

My theoretical premise is that the fundamental desire of the self is to transcend itself in relationship: to the world, to others, to God. But only a developed, powerful self has the strength to realize significant transcendence. My approach, therefore, recognizes two focal points in the fundamental human desire: the drive to be a self, a center of strength [depth]; and the dynamism to move beyond the self in relationship [width] . . . The desires to be a self and to reach out beyond the self must always be understood together: separation and attachment, independence and belonging, autonomy and relationship.[17]

The width dimension is connected with our fundamental desire to extend ourselves into the world around us. The width dimension is about the "We." It's about relationality and communion with other beings and realities. This is the realm of intersubjectivity, which is to say that width engages us and shapes our depth. Our depth dimension could not exist without width. A relationship of some sort is required for any new essence to come into being. And, if essence is to survive, it must be living in communion. People cannot live without oxygen, which in turn requires plants and trees. Plants and trees need minerals and water, and on and on. If we were able to see into the molecular level we would be startled by the degree of communion that exists in every breath that we take. The capacity to effectively channel our desire to join another person and to engage them deeply is the key learning task of the width dimension and an essential step in the dance of spiritual direction.

HEIGHT

Height brings a third dimension into the life and work of a spiritual director. Height represents the transcendent dimension that carries with it otherness, wonder, and awe. It brings with it complexity and mystery, divine transcendence and divine immanence. With the height dimension, the "I" and the "We" enter into the swirl of the great "Thou." Anne Lamott captures the feel of the height dimension as she speaks to the goal of writers. It applies as well to spiritual directors.

> This is our goal as writers, I think, to help others have this sense of—please forgive me—wonder, of seeing things anew, things that can catch us off guard, that break in on our small, bordered worlds. When this happens, everything feels more spacious. Try walking around with a child who's going, "Wow, wow! Look at that dirty dog! Look at that burned-down house! Look at that red sky!" . . . I think this is how we are supposed to be in the world—present and in awe. . . . There is ecstasy in paying attention. You can get into a kind of Wordsworthian openness to the world, where you see in everything the essence of holiness, a sign that God is implicit in all of creation.[18]

The dimension of height, on an experiential level, brings into our lives the mystery and reverence that is always beyond our comprehension and, often at the same time, a presence that is grounding, guiding, and hopeful. We encounter this dimension in the best of our religious and spiritual experiences. We may experience Divine direction as a "calling." We may experience this transcendence in those moments when we feel deeply in love or deeply connected with another, in profound nature experiences, and, of course, in effective spiritual direction experiences. We try to capture height through our carefully articulated theologies and concepts of the Divine. Theologies and concepts are necessary but not sufficient for capturing the Holy. Because conceptual attempts to frame the Divine are partial views of a much greater mystery, spiritual direction seeks to ground and augment discussion of height by staying carefully attuned to our experiences of the Divine and of the "I – Thou" encounter.

ENGAGED PRESENCE

My approach to the supervision of spiritual directors consists of attending to the dimensions of depth, width, and height both within the spiritual director and helping the participants to attend to these dimensions within a client session. When a director simultaneously is accessing depth, width, and height the result is an engaged presence. Jean Stairs, in her book *Listening for the Soul*, provides a helpful description of listening, which I see to be the foundation for engaged presence.

> In placing such a prominent emphasis upon listening, it needs to be said that I am not describing a passive act, but a process that engages us actively in response to what is heard . . . Undeniably, listening for the soul will involve those essential skills normally identified with the act of listening, such as expressing interest by caring behavior, using appropriate facial expressions and posture, posing open-ended questions, closely observing nonverbal clues, responding by paraphrasing, clarifying, supporting, probing understanding, confronting, evaluating, and recommending. Such responses and ways of listening have a necessary function in listening for the soul. To listen for the spiritual dimension in every human experience and life circumstance, however, requires listening with a definite spirit and intentionality. We are listening for more than what is consciously expressed. We are listening for the very voice, presence, or absence of God in the soul, the core of our lives where meaning is created.[19]

Presence is an inner disposition that is grounded and authentic. I believe it is a state of engaged awareness that is simple, relaxed, focused, and purposeful. And, if presence is all of these aspects, it is easy to see why becoming present to self and others is a great challenge! It isn't automatic. We gain it through practice, through our steady attention to the depth, width, and height dimensions within our lives. The following description of teahouse practice within Zen Buddhism reflects nicely the paradoxical challenge and simplicity of the state of presence.

> Teahouse practice means that you don't explicitly talk about Zen. It refers to leading your life as if you were an old woman who has a teahouse by the side of the road. Nobody knows why they like to go there, they just feel good drinking her tea. She's not known as a Buddhist teacher. She doesn't say, "This is a Zen teahouse." All she does is simply serve tea—but still, her decades of attentiveness are part of the way she does it. No one knows about her faithful attention to the practice—it's just there, in the serving of the tea and the way she cleans the counters and washes the cups.[20]

In the spiritual direction context, we move into presence in order to join and engage our clients. Or, to put it more strongly, our job in spiritual direction and supervision *is* engaged presence. When we are authentically present the space between us and the other is altered. There is a tacit but powerful permission given for the other to become more present to their own life: their suffering, fear, hope, joy, etc. If the other is able to be present deeply to her or his life, there will be suffering or fear to hear, to attend to, to care for—because such struggles are deeply human. Engaged presence is a stance that is biased toward struggles because it believes that transformation and renewal usually are constructed out of the building blocks of pain, hardship or loss. Engaged presence leads us into ever-deepening experiences of depth, width, and height, just as these three dimensions are doorways into presence.

CAPACITIES AND CURRICULUM

The big, bewildered eyes that I saw on my daughter's face when first learning to drive have shown up on the faces of many spiritual direction participants when they sit across from a client in a first practicum session. It is overwhelming for most to feel responsible and unqualified for navigating a spiritual direction session with a real, live, unpredictable human being. I remind them that many of the capacities needed for effective spiritual direction are already well-developed within them. Some capacities will need some honing and some capacities will likely be a real challenge to develop. The following table identifies the core capacities that I associate with each of the three dimensions:

	Depth	*Width*	*Height*
Core Capacities	Identity Differentiation Use of self	Compassionate joining Boundaries Guidance	Reverence Devotion Theology/Conceptual framework

Table 13.2

THE DEPTH CAPACITIES AND CURRICULUM

As I view the supervision of spiritual directors, the core capacities that relate to the depth dimension are identity, differentiation, and use of self. Spiritual directors must have a strong sense of "I," a strong sense of identity. This means having an intimate feel for our internal blueprint, what is true and most valued in our personal lives. In the same way that a driver must become familiar with the various knobs and buttons on the dashboard, the capacity of identity grows as we get to know our fears, reactivity, joys, hopes, strengths, weaknesses, compulsions, etc. The more nuanced our view into ourselves is, the more likely we will have a nuanced view of others. The more clarity that we have about our sense of self, the less "at stake" we are with others and the more we have to give of ourselves. Therefore, as our sense of identity strengthens, so grows our capacities for empathy, compassion, and creativity. The stronger our "I" is, the more generative we are able to be toward others and the world.

Differentiation is the capacity to stand apart from others and it is a function of depth and identity. The more clear we are about the "I" within us, the more we are able to be clear with others, the more we are able to differentiate from family, peers, and institutions. As we honor our essential and unique selves we also chart our own course, claim our own perspective, speak our own voice. Differentiation means that our paths at times will be intrinsically lonely because there are no other models for who we are to be. But differentiation becomes a crucial capacity in that it lessens the likelihood that we will get hooked by a client's dynamics. It helps us to separate our agendas from theirs and it becomes an empowering trust that the client is the true change agent.

The third core capacity in the depth dimension is use of self. As we are learning the art of supervision, one of the greatest challenges is to develop a dual focus: one eye on the client and one eye on ourselves. The capacity to observe our intuitions, thoughts, feelings, and body dynamics, and then to incorporate them into our supervision is "use of self." The notion of "use of self" is rooted in our belief that body, mind, and spirit are highly sensitive antennae that guide our listening and our speaking. The self, with all of its mysterious and miraculous abilities, is the primary resource for engaged spiritual direction. We must develop the capacity to listen to it and to let it guide us if we are to be dynamically present to our client.

There are not many university catalogues that include courses in strengthening the "I." Yet this issue of developing our depth dimension may well be the foundation for all spiritual direction learning. Curriculum components that encourage depth speak not only to our own sacred interiors but also to the sacred interiors that are present in all of the created order. Ritual, silence, reading assignments, journaling, art, mindfulness training, the Enneagram and Myers-Briggs typologies, etc., are all means that we use to help participants listen to their lives and further define their identity. Centering activities, such as those that begin each of our days together in our training program, help participants develop the capacity to slow down the self, tune in to breathing, and observe both body and mind dynamics. Finally, peer and leader feedback in spiritual direction practicums is key to the depth curriculum. This feedback helps participants key into the assumptions and feelings that are operating below the surface of their awareness. Furthermore, through the practicum experience, participants often gain a clearer sense about whether or not "spiritual director" is an authentic aspect of their identity.

THE WIDTH CAPACITIES AND CURRICULUM

The capacity to be with another in a deep way is another fundamental aspect of spiritual direction. Spiritual direction is an act of communion where two or more souls come together for support and encouragement, guidance, and blessing. Without the complex skills that come with compassionate joining, boundaries, and guidance, we put clients at risk in the spiritual direction encounter.

Compassionate joining is the capacity to relate to another in a way that is deeply connected. Through this joining, there is genuine sense from the spiritual director that "I am for you in this relationship." There is keen attention paid to verbal and non-verbal signals. A strong message of being attentive and "for" the client gives rise to the development of trust, which is the platform upon which an effective session proceeds. Through compassion, there is a clear current of care and openness to receiving the words of the client in a non-judging way.

When compassionate joining occurs, a client often experiences validation, blessing, and embrace from the spiritual director.

The capacity to set and navigate boundaries is as challenging as it is important. When we think of boundaries we often think of the important issues of touch, the location of direction, dual relationships and roles, and the exchange of money. These issues obviously must be addressed through spiritual direction supervision. At the same time, there is a deeper dimension to boundaries that is even more important, I believe. In the same way that identity sets up the capacity for differentiation, compassionate joining sets up the capacity to create healthy boundaries. Conversely, when we do not join a client well, the conditions are ripe for boundary violations.

Boundary violations are on a continuum and all of us make boundary mistakes. On one end of the continuum are the poor connections which keep us from hearing or honoring the needs of clients. On the other end of the continuum are a range of relationships that occur when we are not "well-joined" to a client: we may equalize the relationship and make the clients into our friends, we may elevate them and give them too much power, or we may diminish them and make them object to be controlled. Recognizing power dynamics and differentials is a core capacity that must be developed before a spiritual director works independently with clients. Marilyn Peterson, in her book *At Personal Risk*, states that professionals use their greater power in the relationship not for their own ends, but to protect the client's greater vulnerability in the relationship.[21] When we are "well-joined," there is clarity about roles and structures, there is one who is compassionately in charge of the session, and there is a caring focus on the issues and the concerns that are brought by the client.

Guidance rounds out the core capacities for the width dimension, and it relates to this notion of "being in charge." There is a common perception among people entering training that a good spiritual director is a good listener who smiles and stays out of the way of the client. We are to be a "non-anxious presence." Listening and non-anxious presence are foundational skills that represent a starting point for spiritual directors. But the spiritual director must be more than a good listener. People come to spiritual direction with real life problems and fears, with deep and complex desires. Friendly listening will be of little help up against these problems or complexities.

This is where the capacity of guidance comes in. Engaged presence means that the spiritual director is passionately involved in a session with a client. As guides, spiritual directors are "in charge" in the sense of creating professional, safe contexts for exploration. They provide a kind of leadership in which the client is joined and carefully guided toward that which is potentially transformative. Guidance brings movement into the width dimension. And, as guide, the primary task is to open the way for the real Guide to be heard within the client, for the Spirit and the resources within the client to do their own spiritual direction.

There is remarkable power and possibility that emerges in the gathered community. Curriculum components that facilitate growth in this width dimension again are the community rituals and storytelling. We have a "check-in" session on the first day of our monthly weekends where each participant shares their lives with the group. We study boundaries, engaged presence, spiritual assessment, active listening, and narrative theory in order to foster in our participants awareness and tools for joining others. We do "fishbowls" in which a leader will model a brief spiritual direction session with a group member, followed by group discussion of the leader's techniques and style. In this context of "We," the community itself becomes the most powerful aspect of a curriculum.

	Depth	*Width*	*Height*
Examples of Core Curriculum Components	- Ritual - Centering - Silence - Journaling - Mindfulness training - Practicums - Personality typologies (Enneagrams, Meyers Briggs)	- Gathered community - Storytelling - Spiritual assessment - Narrative theory - Power and boundaries - Fishbowl observation sessions	- Receiving spiritual direction - Ritual - Religious/spiritual resources - Liturgical or spiritual calendars - Theological and spiritual books - Spiritual practices

Table 13.3

THE HEIGHT CAPACITIES AND CURRICULUM

We may not usually think of transcendence as a capacity because it so often comes to us as a gift. There is, however, a way in which the ability to open oneself to this height dimension is a crucial capacity that can be disciplined and developed. We can think of this through lenses such a James Fowler's stages of faith development, through the development of meditative or prayer practices, or through any number of ways that we emerge from or daily trances to wake up to more fully be in the here and now. I see the core tasks of this height dimension to be the development of reverence, devotion, and theology/conceptual frameworks.

Reverence is the capacity to stay in a sustained state of awakeness, to be attuned to and grateful for the transcendent currents in our own lives and in the world around us. It is an empowered and receptive posture. Devotion is the capacity to surrender to the great "Thou," in whatever religious or spiritual form this might take (God, Goddess, Christ, Buddha, Allah, Gaia, etc.). Many who have left formal religion or not been a part of it find it difficult to recapture or discover devotion. It is my sense that many who seek out spiritual direction or training for spiritual direction are struggling with the vacuum that comes when the "Thou" is lost. A relationship with the Divine and the sense that we are being guided and held is a powerfully life-orienting force that is at the center of spiritual direction work. Spiritual directors must nurture this height dimension. They must be grounded in their own relationship with the Divine, and then trust this Force to be the lead dancer in the spiritual direction work. Goethe writes of the power of this guidance:

> The moment one definitely commits oneself, then Providence moves too. All sorts of things occur to help one that would never otherwise have occurred. A whole stream of events issues from the decision, raising in one's favor all manner of unseen incidents and meetings and material assistance, which no man could have dreamed would come his way.[22]

Finally, theology is important. Theology and other conceptual frameworks that give language to the un-nameable are important because clients will be giving voice to theological questions or wonderings. Spiritual directors do not need to be well-studied theologians, but they do need to have some familiarity with basic theological concepts (e.g. sin, redemption, salvation, grace). Theology is empowering in that it provides spiritual directors with a capacity to variously reference and work with Divine and human attributes and struggles.

Curriculum components that are related to this height dimension include the vast resources from our religious and spiritual traditions (scripture verses, liturgies, prayers, hymns, poems, etc.) These are especially well-utilized in centering activities and rituals. The liturgical calendar and the earlier calendars from Pagan, Celtic, and other ancient sources also provide a powerful way to journey through the seasons, through light and dark, warmth and cold, dying and rising. Such calendars can also be occasions for studying the traditional theological or spiritual themes that are associated with certain holy days or periods (e.g., Easter, Ramadhan, Hanukah, or Imbolc). The reading of theological and spiritual books and articles also has a central place in a spiritual direction curriculum.

Having covered the more objective content related to the height dimension, there is an all-important subjective component to the curriculum. First and foremost, our participants are expected to be recipients of spiritual direction from a seasoned director during their training process. It is also important that practicing spiritual directors are receiving spiritual direction as well. Finally, there is a whole array of practices that we include in our curriculum: prayer, meditation, silence, body movement, drum and mask making, other art, journal writing. These are intended to not only enhance our participants' relationship with the "Thou," but also to be resources for future spiritual direction sessions.

THE DEVELOPMENT OF THE SELF AND SPIRITUALITY

I have found it helpful to view the highly complex issue of self and spiritual development through the simple lens of depth, width, and height. One way to understand human development is in terms of expanding an "I."[23] In this view, infants are basically confined to their depth dimension and are inhabitants of the single-dimensioned ego. As they grow, their depth dimension increasingly adds width. Their ego begins to identify with the ethnocentric context of their mother or family, and they become two-dimensional, as it were. The "I," as the inter-subjectivists know, is now under the influence of the "We" and, accordingly, the self has expanded. This same self becomes three-dimensional as it begins to encounter and integrate the transcendent into its life and view of reality. The self increasingly becomes a vessel of Spirit as it grows in this height dimension, and increasingly gains the capacity to identify with the Divine: it feels the Divine within, it trusts in Divine guidance, its identity becomes shaped by a deep calling.

The depth dimension—the ego, the "I"—are not lost in the midst of this expansion. The dualistic notion of having to rid ourselves of ego in order to develop as a self is avoided in this framework. The ego instead keeps taking on new dimensionality. The "I" expands as it identifies with the "We" and even more with the "Thou." The ego has been compared to a small candle flame that shines bright in a dark room. That flame becomes almost invisible when the curtains are pulled back to let in the brilliant sunlight. In higher states of development and consciousness, the flame of the separate self still burns but it is dramatically eclipsed by the great light of Being. So, the developing self moves from egocentric to ethnocentric to world-centric and on to uni-centric in the case of unitive consciousness (that rare state of identification with Whole of Being which is the aim of most Eastern religions, or with Christ consciousness which is the aim of Christian mysticism). In this light, spiritual direction is nothing other than the process of helping people expand their "I" and increasingly identify their self and spirit with widening circles of reality.

To shift to the other end of the spectrum, we can view the impediments of human development as relating to a self that is stuck on the surface of the depth, width, or height dimensions. A lesser-developed self could be viewed in terms of narcissism if confined to the depth dimension, enmeshment, or co-dependency if caught in the width dimension, and fundamentalism if a reductionistic view of the height dimension is held. Those who are abusive, evil, or ignorant could be said to suffer from a deficiency of self. When confined to such a small self (and this happens to us all from time to time), our responses become limited to defensiveness and reactivity, protecting what little self we have. There is a great cost to our selves, others, and the world when our three-dimensional self is denied or diminished.

THE PROPHETIC DIMENSION OF SPIRITUAL DIRECTION

I believe there is a moral imperative in this age of religious and cultural warfare that we create communities of deep and grace-filled connection, that we find ways to help people of different faith traditions talk to and care about each other, and that we help those who feel spiritually isolated to find community. I believe there is a moral imperative in this age when so many suffer from imprisonment in their small selves that we learn to care for each other in our smallness rather than responding with rage or reactivity. It is essential that we encourage the development of self and spirit as broadly as possible and that we expand our capacity for compassion as a human family.

Spiritual direction is a movement that has tremendous potential in answering these problems and needs. Its power and promise rest in individuals and communities that are expanding their dimensions of depth, width, and height. It is important that we have training programs that can both be a source of inspired and inspiring communities, and can equip spiritual directors to hear and speak into the voids that are so prominent these days. Such communities of spiritual diversity do not reflect a friendly abiding of our differences, but rather an intentional effort to live into a newly evolving human community in which we carry forward the life-giving aspects of our traditions as we simultaneously embrace the new movements of the Divine.

NOTES

1. I am borrowing here from Ken Wilber, who has written extensively about the use of personal pronouns to represent perspectives that can be taken. See *Integral Spirituality* (Boston: Integral Books, 2006), 33-38. This is not to be confused with Wilber's theological work which he calls "The 1-2-3 of God." Here Wilber distinguishes first (I), second (Thou), and third (It) person experiences of God (Wilber, 158-161).

2. A word of clarification is in order related to the use of the terms "Thou" and "height." The pronoun "it" is typically used to represent the third person perspective in Ken Wilber's framework. Given the spiritual nature of the perspectives as I am framing them, I am using "Thou" instead, drawing on Martin Buber's "I-Thou" concept. A limitation of referring to this as a "height" dimension is that is may reinforce the notion of a separate and personified God who resides in the heavens. I view God as present within each of these dimensions. In spite of its limitations, I use the concept of height because it evokes a third and transcendent dimension of self.

3. Joan Borysenko and Gordon Dveirin, *Your Soul's Compass: What Is Spiritual Guidance* (Carlsbad, CA: Hay House, 2007), 235.

4. "Spiritual Director" is a term most commonly used to describe this professional role, but it also is a term commonly disliked. The notion of providing direction may suggest an expert model in which there is a director and a follower, a teacher and a student. Most spiritual directors function with a mutuality model which the "directee" is their own best resource for spiritual understanding and growth. Accordingly, most "spiritual directors" describe their role more in terms of guide, mentor, companion, or midwife. I will use "spiritual director" throughout this chapter, though I want to be clear that I understand this to be modeled after mutuality rather than expertise.

5. William Creed, "Supervision Plus Reflection: A Way to Form Spiritual Directors," *Presence* (Vol. 4, No. 1), 37-42.

6. For a more extensive treatment of the similarities and differences between pastoral care and spiritual direction, see Jean Stairs, *Listening for the Soul: Pastoral Care and Spiritual Direction* (Minneapolis: Fortress Press, 2000), Chapter 7.

7. Walter Conn, *The Desiring Self: Rooting Pastoral Counseling and Spiritual Direction in Self-Transcendence* (New York: Paulist Press, 1998), 5.

8. The Spiritual Guidance and Leadership Program is a two-year training program in St. Paul, MN that meets one weekend a month for eight months of the year. The program, in existence since 1988, generally has between 20 and 25 participants that come from diverse religious and cultural backgrounds.

9. For a sociological assessment of these changes, see Paul H. Ray and Sherry Ruth Anderson, *Cultural Creatives: How 50 Million People Are Changing the World* (New York: Three Rivers Press, 2000). Their research has identified three distinct cultures that are frequently at odds with one another: traditionalists, modernists and cultural creatives.

10. Leigh Eric Schmidt, *Restless Soul: The Making of American Spirituality from Emerson to Oprah* (San Francisco: Harper, 2005), especially Chapter 6.

11. This challenge of whether or not religious traditions can move toward reform and mutual appreciation is one of the most crucial challenges that we face as a global community and our survival may hinge on it. See Wilber, *Op. cit.*, Chapter 9, for an insightful commentary on terrorism and religion.

13. At the Center for Spiritual Guidance, we ground our curriculum in the spiritual cosmology that is represented by sources such as the Universe Story (based on the works of Thomas Berry, Brian Swimme, and Michael Dowd), quantum theology (based on the work of Diarmud O'Murchu), and the nature poetry of Mary Oliver. Michael Dowd's *Thank God for Evolution* (New York: Viking, 2007) is an especially good summary of the New Cosmology.

15. John R. Yungblut, *The Gentle Art of Spiritual Guidance* (Amity House, Inc., 1988), 53.

16. John Tarrant, *The Light Inside the Dark: Zen, Soul, and the Spiritual Life* (New York: HarperCollins, 1998), 11.

17. Conn, *Op. cit.*, 5. Brackets added.

18. Anne Lamott, *Bird by Bird: Some Instructions on Writing and Life* (New York: Anchor Books, Doubleday, 1994), 100.

19. Jean Stairs, *Listening for the Soul* (Minneapolis: Fortress Press, 2000), 17.

20. Attributed to Jane Hirshfield in an interview with Bill Moyer's on *Fooling with Words*.

21. Marilyn R. Peterson, *At Personal Risk: Boundary Violations in Professional-Client Relationships* (New York: WW Norton & Company, 1992), especially Chapter 11.

22. W. H. Murray, *The Scottish Himalaya Expedition* (New York: J.M. Dent and Sons, Ltd., 1951).

23. I was introduced to the concept the expanding "I" or self by Ken Wilber. See *The Eye of Spirit* (Boston: Shambhala, 2001), 210f.

CHAPTER FOURTEEN

CPE Supervision: Past and Present

Judith Ragsdale

My first unit of CPE occurred in 1981; I have had four CPE supervisors and have benefited from the wisdom of each. From the first three, I learned pastoral care skills. From the fourth, I learned the art of CPE supervision. I doubt whether any of my supervisors would have considered themselves purveyors of wisdom. In the *Dictionary of Pastoral Care and Counseling*, wisdom is defined in this way:

> Wisdom is primarily existential, a quality of undeceived understanding and experience won through struggle and effort over time. It is, therefore, largely tacit, only partly reducible to speech and writing—and is marked by qualities of self-knowledge, maturity, perspective, judgment, a sense of the whole, and a capacity to find a certain dialectical wholeness in the contradictory aspects of experience.[1]

In my experience, the process of CPE education came from wisdom and led to the beginnings of wisdom. "To become wise, to transcend one's obstinately self-regarding nature, is understood by wisdom to be a process of education."[2]

I was certified as a CPE supervisor in 1990. This certification indicated that I had demonstrated competence in the education of CPE students at what was then called basic and advanced levels of CPE—we now refer these stages of education as levels I and II CPE. I have supervised students in a congregation-based CPE setting for five years. I have directed a CPE program in a major pediatric medical center for the past 13 years. On average, I currently supervise between six and nine students per year.

Certification as a CPE supervisor also provided the credential allowing me to educate CPE students in supervisory education (SESs). I have supervised four SESs and, through difficult experiences, came to realize that my education had not equipped me to do this type of supervision. I seek to bridge the gaps in my knowledge through consultation with experienced supervisors and through study of the supervisory process.

Although CPE began as a movement in the 1920s and educating supervisors began in 1933,[3] I have found only three articles on the subject published between 1985 and 2005 of the *Journal of Supervision and Training in Ministry* and in the *Journal of Pastoral Care and Counseling*, both in association with the ACPE. All three articles were simple considerations of practice, which could easily have been replicated or expanded. Certification of supervisors, accreditation of education programs, and development of standards for both supervisors and programs have been the focus of the professional organization throughout the history of CPE. However, there has been little empirical evidence to substantiate the value, difference, or effectiveness of such educational programs in producing qualified supervisors. In fact, we know little about how effective supervisors engage in supervision nor do we understand the processes in which they engage.

CPE supervisory education generally takes between two and five years and is provided to students who demonstrate an ability to do competent pastoral care and use the educational tools of CPE for learning. This is to say that students entering supervisory education are competent professionals who are prepared to learn the art and skill of educating others to be practitioners of pastoral care. Pastoral care texts and articles abound—the dearth of literature about educating students to be pastoral supervisors is surprising. Supervisors have tended to rely on literature from cognate disciplines in developing a conceptual framework for teaching pastoral supervision. Continuing to develop literature on pastoral supervision will not only benefit those becoming CPE supervisors as well as those engaging in other kinds of pastoral supervision, it will also add a stronger pastoral voice to interdisciplinary dialogue in supervisory education.

INTRODUCTION TO PASTORAL SUPERVISION

David Steere[4] points out that pastoral supervision has been practiced, taught, and evaluated at least as fully as supervision in any profession: "Among the professions, no group has developed a more thorough system for training, examining, and accrediting competent supervisors than the Association for Clinical Pastoral Education." CPE is an action/reflection model of education for those becoming providers of pastoral care and, subsequently, supervisors. It developed from a grassroots movement that began in the 1920s. Over the next 40 years, various groups evolved—primarily the Council for Clinical Training, the Institute of Pastoral Care, the Lutheran Advisory Council on Pastoral Care, and the Southern Baptist Association for Clinical Pastoral Education.[5] In 1967, these groups united to become the Association for Clinical Pastoral Education (ACPE).

While little focused research has been done on the practice of educating CPE supervisors, supervision is central to the education process of CPE. In 2007, I did a grounded theory research study of the process of educating CPE supervisors. One supervisor interviewed for the study described CPE supervision in this way:

> . . . people need to talk about all kinds of things that aren't immediately related to the exploration of ministry in a process relative to ministry. But in a purist point of view, that's what supervision is. Helping people look inward at how their own inner, you know, their thinking, their values, their emotions, all of that—their history, their relationships—how all of that is affecting their ministry.

To understand the role of CPE supervisors, it is necessary to review the history of CPE.

HISTORICAL DEVELOPMENT OF CLINICAL PASTORAL EDUCATION

CPE began as a radical shift in an approach to theological education in the 1920s.[6] Before the 1920s, theological education focused primarily on classical education in language and systematic theology, but not on applying theological principles to those in physical, emotional, or spiritual distress. CPE reflected a cultural shift towards studying experience—in this case, the experiences of both the student and those to whom he or she ministered. This shift was the result of empirical and pragmatic theologies. The idea of studying theology empirically, by looking deeply into human religious experience, was born of an era of inquiry that insisted on the importance of experience. In his history of CPE, Edward Thornton wrote:

> The intellectual basis for these judgments against traditional theological education was experimentalism in philosophy and its educational expression, progressivism. William James and John Dewey are the best known architects of experimentalism. Experimentalism . . . was pragmatic, depending upon empirical inquiry under the discipline of the scientific method. It was a striking example of men living their way into a system of thinking, rather than the reverse.[7]

CPE resulted from experiments to expand theological education from the classroom into the experiential realm. Table 14.1 depicts a timeline with reference to those events relevant to CPE supervisory education.

Date	Event
1925	Richard C. Cabot, M.D. publishes his article "A Plea for a Clinical Year in The Course of Theological Study."
1930	The Council for the Clinical Training of Theological Students is incorporated in Boston with Philip Guiles as field secretary and interim director.
1938	Guiles and Cabot reorganize their work under the title the New England Theological Schools Committee on Clinical Training.
1940s	The chasm deepens between the two groups offering CPE because the New England group provides a pastoral orientation and the Council for Clinical Training is primarily psychoanalytic.
1944	The New England group is incorporated as the Institute of Pastoral Care.
1947	The Lutheran Advisory Council is formed.
1957	The Southern Baptist Association for CPE is formed.
1967	Unification of the Council for Clinical Training, the Institute of Pastoral Care, Lutheran and Southern Baptist accrediting agencies is accomplished along with establishment of formal relationships with the American Association of Theological Schools and the National Council of the Churches of Christ in the USA. The Association for Clinical Pastoral Education is formed.

Table 14.1 Time of Events Relevant to Supervisory Education in CPE[8]

FOUNDERS OF CLINICAL PASTORAL EDUCATION

The founding fathers of CPE in the 1920s were two physicians and a clergyman, each with a strong opinion about education for clergy. Anton T. Boisen, the clergyman of the trio, suffered from bouts of profound mental illness. Boisen considered himself both a Presbyterian and a Congregational clergyman. He was diagnosed with "schizophrenic reaction, catatonic type."[9] He came to believe that studying his own mental illness as a religious phenomenon would help him understand more about both himself as a clergyman, as well as more about both religious experience and mental illness. Boisen introduced the concept of studying "the living human document" and was a strong proponent of research in the field of religion. Specifically, Boisen was interested in studying the ways religious symbols helped patients with mental illness make meaning of their experience.

One of the physicians instrumental in beginning CPE was William Keller of Cincinnati, Ohio. In 1923, Keller gathered the first small group of theological students and placed them in social agencies of a sort, where they could work with people in pain, acquiring skills from social work and other cognate disciplines. Keller's focus on social problems disappeared from CPE's evolution early in the process, but returned in the 1990s when the ACPE Standards were amended, adding an educational outcome requiring CPE students to demonstrate an awareness of social concerns.

The other physician responsible for developing CPE was Richard Cabot. Changes in medical education led him to imagine an application to theological education.

> Richard Cabot, a Boston physician, was deeply influenced by the Flexner report of 1910 which called for a significant change in medical education. Cabot wrote about and arranged funding for programs providing for a clinical year of training for students of theology.[10]

Cabot applied considerable energy and financial resources to developing a program for educating clergy in the practical application of tools for spiritual care. He founded the discipline of medical social work and transferred the case study, a social work tool, to helping theology students reflect on ministry with patients.

The beginning of clinical training for clergy was set into motion by these men. Although the history of CPE involves splintering the original ideas into two and then three branch organizations, the Association for Clinical Pastoral Education weaves together these three historical strands today.

IMPORTANCE OF CPE SUPERVISION

A key concern of the organizations that ultimately became the ACPE was the education and certification of CPE supervisors. This is because supervision is at the heart of the CPE process of learning. CPE began educating supervisors in the 1920s in the context of interdisciplinary dialogue with medical doctors, psychiatrists, sociologists, social workers, and seminary professors.

SEEDS OF CONFLICT

Boisen and Cabot worked together in the early days. Cabot sponsored Boisen's first program of clinical training with four seminary students in 1925. Thornton noted that "Cabot contributed both to Boisen's developing identity as a professionally trained minister and to his competence as an educator."[11] This is the first reported case of educating supervisors to equip them to provide clinical pastoral education to students.

It appears that Cabot thought Boisen would be one of his protégés, but their individual interests led them to different aspects of pastoral care. Cabot was concerned about Boisen's focus on his own religious experience. Ultimately, Boisen's bouts of schizophrenia caused him to lose favor with Cabot and the financial resources Cabot had available. CPE's enduring emphasis on the individual's emotional, psychological, and spiritual interconnectedness is drawn directly from Boisen. Nevertheless, Cabot arguably had the strongest effect on the evolution of CPE. He emphasized the pastoral aspect of education, stressing pastoral skill development. He felt strongly that clinical training for clergy should take place in the general hospital setting.

THE COUNCIL AND THE INSTITUTE: THE SECOND GENERATION OF CPE

Of the founding fathers, Cabot remained the most influential as the pastoral care training movement began to evolve. Boisen certainly remained active in his research, writing, supervising, and chaplaincy, but his schizophrenic episodes and lack of interest in politics removed him from directly participating in the organizations that emerged. One of Boisen's students, Helen Flanders Dunbar, a physician, psychiatrist, and trained theologian, assumed leadership of the organization that embodied Boisen's philosophy. She became head of the Council for Clinical Training centered in New York. The Council continued to focus on placing chaplains in mental and general hospitals and on having students explore their inner worlds and the inner worlds of their patients as a means to developing a healthier faith. Cabot had a break with Boisen due to his strong opinion that Boisen's illness was organic and therefore beyond healing. Cabot and Dunbar also reportedly had philosophical differences about the developing profession's educational direction. As a result of this conflict, Cabot created another organization for the clinical education of clergy, the New England Group, which ultimately became the Institute for Pastoral Care.

DIFFERENT PHILOSOPHIES OF CARE AND EDUCATION

These two organizations—the Council for Clinical Training and The New England Group—both offered clinical pastoral training, yet had different philosophies of care. The New England Group was closely tied to formal theological education in the form of seminaries. Its proponents believed that clinical pastoral training should be integrated into the academic realm of seminary education. Following Cabot's firm lead, they placed clinical training students primarily in general hospitals. They refused to provide clinical training in mental hospital settings due to Cabot's reaction to Boisen's illness and emphasis on education. The Council for Clinical Training did not align with seminaries, although it certainly provided education for seminary students. The Council, influenced by Boisen and directed by Dunbar, believed its allegiance lay more with placement sites in the mental and general hospitals, as well as in prisons. Members of the Council made use of psychodynamic understanding as a strong component of their curriculum.

The two major histories of CPE[12] [13] look at the process of how CPE became splintered into two groups, adding two other denominational groups along the way, and ultimately united all four groups in 1967 to form the ACPE. As part of the splintering and reuniting, mention is made of how CPE supervisors were accepted as supervisors. This process is referred to as accrediting and, ultimately, is called certifying. The histories do not specifically recount how supervisors are educated to develop the identity and skills necessary for the work of supervision. The consensus of the written histories and those who remember the early days is that supervisor certification took place well before formal education in supervision was available. It is unclear how supervisors came to see the need for certification, yet the practice clearly dates back to the 1940s.[14]

DIFFERENT APPROACHES TO SUPERVISORY TRAINING

This distinction between aligning with seminaries, as did the Institute for Pastoral Care, versus stressing autonomy from the seminaries, as the Council did, becomes important in light of the development of supervisory education. The Institute for Pastoral Care, or the New England Group, largely trusted the seminaries to attend to the quality of supervisors and clinical training programs. Because of their more independent nature, the Council for Clinical Training did not have the kind of relationships with seminaries that invited review or accountability. Rather, the Council provided a way to promote people to the status of supervisors based on personal experiences with them. This process began informally—discussions with the CPE student at a conference—and developed into formal committee meetings to interview the CPE student. The committee meetings resulted in a vote to determine whether the student would be certified as a supervisor.

The standards for clinical training of each organization reflect the approach of each to supervision. In 1944, the Institute for Pastoral Care's requirements for supervisors were described in this way: ". . . the work shall be of a pastoral nature; it shall be done under supervision. It shall be recorded and the notes submitted for criticism." Preference for general hospital centers was stated explicitly. The supervisor was termed a Director of Clinical Training and required to be "an ordained clergyman with parish experience who will have had a minimum of two periods of clinical training under qualified direction." No stipulations were made concerning the length or location of the two required periods of training. This gave rise to serious reservations by supervisors in other groups about the qualifications of the Institute of Pastoral Directors.[15]

Also in 1944, the Council for Clinical Training had this rather lengthy section in its standards. The section is titled "Standards for Selection of Supervisors."

> The Theological Supervisor is the key person in the operation of a training program. . . . The Supervisor, of course, is an ordained clergyman, graduated from a recognized theological school. He must be a well adjusted person himself, emotionally and spiritually stable, with ability to face trying situations calmly and objectively. . . . If the Supervisor is not personally integrated and strong, that which is a period of growth for the student may very easily become a pe-

riod of disorganization and perhaps severe disillusionment. . . . The Supervisor must be sufficiently alive to be capable of enthusiasm, and yet not compulsive, effusive, or overly enthusiastic. He may hold the theology of any communion, but he must have a high degree of objectivity and personal insight, and in belief he must be reasoning rather than polemic, have convictions without dogmatism. He must be interested primarily in the ministry, have sufficient knowledge of other professions and sufficient administrative ability to enable him to maintain the standard program, have the capacity to earn the liking and respect of the staff, students, and patients, and he must have a sustained interest in the bearing of the training experience and theological and pastoral problems upon each other. He should have had at least two competent Supervisors and a period of service and training as Assistant Supervisor. In the latter he must have shown some teaching ability, but primarily the ability to enable others to observe for themselves, to evolve their own conclusions and applications, and above all to grow. . . [16]

LUTHERAN AND SOUTHERN BAPTIST CPE COMMUNIONS: THE THIRD GENERATION OF CPE

As the Council for Clinical Training and the Institute for Pastoral Care were developing clinical education for pastors, two denominations took a significant interest in developing CPE within their own communities of faith. The Lutheran Advisory Council on Pastoral Care was created in 1949 when the National Lutheran Council and the Missouri Synod Lutheran Churches decided to address the need for clinical training for chaplains. The Lutherans had considerable interest in chaplaincy and, when the City Hospital in St. Louis replaced the Lutheran chaplain with a Council for Clinical Training chaplain supervisor in 1945, the Lutherans decided to join the conversation about chaplain education.[17] They were concerned that the Council for Clinical Training did not have a positive relationship with seminaries. The goals of the Lutheran Advisory Council were: 1) promote interest in clinical training as a part of theological education, 2) assist the Lutheran seminaries in creating clinical training centers and hiring clinical instructors, and 3) establish standards in keeping with Lutheran theology for those training programs. The Lutheran Advisory Council was particularly important because of its leadership in calling together the Committee of Twelve in 1951. The Committee of Twelve included three representatives from four groups with a stake in the development of CPE: the Lutheran Advisory Council, the Institute of Pastoral Care, the Council for Clinical Training, and the Association of Seminary Professors in the Practical Field. The Committee's goal was to create national standards for clinical pastoral education.

Seward Hiltner, executive secretary of the Department of Pastoral Services of the Federal Council of Churches, predecessor organization of the National Council of Churches, was instrumental in creating the Association of Seminary Professors in the Practical Field. He "initiated a conference of seminary administrators to consider 'the practical field in theological education with special reference to pastoral care and counseling.'"[18] The inclusion of seminary representation in the Committee of Twelve transformed clinical pastoral education from an outside movement, separate from theological education (at least in the Council for Clinical Training), to an education method combining experiential education with academic preparation for ministry. The Lutherans led the way, integrating clinical training in seminary education. Although they followed the leadership of both the Council for Clinical Training and the Institute of Pastoral Care, the Lutheran Advisory Council also certified its own CPE supervisors. Most of the Lutherans held dual certification by one of the original bodies and by the Lutherans themselves. In the wider realm of seminary education for ministers, Hiltner's leadership called for integrating practical aspects of pastoral education with the rest of the curriculum, which marked a deepening of acceptance of the validity of experiential education in the training of ministers.

The Southern Baptists also created a program integrating CPE into seminary education. Wayne Oates became a clinical training supervisor and was instrumental in beginning the Southern Baptist Association for Clinical Pastoral Education. Oates' request to become a Council for Clinical Training CPE supervisor was denied, as was his application to develop a program of CPE at the Southern Baptist Theological Seminary in Louisville, Kentucky. As no alternatives were suggested, Oates decided to create a program that would be "wholly responsible to seminary educational policies."[19] In addition to the CPE centers and the Southern Baptist Theological Seminary in Louisville, Southern Baptist CPE programs were held in Winston-Salem, North Carolina and New Orleans, Louisiana. The unification in 1967 saw over 70 CPE supervisors in the Southern Baptist Association for Clinical Pastoral Education. The Southern Baptists had created their own certification process for CPE supervisors, none of whom were dually certified. According to *The Dictionary of Pastoral Care and Counseling*:

> . . . by 1956, Southern Baptist leaders recognized that the clinical pastoral education movement was moving toward unification without them. Their concern to become a visible and influential force led them to unite as an association. Having participated in the move toward unification, the members of the Association voted at the annual meeting in 1967 to dissolve the Association in order to fully participate in the nationally unified Association for Clinical Pastoral Education effective January 1, 1968.[20]

CERTIFICATION AS A WAY OF UNDERSTANDING SUPERVISORY EDUCATION

The process of CPE supervisor certification has always been of supreme interest to CPE supervisors because it has been something of a mysterious initiation rite. For many years, certification was called "accreditation." Both CPE supervisors and training sites went through a process of accreditation. The function of accreditation for CPE sites or centers and certification of CPE supervisors eventually came to be separated. The certification process, from the formative years to this day, provides a way of deducing the process of supervisory education.

Charles Hall was the first executive director of ACPE, the organization eventually created from the Institute of Pastoral Care, the Council for Clinical Training, the Lutheran Advisory Council, and the Southern Baptist arm of CPE. Hall wrote a history of CPE[21] 20 years after Thornton's *Professional Education for Ministry: A History of CPE*.[22] Hall's report of the audiotaped comments from the meeting of the Committee of Twelve is fascinating and instructive. The Committee of Twelve met to help the participating organizations work toward unification. The key sticking point noted in all three histories of CPE[23] [24] [25] was the practice of supervision and the manner of certifying new supervisors. The two organizations practicing supervision as the discussion of shared practices began in 1951 were the Institute and the Council; both apparently kept their practices cloaked in a veil of mystery. The process of becoming a supervisor had the feel of initiation into a special club. The philosophies of the two organizations naturally affected the type of supervision each used and defined the style of supervisory evaluation each practiced.

It is impossible to separate the practice of educating supervisors from the practices of evaluating, certifying, and/or accrediting supervisors. Much of the oral history of CPE revolves around certification stories. In his history of CPE, Chuck Hall recounts his own certification story.[26] He was asked a couple of key questions by supervisors who knew and trusted his training supervisor. They then proclaimed him a supervisor and handed him an open bottle of alcohol as a form of "communion;" drinking together signified collegiality and acceptance.

In conversation with John Thomas, former president of ACPE and a long-time member of the ACPE History Committee, I learned that the process of the Council was to move from being an assistant supervisor, to acting supervisor, and finally supervisor. Thomas, who became a CPE supervisor in 1949, said that when he returned from the Navy in 1946, he had already had two units of CPE. His supervisor, Fred Kuether, sent him to a program in Elgin, Illinois to become an assistant supervisor. When he arrived at the program in Elgin where he was to be an assistant, Bill Andrew, the supervisor of the program "discovered that I was not ready yet." Thomas said that Andrew discovered this by talking with him and, in the context of the conversation, Thomas imagined that he "was not doing much personal sharing." Thomas said that although he had taken two units of CPE, he was "not ready for the kind of supervision Bill Andrew was giving in terms of focusing on relationships in the group." After his third unit of training in this program, Thomas began supervising students and attended his first supervision conference in 1948. He talked with the supervisors there and was interviewed to become an acting supervisor. The next year at the fall conference he was interviewed to become a full supervisor. The issue, he said, was that the supervisors wanted to ensure he was not being unduly influenced by his wife, a Rogerian counselor. The personal nature of the review for certification is clear from this story. The emphasis was not so much on what Thomas could do, but on who he was as a person and supervisor. His story emphasizes his relationships with the men who were his supervisors. This story offers insight into the lack of standardization and the practice of fraternalism in the Council for Clinical Training.

OBSERVING THE CERTIFICATION PROCESS

As the move toward unifying CPE into one organization continued, leaders of both the Institute and the Council realized that the education and certification (called accreditation at the time) of supervisors posed a problem. At the 1962 fall conference, where all those engaged in clinical education for ministry assembled, one of the supervisors, John Smith, proposed a method for addressing the difficulty: "I am sure all of us would agree that the only way we can understand the accreditation practice of each other's group is to share in the process. That is the only way of getting the 'feel' of what takes place."[27] The chairmen of the respective accreditation committees agreed and arranged for three joint meetings in the next year. Each group watched the other review candidates for supervision. The two groups felt discouraged, as the Institute seemed overly academic and pastoral, and the Council seemed to overemphasize emotions and inner work.

The experiment became more beneficial when supervisors from each group formed a small committee. Those watching agreed that the combined committee did better work than either group had done alone. Still, the stories are about supervisor certification and not about how those men—in those days, they were all men—learned how to do the work of supervision. John Thomas created a monograph called A "Snap Shot" History (1975-2000) of the Association for Clinical Pastoral Education, Inc. He said that "the late Ernest Bruder of St. Elizabeth's Hospital, Washington, D.C., saw the need for more extensive training for those desiring to become supervisors."[28] Thomas reported that Bruder came up with the idea of a residency year in CPE, but the nature of the education is not defined. In conversation with me, Thomas said that Bruder's residency was a three year program and the beginning of formal supervisory education. Thomas' review of stories he had heard about certification and conversations recorded on the subject reveal a change in the education of supervisors. The move was from informal modeling and learning while supervising to an program designed to educate CPE supervisors.

A Current Perspective on the CPE Supervisor Certification Process

Thomas quoted Bill Russell, a supervisor with "long experience in the certification process":

> The arrival of large numbers of women as well as other races and a more diverse student population began to change the face of CPE as well as challenge the way in which the supervision and education of CPE was carried out. This also challenged the way in which persons were educated in the art of supervision. . . . In the certification process, there came to be more focus on students, group process, and the value of peer interaction as opposed to the dominate supervisor as the dominant personality. Also, there was a challenge to the elevated importance of intuition. Intuition without theory became problematic and, at times, harmful to students. Persons seeking certification needed to be able to give theory to what they practice . . . a challenge in the education of CPE supervisors. Part of this problem is that many of these persons are still being educated by persons who are unable to share with a student in supervisory education why they do what they do . . . This brings challenges from the Certification Commission when candidates arrive unaware that a new day has arrived on the CPE horizon. All of the above, on the whole, have been very positive movements in our organization.[29]

In her book on small group work in CPE, Hemenway reviewed the certification of supervisors with attention to how fully the group element was addressed.[30] CPE includes a significant small group element in the curriculum and Hemenway noted that few of the theories of supervision presented by aspiring supervisors fully addressed group theory. In the review, Hemenway noted that certification was quite subjective. She included Hall's story of his certification to demonstrate that careful review as understood in the 1990s had not been done. Supervisors were intuitively accepted or rejected, and the process felt murky to some, abusive to others, and subjective to most. A task force was created in the mid-1980s to revise the certification process. The revision included a written standardized test as well as position papers on the candidate's theology, personality theory, and education theory. These required academic pieces would be integrated into the candidate's practice of supervision as recorded on tape. The certification committee would know that the test had been passed and that the position papers had been accepted by two out of three anonymous readers (also supervisors). The certification committee would review the supervisory candidate at the National Commission level. If the candidates were successful in the committee meeting, they would be certified as associate supervisors.

The process of getting certified has been refined and is still changing. In August 2006, an ACPE Presidential Task Group produced a report on training and certification. Its process was to have "reflective conversations with ACPE leaders, supervisors, students, and stakeholders." The group collected training curricula and certification data of unspecified origin. In the conclusions section, the report stated:

> We have learned that because our educational methods are often developed autonomously, and because they often reflect diverse practices across the organization, there are often differing expectations between those who provide supervisory education and those who certify. . . . One systemic result may be that our methods of evaluation of supervisory candidates and associate supervisors tend to focus more on subjective assessments of personal integration than on professional competency. Both are essential, but the feedback from those who have experienced the certification process as students and as educating supervisors suggests we have erred on the side of subjectivity, with an "oral tradition" that is difficult to comprehend.[31]

The conflict between professional competency and personal integration that began between the Institute for Pastoral Care and the Council for Clinical Training some 60 years ago is alive and well in the CPE supervisory process today. The report provides specific conclusions about supervisory education in the section entitled "Regarding Supervisory Education and Curricula." Among the 15 conclusions listed, these are particularly relevant to the discussion: 1) We reflect a broad range of practices in our educational theories, methods, and curricula, 2) Our educating supervisors and programs function with a high level of autonomy without clear avenues for cross-fertilization and collaboration, 3) We have not yet developed effective processes and standards for identifying and supporting supervisors who provide supervisory education, 4) We have no consensus on what constitutes "readiness" for supervisory education, and 5) As an organization, we are currently unable to articulate a supervisory education process that will lead to professional certification as an ACPE supervisor.[32]

This task group report reflects the deep need of supervisors in ACPE to learn about the experience of effective CPE supervisory education. The organizational experience of elders has not been gathered, reflected upon, and shared with the wider audience. CPE has become a profession and the profession needs a body of knowledge about what constitutes effective education of students in supervisory CPE.

CONTEXT FOR CPE SUPERVISORY EDUCATION IN 2009

In the early 1900s, theological and cultural changes set the stage for the birth of CPE. Social and theological events in the late 20th century set the stage for changes in the CPE supervisory process. The inclusion of women in professional roles has changed our society in a myriad of ways. Diversity of gender, race, faith tradition, nationality, and sexual orientation has changed the landscape of ACPE in ways that make education at every level of CPE and subjectivity in certification even more problematic. At the National ACPE meeting in October

2007, supervisors serving on national commissions such as certification and accreditation were required to attend a day-long workshop entitled "Multicultural Competencies and the ACPE Standards." The theme of the conference was articulated and explained in this way: "The 2007 conference theme, 'Connecting in a Culture of Complexity: Supervision in the 21st Century,' is symbolized by an Eternal Knot. Used in many cultures and religions, this knot symbolizes the infinite wisdom of the Divine."[33] This theme and requirement for leadership education in multicultural competencies indicates the emphasis being placed on diversity.

The changes in healthcare in the past 20 years continue to heighten ethical issues—they have brought moral decision-making into greater clarity for some and into vast uncertainty for many. The effect on education for pastoral care has been to increase anxiety about the future of the profession, as payment for non-revenue generating services is called into question. As pastoral care providers seek ways to demonstrate the positive difference they make for patients, families, and staff, chaplains have broadened the scope of the profession by adding research as a way to measure pastoral care effectiveness. The founders of CPE focused on patients and families—increasing challenges and needs for pastoral guidance came from hospital staff. The CPE student learning to listen today will take part in conversations that may include daunting levels of technological sophistication. With the advent of the internet, patients and families are much more informed healthcare consumers than they were in earlier eras. Education programs as well as healthcare institutions are more consumer-oriented than before. Authority increasingly rests in the *relationship* between teacher and student, rather than purely in the purview of the teacher. Supervisors face these changes aware that the Standards of ACPE begin with a section on professional ethics which includes material concerning the rights and responsibilities of the student. The Professional Ethics Manual for ACPE is now called the *Processing Complaints of Ethics Code Violations* and is 35 pages long. The first page is devoted to describing the Professional Ethics Commission, and the rest of the manual—apart from the glossary and the appendices—outlines the process of working with complaints. This attention to complaints reflects the struggles supervisors have had with using their power appropriately and the care ACPE has taken to provide students and supervisors with a path for mediation and/or redress. Just as patients in hospitals have become customers, students in ACPE programs have become consumers. In part, attention to needs of those with less power comes from a desire to be more caring; in part, it comes from fear of litigation.

A fine explanation of cultural positioning for pastoral care supervision may be found in the seven essays at the end of the current version of the *Dictionary of Pastoral Care and Counseling*. The purpose of the essays is to reflect on themes of change in the pastoral care climate in the 15 years since the *Diction-*

ary was originally published in 1990. The following series of quotes provide insight into the cultural context at the turn of the century:

> The decade of the 1990s was a time of tremendous ferment and productivity in the United States by women and men of both European American and African American racial identities and differing sexual orientations who together demonstrated increasing nuance and methodological sophistication in their attention to alternative theological, methodological, and practice issues in the field.[34]

The word "ferment" is used in several of these essays. This suggested to me that changes in our culture have resulted in uneasiness in pastoral care communities. Ramsay referred to the attention to diversity and the effect such diversity is having in multiple arenas of pastoral care. As cultural changes persist, supervisors must learn to adapt their CPE programs to respond to the diverse educational needs of CPE students as well as to teach their students to respond pastorally in the midst of diversity issues new to many of them.

> . . . I use the image of the web to depict a major change in the field as a whole, and I describe that change in terms of a modification in primary subject matter from the "living human document" to "living human web." My focus is less on who offers care (clergy or laity) or how care is offered (hierarchically or collaboratively) and more on what care involves today. Genuine care now requires understanding the human document as necessarily embedded within an interlocking public web of constructed meaning.[35]

Miller-McLemore's turn of Boisen's phrase suggests a paradigm shift essential in this millennium. Boisen broke new ground in understanding that individuals teach us so much about themselves, ourselves, and the Divine. In this age of interconnected systems, Miller-McLemore pointed the way to considering how context influences the individual, and demands the attention of the pastoral care provider. In another of the essays, Neuger wrote about a current theme: "The dynamic of power and difference is a central concern of pastoral theology in the postmodern context."[36] As already noted, attention to ethical considerations demonstrates the need for supervisors to be vigilant about their use of power and how they lead students into a relationship to power—their own as well as others'.

The context in which pastoral care is taught has changed dramatically since the early days of CPE:

> Three types of processes seem to characterize developments in pastoral care and counseling on the global scene over the past two decades. These can be described as globalization, internationalization, and indigenization . . . Indigenization, the least recognized of the processes, is occurring on the margins of the global movements. In this process, models and practices indigenous to non-Western contexts are beginning to be re-evaluated and utilized in pastoral prac-

tice. In line with postcolonial cultural, social, linguistic, and political criticism, indigenous practitioners of healing are increasingly encouraged to impact the halls of power in the practice of pastoral care and counseling in several places in the world.[37]

CPE methods are well-suited to consider one's own behavior, but the paradigm exists in a Western Christian context. An ongoing issue in CPE supervision is determining how to meet students where they are spiritually, emotionally, and cognitively while at the same time providing feedback in culturally appropriate ways. As noted, the organization is wrestling in meaningful ways with these issues.

> While other clinical disciplines have changed to reflect new research and changing social contexts, pastoral counseling has not substantially diversified its psychological base. The result is a dated theological anthropology and understanding of human problems embedded in psychoanalysis—a model that is no longer dominant in either theology or psychology. Lester argues that postmodern, contextual, and systemic frames are reshaping theological anthropology in a way that makes this position untenable. He highlights a tendency among CPE supervisors to "cling to a particular theory of personality and methodology as if it were Truth, in the same way that religious fundamentalists cling to a particular dogma, as if it were the life raft that keeps them afloat." Singular commitment to one theory is inconsistent with research that demonstrates no clear advantage of one theory over another. He proposes that AAPC and ACPE must now question training that is not theoretically multilingual.[38]

This is a powerful quote about pastoral counseling, but is equally applicable to pastoral care. Lester's critique of CPE as stuck in one type of theory provides a challenge with which I agree.

CONCLUSION

This chapter situates CPE supervisory education in the history of CPE. The different contributions of the Institute for Pastoral Care and the Council for Clinical Training are still very influential in the practice of CPE supervision today. Supervisors still work on skill development and are often in relationships with seminaries from which many CPE students come. These attributes are the legacy of the Institute for Pastoral Care. CPE supervisors focus on the theological and psychological wisdom and integration of their students. This is the legacy of the Council for Clinical Training. The emphasis on clinical material written in a format that may be studied in the small group of CPE peers is the heritage of both groups and the basis of CPE learning. The student's use of self in ministry and in CPE supervisory education was and remains a strong focus in the CPE process.

As cultural milieus enrich supervisory education and as societal challenges broaden the purview of supervisory education, we supervisors must continue to equip ourselves so we can serve the students in supervisory education who continue seeking to become CPE supervisors. As one of the supervisors interviewed for the grounded theory study of supervisory education said, "I think we have a long and distinguished history and I also think that anything that has a long and distinguished history, if it's smart, is going to keep current and not rest on its long and distinguished laurels."

NOTES

1. R.J. Hunter, "Wisdom and Practical Knowledge in Pastoral Care," in R.J. Hunter and N.J. Ramsay, eds., *Dictionary of Pastoral Care and Counseling* (Nashville: Abingdon Press, 2005), 1325.

2. C.A. Newsom, "Wisdom Tradition, Biblical," in R.J. Hunter & N.J. Ramsay, eds., *Dictionary of Pastoral Care and Counseling* (Nashville: Abingdon Press, 2005), 1326.

3. E.E. Thornton, *Professional Education for Ministry: A History of Clinical Pastoral Education* (Nashville: Abingdon, 1970).

4. D.A. Steere, *The Supervision of Pastoral Care*, 1st ed. (Louisville, KY: Westminister/John Knox, 1989).

5. *Ibid.*

6. Setting the historical development of CPE in context requires acknowledgment of the cultures of both theological inquiry and education in the 1920s. Both stemmed from pragmatism, especially the Chicago School of Pragmatism, founded by John Dewey. Dewey's philosophy of education paved the way for development of the experiential learning that came to be practiced in CPE. The culture of the 1920s represented a shift in focus from externally generated truth to empirical, experiential theology and education.

7. E.E. Thornton, *Op. cit.*, 26.

8. *Ibid.*

9. *Ibid.*, 55.

10. *Ibid.*

11. *Ibid.*, 55.

12. *Ibid.*

13. C.E. Hall, "Head and Heart: The Story of the Clinical Pastoral Education Movement" *Journal of Pastoral Care* (Decatur, GA: 1992).

14. J. R. Thomas, personal communication, November 10, 2006.

15. E.E. Thorton, *Op. cit.*, 104.

16. C.E. Hall, *Op. cit.*, 55.

17. E.E. Thornton, *Op. cit.*

18. *Ibid.*, 155.

19. *Ibid.*, 154.

20. S.D. King, "Southern Baptist Association for Clinical Pastoral Education," in R.J. Hunter & N.J. Ramsay, eds., *Dictionary of Pastoral Care and Counseling* (Nashville: Abingdon Press, 2005), 1204-1205.

21. C.E. Hall, *Op. cit.*

22. E.E. Thornton, *Op. cit.*

23. *Ibid.*

24. C.E. Hall, *Op. cit.*

25. D.A. Steere, *Op. cit.*

26. C.E. Hall, *Op. cit.*

27. E.E. Thornton, *Op. cit.*, 178.

28. J.R. Thomas, "A 'Snap-Shot' History (1975-2000) of the Association for Clinical Pastoral Education, Inc.: A Celebration of the 75th Anniversary of CPE" (Monograph, 2000), 23.

29. *Ibid.*, 24.

30. J.E. Hemenway, "Inside the Circle: A Historical and Practical Inquiry Concerning Process Groups in Clinical Pastoral Education," *Journal of Pastoral Care* (Decatur, GA: 1996).

31. ACPE Presidential Task Group, Report on Training and Certification (August 2006, Unpublished), 1-9.

32. *Ibid.*, 3.

33. ACPE 2007 Conference Information, http://www.acpe.edu/.

34. N.J. Ramsay, "A Time of Ferment and Redefinition," in R.J. Hunter and & N.J. Ramsay, eds., *Dictionary of Pastoral Care and Counseling* (Nashville: Abingdon Press, 2005), 1349-1369.

35. B.J. Miller-McLemore, "Pastoral Theology as Public Theology: Resolutions in the 'Fourth Area,'" in R.J. Hunter and N.J. Ramsay, eds., *Dictionary of Pastoral Care and Counseling* (Nashville: Abingdon Press, 2005), 1370-1380.

36. C.C. Neuger, "Power and Difference in Pastoral Theology," in R.J. Hunter and N.J. Ramsay, eds., *Dictionary of Pastoral Care and Counseling* (Nashville: Abingdon Press, 2005), 1381-1391.

37. E.Y. Lartey, "Globalization, Internationalization, and Indigenization of Pastoral Care and Counseling," in R.J. Hunter and N.J. Ramsay, eds., *Dictionary of Pastoral Care and Counseling* (Nashville: Abingdon Press, 2005), 1392-1403).

38. L.L. Townsend, "Ferment and Imagination in Training in Clinical Ministry in R.J. Hunter and N.J. Ramsay, eds., *Dictionary of Pastoral Care and Counseling* (Nashville: Abingdon Press, 2005), 1404-1415.

CHAPTER FIFTEEN

Intersubjective and Theological Contexts of Pastoral Counseling Supervision: Self, Psyche, and Soul

Felicity Kelcourse

INTRODUCTION: THE ETHOS OF PASTORAL COUNSELING

Pastoral counselors are trained to integrate theological reflection and psycho-therapeutic wisdom. How might this training influence the practice of clinical supervision? Is the general ethos of pastoral counseling and the supervision of pastoral counselors distinct from that of other mental health disciplines, and if so, to what end? How does the pastoral counselor as supervisor balance attention to self, supervisees, and the persons under the supervisees' care in light of God's care for all (Matthew 5:43-47)?[1]

In response to these questions, I offer the following reflections on the integration of theological and psychological perspectives that supports the supervising pastoral counselor's task. I write from my experience in community, congregational, and overseas ministries, including 22 years as a recorded Quaker minister and two decades as a pastoral counselor. Over the last 13 years, my work as a theological educator and supervisor has focused on preparing M.A., M.Div., and D.Min. students for specialized ministries in pastoral care and counseling that may require ordination, chaplaincy certification, and/or counseling licensure.[2] I continually learn from my supervisees and fellow supervisors about effective supervision. I also remember, from my own four year residency as a pastoral psychotherapist at Blanton-Peale Graduate Institute in New York, how exhilarating and challenging the personal transformation that clinical training requires can be.[3] So I write from the position of one who, in mid-career, continues to reflect on the process of becoming a wise supervisor.

The professional culture of pastoral counselors emphasizes respect for persons, in all their particularity, as individuals uniquely loved by God.[4] The ethos of pastoral relationships, of which pastoral counseling is a specialized sub-set, involves intersubjectivity, a sharing of understandings and meanings that arises in the "potential space of exploration" between persons.[5] Pastoral counselors recognize that intercultural as well as interpersonal and intrapsychic receptivity is required for effective communication.[6] While pastoral counselors are expected to maintain clear ties to their respective communities of faith, the care they provide is "non-sectarian and respects the spiritual commitments and religious traditions of those who seek assistance without imposing counselor beliefs onto the client."[7] Although I write in this chapter from a Christocentric perspective, I do not place my Christian beliefs in opposition to those of other faiths. "Good religion" is any faith that builds bridges of understanding across chasms of difference and offers positive meaning and purpose in life.[8] In the Judeo-Christian tradition, the concept of "good" religion can be summed up in the command to "Love the Lord your God and your neighbor as yourself" (Matthew 22:39). But this command cannot be limited to "do as you would be done by." In interpersonal, intrapsychic, and spiritual terms it requires one's best available wisdom to understand the needs of others, to recognize as well one's own desires, and to receptively discern as best one can the will of God.

Following the general ethos of pastoral psychotherapy, supervision that is characteristic of pastoral care and counseling attends to the lives of particular people, loved by God and worthy of respect, in dialogue with theologically informed and clinically trained helping professionals. The supervision of pastoral care has been defined as "an extended relationship in which an experienced clinician help[s] trainees to reflect upon the concrete processes of their care of others in order to increase their competence in the pastoral role."[9] What I find missing in this definition, from the perspective of a training program that places a high value on experiential learning and self-of-the-therapist awareness, is attention to the self of the supervisor. In my understanding, a supervisor's attention needs to be balanced between care for clients, care and monitoring of supervisees, and the care and monitoring of one's self, since the self of the supervisor plays a critical role in the intersubjective space of exploration formed between supervisor and supervisee. I approach supervision from the dual perspective of one who supervises individuals and groups of interns while serving as administrator for a degree program, a role that includes supervision of supervision. From this vantage point, I see the supervisor's training, personhood, and self-care not as a given but rather as a dynamic component of every supervisory relationship.

Pastoral counselors and their supervisors necessarily address the human condition from particular contexts, based on their own experience and training, as formed and sustained by their communities of faith. To ground the theological and theoretical reflections that follow in their postmodern particularity, I'll begin with some brief supervisory vignettes followed by clinical and theological reflections.[10] I do not intend to address in detail the many practical, ethical, and legal aspects of supervision that include attention to diagnosis, intake summaries, treatment plans, medication, family and social support, configuring initial contracts, recognizing legal concerns, or monitoring requirements for Medicaid, Medicare, managed care, etc.[11]

CLINICAL THEOLOGY: VIGNETTES FROM SUPERVISION

Clinical theology can be understood as a "system of thought (built upon) the study of God at work."[12] Anton Boisen, Richard Cabot, Russell Dicks, and other early pioneers in the pastoral care and counseling movement came to believe that "the most helpful expression of the pastor's theology lay not in the facile use of religious terms or even in clarity of belief, but in a certain quality of thought and action."[13] Or as George Fox would have it: "let your lives speak."[14] In practical terms, this means that the supervisor's response to the supervisee in any given situation is an essential aspect of the latter's training.

VIGNETTE 1

A supervisory group of nine with two co-leaders met during the fall of 2008. The co-leaders were European-American: one male, one female. The group members included two European-American women, two African-American men, and five African-American women. During and after the election of Barack Obama, African-American group members, ranging in age from 20s to 50s, openly processed the significance of the election for their self-identity as Black Americans and the impact of this historic election on the African-American community. An older minister recalled childhood humiliations caused by racial segregation in the south. Another intern reflected on the implications for his work with young African-American male clients and their families. As one of the white supervisors, I felt privileged to view this turning point in history through the eyes of my supervisees and to share their hopes for the future.

REFLECTION 1

Just as counselors learn from their counselees about life experiences different from their own, supervisors can broaden their worldviews by listening attentively to the experience of their supervisees. Sometimes in supervision, as in therapy, the supervisor's capacity to listen, respectfully and appreciatively, to the supervisee's story can be more significant than any spoken statement. Like the mirroring of parent to child, the experience of being truly seen and heard is enlivening. At the same time, the supervisor's willingness to acquire multicultural competence depends on the ability to listen and learn from those of other cultures. Tolerance is not enough; genuine hospitality is required.[15] As we approach one another from a phenomenological standpoint, seeking more to understand than to explain, we approach the ways that we are deeply known and understood by God (Psalm 139).[16]

VIGNETTE 2

A faculty practicum supervisor was assigned to work with a first semester D.Min. intern for whom she was also thesis advisor. In the course of a busy semester, the supervisor once rescheduled the intern's supervision hour on short notice because she needed time to finish reading another student's thesis prior to his oral exam. Two semesters later, the intern was able to tell her former supervisor that this had been a hurtful experience, causing the intern to feel disregarded and dismissed. Following that conversation, the faculty member reflected on the insidious nature of power; her action of rescheduling the supervision session had been self-serving and poor modeling of the contract between supervisor and supervisee, as it parallels the contract between therapist and client. The intern, to her credit, did not allow the supervisor's actions to negatively influence her reliable contracting with clients.

REFLECTION 2

In a postmodern world, a supervisor whose theological training includes familiarity with feminist and liberation theologies cannot afford to take refuge in the power and privilege of her or his role. On the contrary; the caution "from everyone to whom much is given, much will be required" applies (Luke 12:48b). The greater one's power and authority, the more one must be mindful of the need to monitor one's own well-being so that the supervisor's anxieties, needs, or personal failings do not impinge on supervisees or their clients unduly. Maintaining appropriate boundaries is a relevant consideration here. If the supervisor had rescheduled the hour without giving a reason the student might still have felt let down but would have been unlikely to see herself as "less than" other students in the supervisor's eyes. The supervisor, for her part, was counting on the student's obligatory acquiescence in relation to the supervisor's dual roles as supervisor and thesis advisor.

Since no one is perfect, similar lapses are bound to arise periodically. The atmosphere of trust necessary for effective supervision can be restored and enhanced when the supervisor is willing to non-defensively admit shortcomings and apologize to the supervisee in all humility. Supervisees need to feel free to raise any manner of concern with their supervisors, just as they would invite their clients to freely share uncomfortable feelings with them. While it is true that "all have sinned and fallen short of the glory of God" (Romans 3:23), it is also true that we are called to become "perfect," meaning whole, complete (Matthew 5:48) to the extent that grace will allow.

VIGNETTE 3

A male intern in his first semester approached his female program director to express his dismay following a shaming experience in a supervisory group where he was the only male. He felt that statements he had made to the group while processing his countertransference to a depressed female client had been misinterpreted. To validate the intern's concern, the program director shared a similar shaming experience of being "one of a kind" in an otherwise all-male research group and noted the tendency of groups to project stereotypes under similar circumstances. An additional difficulty in this instance was that the supervisee's primary theoretical lens was psychodynamic, whereas his female colleagues used theoretical vocabularies in which the term "countertransference" could be viewed in a negative light.[17]

REFLECTION 3

Even when the social location of supervisor and supervisee is similar, everyone's life story is unique. This distinctiveness is underscored by the practice of sharing genograms[18] with supervisees at the beginning of training. At the same time, we are all "much more simply human than otherwise," to cite Harry Stack Sullivan's well-known phrase.[19] The female supervisor in this vignette recognized that the male supervisee was confronted with a training setting in which the majority of interns and most of the authority figures were female. Even persons who enjoy majority privileges in the culture at large can experience minority projections that cause them to feel unsafe under such circumstances.[20] Differences in the use of clinical vocabularies that inevitably arise in the context of a theoretically diverse training program added to this supervisee's sense of being misunderstood. Ideally the supervisor's compassionate response to the supervisee's experience will be replicated in his work with clients who experience discrimination from the dominant culture. At the same time, the supervisor, being confronted in her role as program director with a complaint involving another supervisor's group, must be careful not to encourage triangulation.[21] Following the program director's initial empathic response, the supervisee was advised to openly share his concerns with his group supervisor and peers.

While Christians are called to the vision of Galatians 3:28—"There is neither Jew nor Greek, neither slave nor free, neither male or female, but all are one in Christ Jesus"—it is a difficult vision to honor in practice, whether or not one benefits from having the socially proscribed upper hand. Claiming unity in Christ while recognizing the validity of diverse perspectives can be a challenge.

VIGNETTE 4

An actively suicidal woman grieving a bad divorce refuses to be hospitalized. What are the alternatives for keeping her alive in hopes of buying time to ameliorate her depression? The clinic director and psychiatrist advise the intern that she can either offer to meet the client for therapy daily or have the client agree to call the intern's voicemail daily. The client agrees to the second option without a specified time for her daily call. The intern shares in supervision the burden she feels in this case. She has to carry the client home emotionally and begins to worry if the client calls late in the day. Although the supervisor cannot lift this burden from the supervisee entirely, she suggests a specific afternoon call-in time and a plan to mobilize the client's friends and family if the daily call is not made. This plan at least makes the burden more manageable.

REFLECTION 4

Cases that involve potential harm to the client's self or others necessarily raise anxiety for both therapists and supervisors. It is the supervisor's job not only to support the therapist in managing such anxieties based on the supervisor's broader range of clinical experience but also to recognize when the needs of a given client may be more onerous than a supervisee can bear. If the family history of the supervisee in question included suicide, the supervisor would need to determine whether the supervisee was ready to handle a case that could be powerfully re-stimulating. At Christian Theological Seminary, supervisees are required to be in weekly therapy throughout their two year internship so that they can safely process and contain distress occasioned by their work with clients. Clear boundaries are maintained between individual therapy and supervision. In addition, first year interns attend a "Self of the Therapist" group led by persons who are not part of the regular supervisory group responsible for evaluating supervisees' performance each semester. In these Self of the Therapist groups, which are more structured than the traditional Interpersonal Relations (IPR) groups used in Clinical Pastoral Education, interns share genograms and family histories, both their own and those of clients, in relation to cases they find particularly challenging. Usually the most challenging cases are those that force the intern to confront painful aspects of his or her own experience.[22]

VIGNETTE 5

A supervisee working with at-risk in-patient adolescents is told by his supervisor that the 13 year old boy he is working with will be disowned by his adoptive parents if he fails to behave acceptably during his weekend home visits. The boy behaves well on the unit. At home, the primary conflict seems to be focused between the boy and his adoptive mother. From a family systems perspective, the boy is the identified patient and resolving family issues that concern minor children requires the participation of the parents at a minimum, and ideally siblings or other close relatives as well. Can the conflicts at home be effectively resolved if the boy's in-patient therapist is not able to work with the family as a whole and particularly the boy's mother?

REFLECTION 5

Supervisors are by definition clinicians with more experience than the person(s) they are supervising. The supervisory role includes monitoring the supervisee's care for clients, evaluating the supervisee's work, and serving as a gatekeeper for the profession.[23] But what happens if the supervisor's scope of training is insufficient to effectively guide the supervisee's handling of a case? In this case, a supervisee is being asked to take responsibility for improving the behavior of a minor child without access to the adoptive family. In the case of a younger child, individual play therapy alone might bring some relief to the child in the absence of willing participation from the family.[24] For a 13 year old boy on the cusp of adolescence with a dearth of secure attachment, best practice suggests both individual and family therapy to address the tensions being constellated in the mother-son relationship. Supervisors have a responsibility not to practice beyond the scope of their training, which should ideally include familiarity with the full range of ego-supportive and insight-oriented, intrapsychic and relational-systemic work with individuals, couples, families, children, and groups. If the supervisor is not well-versed in the modalities and techniques required to serve the diverse needs of a wide variety of clients, it is his or her responsibility to consult with knowledgeable colleagues for supervision of supervision, seek additional training, and/or refer the supervisee for supplementary supervision.

CONCLUSION OF VIGNETTES

The above series of vignettes and reflections serves to illustrate some of the complex and demanding challenges supervisors face on a daily basis. Apart from issues of training and experience, noting that many states require supervisors to have at least five years of experience post licensure, I am most interested in the *intrapsychic* and, for want of a less ambiguous term, *spiritual* resources pastoral counseling supervisors need to do their job well. Many of the established models for pastoral supervision focus on the interaction between therapist and client.[25] While this focus is a dimension of the therapist's work that certainly requires attention, I believe that attention to the *intersubjective space* between supervisor and supervisee is of equal importance and that often isomorphisms, or parallel experiences, will be constellated in the supervisory relationship that shed considerable light on the work in therapy. The supervisor must attend, as carefully as possible, to the countertransferential clues that arise in supervision.

To delineate the levels of complexity such attention requires, I turn now to a theoretical consideration of the intersubjective space itself.

CLINICAL THEOLOGY: SUPERVISION IN RELATION TO SELF, PSYCHE, AND SOUL

In each new supervisory relationship, as in each new therapy relationship, one is faced with a person whose life experience is both similar to and different from one's own. Sullivan's interpersonalist saying speaks of our essential human interconnection across boundaries of difference. But in addition to the socially constructed differences that we consciously acknowledge related to gender, class, religion, ethnicity, sexual orientation, generational cohort, socially defined roles, etc., there are also boundaries between what is known and the "unthought known"[26] both intrapsychically and interpersonally, as represented by Johari's window.[27] There will be aspects of myself that my supervisees may perceive more clearly than I do, just as there will be aspects of their being that are more clearly visible to me looking in from the outside. We each contain dimensions of experience that are present in the intersubjective space between us, though consciously unknown.

The supervision of pastoral counselors is therefore a collaborative enterprise that engages both conscious and unconscious dynamics within supervisor and supervisee. In addition to the need for careful attention to the intersubjective field formed by the supervisory pair, there is the ever present concern for the health and well-being of those who are generally not present during supervision—the direct recipients of care. Whether the supervisee is an intern in training or an experienced therapist, the imperative to "do no harm" applies. It is the supervisor's responsibility, as the more experienced clinician, to track ethical and legal considerations, and to do so in such a way that even the beginning clinician feels supported rather than shamed.[28] Ideally, the positive aspects of the supervisory relationship will be replicated in the supervisee's work with clients, though it is also possible for the supervisees to learn from uncomfortable experiences in supervision what *not* to do with clients. In the context of this chapter, I will focus on the broad theological and clinical loyalties that undergird the work of supervision as I've come to understand it.

SUPERVISION AND SELVES: THE INTERPERSONAL DIMENSION OF EXPERIENTIAL LEARNING

My practice of supervision begins with a contextual understanding of persons. Each person's subjective self-awareness is based on the interaction of interpersonal familial, community, and cultural contexts that either may remain largely fixed or continually change over time,[29] as well as internal or intrapsychic "object relations,"[30] "internal family systems,"[31] "parts,"[32] or "voices"[33] that continually mediate the ways in which external sensory data is perceived and interpreted. In this context, I define *self* as our largely conscious sense of *I*, with a bit of "not-me" shadow thrown in, depending on the self-awareness of supervisor and supervisee.[34]

In developmental terms, our perceptions are heavily dependent on "schemas"[35] or "RIGs"—representations of interactions that have been generalized.[36] These basic building blocks of perception begin to form while we are still in our mother's wombs[37] and are largely established by preschool age. The primary challenge of clinical supervision is to offer supervisees the possibility of changing their way of seeing the world, as necessary for their growth as persons and clinicians, and to encourage this transformation in an environment conducive to gradual and substantive reintegration. Like many of the ordeals that traditionally characterize the training of a shaman, the seminary counseling intern is bombarded by theological and psychological demands that serve to destabilize previously unquestioned worldviews.[38] The training community provides a liminal space in which supervisees are both supported and challenged in ways that encourage the personal transformations required to become an effective and experienced healer.[39] These include, but are not limited to, the ability to remain calm under stressful circumstances, or the "non-anxious presence" encouraged in CPE,[40] the ability to receive responses from others non-defensively, and the ability to bracket one's own needs and concerns temporarily so that one can fully attend to the words, presence, and needs of another. Attending to one's countertransferential response to another would also be part of the "evenly hovering attention" originally advocated by Freud.[41] A commitment to receptivity on the part of the psychotherapist is supported by an attitude of humility. We supervisors and therapists are not to see ourselves as the enlightened arbiters of another's fate, but rather as fellow pilgrims on the way, committed to providing a safe space in which persons can discover their own sense of vocation and meaning, trusting that God is at work in the lives of clients as in our own.

In any relationship, including supervisory relationships, persons bring conscious, unconscious, or preconscious systems of perception to bear. An "intersubjective" field is formed when two persons meet, gaining depth and complexity as they continue to interact and learn more about each other.[42] When I enter into a new supervisory relationship, initial impressions based on age, gender, ethnicity, sexual orientation, religious tradition(s) or lack thereof, verbal sophistication, learning preferences, personality traits, and prior relationships with superficially like others, both positive and negative, will initially play a significant role in the way I perceive a supervisee and the way the supervisee perceives me.

As a relationship of trust and mutuality is established, based on openness and respect for the unique gifts and challenges each person brings, it becomes possible for supervisor and supervisee to form a new category of relationship that is based less on prior experience and more on a new experience of self and other. A positive sense of connection develops in which neither party fears being judged and both are open to learning from and about the other. This positive rapport, once established, needs to be continually reaffirmed. Anderson and Goolishian describe intersubjective experience as "an evolving state of affairs in which two or more people agree (understand) that they are experiencing the same event in the same way. . . . It is understood that agreement is fragile and continually open to renegotiation and dispute."[43]

Despite the fact that most interns are known to me from prior course work, the initial phase of each supervisory relationship feels like a new beginning. In the first few supervisory sessions with new practicum students, intakes have not yet accumulated so there are no clients to discuss. As stated earlier, we typically begin by sharing genograms; they talk about their family of origin and I talk about mine. The ostensible purpose of this exercise is to help us be aware of each other's structures of experience beginning in childhood. But it has other uses as well.

At times, after sharing my genogram I have a feeling of exposure, a fear of being judged. What will this student think of me now that they know more about me? When such feelings arise, I have learned to regard them as possible counter-transference clues to the feelings of the supervisee, especially since they are more pronounced in relation to some supervisees than with others. As she/he begins presenting work with clients, I need to be vigilant for any fears of shame or exposure, judgment or criticism that may arise in supervision. If I am not mindful at this point I run the risk of amplifying the chorus of critical voices we often carry with us. I sometimes share my own neophyte experience of attempting to hide my "mistakes" from my supervisor until, following my first semester of training, I realized that those same mistakes were likely to be my best learning opportunities. Shame is inherently a dimension of supervision since, as adult beginners, we fear that more experienced authority figures will see our "back-sides" and judge us.[44]

From a phenomenological standpoint, I respect the given-ness of each person's experience—everyone has a right to what she/he thinks and feels at all times[45]—while recognizing that in social-contextual terms my experience, as well as the experience of others, is culturally conditioned in ways that may not initially promote mutual openness and trust. Some interns have been taught not to "air their dirty laundry in public," particularly when the supervisor's racial, ethnic, or cultural background is different from their own. My approach to supervision is both systemic and intrapsychic in that I attempt to be ever mindful of the external and internal systems that both I and the supervisee must negotiate as our collaborative relationship develops. Just as our North-American culture as a whole must learn to think ecologically about our role as stewards of creation, so pastoral counselors who supervise are called to respect both the hermeneutical challenges of interpreting the "living human document" before us[46] and the ethical challenges of recognizing our shared dependence on the "living human web" that sustains us each and all.[47] If interns face external challenges such as financial hardship, recovery from abuse, or significant loss, the intrapsychic implications of these challenges need to be recognized as well, in ways that promote self-awareness and self-care while simultaneously emphasizing the need to be responsive and responsible in training.

No one becomes a person in the absence of relationships. Each of us is responsible not only for ourselves but also for and with the network of human relationships that sustains us in being. Without relational support of our emerging personhood at birth, we would literally cease to exist, as Spitz' research on hospitalism demonstrated.[48] Lack of relational support in childhood and adulthood is literally crazy-making. Clinical training requires the kind of relational support that encourages persons to grow and change because each of us carry, from childhood on, wounded places that continue to suffer from not being seen, known, heard, or respected in the ways we need to feel whole. The transformative hope of clinical training is that these wounds will be recognized, explored, and understood by both supervisor and supervisee, soothed by reparative experiences, and healed to a manageable degree over time. The fruits of the intern's "self of the therapist" work will become increasingly evident in their work with clients.

An effective supervisor makes good use of his or her wounds, provided of course that one is at the point of being a wounded healer, rather than a wounded wounder. Part of the training required to become a trustworthy psychotherapist and supervisor entails facing one's wounds and embracing them to the point of forgiving past transgressions (one's own) and transgressors, extracting the alchemical gold from every leaden moment of betrayal, sorrow, and loss. To the extent that I can model the process of gleaning wisdom from my own experience of difficult relationships, my own confrontations with inner demons, and my own struggles with grief and depression, I can encourage my supervisees to face suffering in transformative ways, both in their own lives and the lives of their clients. For example, a supervisor who has experienced and extensively processed her own memories of boundary violations, including a willingness to bring repressed memories into consciousness, can bring the sensitivity that she has gained to bear on the experience of both therapist and client when similar issues become the focus of treatment.

SUPERVISION AND PSYCHE: THE PERSONAL AND CULTURAL UNCONSCIOUS

The figure below shows an individual in context. The horizontal line represents a demarcation between conscious and unconscious awareness that is actually permeable rather than rigid, as are all the boundary lines in this diagram. The individual's conscious ego knowing and personal unconscious awareness held in body-based memories, complexes, dream images, etc. is contained within a larger circle of collective conscious knowing and unconscious collective awareness. For example, America is consciously portrayed as a land of equal opportunity for all. To maintain this conscious identity, European Americans tend to repress the bitter legacy of slavery, conquest of Native Americans, and punitive discrimination against successive groups of immigrants that are also part of our collective heritage as Americans. In his successful bid for the presidency, Barack Obama was able to appeal to the national ego-ideal of equal opportunity in a way that helped to heal majority shame and minority pain surrounding our national history of racism.[49]

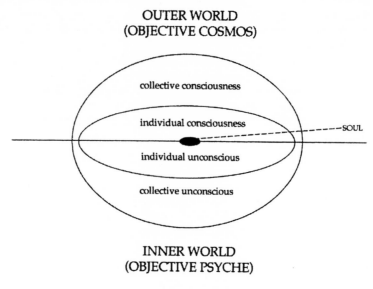

Table 15.1[50]

Beyond collective consciousness is the non-human cosmos that sustains us, and below the collective unconscious is a deeper dimension of shared inner awareness that transcends individual cultures.[51] At the center is the soul, sharing equal knowledge of conscious and unconscious, personal and collective awareness. I define psyche (the province of neurology, psychology, and psychotherapy) as embodied mind and soul (the province of theology, spirituality, religion, and faith) as embodied spirit.[52]

The diagram above is included to illustrate my approach to the integration of spirituality and psychotherapy. To apply this image to clinical supervision, imagine three such embedded spheres that overlap like links on a chain. The center spheres would represent the supervisee and his/her relational contexts, flanked on either side by the supervisor's circles of knowing/unknowing and the client's circles of experience. The areas of overlap would represent intersubjective or shared areas of experience. Unless the supervisor has direct contact with the client, as in live supervision, the client can only be known as mediated to the supervisor by the supervisee. Watching videotape of a counseling session is a step closer to the actual person of the client than either verbal or written case reports, but it never replaces what the therapist can perceive by being in the client's physical presence. All three—supervisor, supervisee, and client(s)—can potentially be linked by means of the soul, which connects the center of all persons to one another in this schematic theological anthropology.[53] The kinds of intuitions that Quakers call leadings require prayerful attention and testing against community wisdom and scripture on the part of supervisor or supervisee, and these leadings are understood as potentially offering wisdom that transcends the abilities of the discursive intellect. With or without such leadings, both members of the supervisory dyad can maintain a client-centered respect for the suffering and potential for healing of persons in their care, even when aspects of that suffering appear self-inflicted, trivial, or unintelligible. The basis of therapeutic receptivity in pastoral counseling is humility. Both care givers and care receivers are children of God. Beyond basic protection of life, we can't presume to know the mind of God with respect to another's welfare. What we can offer is a pastoral presence that lends human form to the Holy Spirit's sheltering wings.

SUPERVISION AND SOUL: MEETING "THAT OF GOD" IN ANOTHER

Beyond the psychological dimensions of existence I've just described, what is the quality of awareness, always present, more or less consciously evident, that I call "soul"? In Christian tradition this awareness relates to the idea of *imago Dei* or "that of God in us." This quality is an aspect of every person's being that, when consciously engaged, has the capacity to increase trust and openness. Soul perception invites receptivity to positive dimensions of non-ordinary experience, a sense of connection within self and with others that is hopeful, enlivening, comforting, and beneficent. These qualities distinguish non-ordinary experience emanating from the soul "part" of us from non-ordinary experiences character-ized by fear, rage, and paranoia as in schizophrenia or dissociation.

Many psychotherapists recognize soul perception as a part aspect of aware-ness while using other names for it. For example, Richard Schwartz' Internal Family Systems model identifies a part of persons characterized by calm and curiosity in the face of traumatic memories. When Schwartz talks about helping traumatized persons access this non-anxious, non-fearful, curious part of them-selves, I believe he is talking about asking persons to look with their soul at as-pects of their experience that require healing.[54] Jung's concept of "Self,"[55] as distinct from the ego and Winnicott's "true self"[56] contain elements of what I am calling soul awareness. Bion talks about K, the known, moving towards O, ulti-mate reality.[57] Perhaps all of these terms are, in some respects, alternate names for soul, our "umbilical cord" to God.[58]

There are no guarantees that soul connections will be consciously appre-hended by any of the participants in therapy or supervision. Still, knowing that this positive dimension of interpersonal awareness is available supports hope in the therapeutic enterprise. Healing potentially begins the moment the decision to make a therapy appointment is made.[59] While clinical training and theoretical knowledge are essential, they are not the only tools the pastoral counselor has available. Intercessory prayer is a resource both pastoral psychotherapist and supervisor can rely on, with or without the conscious knowledge of the client or supervisee. Verbal prayer can be shared when this is welcome by both parties and the supervisor should not hesitate to ask for prayer from peers and mentors, though generally not from students or supervisees lest this request make them hesitant to burden the supervisor with their own concerns.

Freud, the self-identified "Godless Jew," offers the following description of what I would call soul connections in *Group Psychology and the Analysis of the Ego*: "Each individual is bound by libidinal ties on the one hand to the leader (Christ . . .) and on the other hand to the other members of the group."[60]

Freud frames this experience of group unity in relation to Christian belief. I would go a step further to say that all persons are created by God and retain a soul awareness that potentially connects them to God and one another. Saints and other spiritual leaders may develop this shared awareness to a high degree. Others may deny soul awareness or find it inaccessible to consciousness. But as Charcot once observed to Freud in a different context "*Ça n'empeche pas d'exister*"; just because we may not have a psychological theory that adequately describes the existence and function of soul awareness, it still exists for some of us some of the time as an observable phenomenon.[61]

So what? What is the pragmatic "cash value" of soul awareness for supervision, as William James might say?[62] Simply that the supervisor who seeks to be open to the soul dimension of awareness is not limited to theory, discursive logic, rationality, scientific objectivity, or any of the other modes of consciousness that have come to be so highly valued since the Enlightenment. These varieties of left-brain knowing are certainly to be preferred over superstition, stubborn prejudice, culturally sanctioned blindness, or other attitudes that tend to promote lack of understanding between persons. But the right brain awareness that we are all part of God's creation and so part of one another must lead us to approach one another respectfully, tenderly, even tentatively at times, knowing that there are unfathomable dimensions of mystery in every relationship, including our own awareness of ourselves. I agree with a supervisor who said, "If you dislike your client [or supervisee], it simply means that you haven't understood them yet."[63] Diagnoses are superficially useful as a descriptive place to begin but should never be used as a way of distancing us from others. Everyone makes sense to themselves to some degree, if only by way of rationalizations. It is our task as counselors and supervisors to help clients make sense of their lives in more effective ways. If we believe that God is at work in them, as God is in us, luring us towards the deeper fonts of wisdom that connect us all, then the burden of working with suicidal, avoidant, or just plain difficult clients becomes more bearable. Ultimately the work of healing belongs not to us, but to God. Knowing whose we are and whom we serve supports the work of both pastoral counselors and their supervisors.

SUPERVISORY METHODS AND SUPERVISORY GOALS

To return to our opening questions, what supervisory methods and goals are likely to effectively integrate theological reflection and psychotherapeutic wisdom, or, as in the example of soul awareness above, theological wisdom and psychotherapeutic reflection? How is this project of *integrated awareness*, blending as it does discursive and intuitive ways of knowing, likely to influence the practice of clinical supervision?

One of the primary goals of supervision in pastoral counseling contexts is to develop self-of-the-therapist awareness that allows interns to effectively self-supervise. Interns at CTS are required to tape and review their sessions with clients so that they can bring their own self-supervision reflections to individual and group supervision sessions. The individual supervisor serves as mentor, role model, and coach. If the supervisee needs to learn the value of open-ended questions, this is something the supervisor can model as they reflect together on a case. If a supervisee needs to gain real-time awareness of his or her emotional and embodied response to clients, as opposed to thinking more abstractly about a case, the supervisor can invite the supervisee to notice ways in which her or his experience of the client's anxiety, sadness, or anger is replicated in the supervisory session. If the supervisee is intuitively very adept at responding empathically to clients but has difficulty articulating a conceptual framework for care in terms of theoretical approaches, diagnoses, contracts, treatment plans, etc., the supervisor can help to identify the theories most compatible with the supervisee's intuitively empathic approach. If the supervisee is routinely supportive of clients but fails to challenge or redirect when this would be therapeutic, the supervisor can demonstrate the value of departing from a uniform diet of empathic mirroring as needed. The individual supervisor is ideally an experienced healer who helps the intern learn experientially by reflecting on his or her own praxis of care, replicating both the impasses and successes discovered in therapy in a supervisory context that affirms the intern's own healing presence as it develops.

Supervisees also learn from exposure, in group supervision, to peers and supervisors representing diverse theoretical and theological perspectives. Many supervisees find this diversity confusing initially, saying, in effect, "Don't overwhelm me with so many different approaches and options; just tell me what I'm supposed to do with this person!" As clinical learning progresses, supervisees tend to appropriate the suggestions and theories that are most ego-syntonic first, while gradually incorporating a broader range of approaches that will equip them to work effectively with a variety of clients. Most seminary students are NF's (intuitive, feeling) in terms of the Myers-Briggs Type Inventory (MBTI), which means they are generally good at seeing the big picture, imaginatively and empathically entering into the clients' worldview. What they often need is a good complementary dose of ST perception (sensate, thinking).[64] As supervisees learn to shift gears in this way, they begin to pay attention to the concrete details of the case—specifics of family history, life experience, how the person spends his or her day—while addressing conceptual issues in treatment with respect to theoretical and theological considerations. In Live/Interdisciplinary groups, students learn to attend to the process of therapy in real time while receiving specific and theoretically diverse suggestions and instructions from supervisors and

258 Intersubjective and Theological Contexts of Pastoral Counseling Supervision

peers. In Continuous Case groups, second year students reflect in depth on the arc of therapeutic work in a given case, considering the various approaches needed in the beginning, middle, and termination phases of treatment. In Spirit and Therapy groups, interns learn to discern the heart of a client's concern, never equating religious language with actual spiritual concerns in a facile way, nor conversely assuming that questions of faith are absent for agnostic or theologically illiterate clients. In the Group Supervision of Group Therapy, interns learn what it means to be a group, observing the ways in which individual consciousness can shift for good or ill in group settings and supervising each others' leadership of therapy groups in which significant healing can take place in the relationships between group members.

The general ethos of pastoral counseling training tends to include a sincere desire to serve others in ways that are healing to individuals, families, and their communities. Supervisors need to be aware of the pastoral tendencies to "god complexes"—believing that one must be all things to all people at all times to the extent that one becomes a burnt offering rather than a living example of the abundant life promised in Christ (John 10:10b). Many pastoral counselors come from backgrounds in which faith communities are a formative aspect of their identity, but not all faith communities and not all families have offered the respectful support for individuation that personal maturity in faith requires. Often the internalized dictates of faith communities and families of origin need to be unlearned to some degree before crucial aspects of personal transformation can begin. Some interns come into training as seekers or refugees—seekers who have not yet found the communities of faith that might sustain them, and refugees whose faith communities have limited their journeys into wholeness in pernicious ways.

Because the self of the therapist is the means by which God's grace is transmitted in pastoral counseling settings, every supervisor must attend to the therapist's own growth in grace, just as he or she must be vigilant to continue to grow in grace and wisdom rather than rest on laurels earned, stagnate, or become a burnt offering. God's care for all includes care for the supervisor. The work of responding to the suffering of the world one person at a time would prove unbearable were it not for reliance on healthy communities of faith, reliance on the hope of redemption promised in Christ, and reliance on the fact that "the secret is simply this, Christ in me, yes, Christ in me, bringing with him the hope of all the glorious things to come" (Colossians 1:27b).[65]

In short, faith in God's care for all, including the supervisor, makes possible balanced attention to self, supervisees, and the persons under the supervisee's care. The theological context in which these relationships exist, coupled with a healthy respect for the value of discursive knowledge and emerging theories of care, create a unique context for training and supervision in which distinctions and conjunctions between psychic life and the life the spirit can be effectively and usefully identified.

CONCLUSION

In this chapter I have endeavored to state my theological anthropology as it relates to the supervision of pastoral counselors in relational, interpersonal context. My basic clinical orientation as grounded in psychodynamic, intersubjective, and intergenerational theory is open to additional learning and theoretical influences in dialogue with my pastoral values and experience. Contextual sensitivity with regard to all differences among persons is an essential dimension of effective training. Diversity is a quality to be cherished and affirmed since it helps us to learn from one another what it means to be human.

This chapter includes a general description of the methods I typically employ in supervision, as detailed in the following supervisory contract. My primary aim as a supervisor is to develop a positive working alliance with students, lowering anxiety as needed to be supportive, raising anxiety when this is necessary to motivate interns to reach training goals, and holding students accountable for the development of professional standards while recognizing that personal transformation can be an emotionally demanding and "messy" process at times. My philosophy of change is based on the belief that persons generally know at some deep (generally unconscious or preconscious) level what kinds of change are needed for greater wholeness. I think of this deep knowing as "the soul's eye view," only briefly glimpsed at times but precious when it appears for the guidance that it offers.[66] When supervision is both supportive and appropriately challenging, the necessary inner wisdom of persons in transformation, whether clients, interns, supervisors, or supervisory groups, can emerge and flower. The specialized ministry of pastoral counseling is undertaken privately and quietly in hopes that the healing of individuals may one day heal our world.

NOTES

1. All biblical citations are taken from the NRSV, unless otherwise specified.

2. With respect to supervisory credentials, I am an AAMFT Approved Supervisor and an AAPC Fellow, on the way to Diplomate.

3. The term "pastoral psychotherapist" is preferred by some to indicate the distinction between persons with extensive clinical training post-M.Div. and other seminary graduates who may practice brief counseling. Blanton-Peale Graduate Institute was founded by Rev. Norman Vincent Peale and Smiley Blanton, MD, in 1937 as one of the earliest training centers for pastoral counselors, well before the founding of the American Association of Pastoral Counselors (AAPC) as a national organization for clinically trained pastoral psychotherapists and pastoral care specialists in 1963. See the web sites for BPGI, http://www.blantonpeale.org and AAPC, http://www.aapc.org. For a history of AAPC, see Charles A. Van Wagner II, *AAPC in Historical Perspective: 1963-1991*, Allison Stokes, ed. (Fairfax, VA: AAPC, 1992).

4. This attitude of respect for all, a given in Christian communities, in thought if not in deed, is at odds with North American culture at large in which wealth and other forms of prestige are understood to establish the relative worth of persons.

5. This citation from Pamela Cooper-White, *Shared Wisdom* (Minneapolis: Fortress, 2004), vii, alludes to D.W. Winnicott's understanding of potential or transitional space. See, for example, "Transitional Objects and Transitional Phenomena," or "Playing: A Theoretical Statement," in *Playing and Reality* (New York: Routledge, 1971). A theory of intersubjectivity that emphasizes a phenomenological focus on the relational space between persons has been articulated by Robert Stolorow, George Atwood, Bernard Brandshaft, and Donna Orange, among others. See for example *The Intersubjective Perspective*, Robert D. Stolorow, George E. Atwood, and Bernard Brandchaft, eds. (Northvale, NJ and London: Jason Aronson, 1994), or Robert Stolorow, George Atwood, and Donna Orange, *World of Experience: Interweaving Philosophical and Clinical Dimensions in Psychoanalysis* (New York: Basic, 2002).

6. Members of the Society for Pastoral Theology and other theological educators have focused considerable attention on the need for inter- and intracultural sensitivity in recent years. See for example Emmanuel Lartey, *Pastoral Theology in an Intercultural World* (Cleveland: Pilgrim, 2006); Larry Kent Graham, *Care of Persons, Care of Worlds: A Psychosocial Approach to Pastoral Care and Counseling* (Nashville: Abingdon, 1992); Cedric Johnson, "Resistance is Not Futile," in *Healing Wisdom, Ministry in Depth*, Kathleen Greider, Deborah Hunsinger, and Felicity Kelcourse, eds. (Grand Rapids, MI: Eerdmans, forthcoming 2010); Archie Smith, Jr. and Ursula Riedel-Pfaefflin, *Siblings by Choice: Race, Gender, and Violence* (St. Louis: Chalice Press, 2004); Nancy Ramsay, "Navigating Racial Difference as a White Pastoral Theologian," *Journal of Pastoral Theology* (12:2, Fall 2002), 11-27; Lee Butler, Jr., *Liberating Our Dignity, Saving Our Souls* (St. Louis: Chalice, 2006); Joretta Marshall, *Counseling Lesbian Partners* (Louisville, KY: Westminster/John Knox, 2004). For articles specifically related to supervision, see Samuel K. Lee, "A Multicultural Vision for the Practice of Pastoral Supervision and Training," *Journal of Supervision and Training in Ministry* (20, 2000), 111-123; Kathleen J. Greider, "From Multiculturalism to Interculturality: Demilitarizing the Border Between Personal and Social Dynamics Through Spiritual Receptivity," *Journal of Supervision and Training in Ministry* (22, 2002), 40-58; and Curtis W. Hart, "Teaching and Learning Pastoral Counseling: An Integrative and Intercultural Approach," *Journal of Supervision and Training in Ministry* (22, 2002), 75-80.

7. This citation is taken from the American Association of Pastoral Counselor's web site, www.aapc.org.

8. A concept of "good religion" is implicit in James Fowler's broadly ecumenical understanding of faith as articulated in *Stages of Faith: Human Development and the Quest for Meaning* (New York: HarperCollins, 1981).

9. David A. Steere, ed., *The Supervision of Pastoral Care* (Louisville, KY: Westminster/John Knox, 1989), 22.

10. I am using the term postmodern here to connote an approach to clinical experience that does not automatically privilege objectivity over subjectivity and that refuses to automatically privilege one personal or cultural perspective over another, even though it is clear that persons in authority need to make daily decisions that may not reflect the needs and views of everyone in the training community. On the issue of authority, see Brian Grant "Supervisory Power as an Asset," in *Readings in Family Therapy Supervision: Selected Articles from the AAMFT Supervision Bulletin* (Washington, DC: AAMFT, 2000). Regardless of who holds the final authority, a postmodern (and Christian, egalitarian) view avers that everyone in the community has a right to be heard.

11. For an overview of four major traditions represented in pastoral counseling supervision, identified as clinical pastoral education, psychodynamic, humanistic, and sys-

temic, see David Steere, "Supervising Pastoral Counseling," in *The Clinical Handbook of Pastoral Counseling*, vol. 3, Robert Wicks, Richard Parsons, and Donald Capps, eds. (New York: Paulist Press, 2003). Other texts include *The Supervision of Pastoral Care*, David Steere, ed. (Louisville, KY: Westminster/John Knox, 1989) and *The Art of Clinical Supervision: A Pastoral Counseling Perspective*, Barry Estadt, John Compton, and Melvin Blanchette, eds. (New York: Paulist Press, 1987). A sample supervision resource recommended by the American Association of Marriage and Family Therapists is Thomas Todd and Cheryl Storm, *The Complete Systemic Supervisor: Context, Philosophy, and Pragmatics* (New York: Authors Choice, 2002).

12. David Steere, ed., *Op. cit.*, 19.

13. *Ibid.*

14. For a contextual understanding of George Fox's saying, see Elfrida Vipont Foulds, "Let Your Lives Speak," *Pendle Hill Pamphlet* No. 71 (Wallingford, PA: Pendle Hill Publications, 1953). For modern implications, see Parker Palmer, *Let Your Life Speak: Listening for the Voice of Vocation* (San Francisco: John Wiley & Sons, 2000). My basic point in this context is that a supervisor's actions often speak louder than words. The supervisor should be able to model congruence of thought and feeling, reflection and action.

15. K. Samuel Lee, "A Multicultural Vision for the Practice of Pastoral Supervision and Training," *Journal of Supervision and Training in Ministry* (20, 2000).

16. I am using the term phenomenology to connote a broad acceptance of another person's experience as real and significant for them, even in relation to non-ordinary experiences including visions and dreams or psychotic experience. See Medard Boss, *Psychoanalysis and Daseinsanalysis*, Ludwig LeFebvre, trans. (New York: Basic Books, 1963). See also Herbert Spiegelberg, *Phenomenology in Psychology and Psychiatry: An Historical Introduction* (Evanston, IL: Northwestern University Press, 1972). It is my belief that as we approach this deeper way of knowing and accepting another, in the context of their own lived experience, relatively free of our own categories, judgments, and prejudices, we begin to approach the ways in which we are known and understood by God.

17. The intern in question had been exposed to texts such as Pamela Cooper-White's *Shared Wisdom* (Minneapolis: Fortress, 2004) and *Many Voices* (Fortress, 2007) that identify countertransference as an inevitable and potentially very useful response to the therapist's experience of the client.

18. See Monica McGoldrick, Randy Gerson, and Sylvia Schellenberger, *Genograms: Assessment & Intervention*, 2nd ed. (New York: W.W. Norton, 1999).

19. Often misquoted, this is Harry Stack Sullivan's best known saying, taken from *The Interpersonal Theory of Psychiatry* (New York: W.W. Norton, 1953), 4. Sullivan grew up poor, lonely, Catholic, and gay in an anti-Catholic town and knew what it meant to be seen as an outsider.

20. On the topic of sexuality in supervision, see *Journal of Supervision and Training in Ministry*, vol. 21 (2001).

21. The concept of triangulation is associated with the work of Murray Bowen. It identifies the tendency within families and organizations to avoid direct communication between peers, parent to parent, supervisor to supervisor, and intern to intern by drawing in third parties, as when a parent forms an alliance with a child rather than directly communicating with the other parent. See Murray Bowen, *Family Therapy in Clinical Practice* (New York: Jason Aaronson, 1978).

22. For a commentary on the potential pitfalls of IPR groups see Roy Steinhoff-Smith, "The Tragedy of Clinical Pastoral Education," *Pastoral Psychology* (vol. 41, no. 1, 1992), 45-54.

23. Barry Estadt, John Compton, and Melvin Blanchette, eds., *Op. cit.*

24. Vivian Thompson, "Acculturation and Latency," in Felicity Kelcourse, ed., *Human Development and Faith: Life-Cycle Stages of Body, Mind, and Soul* (St. Louis: Chalice, 2004), 183-204.

25. See David Steere, ed.; and Barry Estadt, et al., eds., *Op. cit.*

26. Christopher Bollas, *The Shadow of the Object: Psychoanalysis of the Unthought Unknown* (New York: Columbia University Press, 1989).

27. The Johari window identifies four areas of interpersonal and intrapsychic awareness: known to both self and others, known to others but not to self, known to self but not others, and unknown. See Pamela Cooper-White, *Op. cit.*, figure 1, 6.

28. See Nancy Talbot, "Unearthing Shame in the Supervisory Experience," *American Journal of Psychotherapy* (49:3, 1995), 338-349; also Ann Alonso, A. and J. Scott Rutan, "Shame and Guilt in Psychotherapy Supervision," *Psychotherapy: Theory, Research, Practice and Training* (25, 1988), 576–581.

29. Betty Carter and Monica McGoldrick, eds., *The Expanded Family Life Cycle: Individual, Family & Social Perspectives* (Boston: Allyn & Bacon, 1999); Felicity Kelcourse, ed., *Op. cit.*

30. David Scharf and Jill Savege Scharf, *Object Relations Family Therapy* (New York: Jason Aronson, 1987); Samuel Slipp, *Object Relations: A Dynamic Bridge Between Individual and Family Treatment* (New York: Jason Aronson, 1984).

31. Richard Schwartz, *Internal Family Systems Therapy* (New York: Guilford Press, 1995).

32. Virginia Satir, *Peoplemaking* (Palo Alto: Science and Behavior Books, 1972).

33. Pamela Cooper-White, *Op. cit.*

34. For a basic introduction to Jung's concept of the shadow as "not-me," see "Psychology and Religion," in *Collected Works, Vol. 11: Psychology and Religion: West and East* (1938), 131 and following.

35. Jean Piaget (1896-1980) was a developmental psychologist who theorized that we develop schemas or conceptual models, from infancy on as a way of categorizing and assimilating new information. See, for example, *The Child's Conception of the World*, originally published in 1926, available in English translation by Jacques Voneche, (Lanham, MD: Rowman & Littlefield, 2007). See also Frank Datillio, "The Restructuring of Family Schemas: A Cognitive-Behavior Perspective," *The Journal of Marriage and Family Therapy* (31:1), 15-30.

36. Daniel Stern, *The Interpersonal World of the Infant: A View from Psychoanalysis and Developmental Psychology* (New York: Basic Books, 1985).

37. Anthony DeCasper and Melanie Spence, "Prenatal Maternal Speech Influences Newborns' Perception of Speech Sounds," *Infant Behavior and Development* (9, 1986), 133-150.

38. See Rabbi Yonassan Gershom, "Shamanism in the Jewish Tradition," in *Shamanism: An Expanded View of Reality*, Shirley Nicholsson, ed. (Wheaton IL: Quest), 181-188.

39. Katherine Madden, "The Liminal Space of Pastoral Counseling Supervision," *Journal of Supervision and Training in Ministry* (23, 2003); Craig Nessan, "Internship: A Rite of Passage," *Journal of Supervision and Training in Ministry* (21, 2001).

40. Achieving a "non-anxious presence" as a pastoral caregiver is a goal often cited in CPE and pastoral counseling contexts. Edwin Friedman in *Generation to Generation: Family Process in Church and Synagogue* (New York: Guilford, 1985) mentions the concept in the context of differentiated leadership. What is intended is a true state of inner peace even in the face of highly distressing or crisis circumstances, as opposed to hiding ones emotions: "never let them see you sweat."

41. In his 1912 article, "Recommendations to Physicians Practicing Psycho-Analysis," in *Standard Edition Vol. 12*, 111-120, Freud describes the attitude of "evenly hovering attention" as follows: "The technique . . . is a very simple one . . . It consists simply in not directing one's notice to anything in particular and in maintaining the same 'evenly-suspended attention'. . . in the face of all that one hears. . . . If the doctor behaves otherwise, he is throwing away most of the advantage which results from the patient's obeying the 'fundamental rule of psychoanalysis.'" Cited by Charles Brenner, "Brief Communication: Evenly Hovering Attention," *Psychoanalytic Quarterly* (69, 2000), 545-549. Clearly, it would be important to maintain a non-anxious presence if one wishes to practice evenly hovering attention.

42. Robert Stolorow, George Atwood, and Donna Orange, *Op .cit.*

43. Harlene Anderson and Harry Goolishian, "Human Systems as Linguistic Systems: Preliminary and Evolving Ideas about the Implications for Clinical Theory," *Family Process* (27, 1988), 371-393.

44. See Nancy Talbot, *Op. cit.*; Ann Alonso, A. and J. Scott Rutan, *Op. cit.*; and for a developmental perspective, see also Erik Erikson, on "loss of face" and fear of being attacked "from behind" in "The Eight Ages of Man," *Childhood and Society* (New York: Norton, 1950/1963), 254.

45. Medard Boss, *Op. cit.*; see also L. Binswanger, "Being-in-the-world," in *Selected Papers of Ludwig Binswanger*, J. Needleman, ed. (New York: Harper Torchbooks, 1967).

46. In 1944, Anton Boisen wrote, "We are not trying to introduce anything new into theological curriculum beyond a new approach to some ancient problems. We are trying rather to call attention to the central task of the Church, that of saving souls, and to the central problem of theology—that of sin and salvation. What is new is the attempt to begin with the study of living human documents rather than books, and to focus attention upon those who are grappling with the issues of spiritual life and death," cited on the ACPE web site, http://www.acpe.edu/networks/boisen_bio.htm. More recently, Bonnie Miller-McLemore has added systemic and contextual dimensions to Boisen's thinking with reference to the "living human web." See "The Human Web: Reflections on the State of Pastoral Theology," *The Christian Century* (April 7, 1993), 366-369.

47. See Bonnie Miller-McLemore, *Op. cit.*; and Patricia A. McCluskey, "Weaving the Threads: A Theory of Pastoral Supervision," *Reflective Practice: Formation and Supervision in Ministry* (28, 2008).

48. Renee Spitz, "Hospitalism: An Inquiry into the Genesis of Psychiatric Conditions in Early Childhood," *Psychoanalytic Study of the Child* (1, 1945), 53-72.

49. If the ego is our basic, largely conscious and preconscious sense of self, the ego ideal represents a model of perfection held up for emulation. Christ, for example, is the ego ideal for Christians. See Janine Chasseguet-Smirgel, *The Ego Ideal: A Psychoanalytic Essay on the Malady of the Ideal*, 1st American ed., Paul Barrows, trans. (New York: W.W. Norton, 1985), originally published as *Idéal du moi* (Paris: Tchou, 1975). In 1921, Freud commented on the implications of the ego ideal for group life in "Group Psychology and the Analysis of the Ego," in *Standard Edition* (Vol. 18), 69-143.

50. Felicity Kelcourse, *Op. cit.*, 63.

51. Ernst Cassirer, *Language and Myth* (New York: Dover, 1946).

52. Felicity Kelcourse, "A Phenomenology of Self, Psyche, and Soul," *Global Spiral*, a publication of the Metanexus Institute, (2008), www.metanexus.net/magazine.

53. On the subject of theological anthropology see James Lapsley, "The 'Self,' Its Vicissitudes, and Possibilities: An Essay in Theological Anthropology," *Pastoral Psychology* (35:1, 1986), 23-45; and Frank Milstead Woggon, "The Will To Be Known: Toward a Pastoral Anthology of the Self," *Pastoral Psychology* (44:1, 1995), 45-61.

54. Richard Schwartz, *Internal Family Systems Therapy* (New York: Guilford, 1995) and personal communication following a presentation to AAPC at the 2008 annual meeting.

55. Jung's concept of the Self is often capitalized in English to distinguish it from the small s "self" that is comparable to Freud's "ego." Jung's writes about the Self as the archetype of wholeness and the God-image within the human soul, or *imago Dei*. See "Aion," in *Collected Works* (Vol. 9), Ch. 4, "The Self," 23-35; and Ch. 5, "Christ, a Symbol of the Self," 36-71.

56. D.W. Winnicott, "Ego Distortion in Terms of the True and False Self," *Maturational Processes and the Facilitating Environment* (Madison, CT: International Universities Press, 1965/1987), 140-152.

57. Wilfred Bion, *Attention and Interpretation* (London: Karnac, 1960). See also Brian Grant, *God's Play in Sacred Spaces: A Theology for Pastoral Psychotherapy* (Haworth, 2001).

58. Ana-Maria Rizutto, *The Birth of the Living God* (Chicago: University of Chicago Press, 1979); P. Holliman, "Religious Experience as Selfobject Experience," *Postmodern Self Psychology: Progress in Self Psychology* 18, A. Goldberg, ed. (Hillsdale, NJ and London: Routledge, 2002), 193-205; Felicity Kelcourse, "Prayer and the Soul: Dialogues that Heal," *Journal of Religion and Health* (40:1, 2001), 231-241.

59. Margaret Kornfeld, personal communication.

60. Freud on group psychology, 1921, in Chapter 5, "Two Artificial Groups: The Church and the Army," *Op. cit.*

61. In citing Charcot, I am certainly not intending to equate soul awareness with hysteria. But I do believe that a phenomenological openness to experience invites us to be appropriately curious about aspects of consciousness that have become foreign to Western culture, such as the dreams and visions in the Bible that are cited as instances of God's communication with humankind. See Savary, et al., *Dreams and Spiritual Growth: A Judeo-Christian way of Dreamwork* (Mahwah, NJ: Paulist Press, 1984), 236, for a list of relevant biblical texts.

62. William James, Pragmatism, *A New Name for Some Old Ways of Thinking, Popular Lectures on Philosophy* (New York: Longmans, Green, 1907).

63. Gail Palmer, Emotionally Focused Couples Therapy supervisor, personal communication, 2/7/2009. EFT is considered a marriage and family theory, but it resonates well with the client center approach of Carl Rogers, who was a seminary student at Union Theological Seminary in New York before he became a therapist.

64. David Keirsey and Marilyn Bates, *Please Understand Me: Character and Temperament Types* (Del Mar, CA: Prometheus Nemesis, 1984)

65. *The New Testament in Modern English*, Phillips, trans. (New York: Macmillan, 1958/1966).

66. Felicity Kelcourse, "Discernment, the Soul's Eye View," in Bill Ratliff, ed., *Out of the Silence: Quaker Perspectives on Pastoral Care and Counseling* (Wallingford, PA: Pendle Hill Publications, 2001), 27-49.

CHAPTER SIXTEEN

Supervising the Spiritual Self: The Use of Sustained Empathic Inquiry in Pastoral Supervision

William DeLong

The Clinical Rhombus utilized in the work of Rudulf Ekstein and Robert Wallerstein in *The Teaching and Learning of Psychotherapy* is familiar for most of us trained to supervise in Clinical Pastoral Education (CPE).[1] The rhombus, often used to encourage a broader view and understanding of the multiple layers of supervisory dynamics and accountability, provides a helpful framework for further thinking about empathy and sustained empathic inquiry. Although at times I will be stretching the model originally intended, I believe it will be help-ful in explaining some of my thoughts about the pastoral supervision of the spiritual self. The rhombus, or the use of four quadrants, will assist me in ex-plaining how supervision of the spiritual self can be conceived. I call this a su-pervisory rhombus. After this, and perhaps by laying a foundation for it, I will move to considering the theological implications of sustained empathic inquiry, namely, incarnation as sustained empathic inquiry.

I hope to show in this paper some of the unique perspectives that can be gained when we begin to consider spirituality, or the spiritual self, as an object of empathic inquiry. I wish to say from the outset that I am working out of an understanding of my Christian faith, understood in the particular flavor of the reformed theological tradition, as further handed down by the Presbyterian brand of that movement. As I hope will be demonstrated, I have no intention to bind the widely understood human experience of empathy to any particular religious understanding. Rather, my hope is to further elucidate an understanding of supervision by using the insights gained from the principles of sustained empathic inquiry and other concepts articulated in psychoanalytic intersubjective theory. Further, I hope to show how this particular method used in supervision may convey a different understanding and experience of incarnation that will be liberating to many of us who have experienced the belief of the incarnation of Jesus as toxic, misleading, or nonsensical, particularly as it is understood in the atonement theories of the Christian church. I am speaking then to some of the "Christians in exile" as described by John Spong.[2] In this way I hope to continue and encourage further dialogue about pastoral supervision in the postmodern context.[3]

THE SPIRITUAL SELF

What do I mean by the "spiritual self"? An assumption of mine that requires a bit of explaining is the belief that humans are not so much *homo-sapiens* as we are *homo-religious*. That is simply to say that humans are not so much driven to logic and thinking, as they are driven to faith and spirituality. It is to say that humans seem to seek and experience again and again that which is beyond them. Humans seem to have a need to experience what Rudolph Otto described as the *mysterium tremendum*.

In his well-known book, *The Idea of the Holy,* Rudolph Otto identifies and explores the non-rational mystery behind religion and the religious experience ("non-rational" should not be confused with "irrational"); he called this mystery, which is the basic element in all religions, the numinous.[4]

Otto understood the religious experience as primarily that—an experience. This experience of the "numen" or divine other often leaves the individual with a profound deficit in language to describe the experience. But, for our purposes here it may be sufficient to convey that the experience of the divine leaves the individual with a sense of awe and mystery, as well as a profound sense of fascination and attraction.

Awe and mystery, and the corresponding inability to find words to describe it, are an essential part of any mystical experience. Dorothee Soelle describes this as an essential aspect of mysticism.

> . . . mysticism is *cognition Dei experimentalis* (the knowledge of God through and from experience). What is meant here is the knowledge of God that, instead of being obtained from instruction, tradition, books, and doctrines, comes from one's own life.[5]

Soelle goes on to say that our language to express this kind of experience is deeply inadequate. Yet, because supervision is primarily a "talk method," we can miss our students because they simply may not have the words to describe their own spiritual or mystical experiences. The spiritual self is that part of the person that apprehends this type of mystical experience.

Harold Bronheim, professor of psychiatry at Mount Sinai School of Medicine, suggests in his captivating book, *Body and Soul: The Role of Object Relations in Faith, Shame, and Healing* that humans have, as a part of their character structure, an inherent quest for what we would traditionally call transcendence.[6] Faith, he claims, is:

> . . . a state of self cohesion as a result of an arrangement of internal object relations that reflects the nature and developing maturity of the combined observing and experiencing ego. It is a character structure that serves to maintain psychic stability at times of loss of stabilizing self/objects by allowing for the transcendence of the immediate time and local circumstances while continuing a state of interpersonal connectedness. It may be externalized and directed to an idealized object, for example God, who may then assume qualities of infinite omnipresence. However, it does not require such a projection or assignment, nor does it require objective proof to be true.[7]

Without going too far afield into object relations theory, Bronheim makes some important claims here. First, he says that faith is a character structure, a part of normal maturation, and a part of the biologically predicted aspects of personality. Second, he claims faith is not inherently directed at any particular object. The object to which faith is directed or attached becomes an aspect of culture, family heritage, preference, etc. Faith, he claims, does not have an inherent object—one has faith rather *in a particular object*. Third, he says, faith is an awareness of the initial internalization of the primary object. I want to briefly elaborate on each of these aspects.

As a structural component of character, Bronheim is claiming that faith is a part of each individual and must be accommodated in one way or another. As a "normal" part of development, he claims that faith is not secondary to the individual, but is as basic an element as sexuality, identity, or other aspects of the self. His claim leads us to see each person as struggling not so much about if there is faith or not, but rather centers the individual discussion on the more important question, "What is the object of the faith I already have?"

Faith, he says, is the desire to experience something that is more akin to awe. The human person seeks to experience awe or wonder. And sometimes that is "attached" to a religious object that we call God that is then further re-experienced by the various rituals of religious faith. But, the root of that quest is located as a part of personality structure. It is an aspect of character or the self.

Bronheim suggests that the self experiences a preverbal occurrence of awe. This experience of awe comes he says from the self's initial awareness of internalizing a primary or transformational object. Thus, the initial experience of awe is the felt experience of the self's coming to awareness. It is the original awareness of the self's internalizing a primary object. Bronheim likens this to the question posed by God to Adam and Eve in the creation story in Genesis. When considering that story, we see that Adam and Eve realize that they are naked only after God asks them a question: "Where are you?" Self awareness—the realization of being naked, perhaps vulnerable—is secondary to the act of God seeking humanity. Human awareness comes as a result of God's existential question, "Where are you?"

Bronheim provides intuitive support for these claims by considering the almost universal game of peek-a-boo. In the childhood game, the mother hides her face from the young child, then, when the child is perhaps near panic at the perceived loss of the primary object, the mother suddenly appears, to the squealing delight of the child. When the child once again experiences the restored primary object, she is reawakened to the dawning of that first internalization. She reexperiences awe. In a similar fashion, we term an experience as "awe-filled" when we are reawakened to this foundational experience of our awareness of the internalization of the primary object.

Bronheim makes it clear that faith, as a structure of the person is able to be understood in the same fashion as any other aspect of personality or character. If we are able to observe psychological phenomenon only through the use of vicarious introspection or sustained empathic inquiry as Kohut asserts, then it should also be true that faith, and the part of the self that experiences it, could be the object of that same type of inquiry.

SUSTAINED EMPATHIC INQUIRY

Sustained empathic inquiry is the phrase used by Heinz Kohut and more recently adopted by Robert Stolorow and others working in the area of psychoanalytic intersubjective theory. Sustained empathic inquiry is the use of what I call "clinical empathy" to understand the subjective meaning of another individual.[8] Empathy, according to Kohut, is not simply a feeling. Rather, empathy is the intentional use of the self in attempting to understand the subjective reality of another from within her or his perspective. Kohut describes vicarious introspection, or empathy, by using the example of a very tall man:

> Only when we think ourselves into his place, only when we, by vicarious introspection, begin to feel his unusual size as if it were our own and thus revive inner experiences in which we had been unusual or conspicuous, only then do we begin to appreciate the meaning that the unusual size may have for this person and only then have we observed a psychological fact.[9]

Empathic inquiry, then, is not a feeling associated with compassion or pity. Clinical use of empathy does not so much happen to us, as might pity or compassion, but is rather initiated by us in an attempt to understand the other. Kohut conceives empathy as a method to observe a psychological fact. Kohut so strongly believed in the role of empathy that he claimed that empathy was the only way that another person could apprehend a "psychological fact" in another. He says:

Only a phenomenon that we can attempt to observe by introspection or by empathy with another's introspection may be called psychological. A phenomenon is "somatic," "behavioristic," or "social" if our methods of observation do not predominantly include introspection and empathy.[10]

Empathy is more akin to "fellow feeling" than it is to the emotions of pity or compassion. Further, empathy, or the more extended use of sustained empathic inquiry, is the only way a person can understand the unique perspective of the other. It is only when we enter the unique subjective reality of others that we can begin to truly understand how they make meaning in the world and thus provide for themselves a unique sense of self.

Empathy was also crucial for Kohut because it redirected the emphasis of the therapeutic relationship away from interpretation based on objectivity to a mutual process of understanding. By grounding the therapeutic relationship in the method of empathy, Kohut affirms the subjective reality of the patient leading to a clinical environment of mutual respect and mutual inquiry. Instead of relying on "distortion" and "interpretation," the therapist seeks to understand the inner reality of the patient as she or he understands it. Understanding how the patient makes meaning in his or her inner world became the focus of therapy. The same is true in the process of training. The goal of the supervisee is to understand the patient or client from within his or her own perspective. In similar fashion, the goal of the training supervisor is to understand the student from within his or her unique perspective. The parallel process is supported and understood by empathy. This requires a clinical stance of sustained empathic inquiry. Yet, the question quickly arises: What is the object of sustained empathic inquiry in the supervisory alliance? How do I begin to use the clinical method of vicarious introspection, and what am I to observe? What self is to be the object of that inquiry?

A Supervisory Rhombus

As mentioned earlier, I find it useful to think about the use of sustained empathy by utilizing the notion of a rhombus or four quadrants. The rhombus is, of course, only a representation of what is ultimately the integrated whole of the person. However, as I think of the areas of inquiry within the self in training supervision, I find the model helps me to concentrate on various areas of supervision. In many ways, this depiction violates one of the central tenets of intersubjective theory, namely, making distinct and reified that which cannot be separated or concretized. But, for purpose of explaining my sense of supervising the spiritual self, I believe this artificial distinction is justified.

Development of a supervisor can be conceived as a process that teaches one to become a particular kind of person to others. Acquiring and utilizing theory and particular skills is not sufficient if it is not integrated within the individual. Becoming a particular kind of person for others is most clearly considered in the final process of certification for CPE supervisor as the focus of that process is on the integration of personal history and theory, with the actual practice of supervising. The language we use to talk about that process is indeed centered in "use of self" as the primary teaching tool. Yet, in order to learn the various theories and skills, one must focus on specific goals throughout training. The rhombus outlined below is intended to provide a way of thinking about those goals.

This supervisory rhombus allows us to see how various elements work together to ensure comprehensive supervision. That is, one way the rhombus helps is that it keeps us from splitting apart various aspects needing supervisory attention and integration. At least that is one way that depicting a rhombus has helped me. It is important to remember that my interest at this point is to focus upon the area of the rhombus that illuminates the faith understanding of the supervisory resident or other student. It is quite clear to me that others could assign with equal justification different goals that should be developed in the supervisory process. My hope in using this rhombus is to assist in the use of sustained empathic inquiry as the primary method of supervision.

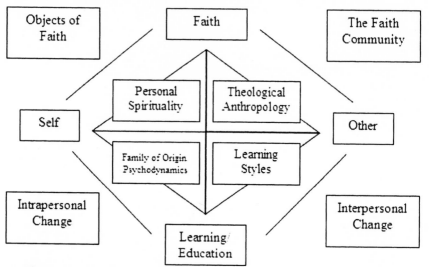

Figure 16.1. Supervisory Rhombus and Corresponding Areas of Inquiry

In the supervisory rhombus depicted here (Fig. 16.1) there are four areas or objects of inquiry, all of them accessed through the use of sustained empathic inquiry. This rhombus is most helpful when attention is paid to each of the sectors and the dynamic interplay between them. Splitting off one aspect or concentrating on one quadrant at the expense of others leads to something other than pastoral supervision of the supervisory resident. For instance, if only the Faith-Self (FS) dynamic is considered in supervision, then we are more likely doing spiritual direction. Paying attention exclusively to the Self-Education (SE) dynamic at the exclusion of the other parts of the rhombus is closer to individual therapy than to pastoral supervision. The Faith-Other (FO) orientation is a closer to community worship or theological anthropology while the Education-Others (EO) dynamic would yield any number of the helping professions depending upon the unique character, nature, and methods of care being taught (i.e., nursing, medicine, social work, etc.).

Having stressed the importance of attending to all aspects of the rhombus, there are times when we must focus upon one aspect that the student may be presenting. Attending means, I believe, the use of sustained empathic inquiry.

THE FAITH-SELF QUADRANT

The Faith-Self quadrant is of particular interest to me as I supervise supervisory residents and the remainder of this chapter will look at this aspect of the supervisory rhombus. This area of supervision clearly overlaps with many current understandings of spiritual direction. That is, the goal of understanding in this quadrant is with the student's spiritual meaning making or the object(s) of their faith dynamic. Understanding the student from within her or his experience of the divine is critical in the formation of CPE supervisors. Since the focus of this chapter is the use of sustained empathic inquiry in supervision and in particular the supervision of the spiritual self, I will limit my comments in this area to the use of empathy in understanding the student in the Faith-Self (FS) sector.

Supervision of the spiritual self is not new to pastoral supervision. Most of us are consciously working with the student's beliefs about the nature of God and the interaction of humanity with God. However, when empathy is used, we move away from understanding the spiritual self of the student in an objective way to what I believe is the more powerful and transformative understanding: the student's subjective understanding of her or his experience of God. That means being more connected to the mystical experience of the student than with their stated formal beliefs such as creeds, doctrines, or learned systematic theology.

Dorothee Soelle's thinking about mysticism has been helpful to me as I seek to understand the experience of awe that students bring to pastoral supervision. In her book, *The Silent Cry,* Soelle articulates the essential nature of mysticism. Quoting William James' four characteristics of the mystical experience, she provides a broad outline of the mystical experience from a subjective viewpoint: 1) The loss of all worry; the sense that all is ultimately well with one; the peace, the harmony and the willingness to be, even though the outer conditions should remain the same, 2) the sense of perceiving truths not known before that make life's mysteries lucid, 3) the objective change that the world seems to undergo, making it seem "new" and never having been seen that way before, and 4) the ecstasy of happiness.[11]

Convinced that mysticism is the life-blood of religion, she outlines several areas one must attend to if they are to understand the mystical experiences of life. They are paradox, negation, and silence. I believe supervising the spiritual self requires we attend to these elements in our supervision and in ourselves.

PARADOX

Language, its use and misuse, is often the enemy of the spiritual encounter. If we are to understand the spiritual experiences of our students, I believe we must move past language or beyond language. Paradox is one way of attending to this important aspect of supervision.

"Heaviness is the root of lightness. Serenity is the master of restlessness."[12] This is a simple example of paradox. The silent cry is another. Paradox has long been used to invite the self to move beyond the "captured thinking of logic." "You have to be strong enough to be weak" as quoted by Jon Kabat-Zinn.[13] Paradox by nature pits two seemingly opposite concepts into a single whole. Soelle says it this way:

> The coincidence of substantive or logical contradictions (*coincidentia opposito-rum*) comes about when in a single statement words are juxtaposed with each other that are insufficient on their own. This creates the paradox, which is an unexpected assertion that goes counter to general opinion or common knowledge. In terms of philosophy of language, the paradox is an attempt to approach from two opposite directions a factor that cannot be perceived or understood.[14]

Paradox is a method well understood by theologians and mystics. Many of the sayings of Jesus use this method to convey deeper truths.

Attending to the nature of paradox provides insight into how the student understands experiences that lie at the edge of reason. Provided that this "attending" is characterized by sustained empathic immersion, we gain insight into how the student makes meaning on the fringes of his or her own logic. Consider the following event with a third unit CPE resident:

> Chris was clearly a talented hospital chaplain. His Southern Baptist religious roots provided him with a sufficient grounding in spirituality to enable him to work with patients in the arena of personal spirituality. For most of the year, the CPE group was working with Chris to move more fully into his feeling and to abandon some of the shame that told him his expressions of feeling were stupid and unimportant to others.
>
> Chris came to IPR after working the previous week with a young man whose 16 month-old boy was brought in to the Emergency Room having stopped breathing. Chris was the first one to begin working with the young father, who was clearly shocked by the events unfolding. Chris formed an appropriate pastoral bond with this young man of his own age. After hugging the man good-bye, the family went home without their son who had died as a result of the anoxia.

Chris came to that IPR after having been contacted by the police regarding his interaction with the young father. As it turned out, the father was the primary suspect in the death of the child and was arrested the same day we were meeting for IPR. Chris was stunned and angry. The group used an empathic stance to support Chris both in his recent discovery of the arrest and of his seeming inability to express his feelings. "You can't kill your own children," he said. "You take the very life you gave?" "What the hell do you do with that?" he concluded.

The paradox presented by this clinical encounter forced Chris to face something that moved him beyond his own internal logic. The paradox of giving and taking life did not make sense to Chris. Had the group focused upon the nature of the paradox and the seeming inability to make sense of the event, they would have missed Chris in the midst of his emotional and learning need. Instead, the group moved to an empathic stance and asked Chris to feel the nonsense of the event. As he did, he began to move more fully and congruently into an understood emotion. The acceptance of the paradox through the use of sustained empathic inquiry helped Chris to feel the event and integrate it.

Paradox, by its nature, quickly removes logic as a means of understanding the event. If we can sit with the nonsense long enough and allow ourselves to be with students in the midst of it, we can be with them in a way that allows them to move with the paradox and perhaps beyond language, rather than to move away from it and to discount it as nonsense.

NEGATION

The philosophy student in me wants to look at the definition of negation before we move further into this aspect of supervising the spiritual self. There are a number of reasons for that, but put most clearly, this is a difficult concept that has long been debated in both philosophy and theology. Given this, I am trying to stay within a manageable discussion of how I understand negation in the supervision of students. So off to brainydictionary.com I went to find a definition. Here is what they say and I think it works for most of what I seek to say here:

Negation
(adv.) The act of denying; assertion of the nonreality or untruthfulness of anything; declaration that something is not, or has not been, or will not be; denial; the opposite of affirmation.
(adv.) Description or definition by denial, exclusion, or exception; statement of what a thing is not, or has not, from which may be inferred what it is or has.[15]

What feels most important to me about this definition is the active use of declaring that "something is not, or has not been, or will not be; denial." Most of us are well-attuned to the unique ways our students deny their reality. Since this is critical to any learning process, I think as a group we are well-prepared to address this aspect in supervision. However, this takes a bit of a twist when we begin to consider denial in the spiritual realm of the self. Questions I pose for myself to begin an empathic inquiry are similar to: Who is the God this student denies? What aspect of God is being resisted? How is God absent from this person's life? In what ways is this student ensuring that she or he does not encounter God differently?

This is only one aspect of negation, however. Soelle sees negation from the aspect of being beyond words. Negation for her is closer to the method of the *via negativa*, the way of knowing that is beyond description because our language is always fixed within the experiential and most of what is deeply spiritual is far beyond our ability to locate words that describe that experience. A mentor of mine describes it this way: "It is about the letting go of the discursive mind as the vehicle for holding one's connection to the mystery." Soelle says it like this:

> The stylistic figure of negation belongs to the experience that is inexpressible in words. It is not this, it is not that, it is not what you already know or have seen or what someone told you before . . . What cannot be named positively can either be left in silence or must be named negatively.[16]

Using a stance of sustained empathic inquiry allows for distinctions like this to become a part of the spoken or unspoken supervisory dialogue. The interplay of negation (the *via negativa,* i.e., that which is denied because of the sheer suffering and darkness of the event and that which cannot be spoken because of the poverty of language) allows for the emergence of what is and what, perhaps, is becoming. A first year supervisory resident taught me much about this process.

> Shawn is a Lutheran student in her first year of supervisory CPE. In one individual supervision she began to talk about the longing she had to communicate a God of love to a hospice patient she had cared for while completing her residency in CPE. As she talked, she began to speak in language of the *via negativa* telling me what she didn't want for the patient. "It's not that I want him to have peace or at least simply peace, or even acceptance. I don't want him to have to find a way to make everyone around him more comfortable with his own death. I don't even want him to have the sacraments of the church, even though I know that is truly important to him. I want him to have that, well, you know, that peace that passes all understanding. I just don't know how to say this..."

Sustained empathy allowed me to be with her as she struggled to find the words, concepts, and meaning that spoke the depth of the spiritual hope she had for this man. The negation, in this instance, was a combination of the denial she herself was experiencing over the care she provided this man two years earlier. But, it was also a struggle to find the way to talk about that which was beyond words. Her own experience of a "peace that passes all understanding" allowed her to move toward this man with the same wordless hope. And it was my experience that was also resonating as I empathically listened to her try to put words to that

experience and hope. In the end, this kind of situation often ends with both partners of the conversation saying something like "You know?" with the only possible response being, "Yeah, I know."

Allowing ourselves to connect empathically with the negation of the student
allows us to feel the depth of angst and hope as the student seeks to communicate that which is often beyond words.

> Tao can be talked about, but not the Eternal Tao. Names can be named, but not
> the Eternal Name.
> As the origin of heaven-and-earth, it is nameless: As the "the Mother" of all
> things, it is nameable.
> So, as ever hidden, we should look at its inner essence: As always manifest, we
> should look at its outer aspects.
> These two flow from the same source, though differently named: And both are
> called mysteries.
> The Mystery of mysteries is the Door of all essence.[17]

SILENCE

The supervision of the spiritual self requires, at least from my perspective, a
profound comfort, understanding, and curiosity with silence. The silence that
emerges in the supervisory encounter is often looked at from a psychodynamic
perspective. And most of us are quite adept at staying with the student in the
midst of this kind of silence. However, as Soelle points out, silence in the spiritual arena can be quite different.

> The third specific element of all mystical languages is silence, which is speak-
> ing coming to an end and producing at the same time an expanse of silence. In
> terms of day-to-day experiences, two kinds of silence may be distinguished.
> One is a dull, listless, apathetic silence; a wordlessness arising from poverty,
> such as exists in culture of poverty or between people who have nothing to say
> to one another. But besides this prediscourse silence, there is also a post dis-
> course means of communication. This silence after speaking does make use of
> words but only in order to leave them behind.[18]

Soelle's notion of a pre- and post-discourse silence is very helpful to me in my
attending to the spiritual self in supervision. Most of us are quite familiar with
the prediscourse silence. If you have ever sat in the quiet of an IPR group as it
moves from anxious chatter to "IPR" and the inevitable silence that occurs. This
is not the silence that is spiritually significant. Rather, as Soelle points out, the
silence that comes over the conversation when words are left behind because a
more powerful and meaningful way of communicating is arriving. Silence can
be the leaving of words not because of resistance or transference, but silence, as
a different kind of language, is beginning. Silence in this manner is more linked
to the beholding of the other in a moment when spiritual awareness is shared.
The supervision of the student in this kind of situation requires letting go of any

predetermined understanding of objectivity (as versus subjective understandings). Sustained empathic inquiry allows for the moments when words leave off being a shared encounter from within the subjective reality of the student. Sustained empathic inquiry is a perspective that would allow for this kind of mystical experience to be shared and understood.

> Henry was completing his second unit of CPE within the context of a year long residency. An older African-American man who had marched in the civil rights struggles of the 60s, Henry had seen much in his life. Central to his learning was a nagging belief that he would be unable to work with patients due to the grief he felt over the death of his own son some 17 years earlier.

> In this individual supervisory session, Henry was telling me the story of his son's death. The depth of pain was clear and present. And so was his grief recovery. But what filled the room was the silence that mirrored the vacuum of loss. The emptiness was beyond words and it seemed the only proper response was the silence we all learned as chaplains in moments of profound grief. Yet, the silence in this encounter was not just grief, it was the silence that comes when words leave off . . . when words have no meaning any longer. The silence gave rise to an understanding that led Henry to say, "Blessed be the name of the Lord."

We sat in silence for maybe half the hour. It was neither rushed nor uncomfortable. A sustained empathic stance allowed me to feel the weight of the moment, the satisfaction with the telling of the story, and the honor being given to his son and himself. At the same time, the final words uttered by Henry leave off the first part of that familiar phrase, "The Lord gives, and the Lord takes away . . ."

INCARNATION AND EMPATHY

Kohut insisted that empathy was the essential language of development and thus psychotherapy. This understanding has been added to by many infant researchers who indicate that long before infants respond to words they are responding to the empathic climate of their surrounding.[19] The childish "coo" of the infant is responded to by the mimic of the parent who repeats the "coo." This mirroring effect provides the infant with an understanding that she is in the world and can find in it responsive others. Empathy, then, is at the very root of our becoming persons. If empathy is at the very root of our becoming persons, then it is not a very far leap to wonder how the divine mystery may also speak the language of empathy. A brief return to the work of Bronheim will help me make this point.

I began this chapter referring to how Bronheim locates faith as a character structure and thus a part of normal development. In that discussion Bronheim quotes a story told by Martin Buber about the Hassidic Rabbi Shneur Zalman. Rabbi Zelman, while in jail having been denounced in Russia, tells this story. It is so good that the extended quote seems worthwhile to me.

While in jail, he was approached by the chief of the gendarmes with the follow-ing question: "How are we to understand that God, the all-knowing, said to Adam 'Where art thou?' Didn't he know where his own creation was?" Rabbi Zalman answered the officer simply and directly that God's question "Where art thou?" seeks to implore Adam to give an account of himself as to what he has been doing with his life, and how he has been hiding himself from truth about himself. Rabbi Zalman continues to say that the question, although asked of Adam, is an eternal one, asking every man through every generation to ex-amine the hideouts and falsehoods in his life and how he hides himself from the face of God. Adam's reply—"I was afraid and I hid myself"—is not so much a submission or surrender to authority as an examination of the truths about him-self that allowed a returning to God.[20]

The eternal question asked by God is not a demand for the accounting of where one has been such as could be expected from a very stern parent. Rather, the question as told by Buber is more like, "Where have you been and what have you been doing?" Or, to use the vernacular of the day, it could be more like "What's up?" The question is designed to provide an opportunity to tell God what it is like for Adam to be Adam. God's inquiry is an empathic one, an at-tempt at sustained empathic inquiry. God is seeking to hear from Adam about his life from within the perspective of Adam.

Christian theology articulates another aspect of empathy. Incarnation, un-derstood as "the word became flesh," is an empathic stance. The belief of the early Christian church was that God became "human." By this, I believe they meant that in the person of Jesus they saw the full nature of God revealed in a human. Marcus Borg makes this a central point of his spiritual teaching.

Jesus is for us, as Christians, the decisive revelation of what a life full of God is like. I see this claim as the central meaning of the Christological language of the New Testament. The human Jesus is the Word Made Flesh. The human Je-sus is the Wisdom of God. The human Jesus is the Spirit of God embodied in human life. In short, the meanings of all the statements regarding Jesus show us what a life full of God is like.[21]

The point is somewhat obvious except when we begin to consider the nature of sustained empathic inquiry. Kohut was clear that empathy was letting go of the desire to understand the other from one's own perspective and shift to the more risky and difficult perspective of the other. The very nature of sustained em-pathic inquiry as articulated in the psychoanalytic intersubjective theory is the suspension of the belief that I can objectively "know" something about the other. Rather, what I can know is only what I can "observe" through sustained empathy. In this way, God's desire as understood through incarnation was to deeply understand humanity, not from the perspective of moral atonement, but from the perspective of being human. Incarnation was God's attempt to answer the question originally asked in the garden, i.e., "What is it like to be you?"

Understanding incarnation in this way allows one to move away from understanding the work of Jesus as one of atonement based on the need to make a payment for sin. Rather, the work of Jesus can be seen as the more empathically motivated understanding of at-one-ment. The notion of God's being at one with humanity as an outgrowth of empathy resonates much more deeply for those of us who are unable to make sense of traditional paradigms of the incarnation. Among these may be our students who are increasingly rooted in a postmodern understanding of truth, agency, and notions of sin. But that will require another chapter.

Concluding Thoughts

My hope in this chapter was to introduce and elaborate on some of the core concepts I am using to supervise what I am calling the spiritual self. Central to this was identifying the spiritual self within the supervisory rhombus. Although only briefly introduced here, more work on the rhombus is needed and welcomed. In addition, understanding faith as a character structure also needs further elaboration. And finally, understanding and articulating other ways of working with the spiritual nature of students is crucial. As the resurgence of spirituality continues, there will be an increasing need for supervisors to understand students from within the perspective of the student's own spirituality. Doing this will allow greater depth in our supervision in this postmodern, multi-faith, multi-cultural context.

Portions of this chapter were previously published in the *Journal of Supervision and Training for Ministry*. Used with permission.

Notes

1. Rudolf Ekstein and Robert Wallerstein, *The Teaching and Learning of Psychotherapy*, 2nd ed. (Madison, WI: International Universities Press), 1972.

2. John Spong, *Why Christianity Must Change or Die* (San Francisco: Harper Collins, 1999).

3. For further understanding of the postmodern perspective, see my article "From Object to Subject: Pastoral Supervision as an Intersubjective Activity," *The Journal of Pastoral Care and Counseling* (Vol. 56, No. 1, 2002).

4. Rudolph Otto, *The Idea of the Holy*, John W. Harvey, trans., 2nd ed. (Oxford: Oxford University Press, 1923), 1950.

5. Dorothee Soelle, *The Silent Cry* (Minneapolis: Fortress Press, 2001), 45.

6. Harold Bronheim, *Body and Soul: The Role of Object Relations in Faith, Shame, and Healing* (Lanham, MD: Jason Aronson Inc., 1998).

7. Harold Bronheim, *Ibid.*, 26.

8. William R. DeLong, *Op. cit.*

9. Heinz Kohut, "Introspection, Empathy, and Psychoanalysis," in Paul Ornstein, ed., *The Search for the Self* (New York: International Universities Press, 1978).

10. Heinz Kohut, *Ibid.*

11. Dorothee Soelle, *Op. cit.*, 21.

12. Lao Tzu, *Tao The Ching*, John C.H. Wu, trans., 26 (New York: St. John's University Press, 1961), 52.

13. John Kabat-Zinn, *Wherever You Go There You Are* (New York: Hyperion, 1994), 65.

14. Dorothee Soelle, *Op. cit.*, 69.

15. www.brainydictionary.com.

16. Dorothee Soelle, *Op. cit.*, 65.

17. Lao Tzu, *Op. cit.*, 1, 3.

18. Dorothee Soelle, *Op. cit.*, 70.

19. Daniel Stern, *The Interpersonal World of the Infant* (New York: Basic Books, 1985).

20. As quoted from Martin Buber, *The Way of Man: According to the Teachings of Hasidism* (Secaucus, NJ: Citadel Press, 1966).

21. Marcus Borg, sermon at Calvary Episcopal Church in Memphis, TN, "Jesus and the Christian Life," March 16, 1999, www.explorefaith.org.

INDEX

CONTRIBUTORS

Mildred M. Best, M.Div.
Mildred Best is Associate Director of the Department of Chaplaincy Services and Pastoral Education and Assistant Professor of Medical Education at the University of Virginia Health System in Charlottesville, Virginia. She is an ACPE supervisor and a board certified chaplain. She holds an M.Div. from Southeastern Baptist Theological Seminary, an M.S.S. from Bryn Mawr College, and a B.S. from Coppin State College. She is a member of the editorial committee of the *Journal of Pastoral Care and Counseling.* Her articles have appeared in *Chaplaincy Today, The Journal of Religion and Health, Bioethics Matters, Baptist Leader,* and *Baptist Informer.*

Beth Burbank, D.Min.
Beth Burbank is Director of Clinical Pastoral Education at VITAS Innovative Hospice Care in Chicago, Illinois. Beth is a member of the Religious Society of Friends (Quaker). She is certified as an ACPE supervisor. Beth was Assistant Editor of the Journal of Supervision and Training in Ministry, ACPE Theory Paper of the Year feature from 1989-2002, and Co-Editor of a Symposium on Story Theology and Ministry for the same journal in 1987. Beth's D.Min. focused upon spirituality and healing. Her qualitative research project followed a 13 month healing circle, "Meeting for Worship for Healing, a contemplative healing service after the manner of Friends."

Donald Capps, Ph.D.
Donald Capps, Princeton Theological Seminary's William Harte Felmeth Professor of Pastoral Theology, earned his B.D. and S.T.M. from Yale Divinity School, and his M.A. and Ph.D. from the Divinity School of the University of Chicago. He draws on his training as a psychologist of religion in both his teaching and his writing. His research interests include pastoral care, psychobio-

graphy, and the psychology of religion, art, and poetry. In 1989, he was awarded an honorary doctorate in sacred theology from the University of Uppsala, Sweden, in recognition of his publications in the psychology of religion and pastoral care and of his leadership role in the Society for the Scientific Study of Religion, which he served as editor of its professional journal from 1983 to 1988 and as president from 1990 to 1992. He is ordained in the Evangelical Lutheran Church in America. Don has written many articles and books, among them are: *Men and Their Religion: Honor, Hope, and Humor* (Valley Forge, PA: Trinity Press International, 2002), *A Time to Laugh: The Religion of Humor* (New York: Continuum Press, 2005), *Fragile Connections: Memoirs of Mental Illness* (Duluth, GA: Chalice Press, 2005), and *Young Clergy: A Biographical-Developmental Study* (London: Haworth Press, 2005).

William R. DeLong, Ed.D.

Bill DeLong is Director of Spiritual Care Services at BroMenn Healthcare System in Bloomington, Illinois. Bill is a certified ACPE supervisor and a board certified chaplain. He is ordained in the Presbyterian Church, USA. Bill's publications include, "Supervising the Spiritual Self," *Journal of Supervision and Training in Ministry* (Vol. 25, June 2005), "From Object to Subject: Pastoral Supervision as an Intersubjective Activity," *Journal of Pastoral Care* (Vol. 56, 1, Spring 2002), "Educating and Certifying Professional Chaplains: A Combined Approach," *Chaplaincy Today, The Journal of the Association of Professional Chaplains* (Vol. 16/2, 2000), "The Prayers of the Faithful: Prayer as a Metaphor for Medicine and Healing," in *Scientific and Pastoral Perspectives on Intercessory Prayer*, Larry VandeCreek, ed. (London: Haworth Press, 1998), and *Organ Transplantation in Religious, Ethical, and Social Context* (London: Haworth Press, 1993).

Carrie Doehring, Ph.D.

Carrie Doehring is Associate Professor of Pastoral Care and Counseling at Iliff School of Theology in Denver, Colorado. She graduated with a B.Mus. and a M.Div. from McGill University, a M.Th. from Wilfrid Laurier University and a Ph.D. from Boston University. Carrie currently is articulating a contextual theologically-based approach to pastoral care that draws upon postmodern approaches to knowledge: *The Practice of Pastoral Care: A Postmodern Approach* (Louisville, KY: Westminster John Knox, 2006). As a feminist pastoral theologian, she focuses on sexual and domestic violence and clergy sexual misconduct in "Taking Care: Monitoring Power Dynamics and Relational Boundaries" in *Pastoral Care and Counseling* (Nashville: Abingdon Press, 1995). Carrie is ordained in the Presbyterian Church, USA and is a diplomate in the American Association of Pastoral Counselors. She is a licensed psychologist in Massachusetts and Colorado.

Mark Hart, D.Min.
Mark Hart is a certified ACPE supervisor and is Director of Clinical Pastoral Education at Baptist Health System in San Antonio, Texas. Mark is a board certified chaplain and has served in a variety of positions within the Association for Clinical Pastoral Education (ACPE). Mark's presentations include: "Transition Times: Confusing Life with Longevity and Confusing Liberty with Location," 60+ Adult Ministry Leadership Conference, Baptist General Convention of Texas.

Gordon J. Hilsman, D.Min.
Gordon Hilsman is an ACPE supervisor, dually certified by the ACPE and the NACC. His publications appear in a variety of journals, indicating his particular interest in the core values of the pastoral care and counseling movement, the essential nature of clinical supervision for enhancement of the professions, and sexual intimacy as a spiritual arena of life. A frequent presenter at professional conferences, he is the author of *Intimate Spirituality* (Lanham, MD: Rowman and Littlefield, 2007). Gordon manages and conducts CPE in the Franciscan Health System of Tacoma, Washington.

Felicity Kelcourse, Ph.D.
Felicity Kelcourse is Associate Professor of Pastoral Care and Counseling and Director of the Psychotherapy and Faith Program. Recorded as a Quaker minister (Religious Society of Friends) in 1987, she holds a Ph.D. in psychiatry and religion from Union Theological Seminary in New York, an M.Min. from Earlham School of Religion and a B.A. from Oberlin College. Felicity's recent articles appear in the *Journal of the American Academy of Psychoanalysis, Chaplaincy Today, Encounter,* and *The Living Pulpit.* She edited and authored several chapters in *Human Development and Faith: Life-Cycles Stages of Change in Body, Mind, and Spirit* (Duluth, GA: Chalice Press, 2004) and contributed chapters to *Kitchen Talk,* Jane McAvoy, ed. (Duluth, GA: Chalice Press, 2003) and *Out of the Silence: Quaker Perspectives on Pastoral Care and Counseling,* Bill Ratliff, ed. (Wallingford, PA: Pendle Hill, 2001). She is a member of the American Academy of Religion, the Society for Pastoral Theology, Quakers in Pastoral Care and Counseling, Spiritual Directors International, and the Forrest-Moss Institute of Disciples women scholars.

David McCurdy, D.Min.
David McCurdy has been Senior Ethics Consultant and Director of Organizational Ethics with Advocate Health Care in Park Ridge, Illinois since 2002. He received a B.A. from Elmhurst College, his M.Div. from Union Theological Seminary, and his D.Min. from Bethany Theological Seminary. An ordained minister in the United Church of Christ, David is a member of the American Society for Bioethics and Humanities, the Association for Practical and Professional Ethics, the Society of Business Ethics, and other professional organiza-

tions. He is a certified supervisor in the Association for Clinical Pastoral Education and a board certified chaplain in the Association of Professional Chaplains. David is coauthor, with four colleagues, of *Organizational Ethics in Health Care: Principles, Cases, and Practical Solutions* (San Francisco: Jossey-Bass and American Hospital Publishing, 2001) and "Ethical Issues in Mental Health Care," for the *Handbook on Ethical Issues in Aging* (Santa Barbara, CA: Greenwood Press, 1999). He has also published "Creating an Ethical Organization," a chapter in *Ethics in Community-Based Care for Elders* (New York: Springer Publishing and American Society on Aging, 2001) and "The Theological Necessity of Informed Consent" in *Faithful Witness: A Festschrift Honoring Ronald Goetz* (Elmhurst College, 2002).

Scott McRae, D.Min.
Scott McRae is Director of the Spiritual Care Department at Park Nicollet Methodist Hospital in St. Louis Park, Minnesota. He received his B.A. from Augustana College and his M.Div. from Yale Divinity School. Scott is an ordained pastor with the Lutheran Church (ELCA) and has served in parish and campus ministry settings in Minnesota and Colorado. He is a supervisor in the Association for Clinical Pastoral Education and a board certified chaplain through the Association of Professional Chaplains. Scott is a spiritual director and leader of the Center for Spiritual Guidance in St. Paul, Minnesota, a training center for spiritual directors.

Francis Rivers Meza, M.Div.
Francis Rivers Meza is Chaplain Supervisor at Wake Forest University Baptist Medical Center in Winston-Salem, North Carolina. He is a Minister of Word & Sacrament in the Presbyterian Church, U.S.A. He graduated with a B.A. from Duke University and an M.Div. from McCormick Theological Seminary. His publications include "The *locus theologicus* of Hispanic/Latino/a Theology and its Implications for Clinical Pastoral Education Curriculum Dvelopment," in *The Journal of Pastoral Care and Counseling* (59, Fall 2005) and "ACPE Theory Papers," *Journal of Supervision and Training in Ministry* (21, 2001), 246-272.

Teresa Snorton, D.Min.
Teresa Snorton is Executive Director of the Association for Clinical Pastoral Education, Inc. (ACPE), an accrediting and certifying agency for programs of Clinical Pastoral Education. She is a certified ACPE pastoral educator and a board certified chaplain by the Association of Professional Chaplains (APC). She is an active member in the Society of Pastoral Theology and the International Congress on Pastoral Care and Counseling. She is an ordained minister in the Christian Methodist Episcopal Church. She is the author of numerous journal articles and book chapters, including "The Legacy of the African-American Matriarch: New Perspectives for Pastoral Care" in *Through the Eyes of Women: Insights for Pastoral Care* (Minneapolis: Augsburg-Fortress Press, 1996) and

"Self-Care for the African-American Woman" in *In Her Own Time: Religion and Women's Life Cycles*, Jeanne Stevenson-Moessner, ed. (Minneapolis: Fortress Press, 2000). A co-edited work with Dr. Stevenson-Moessner, *Women Out of Order: Risking Change and Creating Care in a Multi-Cultural World* is scheduled to be published by Fortress Press in late 2008.

Timothy Thorstenson, D.Min.
Timothy Thorstenson is an ACPE supervisor at Park Nicollet Methodist Hospital in Minnesota. Tim coordinates the CPE program, teaches in the family practice medical residency program, and serves as the lead for clinical and organizational ethics in the Park Nicollet Health System. Tim is a former adjunct professor of health care ethics at William Mitchell College of Law in St. Paul. Tim has previously authored several articles and reflections on supervision, spiritual care, and bioethics, including two book chapters.

M.C. Ward, M.Div.
M.C. Ward is a priest in The Episcopal Church, USA. Her primary work is as a chaplain and pastoral educator at BroMenn Regional Medical Center in Normal, Illinois. She holds a B.A. degree from the University of Oklahoma and an M.Div. from Seabury-Western Theological Seminary and is an ACPE associate supervisor. Prior to entering seminary, Mollie worked for eight years as a journalist, primarily covering the international financial markets and the United Nations.